50+
library services

ALA Editions purchases fund advocacy, awareness, and accreditation programs for library professionals worldwide.

50+
library services

innovation in action

DIANTHA DOW SCHULL

An imprint of the American Library Association
Chicago | 2013

Diantha Dow Schull is an advisor to libraries, museums, and foundations on organizational and program development. She was formerly president of Libraries for the Future and the Americans for Libraries Council. Earlier, she was executive director of the French-American Foundation, director of exhibitions and education at the New York Public Library, director of interpretive programs at the Library of Congress, and assistant director of the Museum Aid Program of the New York State Council on the Arts. Schull serves on the board of the Connecticut Humanities Council. She is the author of numerous articles on cultural institutions and was coeditor, with Pauline Rothstein, of *Boomers and Beyond: Reconsidering the Role of Libraries* (2010).

Printed in the United States of America
17 16 15 14 13   5 4 3 2 1

Extensive effort has gone into ensuring the reliability of the information in this book; however, the publisher makes no warranty, express or implied, with respect to the material contained herein.

ISBNs: 978-0-8389-1119-8 (paper); 978-0-8389-9647-8 (PDF). For more information on digital formats, visit the ALA Store at alastore.ala.org and select eEditions.

Library of Congress Cataloging-in-Publication Data

Schull, Diantha Dow.
    50+ library services : innovation in action / by Diantha Dow Schull.
      pages   cm
    Includes bibliographical references and index.
    ISBN 978-0-8389-1119-8
    1. Libraries and older people—United States. 2. Adult services in public libraries—United States. I. Title. II. Title: Fifty plus library services.
    Z711.92.A35S38 2013
    027.62'2—dc23   2012023720

Cover design by Karen Sheets de Gracia. Image © Khvost/Shutterstock. Inc.
Text design by Kimberly Thornton in Minion Pro and Gotham.

♾ This paper meets the requirements of ANSI/NISO Z39.48-1992 (Permanence of Paper).

CONTENTS

PREFACE

There is a new language addressing this population and it is not "senior." It is about being a mature adult, the third age, the next challenge, productive aging, and much more. . . . We have a lot of ground to cover.

—James Wellbourne, former city librarian, New Haven Free Public Library

This volume documents an important period in the evolution of American library services for older adults, the years 2005–2011. Two milestone events bookend these years: the Designs for Change: Libraries and Productive Aging Leadership Forum held in Washington, D.C., in 2005 and the completion of the IMLS Western States Fellowship program in June 2011. Between these two events librarians began to recognize that traditional concepts of aging and traditional approaches to senior services in libraries were outmoded and needed rethinking for the twenty-first century.

The period 2005–2011 can be characterized as a turning point, a time when librarians started to respond to the aging of America. They became aware of new research on aging and older adults, indicating new possibilities for learning, creativity, and community engagement, and they became aware of the emergence of a new life stage, a period between full-time work or parenthood and the onset of frailty and dependency toward the end of life. Adults in this life stage, including baby boomers, did not seem to fit the profession's traditional definitions of "seniors." Many librarians started to reexamine the profession's traditional definitions of seniors and to rethink approaches for organizing and delivering services to baby boomers and other active older adults. Some even started to coin a new term for a new midlife stage: "50+ services."

During these years the development of 50+ services was encouraged by library leaders in several states, notably Arizona, California, Connecticut, and Massachusetts. Using the tools for institutional change at their disposal—professional development, grants, recognition, and leadership activities—state librarians introduced the professionals in their states to current research on older adult development and provided incentives to translate this research into new models of practice. In California a large-scale initiative started in 2008 that included training, funding, and technical assistance. That initiative, Transforming Life After 50, has inspired new services, programs, and partnerships all across the state and led to wider regional work with other western states to build the capacity of librarians to work with today's 50+ adults.

At the same time, a handful of librarians were moved to experiment in their local libraries. Some had attended the Libraries for the Future Lifelong Access Libraries Leadership Institute, which was held for three years (2006–2008) at the University of North Carolina. Institute fellows gained new perspectives on aging, learned about changes taking place in other professions, and shared ideas about how to transform library services to help boomers through midlife transitions and unexpected "bonus years." Other librarians interested in 50+ services were themselves midlife adults who recognized the lack of relevant library programming for the growing numbers of graying but active adults entering their libraries. No matter their inspiration, these forward-thinking professionals understood the potential for libraries to position themselves as essential centers for learning, creativity, encore careers, and community engagement. Because of their insights and their commitment, a handful of libraries around the country, which I refer to as "50+ Beacon Libraries," are now providing instructive models of change.

As a result of these developments a new movement for older adult services has begun to emerge, a movement that portends restructuring of adult services across the lifespan and promises new relationships between libraries and their midlife constituents. Today, that movement is still in its infancy. The changes taking place are decentralized, uneven, and sometimes invisible even to library colleagues and patrons. Collectively, however, they offer evidence of institutional and professional change.

50+ Library Services: Innovation in Action is intended not only to capture the status of the new movement at a point in time but to help advance that movement. It looks at the societal trends driving change in libraries and considers the implications of these trends for current services and programs. It highlights 50+ initiatives carried out in what I call "Leading-Edge States" and profiles eleven institutions that have taken the lead as "50+ Beacons" in their communities and in the profession. Additionally, it offers examples of the many projects and programs taking place in libraries across the country that can be adapted by creative librarians in other institutions and community settings. Thus, it can provide a foundation for planning and practice for library leaders, practitioners, volunteers, and other current or potential funders. It will also be useful to library educators as a text for use in academic courses or professional development programs on 50+ services.

50+ Library Services has integrity as a holistic work. It can be read from beginning to end, with each chapter providing a snapshot of specific, topical programs or services that contribute to the whole. Alternatively, readers seeking to understand the relationship of libraries to particular themes, such as creative aging or financial planning, may turn first to the relevant chapter.

50+ Library Services is not comprehensive. The landscape of change is too large and too varied to include all possible examples. The examples presented in the following pages were selected to illustrate a key trend or offer an instructive approach for other libraries or library systems. The goal is to prompt librarians to examine the library landscape from their own perspectives and communities, to add their own examples, and to start their own processes of change.

Just as this book is not comprehensive, neither is it neutral. It is my conviction that the American library is uniquely positioned to help mediate one of the greatest demographic transformations in human history—the lengthening of the lifespan, coupled with improved population health. The impact of this transformation is increasingly evident in libraries, from the smallest rural libraries to the largest urban systems. In fact, it is astonishing that in the face of such a transformation there has not been more attention paid by the library profession. Doug Lord, of the Division of Library Development, Connecticut State Library—who was the moderator of the long-running WebJunction Services to Older Adults Discussion Forum and has conducted WebJunction webinars on the same topic—identified the challenge in a WebJunction message in April 2010: "In my experiences so far in considering library services to older adults here in Connecticut, debate has raged about what constitutes 'older.' Is it 55? 65? Older than that? . . . The question for the library community, however, remains: how can we best serve this diverse community that is growing in size?" *50+ Library Services: Innovation in Action* aims to help librarians answer that question and, in so doing, to help reshape the American library as a center for positive aging.

ACKNOWLEDGMENTS

This book was prompted by a paradox. In 2010, after nearly a decade of working with librarians across the country who were experimenting with new programs and services for baby boomers and other active older adults, I did not see their efforts reflected in library literature, librarian training, staff titles, departmental structures, or financial resources. Despite the growing number of innovative and instructive service examples, they were relatively invisible across the profession. Even major initiatives in such states as California and Massachusetts were not widely reported beyond their states or regions. In fact, the amount of innovation in the field seemed inversely proportional to the curriculum development in schools of library and information science and the professional recognition through publications, promotions, and institutional rankings.

50+ Library Services: Innovation in Action is intended to help draw attention to the ideas and accomplishments of the many creative and forward-looking librarians who recognize the potential for libraries to position themselves as centers for positive aging. These librarians have started a movement to rethink services to the aging. As this movement becomes more visible and influential, it will lead to institutionalization of new practices. To capture the movement in its earliest phases, I have consulted with many individuals across the country, all of whom have given generously of their time and expertise. Some have suggested examples, some have reviewed drafts of specific profiles, and some have critiqued draft sections of this book. To all, I am most grateful.

My deepest thanks go to the many librarians, including library directors, state librarians, former librarians, and library educators, who shared their experiences with me, and whose work inspired my research and analysis from start to finish. Among these are individuals who took the time not only to provide information on current activities but also to reflect upon changing attitudes and practices. Among these are Nancy Aberman, Louise Blalock, Brenda Brown, Brigid Cahalan, Kate Cosgrove, Abigail Elder, Suzanne Flint, Carla Lehn, Charity Leonette, Richard Levinson, Melinda Ludwiczak, Douglas Lord, Joanne Gard Marshall, Brenda Miller, Shelley Quezada, Jane Salisbury, Gladys Ann Wells, Bo Xie, and Joan Young. Special thanks go to the late James Wellbourne, whose insights regarding services for 50+ adults were instrumental in the initial concept for the book.

Other librarians and library community leaders who contributed information and ideas include Lori Abbatapaolo, Luz Acevedo, Mary Albro, Mary Altpeter, Katherine Ames, Jennifer Baker, Michael Bice, Norma Blake, Kay Bloom, Cindy Bonaro, Rebecca Bond, Mary Boone, Richard Bray, Sharon Brettschneider, Nancye Browning, Lesley Burger, David Campbell, Carolyn Caywood, Mary Chute, Joan Clark, Gloria Coles, Kathy Cryan-Hicks, Nancy Curtin, Madeline Damell, Elizabeth Dickinson, Mark Donnelly, Jennifer Fenton, Keith Fiels, Lee Fishman, Olivia Frost, Sandra Feinberg, Toni Garvey, Alix Gertz, Kathy Graybeal, Jose Marie Griffith, Peggy Haile-McPhillips, Susan Hansen, Holly Henley, Susan Hildreth, Susan Irving, Marilyn Jenkins, Nancy Johnson, Ed Kieczykowski, Terry Kirchner, Allan Kleiman, Claudia Koenig, Beth Layton, Meryl Leonard, Jane Light, David Lisa, Norman Maas, Ruth Maslin, Kathy Mayo, Gail McGrath, Terri Metros, Mimi Morris, Wendy Moylan, Ellen Myers, Karen Neely, Satia Orange, Kathleen Peiffer, Wendy Pender, Eugenie Prime, Siobhan Riordan, Ann Roberts, Jane Salisbury, Linda Schaeffer, Jim Scheppke, Hagar Sherman, Laura Stone, Sara Strickland, Tracy Toll, Michael Toman, Betty Turock, Kendall Wiggin, Lynn Williamson, and Linda Wilson.

Space limitations prevent my mentioning the many additional librarians whose development of specific 50+ services have inspired my research. It is my hope that this publication will shine a light on their work, bringing it the recognition that it deserves.

Beyond my colleagues in the library profession, I am also indebted for inspiration and conceptual development to others outside the library profession whose work intersects with libraries. They include Andrew Achenbaum, Bruce Astrein, Greg Baldwin, Mary Catherine Bateson, Michael Bice, Donna Butts, Jackie Day, Stacey Easterling, Tom Endres, Lew Felstein, Ed Friedman, Marc Freedman, Judy Goggin, Carol Greenfield, Sarah Griswold, Larry Grossman, Linda Harootyan, Hollis Hedrick, Nancy Henkin, Ruth Holst, Chris Johnson, Margie Lachman, Kali Lightfoot, Robert Maier, Ronald Manheimer, Peter Marimaldi, Victor Marshall, H. Rick Moody, Paul Nussbaum, Maura O'Malley, Greg O'Neill, Katherine Ott, Susan Pearlstein, Steve Ristau, Jeffrey Scherer, Marsha Semmel, Andrea Sherman, Sharon Sokoloff, Martin Sullivan, Jeannette Takamura, Selma Thomas, Robert Tietz, Sabrina Waldron, Olivia White, Kathleen Woodward, Ruth Wooden, and William Zeisel. In addition, the late Robert Butler and Gene Cohen, both leaders in the field of aging, provided important insights regarding libraries and positive aging and encouraged my efforts to generate greater focus on 50+ adults in the library community.

I am especially grateful to my colleague Pauline Rothstein for her thoughtful reading and advice regarding the shaping of this book, and to J. Michael Jeffers of ALA Editions for his wise counsel throughout the editing process.

I am indebted to my husband Walter, my children Bruno and Natasha, and their amazing children, Katja and Ginger, for their patience and insights throughout the course of this project.

INTRODUCTION

The goal of Kaboom! (Knowledgeable & Active Boomers) is to challenge our
assumptions, our language, and the way in which libraries organize adult
and senior library services to find new and engaging methods to address an
emerging third lifephase in transformational ways. Kaboom! will provide new
ideas and help inform the creation of a distinct specialty within adult services,
focusing on active, engaged older adults during this second year of a two-
year library demonstration project of work to serve and engage boomers.

—Multnomah (Oregon) Public Library 2009 LSTA grant proposal

Multnomah County Public Library is one of hundreds of American libraries, particularly public libraries, that are starting to reshape services for 50+ adults, also known as midlife adults. With the blessing of library leaders, new sources of support, and positive responses from their patrons, many imaginative librarians are working toward change. They are testing new approaches to programs, projects, staffing, collections, communications, and partnerships. Some are even revising long-range plans or reshuffling priorities to incorporate goals for meeting the needs of, and working with, midlife adults. In fact, so many libraries are engaged in this process of change that they represent a new movement, a movement affecting the scope, organization, and content of services and programs for midlife and other active older adults.

BACKGROUND

The changes taking place in library services for older adults are driven by one of the largest demographic and social transformations in U.S. history—the aging of the baby boomer generation. In 2011 the first Americans born between

1946 and 1964, 79 million strong, turned 65. For the next eighteen years, 10,000 more boomers will reach that age each day. By 2030 at least 18 percent of the U.S. population will be 65 or over, and a much higher percentage will be 50+.

By sheer numbers alone boomers will play an increasingly dominant role in American society, affecting every aspect of life, from family relationships and housing design to workplace policies and the operations of local institutions. The impact of boomers is already visible in many sectors, such as retail marketing, financial services, and higher education. As a generation known for its willingness to break with social norms and traditions, it is not surprising that the boomer generation is reshaping American life and, at the same time, reshaping our very concepts of age and aging.

Boomers are not the only older adults who are changing how we live and how we think about age. Thanks to general improvements in the health of Americans over the course of the twentieth century, along with advances in medicine and technology, average life expectancy has increased by at least thirty years. Not only are there more adults in their seventies, eighties, and nineties, but they are healthier, more mobile, and more civically and socially engaged than prior generations of "seniors." Many are living vigorous lives well into their nineties, continuing to earn, to learn, to create, and to contribute. These active older adults belie traditional assumptions about later life. They are prompting reconsideration of such fundamental questions as "What is old?" "What is retirement?" and "How do I live a meaningful life?"

The combination of aging boomers and advancing longevity constitutes an unprecedented societal transformation. It provides the basis for what gerontologist Robert Butler termed the "longevity revolution" and what others call "the aging opportunity," "Adulthood II," or "the bonus years."[1] It also provides the basis for rethinking current library services for adults and for seniors. As reflected in Multnomah County's LSTA grant proposal cited above, librarians recognize that they must challenge "our assumptions, our language, and the way in which libraries organize adult and senior library services."

The new thinking about older adult services emerged in the early 2000s, first in Arizona and then spreading to Connecticut, California, Massachusetts, and other states. In 2006, Toni Garvey, director of the Phoenix (Arizona) Public Library and cochair of a newly formed Maricopa County Commission on Age, stated: "Retirement is changing, so we need to evolve to support that change."[2] Other library leaders at the national, state, and local levels were becoming aware of the demographic and social changes taking place and started to use their influence to encourage new attitudes and practices.

By 2006 many adult or senior services librarians were cognizant of the need to reconsider traditional services for older adults. Interviews of local librarians carried out by the University of North Carolina's Institute on Aging in 2009 prompted comments regarding the "perception . . . that the new wave of active seniors ought to bring about a corresponding change in older adult programming." One interviewee stated: "Libraries tend to be serving the slow-goes or no-goes. . . . In the Boomer generation, older adults are goers and they're on the go. They're constantly involved in things. They have no intention of going to the senior center and playing Bingo. I mean that's just too appalling to them."[3]

In recent years the momentum toward change has accelerated, with examples appearing in small rural libraries as well as large suburban and urban systems. The tiny rural Cobleigh Library in northern Vermont has developed "The Plus Side of Life for People Aged 50 and Up," a special section of the library's website with book recommendations, links to national and local organizations, and humorous images. The Tualatin Public Library in Oregon is conducting a library-wide program, Creating Civic Engagement through Library Volunteers, to retrain librarians to work with volunteers who are engaged to help with "high impact" tasks that match their skills and interests. The Hennepin County Library in Minneapolis presented a three-month program on older adult creativity, Art of Aging, that engaged librarians, artists, and members of the public in dialogues on the aging process and featured the work of four local artists 65 and older. Passive entertainment is giving way to participatory programming and peer-led activities that change the relation-

Library Leaders Call for Change

We need to focus on systemic change, on institutionalizing new attitudes and services and integrating them into the culture of our institutions.

—Gladys Ann Wells, then director, Arizona State Library, Archives and Public Records, January 2003 meeting of the Maricopa County Commission on Productive Aging

How can we re-shape our organizations to both meet the changing demands of a maturing population and engage that population in improving our communities?

—Ken Wiggin, state librarian of Connecticut, November 2003 forum Coming of Age: Building Healthy Communities in Connecticut

Time spent now planning and thinking strategically about how to engage with active productive older adults is a necessary investment for the continued vitality of our communities and our institutions.

—Mary Chute, then acting IMLS director, September 2005, National Library Leaders Forum Designs for Change

By 2010, one in five Californians will be 60 years of age or older. And, yet, research has shown that the current paradigm of library services for "seniors" does not match the characteristics and/or interests of the baby boomer generation.

—Susan Hildreth, then state librarian of California, November 2008 Transforming Life After 50 training for California Librarians

Today's active older Americans have learned more and applied this learning to more situations than any previous generation. The library has an obligation to tap into this new national asset.

—David Lankes, "Conversations and the True Knowledge of Generations," in Boomers and Beyond: Reconsidering the Role of Libraries, 2010

ship between librarians and midlife patrons and, ultimately, engage the patrons more substantively in the life of the library.

Some library systems are questioning how they are organized internally to service older adults and are reconsidering the assignment of responsibilities to outreach staff, who necessarily focus on frail and isolated seniors rather than on those who are, or could be, active in-library users. Other libraries are using surveys, focus groups, and advisory councils to learn more about the varied interests of their aging constituents and their capacities for engagement.

One of the most promising trends is librarians' growing understanding that 50+ adults can be assets to their institutions and their communities and can enhance library services by taking on specific tasks that match their unique experiences and skills. Known as "high-value" volunteering, this approach implies new kinds of volunteer recruitment and coordination and new possibilities for enhancement of core services.

As the 50+ services movement emerges, some librarians are taking note of recent research on older adults and ways to help mitigate the aging processes. They understand the importance of participation, social engagement, learning, and creative expression and, especially, the value of peer-led programming. These principles are increasingly reflected in the new services and programs.

The one common denominator of the 50+ services movement is growing understanding that services must match the varied needs and interests of 50+ adults. Within any one community there can be several generational cohorts in the 50+ category and, within those cohorts, diverse interests, cultural backgrounds, linguistic traditions, and economic circumstances. These adults' capacities for engaging, learning, and contributing are not necessarily tied to their ages, but to their interests and experiences. Librarians committed to 50+ services understand the need to avoid preconceived notions about their older patrons and to focus on building a broad portfolio of offerings. Kathy Mayo, who is nationally recognized for her many years in outreach services at the Lee County (Florida) Library System, summed up the challenge in her 2009 Jean E. Coleman Library Outreach Lecture: "Thinking of people as a broad age group can be misleading. In fact, they are identified more by their interests and abilities than their ages."[4]

EMERGING SERVICE MODELS

Because the new service approaches are so varied and so new, there is no one model for what works best. There are as yet no templates for projects or blueprints for institutional change. This volume captures a series of works in progress rather than tried and true "best practices." However, within the landscape of change there are five differing approaches that, if plotted in a curve, reflect a continuum. At one end of the spectrum is an increase in the marketing of current programs to draw in midlife adults; at the other end are system-wide initiatives affecting staffing, programs, communications, and resource allocations.

Increased marketing to attract midlife adults to current programs. Many libraries are in this stage of development, which sometimes also sees an overall expansion of offerings. Current structures do not change in this approach, but it does reflect a recognition that more and varied services and collections are needed to serve today's 50+ populations.

Participation in a national initiative to address specific issues relevant to older adults. Financial planning, health information, and creative arts are typical issues. These signature initiatives usually stand apart from ongoing library programming, but they can and do influence librarians' understanding of demographic changes and prompt reassessment of current practices. Examples include Creative Aging at the Library, a model for instructional arts programs for older adults offered by Lifetime Arts (see chapter 7); and Get Involved!, a partnership between California libraries and VolunteerMatch to stimulate increased local volunteering (see chapter 3).

Development of experimental initiatives to test approaches and community response. These initiatives may be short-lived or sustained. Boomer Connections at the Northland (Pennsylvania) Library, implemented in 2009, had several components, the most successful of which were absorbed into ongoing programming. Live Wires, created with and for active older adults at the Reading (Massachusetts) Public Library in 2007, is an example of a demonstration project that started with grant funds and has been sustained by community donors (see chapter 2).

A deliberate combination of general adult services and specific services for 50+ adults. Some libraries or library systems have both inclusive and specific programs. Rather than change current adult services they are adding new services for boomers or, more broadly, for 50+ patrons. The Metropolitan Library Services Agency (MELSA) in Minnesota is an excellent example of this two-pronged approach (see chapter 2). With special funding from the State of Minnesota, MELSA has increased general adult programs, such as its Community Cinema Programs and Live at the Library (performances)—both of which attract large numbers of 50+ adults—while working with member libraries on targeted programs such as the Art of Aging and First Page: Memoir Writing for Over Fifty.

Systemic 50+ programs with visibility, resources, and library support. This level of institutional support involves dedicated staff, programming, and a clear identity including branding on the library's website and other communications vehicles. New York Public Library's Next Chapter initiative and the Tempe (Arizona) Public Library's Tempe Connections project are excellent examples (see chapter 2).

Distinctions between these approaches are not firm. At the present time libraries are shifting among the above categories depending on staff or leadership changes, responses from key adult constituencies, the capacities and commitment of staff, and the availability of resources. The overall trend is toward a more systemic approach, but that trend is at an early stage of development and will take time to be manifested across the library landscape.

BARRIERS TO CHANGE

Despite the evidence for change, there are still considerable barriers to transformation of library services for aging populations:

Ageism. As Robert Butler so vividly described in his Pulitzer Prize–winning book *Why Survive: Being Old in America* (2002), Americans are acculturated to think negatively about the aging process. The concept of old age as a time of deficit and dependency is entrenched from childhood on. Most of us assume that there is little we can learn, create, or contribute after our years of parenting and paid employment. Our attitudes are hard to eradicate, even when the diversity, productivity, and societal benefits of people 50+ are ever more visible.

Ageism on the part of librarians is reinforced by the classification of all older adults as "seniors" and their inclusion, along with "the underserved," in the service category known as "special populations," who are beyond the sphere of regular adult programming.

Structural organization of services. Libraries' traditional organizational structures reflect the categorization of older adults, or seniors, as special populations that are served through an outreach librarian or outreach department. Most libraries relegate senior services to outreach staff who concentrate on book deliveries to homebound elderly, deposit collections, and programming at senior centers and senior housing. There are few mechanisms to link these services with in-library services and programs that are attracting a higher and higher proportion of 50+ residents who are seeking options for work, learning, and service. Given libraries' existing structures, these midlife adults are not the responsibility of any particular staff person, department, or program. They are relatively invisible and are usually lumped together with other adults and offered services and programs that may or may not be pertinent to their transitional issues and life stage.

The lack of differentiation among different older generations contrasts with librarians' tendencies to break younger age groups into ever-more specific groupings such as "toddlers," "preschoolers," "tweens," and "teens" with corresponding responsibilities, titles, and specialties. If current trends are any indication, librarians will eventually reorganize departments and prepare staff to respond to people wherever they are on the life span.

Lack of a forum for change. The decentralized nature of libraries and the lack of a forum for those working to reshape adult and senior services are another obstacle to change. Excellence and experimentation in one part of the country or even one part of a state are not necessarily known to colleagues in other parts of the country or that state. Despite extensive electronic communications, with WebJunction, blogs, state library e-newsletters, webinars, Facebook, and the like, there is no common mechanism for exchange of ideas and presentation of practices that can inform and inspire librarians across the country. This problem and the likelihood that it would impede librarian responses to aging trends was pointed out by Constance Van Fleet at an early meeting of the Libraries for the Future's Lifelong Access Libraries initiative. Unfortunately, six years later the problem still exists: "The obstacles to progress come mainly from the lack of a cohesive lifelong learning framework and of a way of disseminating innovation throughout the library community. Much interesting work is being in done in libraries scattered around the country but it is still fragmented. We need resources to develop innovative programs and dissemination mechanisms."[5]

Lack of library education courses or certification programs. A fourth barrier to change is the lack of formal training in services for midlife adults. For new librarians interested in specializing in older adult services there are few places to turn. Today there are at most four courses in the nation's library and information science graduate schools that are dedicated to or include midlife services. With respect to professional development opportunities, the situation is only somewhat better. Irregularly, there are webinars on older adult services offered by state libraries or WebJunction. There are also occasional workshops or programs at state and national library association conferences. None of these offer certification; none of them lead to specialization or status within the profession.

There are two notable exceptions to this situation: the Lifelong Access Libraries Institute organized by Libraries for the Future in conjunction with the University of North Carolina's School of Information, and the just completed IMLS-funded Western States Fellowship program led by the California State Library and involving partnerships with five state libraries plus the Pacific Library Partnership.[6] Today, without either program operative, there is no vehicle for in-depth face-to-face professional development. This lack was noted by a student from UNC's School of Information who helped shape the final report on the Lifelong Access Libraries Institute:

> I think librarians definitely will need some training. . . . Because it is a different sense than librarians traditionally have served older adults . . . where you just assumed they don't have or can't have as much going on and you're bringing it all to them. Whereas this is a different model altogether. They have a lot of things going on, and we're going to be competing for their time and interest in the way that we compete for families' time and interest, so we need to understand better what that service model is all about. That's a change.[7]

Economic constraints. Finally, the fiscal limitations that are always a factor in the operation of libraries, especially public libraries, have been magnified recently by the economic recession. At the very time when 50+ services were beginning to gain attention as a distinct specialty and when several influential states were exerting leadership as proponents of change, the recession undermined new initiatives at the local and state levels. With an economic turnaround the momentum that has started should pick up and move forward again.

THE PROBLEM OF LANGUAGE

In addition to the challenges outlined above, librarians seeking to expand their work with midlife adults face another kind of challenge: the problem of language. The pace of demographic change and the unanticipated phenomenon of bonus years in the middle of the lifespan have left librarians without a consensus on the appropriate terms for 50+ or midlife adults. Should they be considered younger seniors? Should they all be lumped together as boomers, even though some are younger and some are older than the strictly year-defined boomer? Are they mature adults, as opposed to frail elderly? Should they include the Silent Generation? Is there a term that can embrace both multiple generations and multiple types of people? These questions reflect the societal changes taking place and the need to convert new thinking about older adults into new language within the profession.

Mimi Morris, assistant director for Branch and Extension Services at Dayton Metro Library and a Lifelong Access Libraries Fellow, asked recently on an online forum: "Does anyone have a better word than 'seniors' to define this population. . . . We want our programming and services to appeal to baby boomers on up, and "Senior" isn't going to cut it. As a Boomer who just turned 60, I know I don't like that reference!"

Despite Mimi's concern, for most librarians the default term for an older adult is still "senior." This has special connotations in the library setting, implying someone who is dependent, infirm, or isolated; who requires outreach services; and who can no longer contribute to community life. In fact, this term contradicts the realities faced by librarians every day as increasing numbers of graying but active midlife adults come into their libraries looking for information on work or finances or health, learning how to use digital cameras, or organizing chess clubs for teens. These adults do not need books delivered to them; they are eager to deliver the books themselves, organize programs, write press releases, design websites, create events, and also show up for the library's morning yoga class. They are not "seniors": they are part of a new population cohort that has yet to find the right name.

> Call them seniors, 50 plusers, older adults, whatever. Just call them.
>
> —Doug Lord,
> Connecticut State Library

Confusion about what terminology to use for nonsenior 50+ people is clearly evident in the range of approaches being taken by libraries today. Some libraries have stopped using "seniors" and are substituting "Adults 50+," "Boomers," or "Boomers and Beyond." Others are continuing to use "seniors" for their traditional outreach to elderly residents while adding "Boomers" or "50+" for in-library activities targeted to midlife generations. Yet others are trying to touch all bases by using multiple terms on their websites and program announcements.

This situation complicates documentation of new services and programs for adults transitioning through the new life stage. Library services that may be relevant to the youngest boomers or newly retired 50+ adults may be classified and titled as "senior" programs. Conversely, community resource information appropriate for dependent and elderly persons may be included in a directory titled "Boomer Resources" or "Fifty Plus Guide." Given the fact that today's titles may be misleading, the selection of projects and programs in this volume is not guided by language as much as by content. Consequently, there are numerous entries that include the word "senior" but that do, in fact, have relevance for younger midlife adults.

For the purposes of this publication, primarily the following terms are used: "50+ services," "50+ adults," and "midlife adults." Although "baby boomers" or "active older adults" are employed as well, use of "50+ adults" or "midlife adults" provides consistency for documentation purposes and may contribute to greater consistency of language by library innovators in the months and years ahead.

INNOVATION IN ACTION: DOCUMENTATION FOR CHANGE

Despite the considerable barriers they face, librarians are making significant changes in how they work with baby boomers and other active older adults. These changes may not be taking place in all parts of the country, they may be uneven in quality, and they may not yet have formal identity within the profession. Nevertheless, the changes are tangible, and they signal the beginning of a new approach to working with midlife 50+ adults.

50+ Library Services: Innovation in Action takes stock of the changes made to date. It captures a shifting landscape of projects, programs, and state initiatives that collectively make up librarians' responses to the aging of America. The first two chapters focus on the national landscape: "Leading-Edge States" looks at the record of four key state library development offices, where leadership in the form of grants and technical assistance helped lay a foundation for change. "Beacons of Change" profiles eleven libraries and library systems that stand out for the scope and quality of their services and the extent of leadership they have provided within the profession.

The remainder of the book comprises ten chapters that focus on particular themes or categories of programming and service development. Each chapter includes an introductory discussion of trends in that subject area and the implications for libraries and profiles of exemplary or unusual programs or projects. Some projects are described in depth, others are listed "In-Brief" in order to capture the range and type of activities in the field. The main profiles all include an overview statement about the activity and its significance, goals, partners, features, and funding sources. Only a handful of the profiles include information on impacts or outcomes. It is a mark of the field's infancy that there is so little available in terms of research or systematic evaluation.

The examples of projects and programs profiled here vary widely in their scope, titles, structure, purposes, partners, and funding sources. Selection of these examples has been guided by the following criteria:

- Illustrate a key trend in service development
- Offer an instructive example that could be adapted for other library systems
- Reflect an effort to innovate, to go beyond business as usual
- Involve activities that take place in the library
- Are targeted for active adults ages 50 to 80 and beyond, thus including but not limited to baby boomers

LOOKING AHEAD

With the accomplishments and changes in midlife services during the period 2005–2011, what can we envision for the next six to ten years of 50+ services? Will we see increased professional recognition of a distinct 50+ specialty in adult services, with associated staff and titles, specialist training, certification programs, and academic research? Will we see some states embracing change and others simply continuing senior and adult services as usual? Will we see midlife adults using libraries more and differently, or will we see commercial or other enterprises positioning themselves as centers for lifelong learning and social exchange? Will we see more and more boomers and other midlife adults becoming partners with the library in the provision of community library services, or will we see them as threats to the library and the profession? Above all, what kind of institutional and cultural changes will take place within the library to support the work of 50+ services librarians?

The answers to these questions are not yet clear. However, with the benefit of the examples brought together in this volume we can begin to envision a roadmap for change. Together, these examples strengthen arguments for staff training, for changes in how adult and senior services are organized, for systematic research and marketing, for the involvement of positive aging specialists in our libraries, and, above all, for investments and incentives to enable change.

As the following examples demonstrate, change is possible, and investments to support change have significant ripple effects.

Roberta Stevens, current president of the American Library Association, recently made the following statement: "For librarians to be 21st century leaders in their communities, they must let go of certain old assumptions and ways of doing things, and fearlessly, and I stress 'fearlessly,' assess their library's audiences, evaluate how 'customer' needs are addressed, and aggressively reach out and communicate with actual and potential library users."[8] The innovative library leaders and librarians whose work is profiled in this volume appear to be following Stevens's advice. They are fearlessly revising long-standing attitudes and practices and creating new approaches to working *with* (not serving) 50+ adults. This publication is dedicated to these librarians as "21st century leaders in their communities."

Notes

1. Robert Butler, *The Longevity Revolution: The Benefits and Challenges of Living a Long Life* (New York: PublicAffairs, 2008). M. Marc Freedman, "The Aging Opportunity: America's Elderly as a Civic Resource," *American Prospect* 7, no. 29 (1996): 38–43. Mary Catherine Bateson, "In Search of Active Wisdom: Libraries and Consciousness-Raising for Adulthood II," in *Boomers and Beyond: Reconsidering the Role of the Library*, ed. Pauline Rothstein and Diantha D. Schull (Chicago: American Library Association, 2010). Maggie Scarf, "The Bonus Years of Adult Life," blog published November 2008 in "Adulthood: Exploring the Newest Stage of the Life-Cycle," Psychology Today, www.psychologytoday.com/blog/the-bonus-years-adulthood/200811/the-bonus-years-adult-life.

2. From the author's notes on the First Lifelong Access Libraries Institute, University of North Carolina, July 2005. Garvey was a member of the panel discussion titled "Leading Change: Lifelong Access Libraries Centers of Excellence and Innovation."

3. Joanne Gard Marshall, Jennifer C. Morgan, and Victor W. Marshall, *Lifelong Access Libraries Centers of Excellence Final Report*, by the University of North Carolina School of Information Science and the Institute on Aging, May 2009, www.aging.unc.edu/programs/lal/reports/CentersOfExcellenceFinalReport.pdf.

4. Kathy Mayo, "The Challenges and Opportunities of Serving America's Elders, 2009 Jean E. Coleman Outreach Lecture, www.ala.org/ala/aboutala/offices/olos/olosprograms/jeanecoleman/index2.cfm.

5. Constance Van Fleet, Remarks at Libraries for the Future's Lifelong Access Libraries National Advisory Committee meeting, New York City, November 2005 (unpublished transcript). Libraries for the Future, also known as Americans for Libraries Council, was an advocacy, research, and program development organization devoted to strengthening public libraries in the United States. It was founded in 1991 and

continued operations until 2009, a period during which it carried out campaigns in support of libraries, produced reports on such topics as library valuation and public perceptions of libraries, and worked with library, community, and philanthropic leaders to design and implement innovative programs to meet emerging information and learning needs. Among these programs were Family Place Libraries, Equal Access Libraries, and Reading America. Libraries for the Future was a leader in advancing new approaches for working with older adults.

6. Sabrina Waldron, *Beyond Bingo for Boomers: An Overview of the Lifelong Access Libraries Model*. Presentation at the Transforming Life After 50 Training Institute for public librarians, Pasadena, California, November 2007, http://transforminglifeafter50.org/files/handout-pdfs/TLAFWaldronppt.pdf; and IMLS Western States Fellowship Program, www.transforminglifeafter50.org/innovators/imls-fellowship.

7. Marshall et al. *Lifelong Access Libraries Centers of Excellence Final Report*.

8. Roberta A. Stevens, *21st Century Libraries: The Challenges and Opportunities*, www.siob.nl/b2d/upload/documenten/b2d10-lezing-roberta-stevens.pdf.

CHAPTER 1

LEADING-EDGE STATES

As stewards of lifelong learning, public libraries are ideally positioned to become cornerstone institutions for productive aging. However, research has shown that library services for "seniors" do not match the characteristics or interests of midlife adults, ages 50+. These adults, many of whom are Baby Boomers, are experiencing a new, extended stage of midlife due to significant increases in longevity. This lengthening of the human life span will have profound effects not only for Baby Boomers but for generations to come, and the implications for libraries and other cultural institutions will be equally profound.

—California State Library, Transforming Life After 50 website

The projects and programs identified in this volume reveal that many librarians are beginning to recognize the aging of America as an opportunity—indeed, a necessity—for new and expanded service. They no longer see all older adults as a monolithic category of "seniors"—retired, isolated, and dependent on traditional outreach services. They no longer assume that all older adults belong to the same generation or economic class or share the same interests, needs, and life expectations. Some librarians are even recognizing older adults as assets, with skills and experience that can benefit their libraries and their communities. Projects such as Creating Civic Engagement through Library Volunteers at the Tualatin (Oregon) Public Library (chapter 3) or the New Haven (Connecticut) Free Library's 50+ Transition Center (chapter 2) demonstrate that libraries are responding to demographic change.

Although these projects are evidence of change, less obvious, and less studied, are the reasons for change. What factors, aside from aging trends, have been responsible for a shift in librarians' perceptions of older adults and the kinds of services they offer or would like to offer? Has change been prompted by individual leaders, new sources of dedicated funds, professional development opportunities, library and information science education, inspiring service models in other professions, or pressure from local patrons?

All of these factors have undoubtedly played a role, with different emphases in different locations. However, it is clear that one overriding factor has affected the pace and type of change more than any other, namely, leadership by state librarians and state library development staff. No matter what particular form that leadership has taken—grantmaking, convening, training, or participation in national and state initiatives—state libraries have been the driving force in provoking the library profession to put aging and longevity on the library agenda.

Given the strength of the profession's current model for senior services, it is surprising that change has started to take hold so rapidly, and it is a testament to the state libraries that are on the leading edge. Changes in how librarians approach their services do not usually come about overnight. Quite the contrary. Sometimes they take decades or even generations. As one example, it has taken more than three decades for public librarians to fully accept infant and toddler services as routine aspects of their services for children. Likewise, recognition of the teen years as a special life phase requiring something different from children's services or adult services also took some years. Thus, it is no surprise that some librarians are hesitant to consider changing the generic service model for seniors. This model, which features outreach to homebound, disabled, underserved, institutionalized, or limited-mobility older adults, is accepted across the profession. There are staff titles associated with these activities, there are professional entities that focus on services for these "special populations," and boards of trustees and municipal officials understand the need to meet the special needs of less active elders.

In fact, as the oldest of the old grow in numbers over the next several decades, outreach and "senior" services must and should continue. Next to baby boomers, the fastest-growing segment of the aging population is that segment that is frail and truly elderly. However, the lack of a distinction between infirm and dependent seniors and all other aging adults means that mobile adults of 50 to 80 years—for the purposes of this publication "midlife" or "50+" adults—are not part of the library service equation. They are essentially invisible.

The invisibility of midlife adults is reinforced by a lack of distinctions between age groups at the other end of the adult spectrum. In most libraries "adult" means all persons between 18 and approximately 65. When librarians do focus on the needs of those who are making midlife or career changes, or new retirees who do not fit the senior mold, many still assume that whatever is provided in adult services is adequate to meet their needs. The size, diversity, and potential of 50+ adults are simply not taken into account. Just as book deposit collections at nursing homes and large-print books for the homebound are not enough to address the diversity of seniors, so AARP tax counseling and afternoon movies at the library are not enough to address the diversity of midlife adults.

It is clear that the new 50+ services described in the following pages constitute an effort to find other ways to organize both senior and adult services. In this context the leadership role of state librarians and their state library development staffs assumes special importance. A few key state libraries have used their influence and resources to encourage librarians in their states to reconsider both adult and senior services. Furthermore, these state libraries have recognized the importance of responding quickly to the demographics of aging. They recognize that the population changes taking place across the country are accelerating and do not allow the profession the luxury of shifting practices over several decades. Their words, actions, and investments, combined, have been responsible for bringing about change.

There are four of these "leading-edge states": Arizona, California, Connecticut, and Massachusetts. In each of these the state library has been a strong advocate for change in older adult practice. Not surprisingly, the states that have taken the greatest leadership are states with high proportions of aging residents. In these states the demographic changes are already more visible, and the diversity and number of the younger older adults cannot be ignored. The library profession's traditional definition of seniors is no longer adequate where there are expanding numbers of workers over 65, new communities organized around residents of 50 or 55, more and more grandparents raising grandchildren, and many midlife and older adults seeking opportunities for learning, service, and creative expression.

The four leading-edge states have each supported change in different ways. The California State Library has developed a major statewide initiative that advances local librarians' understanding of aging while emphasizing support for projects that mobilize older adults as assets to their library or their local community. This initiative has expanded to other western states and has been influential nationwide. The Arizona State Library Archives and Public Records was the first to make investments in 50+ services and has supported projects that promote fitness and learning and engage baby boomers as contributors in their communities. The Massachusetts Board of Library Commissioners emphasizes lifelong learning through its Lifelong Access and Next Chapter projects, with the result that many grant-supported libraries are engaging adults in multidisciplinary enrichment activities. The Connecticut State Library has encouraged experimentation, including allocation of LSTA monies for grants and organization of a special Coming of Age forum held in 2005 at the state capital to promote cross-sector discussion about libraries and aging. Connecticut also played an important developmental role nationally through its leadership of the WebJunction Services to Older Adults Discussion Forum.

These state initiatives vary in scope and emphasis, but they all reflect recognition of the following:

- The need to recognize midlife as a new life stage that merits focused attention from librarians similar to other life stages
- The importance of exposing librarians to current research on brain development and positive aging
- The need to build librarians' capacities to work with midlife adults through training, technical support, and exposure to practical examples of change
- The value of grant funds in helping catalyze change
- The value of leadership buy-in, peer-to-peer support, and professional networking
- The importance of collaborations with other professionals serving active older adults

In addition to the four leading-edge states, several others have undertaken more focused initiatives to improve or transform older adult practice. Both New Jersey and Pennsylvania, for example, have invested LSTA monies in a Senior Spaces grant initiative, affecting both spaces and programming in local libraries. It is important to note that, although the title of the grant programs was "Senior Spaces," in fact the spaces reorganized with grant monies have increased in-library activities as well for mobile, engaged midlife adults who are seeking programs and opportunities for social and civic exchange. Another important program spearheaded by state librarians is the IMLS-funded Western Regional Fellowship. In a partnership with the California State Library, state libraries in Arizona, Idaho, Oregon, Washington, and the Pacific Library Partnership have helped organize and oversee this professional development program, which has provided intensive online and on-site training and technical assistance to library professionals from across the western United States. All of the training materials are now available online, making the rich training content available to librarians nationwide.

There are other states working to build professionals' capacities to meet the coming "age wave." North Carolina supported the participation of eight librarians in the Libraries for the Future 2008 and 2009 Lifelong Access Libraries Leadership Institutes and has collaborated with the Institute on Aging at the University of North Carolina. Texas has offered several continuing education webinars on boomer services. Missouri, which took the lead some years ago in promoting more systematic senior services, is now supporting local projects for midlife adults as well. West Virginia has worked with the National Network of Libraries of Medicine (NM/LM) to carry out a health information initiative focusing on older adults, and Montana worked with NM/LM to implement a major public relations campaign, along with staff training, that built awareness and use of health information resources for boomers in the state's libraries. Several of these projects are profiled in the chapters that follow.

Recent developments indicate that state-based leadership for 50+ services will continue. The Idaho Commission for Libraries, for instance, has created the website Mid-Life Adults (http://libraries.idaho.gov/landing/mid-life-adults), which includes the following introduction:

> The ICfL is dedicated to providing information, training, technical assistance, and resources for Idaho libraries and their community partners for all areas relating to mid-life adults. . . . Our goal is to help libraries better serve and engage midlife adults by positioning libraries as catalysts, resources, meeting places, and partners in creating opportunities for midlife adults to learn, teach, lead, build skills, re-career, and become civically-engaged.

Most recently, in December 2011, as this publication was going to press, the New Jersey State Library hosted a Boomer Generation conference in Atlantic City that included presentations on economics, the aging brain, generational characteristics, and "how libraries should respond to remain viable and valuable to this generation."[1]

Collectively, these state initiatives reflect the powerful role played by state librarians and their staffs in fostering systemic change in how libraries understand and work with midlife adults.[2]

Notes

1. See Kelly Nicholaides, "Baby Boomers' Recareering Challenges and How to Meet Them," *South Bergenite*, December 7, 2011, www.northjersey.com/news/135228683 _Libraries_gear_up_to_help_boomers_into_the_new_age_of_retirement.html.

2. Unless otherwise indicated, all population statistics for the following profiles derive from American Community Survey 5-year estimates, accessible through http://factfinder2 .census.gov/faces/nav/jsf/pages/index.xhtml.

ARIZONA

Arizona State Library, Archives and Public Records www.lib.az.us

The Arizona State Library, Archives and Public Records (ASLAPR) has carried out a sustained effort over eight years to promote development of library services and programs responsive to the needs and potential contributions of Arizona's midlife adults. Under the leadership of former state librarian Gladys Ann Wells, the agency has advanced this goal through professional development, allocation of LSTA funds for special projects, leadership in other state and national projects, technical assistance, collaboration with philanthropic initiatives, and organization of model programming. Many of the Arizona library projects profiled in this volume are the result of direct or indirect ASLAPR support.

FACTS

State population (2010):
6,324,865

% population 50+: 31.7%

Trend: According to the Office of the Governor, by 2020 a quarter of Arizona's population will be over 60.

In addition to helping transform library practices with and for 50+ adults, ASLAPR has worked with outside agencies, both private and public, to position libraries as key centers for positive aging. The agency has built new connections between libraries and others working with active older adults.

ASLAPR's efforts to advance 50+ services were the first systematic state-level efforts in the nation. Senior staff provided leadership within and beyond the state to help transform traditional senior services and to recognize the special opportunities for working with midlife adults in transition to a new life stage. Through participation in national and regional conferences, extensive librarian training, and collaboration in national projects, ASLAPR staff have had an unusually strong impact on the profession.

BACKGROUND

Since 2003, ASLAPR has promoted midlife adult services in the library community and provided leadership, both directly and indirectly, to foster new practices. ASLAPR's professional development and funding initiatives, started in 2003 and continuing today, have complemented and extended other projects to improve opportunities for midlife adults in many Arizona institutions. Key components of ASLAPR's midlife adult initiatives include the following:

Leadership. ASLAPR participated in the Maricopa County Commission on Productive Aging (2003) and the Life Options Libraries Training Institute

[6]

(2004) funded by the Virginia G. Piper Trust and organized by Libraries for the Future (www.lff.org).[1] ASLAPR was a key collaborator in the design and implementation of these activities, both of which helped stimulate subsequent changes in Arizona libraries' approaches to older adult services.

Grants. Between 2004 and 2010, ASLAPR provided LSTA grant funds totaling more than $300,000 for 50+ services. Projects were funded at some of the state's smallest and most remote libraries as well as the largest metropolitan libraries. Funding supported a wide range of activities, from information needs assessments to recareering services. Today, ASLAPR continues to fund 50+ projects such as cultural programming, literacy and computer classes, access to digital content, and, most recently, job help projects.

Professional development. From 2003 to 2007, ASLAPR worked closely with Libraries for the Future to provide training in Equal Access Libraries, a methodology for community librarianship involving special training in Lifelong Access Libraries, an approach to midlife services that emphasized needs assessment, advisory committees, community partnerships and peer-led programming.[2] EqualAccess in Action: Experts & Practitioners in Lifelong Learning was a final workshop program, held in February 2007, that showcased success stories. New

Selected LSTA-Funded Projects, Arizona

Directions and Connections (2004), Glendale Public Library
A project with multiple components: formation of a community network linking residents with organizations and agencies providing information for 50+ adults; programs addressing main issues of boomers, such as retirement planning, health and wellness, and availability of Spanish-language materials; and a senior advocate staff position to link seniors and their families or caregivers with community agencies. (www.glendaleaz.com/library)

Life Changes: The Future Is Now (2005), Parker Public Library
Parker Public Library, a small library serving a large rural area of western Arizona, worked with Arizona Western College to offer computer training and consumer health classes that enabled older community members to access accurate and timely health information independently. (parkerpublic libraryaz.org)

Baby Boomer Grant (2006), East Flagstaff Community Library
Working with the Nonprofit Resource Center of Northern Arizona and the Northern Arizona University Senior Corps, the library reached out to local boomers to encourage community service. Funding supported acquisitions, marketing, and public relations. (www.flagstaffpubliclibrary.org)

The Best Part of Life (2006), Phoenix Public Library
Funding supported research on service needs and interests for 50+ residents. Through data collection and focus groups the library identified the most pressing issues for midlife and older residents.

Community partners included Phoenix College, Jewish Family and Children's Services, and OASIS. Research results led to a program plan with community partners and the purchase of additional library resources. (www.phoenixpublic library.org)

Kaboom! (Keeping Boomers Options Open and Manageable) (2007), Apache Junction Public Library
The library established a "next step" program for community members 45 years and older. Funds were used to outfit a room for discussion and programming and an outdoor multimedia area. Partners included the Volunteer Center of Pinal County and Apache Junction Chamber of Commerce. (www.ajpl.org)

approaches to working with midlife adults have been featured in subsequent leadership academies and library institutes organized by ASLAPR.

ASLAPR sponsored seven Arizona librarians to take part in the IMLS Western States Fellowship program, a part of the California State Libraries Transforming Life After 50 initiative during 2010–2011. Two Arizona participants helped organize ASLAPR's Adult Services for the 21st Century: Living Longer, Living Better Summit held in August 2011, attended by seventy librarians from across the state, which featured emerging practices in 50+ services.

Collaboration. ASLAPR has collaborated with public agencies, private funders, and national organizations to expand opportunities for learning and community engagement by baby boomers and other active older adults. ASLAPR staff encouraged libraries to take part in the 2006 Life Options Libraries project and subsequent Next Chapter projects, both funded by the Virginia G. Piper Trust and organized with the assistance of Libraries for the Future and Civic Ventures (www.encore.org/about).[3]

"Bonus Years" programs. ASLAPR staff created a program series titled Bonus Years at the Carnegie Library Center, a facility of the state library (see chapter 9). The series was targeted to state workers and residents located nearby in downtown Phoenix. They also created a *Core Bibliography Information Guide for the Bonus Years* (www.lib.az.us/carnegie/bib/Default.aspx).

Technical assistance. In addition to its extensive training activities, ASLAPR provides technical assistance for Arizona libraries considering new or expanded 50+ initiatives.

FUNDING

Grant monies for individual library projects derive from the federal LSTA funds administered through the IMLS and allocated on a competitive basis by ASLAPR. In some cases the LSTA monies have been matched or extended through local funding from library Friends groups or local philanthropies. The collaborative ASLAPR–Libraries for the Future Equal Access and Lifelong Access Libraries training was funded in part by Atlantic Philanthropies and the Bill and Melinda Gates Foundation.

STATUS

ASLAPR's leadership and funding for 50+ service are ongoing; the agency continues to accept grant proposals for LSTA funds. In addition, many of the libraries that received LSTA grant monies or participated in ASLAPR professional development activities continue to focus on midlife adults. Through classes and programs, advisory councils, community partnerships, online resources, and in some cases dedicated spaces, the libraries continue to improve and expand services for Arizona's large numbers of 50+ residents.

Notes

1. See *The Next Chapter Network*, www.encore.org/files/blueprint-supplement.pdf.

2. Waldron, Sabrina. *Beyond Bingo for Boomers: An Overview of the Lifelong Access Libraries Model.* Presentation at the Transforming Life After 50 Training Institute for public librarians. Pasadena, California. November 2007 http://transforminglifeafter50.org/files/handout-pdfs/TLAFWaldronppt.pdf

3. Next Chapter projects took place in four communities: Chandler, Scottsdale, Mesa and Tempe. In each community the local library was a key partner in a multi-agency collaborative to advance community engagement by older adults living in Maricopa County.

LEADING-EDGE STATE

CALIFORNIA

California State Library, Transforming Life After 50

www.cla-net.org, www.transforminglifeafter50.org

Transforming Life After 50 (TLA50) is a sustained, multifaceted initiative of the California State Library (CSL) that is helping the state's public libraries transform services for midlife adults. TLA50 aims to "inspire library innovation that is responsive to the changing nature of adult aging in America and to help libraries become true cornerstone organizations of productive aging."

As a catalyst for professional change, TLA50 is unique within the library profession. It includes a combination of training, online resources, project implementation grants, networking forums, and, most recently, a related program that extends the work in California to neighboring states. Whereas the ASLAPR was the first state library to promote new approaches to the growing 50+ population, California took several more steps with its large investment of dollars and professional staff time, its efforts to engage as many of the state's libraries as possible, and its emphasis on transformation rather than routine change.

TLA50 has also spawned two other initiatives with national impact: Get Involved: Powered by Your Library, a partnership with the national organization

> **FACTS**
>
> **State population (2009):** 36,308,527
>
> **% population 50+ (2009):** 22.3%
>
> **Trend:** The number of residents 65 and older is expected to increase 107% from 2010 to 2030.

VolunteerMatch (www.volunteermatch.org) that benefits libraries and communities statewide (see chapter 3); and the IMLS Western States Fellowship (see below.) In addition, the TLA50 website, with a wide range of practical information and training materials, is now a major resource for 50+ library services nationwide.

In its scope, depth, and continuity TLA50 is unprecedented and is leading to systemic change in how public librarians perceive and work with 50+ adults.

BACKGROUND

Since 2006, CSL has been developing ways to help libraries respond to the rapid increase in 50+ adults in California. The state librarian, Susan Hildreth, participated in the Libraries for the Future/IMLS Designs for Change: Libraries and Productive Aging forum in 2005.[1] Along with other state librarians, she recognized the potential for libraries to become centers for positive aging and the need for leadership at the state level. CSL's initial investment enabled a staff consultant, Suzanne Flint, to attend the first weeklong Libraries for the Future Lifelong Access Libraries Leadership Institute. After this experience, Flint spearheaded development of TLA50, which has exerted considerable influence over California librarians' responses to aging and proven to be the most substantive and sustained of all 50+ state efforts.

Key TLA50 features include the following:

Professional development. The three-day TLA50 Institute, held in Pasadena in 2007, brought together two staff members, including the library director, from

Transforming Life After 50: Selected California State Library LSTA Grants

Be More @ your library, Tuolumne County Library

Library staff developed new cultural enrichment and educational opportunities for older residents of their small rural county. They designed and launched twenty new library programs responsive to boomer interests, including weekly games activity, computer classes, lectures and readings, and viewings of dramatic productions. Two large community events, an art show and the Caregivers' Information Fair, were also offered in collaboration with community partners. To carry out these and other activities, the library recruited and prepared twenty community volunteers who taught several of the new programs, with forty-five additional volunteers assisting in other ways. A six-member advisory board was created that also assisted with the new programs. (www.library.co.tuolumne.ca.us)

Kern County Library

During the first round of TLA50 grants in 2008, library staff conducted a community needs assessment that elicited more than three hundred responses. Staff then created a gathering place at all seven Bakersfield libraries for boomers to meet, exchange ideas, get information, socialize, and attend lectures (see chapter 12). The library also experimented with nontraditional means of publicizing project activities via TV, radio, print, and digital media in English and Spanish. (www.kerncounty library.org) each of fifty libraries across the state.[2] The institute was a cooperative effort of CSL, Libraries for the Future, and the California Library Association. Training goals were to promote an understanding of older adults as resources for their communities; offer an alternative to the predominant deficit-based model of aging; and introduce participants to a new framework to promote productive aging through learning and civic engagement.

Participants were invited to follow up by conducting a needs and assets assessment of their own community. They were then encouraged to apply for an LSTA grant to implement promising practices. A consulting team provided technical assistance for applicants.

Grants. CSL awarded twenty-four implementation grants of $15,000–20,000 in the 2008/09 LSTA grant cycle. Twelve additional LSTA grants were awarded in subsequent annual rounds, for a total investment, to date, of approximately $536,000 in LSTA monies. Grants continue to be available for 50+ services.

Forums. During the spring of 2010, TLA50 libraries were invited to regional forums where they participated in panel discussions and plenary meetings about their progress toward achieving their local objectives and the goals of the overall initiative. Promising practices and lessons learned continue to be posted on the TLA50 website and social networks.

Communications. Communications and identity building within the profession, especially online, have been important aspects of the TLA50 initiative. A robust website was developed that supports the initial training and grants programs. The site has become a resource for exchange on best practices in the

---

Orange County Public Libraries
Orange County Public Libraries (OCPL) developed a range of special programs designed for boomers that covered topics such as health and nutrition, work, and lifestyle choices. The health component involved production of twelve information packets on boomer health concerns that were distributed to all OCPL branches. The library also partnered with the Parks Department to offer a "walk and learn" event, and it expanded business development workshops with SCORE (see chapter 11) and marketed them to older adult business entrepreneurs. Lifestyle programs included a literary event with mystery writers and a community book read of *Three Cups of Tea* in which almost three hundred people participated The book read resulted in the creation of a social networking blog. In addition, OCPL organized a half-day training program for staff to prepare them to meet the growing demand for job search assistance from 50+ patrons. (http://egov.ocgov.com/ocgov/OC%20Public%20Libraries)

Santa Fe Springs Library
The library carried out a survey of lifelong learning interests identified by local boomers and organized a wide variety of workshops, lectures, film screenings, and book discussions as well as classes on crafts, fitness, and job searching to address those interests. Materials were added to the collection on related topics. The library gained important insights into the dual needs of its primarily Hispanic adult user population who wanted both nonformal learning opportunities and inclusive family events. Participation at events was very high—higher than ever before—and the library also recruited forty-three new volunteers. (www.santafesprings.org/library)

state and has recently expanded to function as the base for the Western Regional Fellows initiative including online training courses.

Expansion projects. In addition to the above, CSL has worked with partners to develop two complementary projects that enhance TLA50 and extend its impact: Get Involved: Powered by Your Library (see chapter 3), and the Western Regional Fellowship: Transforming Life After 50. For both of these projects, CSL has taken the lead in providing an administrative center, funding, and professional training for librarian participants.

Leadership. CLS senior staff have provided encouragement, technical assistance, and a training base for California librarians and many others who have benefited through the Western Regional Fellowship program and online resources. In addition, through presentations at national and regional conferences, and through printed and online communications, CSL senior staff have helped advance the development of 50+ services as a new specialty within adult services.

PARTNERS

In the initial stages of TLA50, CSL worked in partnership with Libraries for the Future to provide initial concepts and materials for the initiative. The first institute also involved the California Library Association. Many organizations, such as AARP California (www.aarp.org/states/ca) and the Stanford Center on Longevity (www.longevity.stanford.edu), have participated in TLA50 events or webinars. Get Involved, a result of TLA50, includes a partnership with VolunteerMatch. The Western Regional Fellowship involves collaboration with state libraries in Arizona, Idaho, Oregon, Washington, and the Pacific Library Partnership.

FUNDING

Funding for TLA50 has derived primarily from federal LSTA funds allocated to the State of California by the IMLS. The Western Regional Fellowship was funded through the IMLS Laura Bush 21st Century Librarian Program and in-kind contributions from state partners. Several of the TLA50 libraries that received initial implementation grants have successfully incorporated these initiatives into core programming operations or have received continuing support from their Friends group or local businesses.

STATUS

TLA50 continues as an important part of CSL's Library Development Services division. California librarians use the TLA50 website as a resource for ongoing project development, and they may apply for LSTA grants for 50+ library services. Many are participating in Get Involved: Powered by Your Library, and others are participating in the Western Regional Fellowship program. In addition, most of the libraries that took part in the original TLA50 training and received early grants have continued their project work in one form or another. The California library projects here are a direct result of CSL's leadership in 50+ services.

Notes

1. See *Designs for Change: Libraries and Productive Aging*, a report on the National Library Leaders Forum cosponsored by Americans for Libraries Council and Institute for Museum and Library Services, September 26–27, 2005. www.imls.gov/assets/1/AssetManager/DesignsforChange.pdf.

2. *Transforming Life After 50: Public Libraries and Baby Boomers*, Project Overview, www.transforminglifeafter50.org/files/TLAFOverviewAgendaGoals.pdf.

LEADING-EDGE STATE

CONNECTICUT

Connecticut State Library www.cslib.org

The Connecticut State Library (CTSL) was one of the first state library agencies to advocate expanded services and programs for 50+ residents. Like ASLAPR, CTSL took the lead in promoting new service development within libraries and also in promoting libraries as key centers for positive aging with other public and private agencies. Connecticut was one of the first states to provide LSTA funding for local projects serving midlife adults, such as the New Haven Free Public Library's 50+ Transition Center (see chapter 2) and has continued to support experimentation in services for and with 50+ residents. CTSL's 2003 Coming of Age forum, carried out in partnership with Libraries for the Future and Civic Ventures, was an early model for convening library leaders with leaders from other sectors to discuss strategies for serving and engaging older adults. In addition, CTSL con-

FACTS

State population (2009): 3,518,288

% population 55+: 25.1%

Trend: The U.S. Census Bureau estimated in 2008 that by 2015 the number of residents age 65 and over will increase by 11.9% while the number of residents age 18–64 will grow by less than one tenth of one percent.

tributed to change at the national level by dedicating time and expertise to WebJunction Services to Older Adults Discussion Forum. Without these forums local librarians would have less access to case studies, new research, and peers, all of which are essential for advancing professional change.

BACKGROUND

CTSL has played a leading role, both statewide and nationally, in advancing new attitudes and practices with respect to 50+ adults. Through a combination of professional development, grantmaking, consulting services, and communications, staff of the Division of Library Development have supported librarians' efforts to meet the emerging needs of baby boomers and other active older adults.

CTSL's work to encourage 50+ services emerges from a long-standing commitment to improved services and programs for all Connecticut seniors. In 2004 it organized a special interest group, SOAR (Services to Older Adult Roundtable), which continues to meet regularly and provides a forum for professional exchange. Beyond SOAR, the work on midlife adults includes the following components:

Coming of Age forum. As Connecticut's population of 50+ adults has expanded over the past decade, including many who do not fit the traditional "senior" stereotype, CTSL has recognized the importance of reexamining traditional senior services as well as adult programming. To this end, CTSL helped present a 2003 forum at the state capital in Hartford titled "Coming of Age: Building Healthy Communities in Connecticut."

> If you wait for the "right time," you'll be waiting forever. Right now is the time for libraries to get on the ball and target older adults with services and programs. . . . Try out ideas like you're throwing spaghetti at the wall—see what sticks. Listen to feedback, incorporate it into your process. Hook people with good programming and clearly explain that you need their support (time, attendance, effort) in the future. Get results-based accountability (RBA) data to prove worthiness to funders.
>
> —Douglas Lord, older adult specialist, Connecticut State Library

The forum was designed to "initiate a dialogue among the public, private and non-profit sectors—including numerous librarians—concerning opportunities and approaches for tapping the skills and experience of the state's growing population of older adults." In opening the forum Kendall Wiggin, state librarian of Connecticut, posed a challenge: "How can we reshape our organizations to both meet the changing demands of a maturing population and engage that population in improving our communities?"

Professional development. After the Coming of Age forum, CTSL worked with Libraries for the Future for three years to offer librarians training in new approaches to community librarianship, including the Lifelong Access Libraries model for working with midlife and older adults. Librarians from across the state learned about the importance of needs assessments, advisory committees, partnerships, marketing, and other strategies for work with active older adults. Participants who were part of SOAR brought new perspectives to those discussions, stimulating increased attention to work with active midlife adults as distinguished from outreach to dependent elderly clients.

Grants. Since 2004, CTSL has awarded LSTA grants to support services and programs for midlife adults. The funded programs, each of them quite different in approach, offer examples of experimentation and outreach to the state's growing 50+ population. Examples of funded projects include Arts and Archives at the Hartford Public Library (see chapter 7) and the 50+ Transition Center of the New Haven Public Library (see chapter 2).

Communications. CTSL has provided significant state and national leadership through its communications work regarding 50+ services. For six years, Doug-

Selected LSTA Projects, Connecticut

Community Needs Assessment (2010), Ferguson Library, Stamford

In 2010, Ferguson Library staff decided that they needed to consider improvements to older adults services. Before developing any new programs or services, they decided to learn more about local older adults' interest and information needs. With LSTA support and pro bono assistance from a major marketing firm headquartered in Stamford, they carried out two focus groups of mobile older adults. The sessions were designed to elicit feedback on their viewing, reading, and listening habits and to gather suggestions for new or reorganized activities. The library is now designing services that respond to the suggestions. (www.fergusonlibrary.org)

Lunch and Learn (2006), Russell Library, Middletown

The Russell Library initiated Lunch and Learn in 2006 with an LSTA grant that also helped support a part-time older adult coordinator. The midday programs, led by knowledgeable local adults, range from thematic film series to gardening and cooking topics involving hands-on demonstrations. The programming benefits from guidance by the library-wide older adults team. (www.russelllibrary.org)

Senior Savvy, West Hartford Public Library (2008)

Senior Savvy takes advantage of young adults' skills in communications technologies to assist boomers and other older adults who aim to become more

competent computer users. West Hartford received an LSTA grant for weekly one-on-one tutoring—a teen and an older adult—in the areas of basic computer use, word processing, and Internet use. Each participant receives customized, individual instruction. According to project leader Doreen McCabe, "we teach exactly what each person really wants, rather than giving them formalized preset lessons on a particular computer topic." (www.westhartfordlibrary.org)

Arts and Archives at the Hartford Public Library

(see chapter 7)

The 50+ Transition Center at the New Haven Free Public Library

(see chapter 2)

las Lord, CTSL's specialist on older adult services, moderated the national Services to Older Adults Discussion Forum on WebJunction as well as Connecticut's SOAR.[1] Lord has spoken at library conferences and professional meetings, including the 2009 regional Lifelong Access Libraries Leadership Institute and has offered national WebJunction webinars such as "Libraries Go Boom!"

FUNDING

Grants for local projects approved by CTSL have derived from federal LSTA monies funded through the IMLS. The Lifelong Access training offered jointly with Libraries for the Future was funded by Atlantic Philanthropies and the Bill and Melinda Gates Foundation.

STATUS

Connecticut's commitment to 50+ library services and programs is ongoing, with continued leadership by the state librarian and the staff of the state library development office. The SOAR group meets every other month under the aegis of the Connecticut Library Consortium; during each recent round of LSTA grants, programs involving 50+ adults have been approved for funding; and Douglas Lord continues to lead discussions on older adult services at the state and national level. Although the recent economic downturn has slowed new program development in the state, the Division of Library Development works to mitigate the impacts of the downturn and to ensure that 50+ adults are an important focus for Connecticut librarians.

Note

1. This forum is no longer active, but WebJunction now provides the web page "Older Adults & Seniors," a list of resources that includes webinars by Lord.

MASSACHUSETTS

Massachusetts Board of Library Commissioners   http://mblc.state.ma.us

Since 2005 the Massachusetts Board of Library Commissioners (MBLC) has carried out a sustained effort to prepare Massachusetts librarians for an increased presence of active older adults. Through training and project funding MBLC has stimulated many libraries and library systems to develop new approaches to working with baby boomers and other active older adults. MBLC's training and funding initiatives have had, and continue to have, widespread impact on how older adult services are carried out in the state. In addition, MBLC staff have contributed to regional and national initiatives designed to build librarians' capacities for midlife services, providing leadership and practical examples of value to colleagues nationwide.

> **FACTS**
> **Population (2009):** 6,512,000
>
> **% population 55+:** 24.6%
>
> **Trend:** As the Massachusetts population ages, older workers will constitute a larger share of the labor force. The U.S. Census Bureau estimated in 2005 that, between 2010 and 2030, 100 percent of the growth in the Massachusetts labor force will come from workers who are 55+.

MBLC's investments in 50+ services are distinctive in several ways. First, they are designed to include both training and related seed monies to implement programs. Second, the projects engage librarians from all sizes of libraries throughout the state, including libraries serving small communities. Third, MBLC has provided sustained support for this work and plans to continue doing so, enabling numerous librarians to develop new skills that can be applied in different settings and to function as a cohort group within the larger Massachusetts library community. Most of the Massachusetts libraries profiled here received initial training and funded through MBLC.

BACKGROUND

MBLC has a tradition of supporting professional development and of encouraging community responsive services in such areas as literacy, health information, technology training, and services for new immigrants. In 2005, MBLC offered a workshop introducing library directors to the concept of "The Experience Library," based on the work of Joseph Pine, author of *The Experience Economy* (1999). After this workshop the Northern Massachusetts Regional Library System (NMRLS) was awarded an LSTA grant to carry out the Experience Library for Older Citizens Project, which was designed to train staff from member libraries in new approaches to working with older adults. NMRLS also received funds to create the Lifelong Access Xchange, a clearinghouse of information and service examples for member libraries. Although NMRLS was subsequently disbanded during reorganization of the state's library systems, the training and the Xchange were important sources of professional communications for early adopters within the NMRLS system and beyond.

Building on the NMRLS initiative, MBLC recognized the need to strengthen 50+ library services across the state. The board embarked on a series of training and funding initiatives that have enabled numerous Massachusetts libraries to experiment with new service approaches and to build new constituencies. Key components of MBLC's work in this area include the following:

> It is not enough to just do the training. We must also provide incentives so that librarians can apply the new concepts and skills.
>
> —Shelley Quezada, MBLC consultant to the underserved

Professional development. A partnership with Libraries for the Future involved the provision of training in the Equal Access method of community librarianship, including services for active older adults. Two yearlong statewide initiatives—Equal Access Libraries (2008) and Lifelong Access Libraries (2009)—combined training with follow-up seed grants to enable trainees to implement new service concepts in their local communities.[1]

Libraries selected for the training and funding initiatives sent at least one staff member to a multipart training program. Participating libraries could opt for three different service emphases, including work with active older adults. Those that chose to focus on active older adults then received LSTA grants of $5,000 to create and implement new community programming and services.

Over two years, MBLC supported twenty-one Lifelong Access libraries, each of which carried out community needs and assets assessments and designed programs responsive to local needs. Programs varied from the Oak Bluff Library's Illumination for Lifelong Learners series (see chapter 8) to the Paul Pratt Library in Peabody's Next Chapter workshops on using new social media (see chapter 6).

In 2009, MBLC and Libraries for the Future cosponsored a one-day New England Lifelong Access Libraries Institute for librarians from Massachusetts and several other New England states. The program introduced participants to recent research behind new service concepts and provided examples of new practices.

Grants. As of January 2011, MBLC had made twenty-six Lifelong Access grants, allocating a total of $105,000 in LSTA funds. This total includes six grants of $5,000 in 2007, sixteen in 2008, and four grants of $7,500 in 2010. Although the individual grants are relatively small, they are intended as seed grants, enabling librarians who have been exposed to new ideas and practices to experiment with new approaches in their local settings. As described by MBLC's Shelley Quezada, "completed projects helped libraries focus on adults ages 50–70+, the baby boomer generation, who are active and eager to be engaged. An emerging community of practice now provides a network to discuss services to this older active population."

MBLC was engaged in a two-year funding program (2010–11), titled "Next Chapter": Vital Aging for Older Active Adults, in 2010–11[2] This initiative built on prior grant programs and encouraged additional libraries to engage and inform 50+ adults. Four libraries received Next Chapter grants in 2010 and four additional libraries in 2011. The libraries approved for funding had to

- Complete a preliminary needs assessment
- Develop an advisory group and engage members in program design
- Develop multiformat collections to match local interests
- Examine ways in which new information technology can be used to benefit the target audience
- Attend a special training meeting

Selected MBLC LSTA Grants

Experience Library for Older Citizens Project (2007), Northern Massachusetts Regional Library System
NMRLS received support to train member libraries in the Lifelong Access service approach, in collaboration with Libraries for the Future. The grant also enabled creation of the Lifelong Access Xchange, an online communications center. Although NMRLS no longer exists, several member libraries continue to offer targeted 50+services.

The Retirement Puzzle: Conversations for a Successful Transition (2009), Cary Memorial Library, Lexington
How can individuals and couples make decisions that lead to satis-

faction and fulfillment in the next chapter of their lives? This question was the basis for a "conversation" on retirement transitions held November 2011. The program was led by Roberta Taylor, a psychotherapist and transition coach. The program was one activity undertaken by the library as part of a Next Chapter grant awarded by the Massachusetts Board of Library Commissioners. (www.carylibrary.org)

Fifty Plus Resource Directory (2010), Wayland Free Public Library
Staff created a special online directory, listing a wide variety of activities and services available to middle-age and older adults in Wayland covering education,

financial planning, nutrition, and housing. (www.waylandlibrary.org)

Golden Opportunities at the Holmes (2010), Holmes Library, Halifax
The grant supported writing, web and craft workshops, and the drop-in Technology Café, which offers opportunities to "become confident in using laptop computers as you blog, skype, tweet and Facebook your writings and experiences." (www.holmespubliclibrary.org)

Leadership. Through participation in state and regional forums pertaining to aging trends in Massachusetts, MBLC has fostered closer connections between the library community and other agencies and organizations focused on positive aging. Libraries are now "at the table" in Massachusetts.

FUNDING

Grant monies provided by MBLC were derived from LSTA monies funded through the IMLS. The professional development work of Libraries for the Future was funded by Atlantic Philanthropies and the Bill and Melinda Gates Foundation.

STATUS

Many of the libraries that received NMRLS training in 2006 and received direct grants from MBLC in 2008–10 continue to focus on active older adults, maintaining special online resource centers and offering classes or events for this population. The Reading Public Library's Live Wires program, for example, continues to evolve, attract local support, and provide an instructive example for other libraries in the state and the nation. Several libraries that took part in Equal Access and Lifelong Access training have sustained or adapted their funding projects.

With the new funding for Next Chapter libraries in 2010 and 2011, MBLC leveraged the accomplishments of early adopters and enlarged the network of Next Chapter libraries across the state. MBLC intends to continue funding Next Chapter requests as long as funds hold out and libraries indicate interest.

Notes

1. See Kimberly Shigo, "LFF Wins Grant for Equal Access Libraries," *AllBusiness*, October 1, 2003.

    Lifelong Access is an approach to community librarianship that focuses on mid-life and other active adults and emphasizes the provision of opportunities for learning, interaction, expression and community engagement. *Lifelong Access* employs the *Equal Access* method of community librarianship, developed by Libraries for the Future, that involves needs assessments, community partnerships, patron participation in program development and multi-format programming.

2. For background, see http://mblc.state.ma.us/grants/lsta/opportunities/mini-grants/fs_next_chapter.pdf.

CHAPTER 2

BEACONS OF CHANGE

Libraries throughout the United States constantly retool to meet the needs of library users and, as librarians, we welcome the 50+ population, in its millions of manifestations, through our physical and virtual doors.

—Brigid Cahalan, New York Public Library

The library landscape is filled with examples of programs and services for older adults, ranging from arts and humanities courses and workshops on retirement planning to job fairs for boomers, computer classes for seniors, and activities for grandparents and grandchildren. Though some of these are offered as part of ongoing "adult programs" or "senior services," more and more are designed and marketed specifically for midlife adults. They reflect librarians' growing recognition that people are living longer, healthier lives; that concepts of "retirement" are changing; and that library services must meet the realities of a new life stage.

The number and variety of entries in the following chapters attest to the emergence of a movement to respond to this new life stage, a movement to create 50+ services. Librarians are clearly starting to pay serious attention to midlife adults, a diverse group that includes baby boomers but also individuals who are older than the boomers but still active and engaged in work, learning, or community pursuits. Midlife adults can also include "Younger Boomers" (defined by the Pew Internet and American Library Project as ages 46–55). Librarians are starting to recognize not only that midlife adults are multigenerational but that most do not fit the current paradigm for "senior services." Instead of being isolated or infirm and depending on outreach services, the majority are active, engaged, and mobile. Some even have valuable life experiences and skills that they are interested in applying for the benefit of their communities. These realizations are fundamental to the development of 50+ library services.

As with other types of institutional and professional change, the emergence of 50+ library services is not a dramatic transformation but rather a gradual evolution in attitudes and practices. Change depends on a host of factors: library leaders' awareness of new needs, economic climate, governance structure, institutional traditions, social and geographic environment, and opportunities for professional development. Change can also be impeded by the kinds of barriers discussed in chapter 1, including but not limited to ageism, institutional traditions, lack of leadership, minimal resources, and lack of professional development or incentives for change. In addition, instructive examples of new service approaches are located in various parts of the country, have different emphases, and lack the benefit of a connective mechanism to create critical mass. In the context of these challenges, the remarkable movement to create 50+ services attests to the tenacity, commitment, and imagination of the leaders and practitioners who are paving the way for change.

A scan of the national landscape reveals eleven libraries or library systems that reflect change at the institutional level. They demonstrate high and sustained commitment to 50+ services. These "50+ Beacon Libraries" are not simply trying out one or another project depending on the availability of grant funds. They are committed to meeting the needs of their 50+ patrons on a continuing basis and are working to ensure that services are organized in such a way that they are responsive to the communities the library serves, integrated into the library in terms of planning priorities, staffing, and resource allocations, and sustainable.

The eleven 50+ Beacons are profiled below. Widely divergent in terms of community settings and local resources, they all represent a new attitude about older adult services and they all provide instructive examples for other libraries in terms of the scope, depth, and particulars of their approaches. They are harbingers of a transformation in adult and senior services to focus on midlife adults.

The eleven Beacon libraries do the following:

- Understand that traditional models for senior services are no longer adequate for today's diverse aging populations

- Seek input about library services and programs from midlife adults, including nonusers
- See midlife patrons as library and community assets and engage them in designing and implementing programs
- Demonstrate awareness of new research on positive aging through activities that emphasize participation, engagement, and expression rather than passive consumption of information
- Integrate 50+ services and programs across the library
- Respond to diverse midlife patrons, including those with varied linguistic, economic, and cultural backgrounds
- Offer activities and programs that cross generations and promote social, intellectual, and cultural exchange
- Collaborate with other institutions and agencies concerned with positive aging
- Experiment with new structural or staffing approaches for 50+ services
- Reflect commitment to ongoing, sustained programming rather than one-time events
- Assess and refine 50+ services on a continuing basis

In addition to meeting these criteria, the 50+ Beacons also demonstrate a willingness to help move the profession in a new direction. Many of them have sent staff to professional meetings and conferences to share their experiences and findings. Their library staffs often participate in electronic forums on older adults services, and they sometimes advise or mentor colleagues in other communities on development of new approaches to serving and working with midlife adults. Some Beacon libraries or library systems have even created training programs

50+ Beacons: Keys to Success

SUPPORT FROM THE TOP

You need not just support but enthusiasm from the Library Director—someone to say "this is a priority" and really mean it. The excitement and the message will trickle down to staff.

—Kate Cosgrove, manager, 50+ Transition Center, New Haven Free Public Library

INPUT FROM 50+ PATRONS

Focus groups were essential in challenging our assumptions about what people want and need for their transition years.

—Nancy Aberman, coordinator, Live Wires, Reading Public Library

INVOLVEMENT OF LIBRARY STAFF

These programs cannot be successful as sole-person operations. You need staff that recognize the value of programs and the value of re-thinking programs for older adults.

—Melinda Ludwiczak, legacy project manager, Metropolitan Library Services Association

PARTNERSHIPS

Community partnerships are the lifeblood of our programming. Partners provide expertise, help market programs, and share resources for mutual benefit.

—Charity Leonette, community partnerships coordinator and webmaster, Allegheny County Library Association for their own staff and colleagues from other institutions. In the absence of other systemic efforts to promote change—aside from the state library initiatives profiled in chapter 1—the professional assistance provided by the 50+ Beacon libraries is an essential tool for change.

The libraries profiled below provide powerful evidence of institutional change. They are not only making changes to their core work by creating a new genre of library service for a new life stage but also creating new program and project models in a broad array of formats and subjects. Many of their projects are included in later chapters on specific service categories. Although the eleven Beacons are dispersed across the country and do not represent an official network or leadership group, their collective impact on the profession is tangible. They are truly beacons of change.

ALLEGHENY COUNTY LIBRARY ASSOCIATION

Pittsburgh, Pennsylvania www.aclalibraries.org

The federated Allegheny County Library Association (ACLA) demonstrates what is possible in terms of service innovations and community connections when a library system is committed to meeting the changing needs of a diverse aging population. ACLA's leadership in 50+ services derives from its extensive partnerships with varied organizations and sectors in the Pittsburgh area; the many experimental programs it has undertaken to advance intergenerational contact, healthy aging, and creative expression; its attention to programs that engage low- and mixed-income midlife adults; its sustained support of peer-led book clubs and discussion groups; and its provision of training and collegial networking for member librarians.

FACTS

Member libraries: 45

Service area: Allegheny County

Population (2010): 1.2 million

% population 55+: 28.7%

Trend: There are numerous communities in Allegheny County where a high proportion of the population is age 65 and over. These NORCs (naturally occurring retirement communities) will grow as baby boomers turn 65.

BACKGROUND

ACLA is unusual in having had a strong commitment to older adult services dating from the mid-1990s, including services for active older adults as well as homebound seniors. Led by director Marilyn Jenkins and a highly committed staff member responsible for programming and community partnerships, ACLA developed two signature programs in 2006 that provided the foundation for later program development. Both programs continue today: Conversation Salons engage older adults in regular, facilitated conservations on topics of interest to participants. There are now fourteen such salons in libraries across the county, one of which is facilitated by a nonagenarian. PALS Book Clubs provide older adults who are eligible for Medicare the opportunity to join a book discussion in one of three locations: high rises, senior centers, and libraries. There are now more than twenty PALS clubs in member libraries.

> Aging well and never ceasing to grow is what we all hope to experience. At ACLA we focus on creating opportunities that stimulate curiosity, expand horizons, and add richness to the everyday lives of our 50+ neighbors.
>
> **—Marilyn Jenkins, executive director, ACLA**

The success of these programs when they were initially offered prompted ACLA to consider other ways to engage the growing population of 50+ adults in Allegheny County. In 2006, ACLA sent a staff member to the Libraries for the Future Lifelong Access Libraries Institute. Her participation in the weeklong program, and in the Intergenerational Training Institute at the University of Pittsburgh, strengthened ACLA's commitment to expand 50+ programs and services.[1] In addition to the Conversation Salons and PALS Book Clubs, key components now in place include a highly successful One Book, One Community program that especially engages midlife adults and intergenerational groups; the Older Adult Forum, a meeting group and blog for librarians; and several intergenerational programs including the new ACLA Intergenerational Academy. Many of ACLA's member libraries have adopted these programs, and some have been inspired to create their own services for and with midlife adults.

SCOPE AND STATUS

The number of ACLA projects profiled in this volume suggests the depth of ACLA's commitment to 50+ services and to continual development of these services as needs and opportunities arise. As ACLA and its member libraries have designed, tested, and evaluated programs, their formats and content have evolved. As one example, ACLA has continually developed new approaches to intergenerational activities. 50+ services and partnerships have become an integral part of ACLA's core functions—they will not disappear with the loss of a grant or change in staff—and ACLA member libraries are also devoting staff time and other resources to midlife adults and integrating 50+ activities into their service routines. For example, in 2010 two ACLA libraries received LSTA grants from the Commonwealth Office of Library Development to create Senior Spaces.[2] With leadership from ACLA, these libraries are promoting positive aging and lifelong learning for their local 50+ residents and will continue to do so at the local level.

PARTNERS

ACLA's 50+ services also reflect strong commitment to partnerships. In fact, the individual who is responsible for 50+ programs and services bears the title "community partnerships coordinator." ACLA staff state that partnerships are vital to reaching and engaging older adults. Indeed, ACLA's emphasis on partnerships is a distinctive feature of its work and one reason for its success. Partners range from the Osher Lifelong Learning Institute at the University of Pittsburgh and AARP Pennsylvania to Generations Together, Barnes & Noble, and OASIS.

FUNDING

Funding for ACLA's work with older adults derives from multiple sources, primarily sponsorships for particular programs. For instance, One Book, One Community has been sponsored by several agencies and businesses, including Allegheny County, Highmark, and Dollar Bank. In addition, the time and resources committed by each of the partners involved in particular programs or projects have made these activities possible.

KEYS TO SUCCESS

Charity Leonette, ACLA's community partnerships coordinator, has developed and managed most of the program initiatives for active older adults. She identifies four primary factors that account for ACLA's success:

- Support and encouragement from ACLA's leaders
- Community partnerships, "the lifeblood of our programming"
- Creative library staff, willing to try new concepts in their communities
- A staff position dedicated to partnerships and programs at the system level

FEATURED ACLA 50+ SERVICES
- Conversation Salons (chapter 4)
- PALS Book Clubs (chapter 9)
- Intergenerational PALS Book Clubs (chapter 10)

- One Book, One Community (chapter 10)
- Create Together: An Intergenerational Art Program, and the ACLA Intergenerational Academy (chapter 10)
- Osher Lifelong Learning Institute Collaboration (chapter 9)

Notes

1. The course "Introduction to Intergenerational Programming" was offered through the University of Pittsburgh School of Social Work Continuing Education program in partnership with the Generations Together Intergenerational Studies Program; see www.gt.pitt.edu.

2. See Claudia Koenig's presentation "Senior Spaces Pennsylvania Style": http://senior spaces.pbworks.com/f/ClaudiaKoenig_Presentation.ppt.

BROOKLYN PUBLIC LIBRARY

Brooklyn, New York www.brooklynpubliclibrary.org

Brooklyn Public Library (BPL), the fifth-largest library system in the United States, has been in the forefront of services to older adults since it founded a special department, Service to the Aging, in the late 1970s. It has served as a model for libraries nationwide based on its sustained commitment to older adult services and the organization of these services. It has also served as a model through the scope and quality of its general adult programming, programming that also benefits 50+ adults. Today, with so many midlife and older adults who do not fit the traditional stereotype of dependent, frail elderly, BPL is seeking ways to adapt and extend its current services for those who are mobile and engaged. In so doing, the library can draw on a strong foundation that includes both traditional outreach and adult programming.

FACTS

Service area: The borough of Brooklyn (Kings County), the most populous of New York City's five boroughs

Total population (2010): 2.5 million

% population 55+: As of 2003, about 20%

Trend: Between 2010 and 2030, the percentage of adults 65+ will increase from 11% to 15%.

BACKGROUND

Patron interest prompted formation of the Service to the Aging department, and responsiveness to patrons has been a hallmark of the program since its inception.[1] Based at New Utrecht Library, BPL Service to the Aging has its own office and staff. In fact, for some years BPL was the only library system in the country with a full office dedicated to senior services. Outreach is extensive, including delivery of library materials to more than 170 designated sites all around Brooklyn, a books-by-mail program, and informational and cultural programs that provide speakers and presentations at senior sites. Three programs suggest the extent and variety of library outreach services for older adults:

Young at Heart: Events for the Active Adult offers or supports musical performances, lectures, or workshops at Brooklyn Public Library locations; senior and adult day-care centers; and assisted living and rehabilitation facilities, hospitals, and nursing homes. For entertainment components, the library uses older adult performers when possible.

Words and Memories, presented in nursing homes and other senior sites, provides poetry readings, film, short stories, history, and art to inspire older adults to reminisce about their life experience.

Creative Writing is a program in which professional poets work with older adults in assisted-living centers to write poems. The resulting anthologies are published for participants and their families.

BPL's Service to the Aging department maintains a web page with numerous information resources including resource guides that point to websites and community agencies put out by its Education and Job Information Center on topics such as education and employment opportunities for seniors.

In addition to full-time staff members, Brooklyn's Service to the Aging department provides older adult patrons the opportunity to serve as paid senior assistants. These assistants implement programs or events at different locations throughout Brooklyn, each one being assigned to a particular location, such as a nursing home or public library. The assistants are encouraged to suggest programming that relates to their constituents. They are described by library staff as "The Heart and Soul of Brooklyn Public Library's Service to the Aging Program."

Along with Service to the Aging, programming is a strong area of service at BPL that benefits 50+ adults. Reflecting the diversity of Brooklyn residents, programming is extraordinarily varied in both content and format, from live entertainment and lifelong learning to practical information and computer training. The programs take place at Central Library, some in the Dr. S. Stevan

Dweck Center for Contemporary Culture, and in neighborhood libraries. Many midlife and older adults take advantage of these programs, especially when they offer opportunities for learning and social engagement. The range of options is considerable: "Get Smart, Get Connected"; "Meet One on One with a Business Counselor"; "Growing Dollars and $ense for Adults"; tango lessons; and free blood pressure clinics.

The library's overall commitment to older adult services is indicated by development of a special training program for staff across the system who interact with seniors. With an LSTA grant through the New York State Department of Education's Office of Library Development, the library created a training curriculum and a guide, *Everyone Serves Seniors*, which is one of the most comprehensive of its type in the country.

SCOPE AND STATUS

With strong traditions of both outreach services and adult programming, it is no surprise that Brooklyn is responding to the increase in the number of 50+ adults with more targeted programming and more specific marketing of current services to reach younger seniors. For instance, the library's website description of Service to the Aging states, "We offer many special programs and events especially tailored to the 55+ audience. These include lectures, films and performances that reflect the wide interests of today's seniors." In addition, the home page link for events is titled "Events for the Active Adults."

Though the use of "55+" and "active adults" rather than "seniors" may seem a small matter, the change can make a difference in how potential library users view the library and its attitudes toward older adults. The current description suggests a shift from a total focus on seniors to a broader focus that includes baby boomers and mobile, active adults.

Another indication of BPL's interest in 50+ services is its new partnership with Lifetime Arts to carry out Creative Aging in Our Communities: The Public Libraries Project. Begun in fall 2011, BPL is hosting Creative Aging projects in thirteen neighborhood libraries and will involve staff in training provided by Lifetime Arts.[2]

PARTNERS

Both adult programs and the Service to the Aging department maintain a multiplicity of partnership relationships with community agencies, nonprofit and for-profit organizations, educational institutions, and cultural and service organizations. A few of Service to the Aging's current partners are the Amico Senior Center, Department for the Aging, Go Direct, Lifetime Arts, Maimonides Hospital Medical Center, Millennium Development, and the VA hospital.

FUNDING

Activities carried out by the Service to the Aging department are funded in part through the New York State Coordinated Outreach Services Grant, the City of New York, and Con Edison. Support from the private sector helps to make up the balance of funding needed to sustain the range and quality of Service to the Aging's major programs. Staff training and the *Everyone Serves Seniors* guide were funded by an LSTA grant administered by the Office of Library Development at the state's Department of Education. The new Lifetime Arts' Creative Aging in Our Communities Program is funded by the Fan Fox and Leslie R. Samuels Foundation.

KEYS TO SUCCESS

BPL's services for older adults, including its traditional outreach to seniors and its newer programs for 50+ residents, position the library as both a pioneer in senior services and an innovator with respect to midlife residents. Several features help account for BPL's distinctive position:

- The longtime identity of the Service to the Aging department, its acceptance as an essential unit of service within the library, and its dedicated staff
- Efforts to train all staff regarding the value of serving older adults
- The wide range of program options available for all adults, including midlife and older residents
- Targeted marketing of educational and cultural programs to 50+ audiences

An additional strength of BPL's service approach is the engagement of older adults as assistants in the Service to the Aging department. With this approach BPL is not only leveraging staff capacities to reach more people and organizations but demonstrating that older adults bring skills and experience that can be applied for the benefit of community members.

FEATURED BPL PROJECTS AND PROGRAMS

- Senior Assistants (chapter 3)
- Creative Aging in Our Communities (chapter 7)

Notes

1. For more on the Service to the Aging department, see Katelynn Angell, "A Senior Program Grows in Brooklyn: Brooklyn Public Library's Service to the Aging," Public Libraries Online, www.publiclibrariesonline.org/content/senior-program-grows-brooklyn-brooklyn-public-librarys-service-aging.

2. See the Creative Aging schedule of events at http://lifetimearts.wordpress.com/tag/brooklyn-public-library-system.

CHANDLER PUBLIC LIBRARY

Chandler, Arizona www.chandlerlibrary.org

Chandler Public Library has been a leader in 50+ services since 2004, when the library first served as coordinator of Boomerang, a community-wide initiative designed to engage baby boomers. Today that leadership continues, with an emphasis on mobilizing boomers as volunteers and stipended workers. In 2010, four hundred adult volunteers committed 24,000 hours to the library; more than 90 percent of them were baby boomers. Library director Brenda Brown has provided leadership nationally and statewide, sharing the library's experiences. Overall, Chandler offers an instructive example of how a broad-based experiment to support boomers during life transitions can evolve into a focused program that consistently and effectively engages 50+ adults in helping to meet the needs of the local community.

FACTS

Service area: City of Chandler

Total population (2010): 238,041

% population 50+: 21.7%

Trend: Chandler is one of the fastest-growing cities in the nation, with 40% growth between 2000 and 2008. Growth has been driven in large part by baby boomers relocating from other parts of the country.

BACKGROUND

Chandler Public Library was one of a group of Phoenix area libraries that took part in a groundbreaking initiative in 2005–2008, the Maricopa County Next Chapter Initiative. Funded by the Virginia G. Piper Charitable Trust and developed with support from Libraries for the Future and Civic Ventures, four community-based coalitions created new models designed to increase baby boomers' participation in and contributions to their communities. The Chandler Next Chapter coalition, lead by Chandler Public Library, developed the Boomerang project, which was a distributed project without a single physical center. The goal was to assist boomers and their families through life planning, re-careering, lifelong learning, wellness, and community service during the "Third Age" of life.

Boomerang involved multiple points of entry, including four Chandler library sites (including the downtown library), two community colleges (Chandler-Gilbert Community College and Sun Lakes Education Center), a website, and community programs and forums. The website was the primary information source, offering a resource navigation tool with links to project partners, local programs and services, and other relevant information sources.

Boomerang was a complex project that provided a laboratory for experimentation and learning. Day-to-day organization was carried out by a grant-funded part-time coordinator. Library administrators provided leadership within the overall coalition. An advisory network of preretired, recently retired, and fully retired community members advised the coalition on program design and the website. Boomerang programs included book discussions, seminars, a Conversations Café for informal discussion, and special events. Programs took place at all four library locations, with a concentration of activities at the downtown library where a "Lunch and Learn" series with presentations on historical and cultural topics drew robust audiences.

The project also created the Experience Bank, an approach for helping to link potential volunteers with organizations or causes that match their backgrounds and interests. Participants entered their profile in the online Bank and were then notified of a range of matching opportunities.[1]

When special funding for the full Boomerang project ended in 2008, the library faced the question of how to focus its continuing work with baby boomers. Based on their experience with the Boomerang project, librarians knew that many 50+ adults were searching for something meaningful to do. They also knew that demand was rising for adult English tutors and for assistance in using the library's Job Resource Center. They decided to focus on boomer civic engagement, specifically, on recruiting and preparing 50+ adults to assist the library in meeting the needs of newcomers and job seekers. It worked. According to Brown, "the practical benefits of having large numbers of boomer volunteers are far greater than I could have envisioned years ago."

SCOPE AND STATUS

Since 2008 the Chandler Public Library has built a large cadre of volunteers whose involvement has made it possible for the downtown library to expand its Job Resource Center. Demand for assistance with job searches and other employment-related services far outstrip current staff capacities. Volunteers are also "the backbone of the Adult Literacy program," which also faces growing demand. Intel Corporation has three major plants in Chandler, and there are other corporate operations in the area. People come from all over the world to work at these businesses, but their families often have difficulties assimilating. Using volunteers, the library can offer classes, one-to-one assistance, as well as "Talk Time," where newcomers can gain confidence in speaking English through informal small group discussion. Volunteers also lead the library's Citizenship Workshops and other adult literacy activities. According to Brown, "the volunteer retention is amazing. People love what they are doing, especially the Talk Time interactions."

The Job Resource Center is the other focus of volunteer activity. When the economic downturn occurred, the Maricopa County Workforce Connections agency provided a grant to help the library expand its services for job seekers at the downtown library. Depending on the availability of grant funds, some boomers recruited to help at the Center, who themselves had lost jobs, are paid stipends.

When the library started to expand its volunteer capacity through boomer recruitment, they had approximately two hundred volunteers. Today there are four hundred, nearly 90 percent of them boomers.

PARTNERS

Community partners for the original Boomerang project included the City of Chandler, Chandler Chamber of Commerce, Chandler Regional Hospital, Chandler Non-Profit Coalition, Chandler Gilbert Community College, and Maricopa County Community College. Current partners include a variety of local corporations, Maricopa County Workforce Connections, and the Chandler Education Coalition.

FUNDING

The original Boomerang project was funded by the Virginia G. Piper Trust as part of its Maricopa County Next Chapter initiative. Currently there is no direct support for the volunteer activities or stipended positions other than an occasional government grant for the Job Resource Center.

KEYS TO SUCCESS

Reflecting on the evolution of the library's work with 50+ adults, Director Brown has identified several practices that helped bring about success in positioning the library as a vital center for boomer engagement:

- Know your community—what it needs and who can help.

- Provide flexible schedules for volunteers. Baby boomers will be consistent in their commitment, but they need a certain amount of flexibility.
- Collaborate—work with other nonprofits, government agencies, educational institutions, and businesses.
- Define your desired outcomes—be specific about goals in order to measure progress.
- Be imaginative about how to use the reservoir of boomer talent in your community.

Note

1. For details, see Brenda Brown, "Designs for Change: Libraries and Productive Aging," Report on the National Library Leaders Forum, September 2005, www.imls.gov/assets/1/AssetManager/DesignsforChange.pdf.

FREE LIBRARY OF PHILADELPHIA

Philadelphia, Pennsylvania www.freelibrary.org

In August 2009, the Free Library of Philadelphia (FLP) opened Central Senior Services (CSS), a spacious resource center in the Central Library that augments current outreach services and provides a focus for expanded and enriched services and programs for Philadelphia's growing older adult population. The CSS mission is to create a place for seniors that blends a warm, welcoming environment with state-of-the-art knowledge and information resources. Since opening, the CSS has demonstrated success in terms of the volume of requests for assistance, the varied uses of the resource center, and strong participation in the public programs.

FACTS

Service area: City of Philadelphia

Population (2009): 1,531,112

% population 55+: 22.5%

Trend: Over the next twenty years, 55+ residents will grow by 11%.

BACKGROUND

FLP has a long tradition of serving older adults through extensive "senior" services and outreach to homebound and dependent adults. The library is also a leader in adult programming, serving many 50+ patrons through programs and services at the Central Library or one of the fifty-four branches. Over the past decade, the number and diversity of the city's older residents have increased, including more baby boomers planning for their next life stages. In response to these changes, FLP recognized the need to develop new approaches to older adults by broadening and deepening services.

SCOPE AND STATUS

CSS is housed in a 480-square-foot dedicated space in the Parkway Central branch, equipped with comfortable seating, laptop computers, magazines, a semiprivate conference area, and a collection in multiple formats addressing multiple topics. The Center is adjacent to the library's access technology workstations for the visually impaired and the government publications department. A reference librarian is available at the Center from 9 a.m. to 5 p.m. each day the library is open.

Dedicated staff include a part-time CSS coordinator and a reference librarian who is available at the Center from 9 a.m. to 6 p.m. each day the library is open. The coordinator provides assistance to individuals in the Center and serves as outreach coordinator for promotions and programs. He works closely with other library departments and Philadelphia organizations to design special programs.

A dedicated section of the FLP website offers links to useful information in such categories as paid employment, volunteer work, brain power, entertainment, creative expression, travel, and education. Special one-to-one computer tutoring is available with an experienced professional, a volunteer who works with clients three days a week, helping 50+ adults become more comfortable with electronic communications.

Programs and events are designed in response to resident and patron interests and augment current adult programs. CSS activities include one-time special events as well as topical series; many are carried out in collaboration with other agencies and organizations. The free monthly programs "invite

Central Senior Services at the Parkway Central Library offers a variety of programs to help you thrive at any age. You can count on us to help you find reliable resources for maintaining a healthy, active lifestyle. Get useful information about estate planning or filing for Medicare. Join us for one of our regular workshops to learn a new skill or reinvigorate interest in an old hobby.

We also present free public programs designed for lifelong learners. Become inspired during a seminar or take part in a lively book discussion. Find camaraderie playing bridge or learn how you can become more involved in your community through an exciting volunteer opportunity. We can even provide you with additional computer assistance so that you can email your grandchildren or use the internet to keep updated on the latest events. Of course, you can always visit us just to relax and explore our growing collection of large-print books, leisure magazines, and classic films—some things just get better with time!

—FLP Central Senior Services web page

Philadelphians to learn more about the health care system, fitness and nutrition, theater, travel, international issues and legal matters."

CSS programs are billed as "programs for lifelong learners" and are marketed to and through community organizations as well as through the library's vehicles for reaching general adult audiences. As one example of CSS programming, the Focus on Health series in fall 2009 offered seminars on such topics as "Live to be 100" and "Doctors are from Mars . . . Communicating with your doctor." During the spring of 2011, CSS offered "The World at Your Door," six programs featuring area diplomats discussing global policy issues from their respective national perspectives. According to CSS coordinator Richard Levinson, this was an effort to diversify and enlarge the sources of information available to older FLP audiences.

PARTNERS

Since opening in 2009, CSS has worked with numerous partners to design and carry out programs, including the Philadelphia Bar Association, Creative Arts and Aging Network, School of Nursing of the University of Pennsylvania, Jewish Federation of Greater Philadelphia, Philadelphia Gray Panthers, United Way, Mayor's Office of Community Services, and League of Women Voters.

FUNDING

CSS is funded by a grant from the Christian R. and Mary F. Lindback Foundation. In 2009 the library received start-up assistance with LSTA funds administered by the Office of Commonwealth Libraries.

KEYS TO SUCCESS
- Commitment from the library's governing structure and management
- Dedicated space, with dedicated staff, that provides a focus for 50+ services
- Organization of CSS as a separate unit that expands the library's capacity to work with midlife/50+ adults while complementing current work with seniors
- Extensive outreach to current and potential patrons, and other community organizations, during development of CSS
- High-quality programs that complement the library's adult programs, thereby expanding options for multiple generations of adults

FEATURED PROGRAMS
- World at Your Door (chapter 9)
- You Are Always a Son or a Daughter: Experts Discuss (chapter 4)
- One Book, One Philadelphia (chapter 10)
- Arts program—panel discussion (chapter 7)

HARTFORD PUBLIC LIBRARY
Hartford, Connecticut www.hplct.org

Since 2006 the Hartford Public Library has been a leader in the development of services and programs for midlife adults. With a growing number of older adults living in Hartford and surrounding areas, the library recognized the need to move beyond traditional services for seniors and to work in different ways with 50+ adults seeking options for learning, work, and creative expression. The programs developed by library staff reflect their awareness of key features for successful midlife programming: the importance of participatory activities, community partnerships, and opportunities for creative expression. They also reflect unusually creative thematic approaches and the special leadership of the library's Hartford History Center.

FACTS

Service area: City of Hartford

Population: 120,000

% population 50+: around 25%

Trend: Over the next twenty-five years, Connecticut's older adult population (65 and older) is expected to double in number.

BACKGROUND

The Hartford Public Library is well known for high-quality services and programs. In 2001 librarian Louise Blalock received the Librarian of the Year Award from *Library Journal*, and in 2002 the library received the National Award for Library Service from the IMLS.[1] Director Blalock was instrumental in the library's initial efforts to design programs focusing on 50+ adults. She encouraged two staff members to attend the Libraries for the Future Lifelong Access Libraries Leadership Institute in 2006 and 2007 and subsequently supported new program development.

The first programs dealt with older adult cognitive development. In 2007, Active Wisdom: Building Brain Power was a series of four workshops on techniques for increasing concentration, memory, reasoning and processing skills. Active Wisdom and Creative Wisdom (2008) were two series of dialogues on the process of aging and how individuals can discover their own capacities, insights, and creative potential during their later years.

The response to these programs was strong enough to convince the library's senior staff of a growing midlife audience eager for similar activities. Under the aegis of the History Center, the library has offered the following unique projects:

... **Age,** an intergenerational community history/community arts program, involved collaboration between the History Center and the Amistad Center for Research and Culture at the Wadsworth Atheneum. The project was designed to stimulate public awareness of "age" as a historical and cultural phenomenon (see chapter 10).

Arts and Archives offered two series of instructional arts classes for older adults in six different media, from sculpture and photography to pen and ink drawing (see chapter 7).

Cooking It Up: Hartford Health and History, organized by the History Center and the Adult Learning Department, is a series of ten cooking demonstrations by local chefs from traditional Hartford restaurants that involve professional nutritionists and use of family recipes contributed by members of the public (see chapter 5).

In addition to these special projects, Hartford Public Library has refocused several ongoing programs in ways that are meaningful to 50+ adults. As one example, the library offers book discussions on historical topics of interest to local residents, such as "Memory of Place," a book discussion on Hartford's North End. The library has also created a directory of resources for job seekers titled "Especially for the Over 40."

SCOPE AND STATUS

The Hartford Public Library projects profiled in this volume reflect a continuous effort since 2006 to address the needs and interests of Hartford's 50+ adults. As the library's understanding of residents' interests has grown, the programs have become more participatory and also more interdisciplinary. There has been strong public response to the library's offerings, with waiting lists for some activities. As a result of the response, senior staff are more than ever convinced that the library is a natural hub for older adult learning. Brenda Miller, curator of the Hartford History Center stated in an interview that the Arts and Archives program "reminds me and reaffirms to the community that the library is a safe and welcoming place. Ideas bounce around in libraries like neurons, and there is a true connection to ideas at this program. Serendipitous learning tends to be the best learning; that's what this is all about."

Looking forward, there is strong evidence that 50+ programs and services will be sustained. For instance, several of the partnerships that came about as a result of ". . . Age" are contributing to ongoing programming. The ". . . Age" exhibition that inaugurated use of the walkway connecting the Hartford History Center at the library and the Amistad Center at the Wadsworth Atheneum has subsequently become an art walk used for other collaborative exhibitions. The connections established with the Hartford School of Art through ". . . Age" have been helpful in recruiting teaching artists for Arts and Archives. In these and other ways the community connections that began as a result of the library's programs for midlife adults are helping sustain these kinds of programs and ensuring their place on the library's agenda.

PARTNERS

From the outset, Hartford's midlife programs have involved partnerships with community agencies and institutions, many of them new to the library. For the first three programs, on cognitive development and aging, the library worked closely with the New England Cognitive Center and the International Center for Creativity and Wisdom. The ". . . Age" project involved a primary partner, the Amistad Center for Art & Culture, as well as five other partners ranging from the Hartford Art School at the University of Hartford to *Connecticut Explored*, a magazine devoted to Connecticut history.

FUNDING

Funding for Hartford's work with older adults has been mainly from public sources. For the ". . . Age" program the library shared a grant with the Amistad Center that derived from federal funds awarded to the national Re-Imagining Age Project. The two phases of Arts and Archives classes and the current program Cooking It Up! received LSTA grants awarded by the Connecticut State Library.

KEYS TO SUCCESS

Brenda Miller of the History Center, Penny Rusnak, former Hartford community librarian, and Mary Albro, former adult services librarian, were primarily responsible for the library's 50+ program initiatives. Based on their experiences, they recommend the following as critical for success:

- Support is required not only from the library director but also from key colleagues.
- Creative and collaborative partners are essential, "but you need to leave time to work closely with partners."

- Emphasize that the programs are free. This makes it possible for many people to attend who have no alternative opportunities to develop their creative talents.
- Use a microphone. "Sound is critical with older adult programming in library spaces."
- "Mix it up! Don't run too many programs where you are talking to the audience; let them talk to each other. . . . the social connection is big. Folks are getting out and mixing with people they wouldn't otherwise have had a chance to meet."
- Document the programs, especially the final session of a workshop series when participants can reflect on what the program meant to them.

Note

1. See "Louise Blalock Is Named 2001 Librarian of the Year by *Library Journal*," http://198.134.159.33/Librarian2001.html; and "Hartford Public Library Receives the 2002 National Award for Distinguished Library, October 2002," http://198.134.159.33/Service Award.shtm.

METROPOLITAN LIBRARY SERVICES AGENCY

Minneapolis–St. Paul, Minnesota www.melsa.org

Metropolitan Library Services Agency (MELSA) is an alliance of 103 libraries (eight library systems) in metropolitan Minneapolis and St. Paul. It is one of two regional library systems designated in the book as a Beacon library. Three aspects of MELSA's work to advance midlife programming stand out: the system's emphasis on collaborations with nonlibrary organizations and agencies, which help ensure public access to expertise and activities that would not otherwise be possible; the emphasis on professional development for staff of member libraries; and the outstanding, original programs developed by MELSA and its 50+ Interest Group (made up of representatives from member libraries). As one example, the public program series Brain Fitness, with accompanying Brain Stations, introduced midlife adults and other Twin Cities residents to the possibilities for maintaining brain health during the aging process (see chapter 5).

BACKGROUND

MELSA's mission is to enhance the quality and accessibility of library services for Twin Cities residents by enabling cooperation among the eight metro area library systems. Through MELSA, many local libraries are able to provide special programming beyond their usual offerings. They also have access to professional development opportunities, promotional initiatives, and partnerships that they could not undertake on their own.

Adult programming has always been a strong focus for MELSA, and in recent years there has been an increase in adult programs with special benefit for aging adults. In 2009, MELSA members organized the 55+ Interest Group—library staff who have a special interest in new approaches to working with midlife adults. Members of this group help select regional projects such as Brain Fitness.

The trend to create programs that enrich the lives of active older adults has benefited from substantial funding available to MELSA and its member libraries through the Minnesota Legacy Amendment Arts and Cultural Heritage Fund (ACHF), a fund supporting the arts and the environment approved by voters in 2008. The impact of the ACHF, or "Legacy," funding on MELSA, its members, and their clients cannot be overestimated. MELSA receives a substantial annual ACHF allocation, which has been used for development of numerous regional cultural programs.[1] As a result, MELSA and its member libraries have developed new organizational allies, reached new audiences, and offered an extraordinary array of opportunities for arts, cultural, and literary participation, from live performances and librarian trainings to book and film discussions.

FACTS

Service area: Seven Minnesota counties in the Twin Cities area

Population (2010): 2,849,567

% population 55+: 21.65%

Trend: According to the *Not Yet Gazette* (www .demography.state.mn .us/notyet/index.html), after 2010 the number of people over age 65 will grow dramatically as baby boomers reach this age bracket.

SCOPE AND STATUS

Like many libraries and library systems, MELSA is moving toward a greater focus on 50+ adults, even as it offers enriched services and programs for all adults. Both types of projects benefit midlife participants and are highlighted in this volume. The combination of targeted programs and general adult programs provides a rich menu from which member libraries can select depending on the demographic profile, needs, and interests of their communities. For example, older adults make up a significant proportion of MELSA's Community Cinema at the Library program, which involves film screenings and discussions from Independent Lens. For this program, MELSA and the host libraries do not distinguish between age groups in their program marketing. They do, however, offer creative writing classes and workshops designed specifically for 50+ adults.

As MELSA continues to develop and circulate programs in the metropolitan Twin Cities region, it is likely to continue to offer both general and targeted programs. MELSA officials believe there is a need for both approaches, which are complementary and offer more participation options.

PARTNERS

MELSA exists to facilitate collaborations and partnerships between member libraries. This commitment to partnerships carries over into projects undertaken with nonlibrary groups. When the ACHF, known as the Legacy Fund, came into being, MELSA and the other regional library systems were appropriate agencies to help carry out the fund's mandate to advance partnerships among the state's cultural organizations, historical agencies, and libraries. Accordingly, the MELSA Legacy Committee included the following in its guidelines for use of the monies: "Develop sustainable partnerships between public libraries and other arts, cultural and educational organizations throughout the state."

MELSA has reached out to numerous state, regional, and local organizations to carry out the ACHF and other programs benefiting midlife adults. Partners include the Minnesota Historical Society, Minnesota Creative Arts and Aging Network, Vital Aging Network, Loft Literary Center, Library Foundation of Hennepin County, COMPAS, Minneapolis Institute of Arts, and Minnesota Public Television.

> I think the paradigm will shift. People will not be interested in programs because they are labeled for "seniors" or for "adults." They will be attracted to programs because of their content and their schedule.
>
> —Melinda Ludwiczak, Legacy projects manager, MELSA

FUNDING

Through the ACHF, Minnesota's three hundred plus public libraries receive monies distributed through existing formulas to the state's regional library systems to provide programs and services in four areas: arts (visual, performing, and media), culture, literary, and Minnesota history. MELSA has received grants through 2011 and will continue to receive Legacy Funds through 2013. Many adult programs developed by MELSA for and with member library systems, including those targeting 50+ adults, are supported by these funds. Other sources of project support are federal LSTA grant funds allocated to MELSA through the Office of Library Services, Minnesota Department of Education, local library foundations or Friends groups, and local businesses.

KEYS TO SUCCESS

MELSA and its member libraries are learning that programs designed to meet the needs of midlife adults are having positive results: attendance is strong, there are measurable impacts, and the programs are well received throughout the metropolitan region by participants and partners alike. These results may be due to the fact that MELSA is well positioned to organize and distribute new programs across multiple libraries, that MELSA's history of partnerships within and outside its structure helps attract partners and constituents, and that MELSA works with member libraries on marketing to ensure wide program visibility. In addition, the substantial ACHF monies made available for partnerships through MELSA have had an immense impact on the scope and quality of MELSA's recent offerings, including those targeted for active older adults.

FEATURED MELSA AND MEMBER LIBRARY PROJECTS
- Art for Life Residencies (chapter 7)
- Brain Fitness project (chapter 5)
- Club Book, Community Cinema (chapter 9), and Live at the Library (chapter 7)
- Creativity and Aging forums (chapter 7)
- Hennepin County: Art of Aging (chapter 7)

Note
1. For more on the Arts and Cultural Heritage Fund, see "Legacy Amendment & Libraries," www.melsa.org/melsa/index.cfm/programs/legacy-amendment.

MULTNOMAH COUNTY LIBRARY
Portland, Oregon www.multcolib.org

Multnomah County Library is a leader in the provision of focused services for baby boomers. With an emphasis on partnerships and on innovative, relevant programming, the library has attracted a new audience of midlife patrons interested in learning, volunteering, and discussing transition issues with peers. Although the City of Portland has unusually strong educational and service opportunities for it 50+ residents, the library has creatively augmented these opportunities with its own special resources and partners. In addition, library staff who work with midlife adults have willingly shared their knowledge with professional colleagues at conferences and meetings, enabling other libraries to benefit from their experiences and insights.

BACKGROUND

Multnomah County has been in the forefront of 50+ services since 2007, when then library director Molly Raphael encouraged two outreach services staff members to attend the first Libraries for the Future Lifelong Access Libraries Leadership Institute held at the University of North Carolina. Jane Salisbury and Abigail Elder returned from the Institute armed with tools and concepts to help the library engage Portland's growing population of midlife and older active adults.

Before the Lifelong Access training, Salisbury and Elder had recognized the need for new approaches to programs for mature adults, beyond their ongoing outreach services. However, they knew they had to overcome some internal objections, such as staff assumptions that the library was already serving boomers effectively or that boomers would become "another juggernaut like youth services." To help in the process of convincing administrators and colleagues, they marshaled demographic data and carried out focus groups of boomers and other active adults that affirmed the number and diversity of older adults and their need for a neutral space for learning, information, and civic engagement. At the same time, they reached out to other groups. They "invited themselves to the party, made connections within their community, found out what was needed and convinced Library leadership."[1]

The groundwork laid by Salisbury and Elder resulted in two complementary and overlapping programs. The first, Life by Design @ your library, was a partnership with the regional initiative Life by Design NW (www.pcc.edu/climb/life/), which included two years of support for a half-time staff position in Library Outreach Services. That position was extended through Kaboom! (Knowledgeable & Active Boomers): Harnessing the Energy and Engagement of Older Adults at the Library, a two-year demonstration project funded by an LSTA grant awarded by the Oregon State Library Development Office. The goal of Kaboom! was to "challenge the assumptions, the language, and the way in which the Multnomah County Library organizes adult and senior library services. The project will find new and engaging methods to address an emerging 'third life' phase. It will provide new ideas and help inform the creation of a distinct specialty within adult services, focusing on active, engaged older adults."[2]

Both Life by Design @ your library and Kaboom! offered public programs, workshops, and issues forums of special interest to diverse boomers and other older adults. They also created new volunteer opportunities for 50+ adults and recommended books and other resources for those in life and work transitions. The emphasis in all programs was on freewheeling discussion and open, relaxed presentations rather than formal readings or lectures. Programs were promoted via traditional channels, including media ads, promotional flyers, brochures, and postcards as well as through social network sites such as Facebook and Twitter. The library also reached new constituencies through publicity on the Life by Design NW website and its mailing lists.

SCOPE AND STATUS

The many lectures, workshops, discussions, and service opportunities offered by the library through Life by Design @ your library and the Kaboom! project emphasized community participation and issues relevant to adults in midlife. Programs ranged from Books-to-Action, a series of readings and discussions with related community service projects, to Caring for Your Aging Parent, presentations, and group discussions.

Despite the success of these and other programs, which provided new educational opportunities and helped connect multiple volunteers with service opportunities, Multnomah has not been able to continue the depth of programming made possible with dedicated grants. However, part of the library's goal was to make programming of the sort carried out under the Kaboom! project a regular component of library services. To that end, the library's program department is now taking on several of the key activities, with the expectation that they will be carried out using regular staff and resources. They plan to go on recruiting and using highly skilled midlife volunteers and to put on programs that have been proven to be of strong interest through Life by Design @ your library and Kaboom!

Over the course of their work to develop programming for midlife adults, Multnomah staff have generously taken time to make presentations at library conferences and professional meetings. During 2007/8 outreach staff made presentations at three professional development conferences—in Pasadena, Minneapolis, and Chapel Hill—and Portland was recently the site of the initial training for the Western States Fellowship Program, an extension of the professional development activities led by the California State Library through its Transforming Life After 50 program.

PARTNERS

The majority of Multnomah County Library's 50+ programming has been carried out in partnership with Life by Design NW, a regional initiative dedicated to helping boomers achieve fulfillment by engaging in their communities in meaningful ways. Life by Design NW "empowers people to find their passion and purpose while giving back to the community." In addition to the library, other Life by Design partners include AARP Oregon, Express Employment Professionals, Hands on Greater Portland, NW Natural, Oregon Public Broadcasting, Portland Community College, and Portland State University. Many of the specific programs carried out during the Life by Design @ your library program and the Kaboom! project involved one or more of these partners. Another key partner has been Portland's Vital Aging Network. The library's relationship with Life by Design NW was instrumental in reaching a broader range of constituencies for library programs and deepening coalition partners' awareness of library resources.

> The demographics are undeniable, but it really takes talking about it over and over locally and nationally to make something happen.
>
> —Jane Salisbury, outreach services supervisor, Multnomah County Library

FUNDING

As a result of its partnership with Life by Design NW, Multnomah County received funds from Atlantic Philanthropies to support a dedicated part-time staff member in Library Outreach Services. The library leveraged that support through a subsequent two-year federal LSTA grant for the Kaboom! project, administered by the Oregon State Library.

KEYS TO SUCCESS

Multnomah staff cite several factors that have helped advance their 50+ services:

- The interest and support of the former director, who was one of the funders of Portland's Life by Design initiative
- Participation by two staff members in the Libraries for the Future Lifelong Access Libraries Leadership Institute
- Networking with other groups locally and nationally, including opportunities to make presentations at professional development meetings
- Grants to help support initial staffing

- Recruitment of boomer staff as allies
- Relationships with other community groups with complementary goals
- Involvement of boomers in design and implementation of programs

FEATURED PROJECTS AND PROGRAMS
- Books-to-Action (chapter 9)
- Gift People (chapter 8)
- Perspectives on Positive Aging (chapter 4)

Notes

1. See the slide presentation by Abigail Elder and Jane Salisbury at http://transforming lifeafter50.org/files/handout-pdfs/TLAFElderSalisburyppt.pdf.

2. Kaboom! (Knowledgeable & Active Boomers), Year 2 Brief Grant Proposal for Continuing Projects, April 10, 2009. See www.oregon.gov/osl/LD/LSTA/2009LSTAgrants funded.htm.

NEW HAVEN FREE PUBLIC LIBRARY / 50+ TRANSITION CENTER
New Haven, Connecticut www.cityofnewhaven.com/library

The New Haven Free Public Library (NHFPL) was one of the first libraries in the nation to create a specific space and dedicated services for midlife adults. Established in 2004, the 50+ Transition Center has provided a conceptual and practical model for other libraries and helped advance librarians' understanding of the differences between traditional services for seniors and services for midlife adults.

BACKGROUND
The Center grew out of New Haven's involvement in state and national projects aimed at stimulating new approaches for older adult library service. One initiative, the Life Options Libraries project, was a joint 2003 initiative of Libraries for the Future and Civic Ventures—a national organization that works with communities to redefine aging—designed to test approaches for older adult civic engagement through library services. The NHFPL component of Life Options included Community Conversations on topics relevant to retiring or already retired older adults and a partnership with the New Haven Volunteer Center that

matched midlife library patrons interested in community service with local organizations and causes.

Building on the Life Options project, NHFPL developed the concept for a 50+ Transition Center that would provide a place for active older adults to mingle and gain information on work and service opportunities. Started in 2005, the Center was to provide programming on life transitions, health, finances, new careers, and other topics suggested by peer advisors as well as encourage community involvement by midlife adults.[1]

SCOPE AND STATUS

Since opening in 2005 the Center has fulfilled its vision, with a dedicated physical space for midlife adults, a part-time manager, and a full complement of programs and services. Working closely with library staff and with patrons of the Center, the Center's manager has experimented with approaches for providing the right balance of permanent and changing offerings, including collections, information on local services and other resources for older adults (in print and online), opportunities for social contact and civic engagement, and, above all, programs that enrich the lives of New Haven's older adults.

The Center has been responsive to changing needs in the community. For instance, with the economic downturn and greater numbers of midlife adults requiring employment, the Center has shifted its emphasis on volunteering to a greater emphasis on job-related information and support, along with financial planning. Center staff have also worked to ensure that 50+ patrons benefit from the expertise of librarians in other departments who can help them with job searching, small business development, grant information, and health information.

Staff have cross-marketed 50+ Transition Center programs with the library's adult programs, and vice versa, with the expectation that the audiences for the two strands of programming often overlap and benefit from having a wider set of program options. 50+ patrons, for instance, participate in the library's "Author Talks" and "Cinema at 6" screenings, and general adult patrons have taken part in some of the financial and health programs offered by the Center.

Libraries for the Future designated NHFPL "a Center of Excellence and Innovation" in 2006, citing efforts to provide meaningful connections to work and community for midlife adults and to help them "discover new potential for personal transformation at any age."[2]

The range and depth of offerings, the dedicated space, and the effort to integrate 50+ services into the overall library make the New Haven Center an important model. New Haven staff have been asked to present at national conferences, trainings, and workshops, including Libraries for the Future's Lifelong Access Libraries Leadership Institutes. The Center's manager participates in Connecticut's SOAR (Services to Older Adults Roundtable (www.ctlibrarians.org) and has advised other libraries on programming for 50+ adults.

PARTNERS

Through the early Life Options Project, the Community Conversations and civic engagement activities, and the 50+ Transition Center, the library has developed partnership relationships with a broad array of organizations and agencies including Connecticut Public Television, Community Foundation of Greater New Haven, Dialogue Project & Mediation Center of Greater New Haven, Empower New Haven, Gateway Community College, Mentor New Haven of the New Haven Office of Elderly Services, SCORE, Senior Service America, AARP, and Yale University.

> Participants will experience giving back to the community in a meaningful way, they'll be able to pursue a greater awareness of life options, and be better able to make informed decisions about their finances, health, re-careering and leisure and civic activities. . . . We hope other libraries will replicate it.
>
> —Kate Cosgrove, manager, NHFPL 50+ Transition Center

FUNDING

The Life Options Libraries project, a joint initiative of Libraries for the Future and Civic Ventures, was funded in part by the William R. Graustein Memorial Foundation. Funding to launch the 50+ Transition Center was provided by the Connecticut State Library through an LSTA grant in 2004. In-kind support for the Center during its development was made possible by ongoing support for library operations from the City of New Haven. Libraries for the Future funding for the Center as a national "Center for Excellence and Innovation in Productive Aging" derived from Atlantic Philanthropies. Recent programming on financial planning has been made possible by a grant from the Financial Industry Regulatory Authority Investor Education Foundation and ALA.

KEYS TO SUCCESS

Over the course of its development the Center has become a fixture in the library and the community. It is not a one-time grant-dependent project but an integral part of the library's agenda. Despite citywide budgetary constraints, the Center has been sustained and has grown. Interviews with the former city librarian, the 50+ Transition Center manager, and senior library staff have revealed a variety of reasons for its success, including the following:

- Strong support from the city librarian and other library leaders
- High community interest and expectations
- A separate identity for the 50+ Transition Center including a special icon on the library's home page
- Support from the state library, in the form of not only grants but also professional encouragement
- Paid staff with authority to organize programs and partnerships
- Diverse programs and partnerships
- Encouragement from and collaboration with staff in other library departments
- Regular programming, such as the same time each week or month for a particular type of assistance or activity
- Willingness to experiment and to evolve in response to new needs and interests

FEATURED PROJECTS
- 50+ Transition Center (chapter 12)
- Finances @ Fifty and Smart Investing (chapter 11)
- Head to Toe: A Health Care Series for Older Adults (chapter 5)
- Technology Across Generations (chapter 6)

Notes

1. Douglas Lord, "BOOM! The 50+ Transition Center at the New Haven Free Public Library," WebJunction, March 23, 2007, http://webjunction.org/documents/ct/BOOM_The_50_043_Transition_Center_at_the_New_Haven_Free_Public_Library.html.

2. See Joanne Gard Marshall, Jennifer Craft Morgan, and Victor H. Marshall, "Lifelong Access Libraries Centers of Excellence Final Report," May 2009, Lifelong Access, www.aging.unc.edu/programs/lal/reports/CentersOfExcellenceFinalReport.pdf.

NEW YORK PUBLIC LIBRARY /
NEXT CHAPTER

New York, New York www.nypl.org

The Next Chapter program of the New York Public Library (NYPL) is one of the country's most extensive and effective midlife initiatives. It is outstanding in terms of scope, offering a wide array of themes, activities, and options for midlife adults. It is also outstanding in terms of its varied community partnerships, the number of neighborhood branches involved, the staff training, the many volunteers or stipended midlife adults who have been mobilized to work with peers, the program's visibility on the library's website, the support it has received internally, and the extent to which it has contributed to New York City's "age-friendly" initiatives.

BACKGROUND

In 2006 and 2007, NYPL sent two adult services managers to the weeklong Libraries for the Future Lifelong Access Libraries Leadership Institute. Subsequently, one of the Lifelong Access Fellows, Brigid Cahalan, was appointed to a newly created position, older adults services specialist. This appointment sparked the evolution of a multifaceted program that has enriched the lives of thousands of aging New Yorkers and that positions NYPL as one of the nation's most important 50+ library services systems.

The evolution of the NYPL initiative demonstrates what is possible when a library system confronts the question posed by Cahalan in a 2008 Lifelong Access Libraries blog: "Since participating as a Fellow in the 2007 Lifelong Access Institute, I've been giving a lot of thought to the question of how libraries can contribute to enhancing the lives of active older adults in the community. What tools can we provide to promote civic engagement, healthy aging, and creativity and growth throughout the lifespan?"

To answer this question, NYPL started by reaching out to other agencies and organizations serving aging adults. It worked with the New York City Department of Aging to map senior centers and branch libraries and to host a series of first-time joint meetings between branch librarians and senior center directors to foster new connections. This effort led not only to several local library–

FACTS

Service area: Three New York City boroughs: Bronx, Manhattan, Staten Island

Total population served (2010): 3.5 million

% population 55+: 40.4%

Trend: The New York City Department of City Planning projects the number of persons 65 and over in the city's five boroughs to rise 44.2% from 2000 to 2030.

senior center partnerships but also to system-wide programs such as the Stay Well health promotion workshops now in place at ten neighborhood libraries across three New York City boroughs (see chapter 5). Other partnerships with city agencies have developed as well, including work with New York City's Age Friendly Initiative (www.nyam.org/agefriendlynyc), in which NYPL is talking a leadership role and has helped to define new guidelines for age-friendly public institutions.

Special programming has helped focus public attention on the library's commitment to midlife and older active adults. In 2008 the library hosted the award ceremony for the Purpose Prize, a major national award that recognizes 50+ social entrepreneurs. It also organized a large resource fair, enabling eighteen local and national organizations to connect with individuals seeking volunteer opportunities. During 2008 and 2009 the library offered extensive book talks and informal learning programs at the Mid-Manhattan Library and local libraries, featuring prominent authors or representatives of key national organizations focusing on aging adults. During 2010 it offered four fitness fairs, a series of financial literacy presentations, Memory Day screenings, and ten Consumer Choice 50+ Summer Seminars. A partnership with the national organization Lifetime Arts has enabled branch libraries to offer Creative Aging in Our Communities, a model for library-based creative aging programming (see chapter 7).

Most recently the library received LSTA funding through the New York State Library Development Office to collaborate with the Older Adult Technology Services agency to offer twenty-session computer courses—including one in Spanish—in a project titled "Becoming an Age-Friendly Library: Enhancing Technology Services of Older Adults." And in 2011 the library established a partnership with ReServe (www.reserveinc.org) to engage midlife adults as tutors helping peers learn about new communications devices in a series of "petting zoos."

At the outset of the library's work with active older adults, staff acknowledged the importance of building an identity for the initiative, titling it "Next Chapter," a name also used for a widely read blog and a Facebook page and for special events and numerous other activities for 50+ adults. In addition, the li-

> The Library strives to meet the needs of all New Yorkers, as well as its virtual community world-wide. As the average age increases with the aging of the Baby Boom generation—generally accepted as those born 1946-1964—the Library has added links and programs targeting those 50 and over. Also, a Next Chapter blog channel focuses on the 50+ population and many related library programs and services.
>
> —NYPL website

brary placed a special logo on the library's home page, giving the Next Chapter further status as a key service area.

SCOPE AND STATUS

The NYPL commitment to sustain its myriad programs and services is reflected in its cultivation of partnerships, outreach to new funders, targeted marketing, and professional development. For instance, the library's ongoing computer classes for older adults are now being expanded through an LSTA grant administered through the New York State Library. The pilot Creative Aging project carried out with Lifetime Arts has now received significant new funding that triples the number of sites. And the partnership projects with the city's Department of Aging are succeeding because they involve volunteers who constitute a cadre of dedicated workers and a constituency for the programs. Through new training opportunities the library is helping staff members, especially public service librarians in the branch libraries, adjust their thinking and practices with respect to older adults, broadening services from "senior services" to include specific activities for baby boomers and other active, independent, and socially engaged older adults.

PARTNERS

NYPL's extensive Next Chapter programming has involved many partnerships, from the New York state AARP and Fordham University's Coalition for Debtor Education to the Transition Network and the New York City Office of the Global Age-Friendly Cities initiative.

FUNDING

Funding for the library's Next Chapter initiative has derived from multiple sources. The partnerships with city agencies have involved commitments of time and staff from those agencies, including professional oversight staff for the Stay Well workshops. Federal funds have been provided in the form of an LSTA grant administered by New York State's Office of Library Development. Private funds include monies from the Fan Fox and Leslie R. Samuels Fund for Creative Aging in Our Communities Project, a partnership with Lifetime Arts.

KEYS TO SUCCESS

According to library staff, success of the Next Chapter initiative can be traced to several key factors:

- Support and encouragement from library leaders

- The position of older adult services specialist, which enables staff to dedicate time to 50+ services planning and implementation
- Partnerships that enable the library to extend its offerings, reach new constituencies, and build new sources of direct and indirect support
- A system-wide approach, enabling some flexibility of offerings and engaging multiple local librarians in rethinking their work with active older adults

FEATURED NEXT CHAPTER PROGRAMS AND SERVICES

- Creative Aging in Our Communities: The New York City Libraries Project (chapter 7)
- Book Talks and Informal Learning Programs (chapter 9)
- Becoming an Age-Friendly Library: Enhancing Technology Services to Older Adults (chapter 6)
- Next Chapter blog (chapter 8)
- Reflection and Re-invention (chapter 4)
- Campaign for Financial Literacy Now (chapter 11)
- Stay Well exercise classes (chapter 5)

READING PUBLIC LIBRARY
Reading, Massachusetts www.readingpl.org

Reading Public Library stands out for its commitment to enriched learning services for and with active older adults. Although Reading is relatively small in relation to some of the other Beacon libraries, its LiveWires program was one of the first educational enrichment programs for midlife adults in the country and has influenced the development of 50+ services at other libraries. LiveWires is distinguished by participation of patrons in program planning, regularity of core activities, inclusion of a social component, interdisciplinary program content, and varied program formats. In addition, Reading Public Library staff have influenced others in the profession through presentations at professional conferences and trainings, such as the 2008 New England Lifelong Access Libraries Institute,

FACTS

Service area: Reading, Massachusetts

Population: 24,747

% population 50+: 36.9%

Trend: Projections for 2020 show that 42.5% of residents will be 50+.

where they have shared insights regarding the challenges and benefits of working differently with midlife patrons.

BACKGROUND

In 2005, Reading Public Library, as a member of the Northern Massachusetts Regional Library System (NMRLS), participated in a professional development workshop for NMRLS members through a special grant to NMRLS from the Massachusetts Board of Library Commissioners (MBLC). The grant, titled "The Experience Library: Older Citizens," was designed to strengthen the capacities of member libraries to respond to aging trends in Massachusetts, particularly the increasing number of midlife adults. The Experience Library workshop was conducted in partnership with Libraries for the Future through its Lifelong Access Libraries national initiative to advance librarians' capacities to respond to aging in America.

In 2006, Reading Public Library also participated in another training program, offered jointly by MBLC and Libraries for the Future, that focused on the Equal Access model of community librarianship. Reading library staff opted to use their follow-up implementation grant to focus on boomers and other active older adults. Led by Nancy Aberman, adult services librarian, Reading created LiveWires: Boomers and Beyond. According to Aberman, one of the most successful program series the library has ever offered is the twice-monthly LiveWires lifelong-learning programs, which attract people who bring their curiosity and interest "in everything from charitable giving to Cape Ann artists and more." This program series was originally established through a special grant and has been continued through generous private donations.

As a result of LiveWires, Aberman was invited to make a presentation at the 2007 Libraries for the Future Lifelong Access Libraries Leadership Institute at the University of North Carolina. Also in 2007, Libraries for the Future awarded a grant to NMRLS as a "Center for Excellence and Innovation in Lifelong Access Libraries." NMRLS used the funding to provide two member libraries, including the Reading Public Library, with implementation grants for new practices in older adult service. The grant was used to strengthen the LiveWires program and to offer two in-depth workshops focusing on aging issues.

SCOPE AND STATUS

Since LiveWires started in 2007 it has become a model for other libraries, especially mid-sized and smaller libraries. It has also continued to evolve in response to patron input. Focus groups and surveys have helped to inform library staff and older adult advisors regarding patron interests.

Today, Reading continues its commitment to create programs with and for active older adults. LiveWires is still the core program, but its title has shifted to emphasize learning—"LiveWires: Lifelong Learning at the Library"—and it has expanded topics beyond the initial focus on aging issues. Past and current offerings include the following:

- LiveWires: Coffee and More, monthly mid-morning presentations that include discussion, a social component, and an overview of relevant library resources
- LiveWires Presents, monthly evening events that include talks by authors, specialists, and performers and viewings and discussions of films that address a wide variety of topics
- Workshops on Aging, one-time in-depth workshops on issues particular to older adults, such as the 2007 workshops Purpose and Legacy

> Library administration is very enthusiastic about this program and see it as a cornerstone of our service to older adults. Trustees are supportive and many attend our program series. Staff is supportive and helpful in generating ideas for programs and assisting.
>
> —Nancy Aberman,
> adult services librarian,
> Reading Public Library

In addition to these core LiveWires activities, Reading offers diverse adult programs that complement LiveWires offerings and extend the learning opportunities available to older adults. These include intergenerational programs such as the Intergenerational Walk in the Woods; a foreign affairs discussion series of monthly programs from September to May that feature public policy experts and scholars on topical issues; and American Voices—"lively discussions of books relating to the theme of what defines us as Americans" led by a local scholar.

With growing interest in the library community regarding new approaches to services for midlife adults, Aberman has made presentations at numerous professional meetings and conferences, including her most recent talk "Please Don't Call Them Seniors," at the Massachusetts Library Association's 2008 Annual Conference.

PARTNERS

Aside from its original affiliation with NMRLS, which was discontinued after reorganization of Massachusetts library systems, Reading Public Library has not had any official partners in planning or carrying out LiveWires.

FUNDING

Financial assistance for the first year of LiveWires was made possible as a result of the MBLC/Libraries for the Future Equal Access training and grants program, with LSTA funds from the IMLS administered by MBLC. Subsequent support has been provided by the Friends of the Reading Public Library, the Reading Lions Club, a local business, and an anonymous donor.

KEYS TO SUCCESS

According to Aberman, there are several reasons for the success of the program:

- A sustained commitment by the library to carry out programming that achieves three goals: increased awareness of productive aging issues, increased knowledge of available resources on aging, and increased opportunities to discuss productive aging with others
- Strong internal support for the program at all levels
- Involvement of patrons in selecting program topics and formats, and efforts to continually assess older adult needs and interests
- The social component
- Staff time allotted for planning and executing the LiveWires program series

FEATURED PROJECTS
- LiveWires (chapter 9)
- Workshops on Aging / LiveWires (chapter 4)

TEMPE PUBLIC LIBRARY / TEMPE CONNECTIONS

Tempe, Arizona www.tempe.gov/library, www.tempeconnections.org

Tempe Connections, based at the Tempe Public Library and funded by the Friends of the Tempe Public Library, is the most comprehensive library-based program for 50+ adults in the country. It consists of a specially designed physical space that provides a focal point for a rich array of programs, services, and volunteer opportunities. Appropriately situated in a city with a high percentage of baby boomers and older retirees, Tempe Connections is a separate nonprofit organization governed by a board of community members and representatives of partner organizations.

FACTS

Service area:
City of Tempe

Population (2010):
161,719

% population 50+: 23.2%

Trend: Tempe had a population growth of over 10% between 2000 and 2010; growth has slowed considerably but the percentage of older adults remains high.

BACKGROUND

Tempe Public Library is one of the busiest libraries in the Phoenix metropolitan area, with over a million visitors each year. The library is known for its diverse and high-quality services and its commitment to community collaboration. In 2003, Terri Metros, then director of the library, participated in the Maricopa County Commission on Productive Aging, which was formed to examine the county's services for baby boomers and to explore mechanisms for strengthening the environment for boomers and encouraging their engagement with local communities. At the time, Maricopa County was one of the fastest-growing counties in the nation, due in part to the increase in the number of 50+ adults.

One outcome of the Commission's work was the Next Chapter initiative through which the Virginia G. Piper Charitable Trust provided grants to four community coalitions organized to "help people in the second half of life set a course, connect with peers, and find pathways to significant service." Civic Ventures, a national nonprofit organization focused on civic engagement of older adults, provided expertise and assistance to the grantees. Tempe Connection, a coalition of community organizations formed under the leadership of the Tempe Public Library and the Friends of the Tempe Public Library, was one of the four Next Chapter grantees. Formally incorporated as a 501C3 organization in 2006, Tempe Connections is "a nonprofit community service program that seeks to enrich our community by providing adults with opportunities to discover new purpose through access to a wide range of learning programs, and volunteer participation. . . . Purpose, Programs, Participation—Brewed in One Place is more than just a tagline—it's our mission, our commitment, our passion."

SCOPE AND STATUS

Tempe Connections offers information, services, and programs on learning, social connections, and civic engagement. Program formats range from formal academic classes and seminars to workshops, one-to-one coaching, small group activities, and informal and independent learning. Almost all of the programs involve partnerships with other community agencies, organizations, or institutions of higher learning. Key offerings include the following:

- Lifelong learning and new career opportunities in partnership with Maricopa County Workforce Development, Arizona State University, and other partners

- Life planning workshops
- Wellness classes, screenings, and exercise programs provided by St. Joseph's Hospital and Medical Center
- Volunteer information and opportunities through Tempe Connections Talent Connection, Civic Ventures' Experience Corps, and Tempe Public Library's volunteer office. Tempe Connections assists in recruiting interested adults age 55+ who want to use their experience and skills to make a positive impact on their communities

In addition to offering extensive programs and services, Tempe Connections is also a physical space—a café, meeting room, and patio area where 50+ adults can find information, read, browse the Web, socialize, and discover programs that meet their interests and needs. The Tempe Connections Café provides a focal point for the overall initiative and helps transform the library into a center for 50+ adults. The café has received widespread attention in the profession and helped inspire other libraries to develop physical spaces dedicated to midlife adults.

As a nonprofit organization operating under the aegis of the Friends of the Tempe Public Library, Tempe Connections is quite unusual in the library community. An independent entity, it is directed by an advisory council that sets project goals, hires staff, and plans for operations. A full-time paid director manages activities.

The Rest of Your Life Begins with a Cup of Coffee

6 million of us are looking at the next chapters of our lives in ways that are completely different than our parents. We no longer look forward to a traditional "retirement" phase, but seek activities that involve purpose, passion and programs for improving life.

- **Learning programs** for intellectual stimulation

- **Supportive planning** for a variety of life changes

- **Encore work options** for continued meaningful engagement

- **Volunteer participation** to effect positive community change

It's not just about baby boomers. The hallmark of Tempe Connections is giving back to our community. We connect people with volunteer opportunities that enrich our neighborhoods and schools. *—Tempe Connections website*

PARTNERS

More than two dozen community organizations and educational institutions partner with the City of Tempe and Tempe Connections to provide program offerings, including the Arizona State University Department of Continuing Education, St. Joseph's Hospital, Experience Corps, Tempe Chamber of Commerce, Southwest Institute of Healing Arts, Boys and Girls Club of the East Valley-Ladmor Branch, Tempe Elementary School District 3, and Changing Hands Bookstore.

FUNDING

Funding for the construction and operation of the Tempe Connections Café and initial programming was provided by the Virginia G. Piper Charitable Trust. The Friends of the Tempe Public Library operate the café and program space, with all profits used for the support of Tempe Connections programs and services. Community donations help support programming and volunteer activities.

KEYS TO SUCCESS

Establishment of Tempe Connections was due in large measure to a generous grant from the Virginia G. Piper Trust. However, when that grant was used up, it was up to the library and its partners to sustain the activities without substantial, dedicated funds. There are many reasons for the ongoing success of the initiative, including the following:

- Strong support from library leaders and from the Friends of the Tempe Public Library
- A culture of collaboration in the city of Tempe and in the library
- The availability of space for the Tempe Connections Café and other meeting areas
- The capacity to have paid staff
- Commitment of library staff to make the project work
- The talent and experience of the individuals who have volunteered to make the program possible

FEATURED PROGRAMS
- Academic Connections: Learn for the Love of Learning (chapter 9)
- Health and Wellness (chapter 5)
- Tempe Connections Café (chapter 12)
- Tempe Connections Talent Connection (chapter 3)
- Transition Talks: Prepare for the Next Chapter of Life (chapter 4)

WORK, CAREERS, AND SERVICE

For baby boomers . . . retirement may just be a transition to an all-new encore career or "a new stage of work after a midlife career." . . . It combines compensation, personal meaning and social impact.

—Phyllis Segal, vice president, Civic Ventures

When the first baby boomers turned 65 on January 1, 2011, they were already well on the way to redefining traditional concepts of work and retirement. Rather than opting out of the workforce altogether or withdrawing from civic life, they are continuing to participate, often in new ways, bringing skills, experience, and creativity to the workplace and the community. Their approaches to extended work, second careers, and community service are causing economists, labor specialists, sociologists, nonprofit leaders, government officials, employers, and librarians to reconsider existing policies and practices with respect to older workers and volunteers.

TRENDS

In the dynamic environment of newly active, older members of society, three primary trends can be identified: a set of more mature workers, people seeking new careers, and an enriched source of community servants. Each has implications for libraries.

MATURE WORKERS

The first and most obvious trend is the tendency for more and more adults to continue as full- or part-time workers beyond the typical age for retirement. Research shows that as more and more people are living longer, healthier lives they are also choosing to stay in the workforce longer or reentering it at different levels and in different roles.[1] Almost two-thirds of people 55 and over in a recent national survey said they would like to remain productive in either full- or part-time work, some for personal fulfillment, some for social or civic purpose, and others out of necessity.[2]

Many older adults simply cannot afford to give up paid employment. They do not have the asset base or the level of retirement income to leave paid employment. For those who have secure jobs, the choice is less fraught than for those who have lost jobs because of changing economic conditions or contractions in a particular industry or sector. Finding work in midlife can be particularly challenging and may require new skills and new contacts.

Beyond economic necessity, there are other motivations for continuing to work. Some individuals find it important to maintain their identities as participants in the workforce. Some find that they need paid employment as a structure for their daily lives, although there are other means of creating that structure. Yet others are motivated by an entrepreneurial bent and decide to start an entirely new business or organization. Whatever the reasons—economic, personal, or a combination of these—a high percentage of midlife Americans are looking for options that allow their continued participation in the labor force.

ENCORE CAREERS

Another trend is for midlife adults, as they approach their sixties, to change careers, start new organizations, or move from the profit to the nonprofit sector. For these individuals, especially those with the financial resources to experiment with options, the motivation to work is not primarily economic or even entrepreneurial; the motivation is to apply their skills for social purposes. Many are choosing to shift professions, moving into socially oriented careers such as teaching, nursing, and spiritual or religious positions. Although the current economic recession makes these changes more challenging, there is a continuing surge in enrollment by midlife adults in community colleges and continuing education and certification programs.

There are some career changers who are using their professional or financial expertise to tackle large-scale social issues, such as environmental or health challenges or school reform. These individuals represent a new type of entrepreneur: the social entrepreneur. Civic Ventures, a think tank dedicated to "Boomers, work and social purpose," has helped lead the movement toward encore careers and social entrepreneurship. In his latest book, *The Big Shift: Navigating the New Stage beyond Midlife*, the CEO and founder of Civic Ventures, Marc Freedman, presents the stories of individuals who exemplify the trends.[3]

The trend toward encore careers is fundamentally altering the perceptions and realities of the middle years. A 2008 Civic Ventures–Metlife Foundation survey found that more than five million people ages 44–70 have begun encore careers, and of those not already in encore careers half say they want them.[4] This trend has gained traction in the media, with mainstream publications such as the *Wall Street Journal* publishing a regular column titled "Second Acts." There is also a new genre of literature consisting of testimonials by individuals who have negotiated the shift from primary careers to work that matters in the second half of life. Examples include *Inventing the Rest of Our Lives: Women in Second Adulthood*, by Suzanne Braun Levine (2005), and *The Third Chapter: Passion, Risk, and Adventure in the 25 Years after 50*, by Sara Lawrence-Lightfoot (2009).

COMMUNITY SERVICE

Even as some midlife adults are shunning retirement to develop new careers or take part-time jobs, others are engaging in volunteer activities of all kinds. This trend includes volunteering in a traditional sense, that is, providing an extra pair of hands wherever help is needed, as well as more "high value" volunteering that involves applying particular talents and experience for the benefit of an organization or cause.

Unless you've been living under a rock, you know that in 2006 the first of America's 77 million baby boomers turned 60. When retirements peak around the year 2020, the workforce will be changed drastically enough to be unrecognizable. Amid our collective teeth gnashing about evaporating Social Security and the graying of the profession, what librarians might consider are those 77 million potential library users transitioning from one major life activity to the next. Specifically, how libraries can help them and how they can help us.

Because straight-to-rocking-chair retirement is relatively rare these days, part-time work and the retooling of skills into second careers (re-careering) are important to most of today's transitioners, the most active and healthy of any generation to date. As the Urban Institute recently noted, "Retirees are happier when active." Grandparenting, health, social networking, travel, and exploring new technology are among the top nonwork issues for boomers. So is civic engagement—the new buzzword for volunteering.

—Doug Lord, older adult specialist, Connecticut State Library

> Civic engagement involves a citizen's active participation within a community, such as volunteering or political organizing. As the Baby Boomers are verging on retirement, they may be looking for ways to keep active through meaningful work. Older workers are an amazing resource to provide advice on and help to address community needs. They have unique perspectives on social issues and wisdom on how to strengthen community life.
>
> —Everyone Serves Seniors, a Brooklyn Public Library staff guide

The trend for midlife adults to engage in community service results in large measure from their motivation to apply their skills to help improve the lives of individuals and to stay active. A national survey of adults 55 and over sponsored by Metlife Foundation and Atlantic Philanthropies indicated that a majority of respondents would prefer a volunteer opportunity that makes use of their personal or professional skills to make a difference rather than jobs that can be done by anyone.[5] The movement to "give back" has gained momentum from other research showing that volunteering is not only socially beneficial but also beneficial to health. Those who volunteer have lower mortality rates, greater functional ability, and lower rates of depression later in life than those who do not volunteer.[6]

The trends outlined above have all gained traction from philanthropic and governmental initiatives promoting older adult engagement through stipended work, encore careers, and civic engagement. Senior Corps (www.seniorcorps.gov), a program of the Corporation for National Service, provides stipends and assignments that mobilize "the energy and efforts of citizens aged 55 and over" for the benefit of local communities. The Purpose Prize, a key component of the Encore Careers initiative of Civic Ventures funded by Atlantic Philanthropies, has helped draw attention to the many 50+ social entrepreneurs who are addressing key social problems.

These trends have also spawned new organizations geared to promote older adult engagement through community work. ReServe, based in New York, matches individuals with organizations seeking professionals to enhance their core services. ReServe orients, supports, and provides stipends for these individuals. As described in a profile below, ReServe has placed several "ReServists" in the Queens Library, where they are performing varied tasks: helping immigrants start new businesses, recruiting new adult literacy tutors, organizing cultural programs for homebound seniors. VolunteerMatch, also profiled below, is a national organization that works with employers and nonprofits to increase the connections between individuals and the organizations that could use their talents. VolunteerMatch and the State Library of California are working together on a statewide initiative, Get Involved: Powered by Your Library, that enables 80 percent of California's libraries to offer VolunteerMatch software. Other organizations that are effectively deploying older adults in community work include OASIS, SCORE, RSVP, and Civic Ventures' Experience Corps.

IMPLICATIONS FOR LIBRARIES

The trends outlined above have particular relevance to libraries, which are well equipped to provide job and career information, community referrals, and matching services for midlife adults considering second careers or community service. Whether it is helping a laid-off industrial worker in his fifties find the training required for different work or providing a former executive in her seventies options for applying her skills in a community setting or learning new skills altogether, libraries can leverage their current expertise in a variety of ways, including the following:

- Assistance in getting started with a job search
- Free access to online job search sites
- Resume help, including personal assistance, workshops, and online sources
- Information and referral services for adults seeking volunteer opportunities
- Books and online information about careers and community service
- Salary information
- Computer classes to prepare for online applications and for jobs requiring computer skills
- Company profiles and contact information
- Information, books, and workshops on interviewing techniques
- Access to want ads, both local and national

By adapting, expanding, and marketing these services to meet midlife adults' needs for options, information, and connections, libraries will become essential service hubs for 50+ adults seeking work, careers, or community service. For instance, job and career information guides and directories can be tailored to the needs of mature workers and—with appropriate titles and promotion—can be made visible to this age group. *Career Information for Seniors*, compiled by the Johnson County (Kansas) Public Library, is a good example of how a library can tailor information services to support older jobseekers.[7] Other libraries have created similar additions to their online directories with sections devoted to "50+ adults," "seniors," "over 40," and the like. It is important to note that some online resource centers with specific information for midlife adults are still promoted as sites for "seniors," reflecting the fact that many libraries continue to use this term as an umbrella term for all older adults.

Job and career workshops and programs are other core activities that can be adapted or expanded to benefit career changers and older workers. For instance, some libraries are offering job counseling services for unemployed older adults separately from those for younger individuals entering the workforce for the first time. They are also offering mock interview clinics, online job preparation programs for those making career or industry transitions, resume preparation workshops for older workers who need help editing or updating prior resumes, and career presentations or job fairs featuring employers interested in older workers.

For social and civic entrepreneurs, the library's core resources are being tapped in different ways, through the provision of databases and other research sources on particular issues or sectors. Some libraries are offering forums on issues of interest to these entrepreneurs or encouraging peers working on socially oriented projects to meet and share information and expertise. The Next Chapter initiative at New York Public Library recently hosted a panel of Purpose Prize winners, all 50+ social entrepreneurs, at a program titled "In Search of Purpose, Passion, and a Paycheck: Finding Work that Matters in the Second Half of Life."[8]

With respect to community service, libraries are drawing on their core skills in information and referral to connect individuals with unique talents to the local organizations, institutions, and services that could benefit from their involvement. They are organizing expos, resource fairs, or meet-ups to connect 50+ residents with potential volunteer opportunities, such as the Fairfax County (Virginia) Public Library's Venture into Volunteering Fair. In addition, more and more libraries are taking advantage of matching software to link organizations and people for community benefit. Leadership in this regard is coming from California libraries as a result of the state library's partnership with VolunteerMatch (http://californialibraries.volunteermatch.org).

Beyond the possibilities for libraries to assist midlife adults seeking work and service opportunities, libraries themselves stand to benefit from current trends in 50+ work and service. For instance, the graying of the library profession is a challenge for library leaders and planners, and some institutions are eager to recruit second careerists while retaining midlife workers through flexible schedules or part-time work. Unfortunately, current economic conditions are undermining these efforts, making it difficult or impossible to replace retiring librarians. Given the numbers of midlife adults who are looking for work with direct social impact, this situation is a loss for those libraries that could benefit from the talents of motivated encore careerists.

In terms of volunteers, there is also the potential for libraries to benefit from midlife adults' interests in giving back and, in particular, "high value" volunteering. Recognizing this potential, there are numerous efforts under way to revise existing approaches to recruiting and deploying volunteers. Rather than assigning all volunteers to certain support tasks such as reshelving books, staffing information desks, or providing administrative support, some libraries are matching volunteers with particular skills to tasks such as public relations, program planning, adult literacy teaching, website or graphic design, and other activities that enhance basic library services while engaging motivated and skilled constituents.

> The library offers a wealth of opportunities for people to volunteer to make our society a better place. We need people who have a variety of skills, who want to help people, who want to devote their energy to something important, who want to connect with people.
>
> —Trudy Toll, Refresh Your Life blog, Hayward (California) Public Library

In Chandler, Arizona, library director Brenda Brown reports that 90 percent of the library's 390 adult volunteers are baby boomers. "Baby Boomers are the backbone of the library's Job Resource Center and English language teaching programs. They make Chandler a library and a community that supports adult education."

Many other libraries confirm the continuing interest and growth in library volunteering by midlife adults. As the following examples demonstrate, their engagement in libraries is in itself fostering new appreciation and use of libraries by peers—a win-win situation for libraries and their communities.

Overall, libraries are starting to focus on midlife adults as an important category of workers and volunteers. From workshops and online resources offered by job and career information departments in large urban libraries to changes in how volunteers are recruited and deployed in smaller libraries, there is a shift in perspective about 50+ adults. There is, however, also a significant problem that becomes evident in the following examples: visibility. Even though many libraries are regearing what they do with respect to job information, career services, and volunteer matching, they have not yet communicated these changes in their language and marketing. Too many libraries are subsuming their "over 50" pages under traditional umbrella titles such as "Senior Services." Too many continue to use "seniors" in their public relations and on their web pages when, in fact, they are investing new resources in reaching baby boomers and other active midlife adults. And too many continue to see marketing primarily in terms of in-library signage or library newsletters rather than external promotions to reach new audiences. With more intentional promotion of the 50+ services actually being offered, more midlife adults will become aware of what is available and will help fulfill libraries' natural potential as information hubs for mature workers and volunteers.

Notes

1. Anne Shattuck, *Older Americans Working More, Retiring Less*, Carsey Institute (University of New Hampshire), issue brief 16 (Summer 2010), ww.carseyinstitute.unh.edu/publications/IB_Shattuck_Older_Workers.pdf.

2. *The SunAmerica Retirement Re-Set Study*, Sun America Financial Group (2011), http://retirementreset.com/the-study.

3. Marc Freedman, *The Big Shift: Navigating the New Stage beyond Midlife* (New York: PublicAffairs, 2010). Find details on this book at http://www.encore.org/thebigshift.

4. *Encore Career Survey*, MetLife Foundation/Civic Ventures, 2008, www.encore.org/files/Encore_Survey.pdf.

5. *Great Expectations: Boomers and the Future of Volunteering*, VolunteerMatch, http://cdn.volunteermatch.org/www/nonprofits/resources/greatexpectations/GreatExpectations_ExecutiveSummary.pdf.

6. *The Health Benefits of Volunteering: A Review of Recent Research*, Corporation for National Service, April 2007, www.nationalservice.gov/pdf/07_0506_hbr_brief.pdf.

7. *Career Information for Seniors*, Johnson County Library, www.jocolibrary.org/upload/library/docs/doc/research/career_info_seniors.pdf.

8. For details, see "In Search of Purpose, Passion, and a Paycheck: Finding Work That Matters in the Second Half of Life," New York Public Library, www.nypl.org/blog/2011/06/10/search-purpose-passion-and-paycheck-finding-work-matters-second-half-life.

American Association of Retired Persons Work and Retirement Resources

National Programs

www.aarp.org/work

WHAT AARP, a national nonprofit organization that helps 50+ adults improve the quality of their lives, offers online information to assist older workers in finding meaningful employment. Some state and local AARP offices also offer in-person services. Most libraries offer access to the online resources; others partner with local AARP offices to offer orientation workshops on AARP job search resources or job counseling by AARP volunteers or staff.

GOAL To enhance awareness and use of AARP's WorkSearch and other job and career development resources.

FEATURES AARP provides extensive information for 50+ workers, including ideas for part-time employment, career change opportunities, help on writing resumes and cover letters, and articles on retirement planning. Key offerings:

Sample Library-AARP Partnerships

Arlington (Virginia) Public Library

A partnership between the AARP Foundation and the Arlington Public Library enhances use of AARP's WorkSearch by offering demonstrations of the website by trained volunteers, conducting on-site individual assessments, and providing one-on-one job coaching. (http://library.arlingtonva.us)

Louisville (Kentucky) Free Public Library

Louisville's Library Job Shop partners with AARP to offer "AARP: The Power of Promoting Yourself at 50+," a workshop for 50+ jobseekers

who are making age an asset. The program covers the "new reality of job hunting, how to sell your personal brand, the value of an 'elevator speech,' and much more." The program is useful for those seeking full-time, part-time, seasonal, or temporary work. (www.lfpl.org)

New York Public Library

New York Public Library's Job Search Central at the Science, Business and Industry Library offers orientations to WorkSearch with local AARP volunteers, along with job coaching and counseling services tailored to the needs of 50+ job seekers. Volunteers

focus on targeting clients' transferable skills and the needs of adults who wish to return to the workforce. (www.nypl.org)

Tigard (Oregon) Public Library

Tigard offers a seminar by experts from Oregon AARP on job searching strategies and tactics for 50+ adults. Aimed at both those who are unemployed and those looking to change careers, the workshop provides advice on how to present your experience as assets to potential employers. Networking opportunities are available before and after the presentation. (www.tigard-or.gov/library)

AARP WorkSearch provides community-level job and career information and services to individuals who are seeking to remain in, or reenter, the workforce. WorkSearch includes skills assessments, interest and ability inventories, information about the community job market, and connections to free local training and employment opportunities.

AARP Job Search Board is a free job search website, designed for adults age 40 and over, who are unemployed or underemployed.

Quintessential Careers has a comprehensive list of job and volunteer sites and relevant articles.

PARTNERS AND FUNDING Libraries build partnerships with local and state AARP offices to offer on-site programs. Funding varies from location to location. Services provided by the Louisville Free Public Library's Library Job Shop are supported by the Louisville Library Foundation. The AARP Foundation supported the Arlington Public Library programs.

Boomer Connections @ Northland Library
Northland Library, Pittsburgh, Pennsylvania
www.northlandlibrary.org

WHAT Special programming that targeted "boomer adults" was carried out over two years, 2008 and 2009. The programs attracted new patrons and established the library's commitment to better serve the boomer population.

GOAL To connect the baby boomer generation with new opportunities for learning, work, community service, and social interaction.

FEATURES Boomer Connections programming concentrated on three areas: re-careering, civic engagement, and the "sandwich generation." At the outset of the program, in 2008, the library invited the public to use a new Boomer Connections website to recommend programs and join the library's internal planning committee for boomer programs. One of the most successful program components was an evening of "Volunteer Speed Matching." Modeled after speed dating, this event provided an opportunity for older adults, as well as other interested parties, to "interview" with nonprofit organizations. Boomer Connections has helped more than thirty community organizations and several local libraries rethink their use of midlife volunteers and expand their volunteer base.

In 2009, Northland Library offered a series of programs on workplace issues for midlife adults, including "Presenting Oneself for Success," "Dealing with Multiple Generations in the Workplace," and "The Employer Perspective."

Since offering the Boomer Connections programs, the library has integrated many program elements into its rich array of adult programs. According to library leaders, Boomer Connections helped the library strengthen its connections with boomers, who now make up a high percentage of program attendees. Northland Library was recognized by AARP Pennsylvania for Boomer Connections, receiving the 2008 Library Services for Older Adults Award.

FUNDING AND PARTNERS Boomer Connections was supported by the Northland Public Library Foundation. The Volunteer Speed Matching event involved many local nonprofits.

Creative Job Search for Workers over 50
Ramsay County Library, St. Paul, Minnesota
www.rclreads.org

WHAT A class for 50+ patrons offers hands-on experience in using the library's resources for changing careers and finding jobs.

GOAL To introduce midlife adults to library and online resources for job hunting and build their capacities to use these resources effectively.

FEATURES The Creative Job Search for Workers over 50 program builds participants' capacities to take advantage of employment resources on the library's website, including the *JobsNow!* database, which offers individualized help with resumes, interviews, and other topics of interest to job seekers. The class presents tips and strategies for finding job openings and applying for jobs online. In addition to Creative Job Search for Workers over 50, the library offers these complementary classes: "Resume and Cover Letter Fundamentals," and "How to Get a Job in the New Economy (and Keep It)."

PARTNERS AND FUNDING Ramsey County Library is partnering with Goodwill–Easter Seals of Minnesota and Workforce Solutions to offer Creative Job Search for Workers over 50 and related programs for midlife job seekers. These programs are sponsored by the Friends of the Ramsay County Library.

Employment Roundtable / Phase2Careers
Peninsula Library System, San Mateo, California
http://www.plsinfo.org

WHAT Career presentations are offered by local career experts, managers, and human resource specialists, developed by Phase2Careers (www.phase2careers .org), a San Francisco Bay area nonprofit. Sponsored and promoted by the regional library system, these discussions demonstrate how collaboration with a nonprofit specialist organization can enhance a library system's services to member libraries and to midlife adults in the region.

GOAL To assist midlife workers in the Bay Area find new career opportunities and to help companies connect with qualified and experienced applications.

FEATURES Libraries in the Peninsula Library System host Employment Roundtables, panel discussions with five to seven specialists in different industries. The presentations are for adults over 40 who are searching for jobs and careers or considering changing careers. Participants learn about specific companies, network with hiring managers, and obtain a snapshot of various Bay Area industries and companies. They also introduce participants to library resources for job searches and career development. Peninsula libraries offering Employment Roundtable include the Belmont Library, Burlingame Public Library, Daly City Public Library, Redwood City Public Library, San Bruno Public Library, and San Mateo Public Library.

In addition to the Employment Roundtables, several libraries also offer mock interview clinics, which are opportunities to practice job interviewing skills with experienced human resources professionals from Phase2Careers.

PARTNERS AND FUNDING The programs involve collaboration between the Peninsula Library System and Phase2Careers. They are supported directly by the local libraries or by library support organizations. In Burlingame the Employment Roundtable was sponsored by the Burlingame Library Foundation, in Redwood City by the Friends of the Redwood City Public Library.

Job Center

Richland County Public Library, Columbia, South Carolina

www.richland.lib.sc.us

WHAT The Job Center of the Richland County Public Library (RCPL) assists residents looking for work, including midlife adults. Created in 2010, it provides access to job information using the latest communications technology and online resources as well as personalized assistance with job searches and research on industries, training, and employers. The Job Center was developed in response to the high number of unemployed in the Midlands region of South Carolina and the fact that a high proportion of these individuals are in their late forties and fifties. Collaboration with AARP South Carolina enhances the Job Center as a resource for midlife and older adults.

GOAL To provide critical resources and virtual or on-site assistance for those looking for work.

FEATURES With grant support, RCPL has developed on-site and virtual tools for job seekers, along with programming to support individual job and career planning. Job Center features include free classes and personalized help with resume writing, interviewing, and job searching; online resources on looking for a job, learning about an industry, starting a business, or researching employer information; and a copy center (copier, printer, scanner, and local fax). To complement the Job Center services, the library also expanded access to computers at all locations and provides regular "Tech Training."

> Older workers who are looking for employment will benefit greatly from the Job Center.
>
> —Jane Wiley, AARP South Carolina state director

A section of the Job Center is set up for patrons to practice job interviews using interviewing software. Biweekly "Interview Practice" sessions are offered to provide constructive feedback. RCPL also offers a Virtual Career Resources web page to allow users to research occupations, learn interviewing skills, search current job listings, and create professional resumes. In addition to the research resources and interactive tools, job seekers can schedule appointments with a career specialist or attend weeklong networking sessions with other job seekers in a facilitated Job Help Club.

PARTNERS AND FUNDING Through a partnership arrangement, AARP South Carolina provides the library's Job Center with speakers and materials appropriate for older workers who are looking for jobs and career assistance. Funding for the Job Center and computer upgrades at all RCPL locations was provided by the John S. and James L. Knight Foundation.

Job Help
Pima County Public Library, Tucson, Arizona
www.library.pima.gov

WHAT This joint venture of the Pima County Public Library (PCPL) and Pima County ONESTOP Career Centers (ONESTOP) creates programs and identifies technology-based solutions that meet the needs of the county's growing displaced worker population, including refugees of all ages and, especially, the large numbers of 50+ adults who have recently moved to the state and are looking to reenter the workforce. The partnership demonstrates the possibilities for integrating library resources for job seekers with another community specialist in community-based job support. The PCPL coordinator of adult services, Beth Matthias-Loghry, notes that "many of the individuals over 50 currently looking to reenter the workforce lack some of the fundamental skills that conducting a job search today requires. And while the Job Help platform is geared toward computer-related skills necessary to conduct a job search, the program also introduces e-mail and social networking as a way to stay connected with friends and family to this demographic."

GOAL To combine the resources of PCPL and ONESTOP to help displaced workers, both refugees and 50+ adults, gain the information and skills they need to become effectively employed.

FEATURES In 2009, the Pima County administrator challenged PCPL and ONESTOP to integrate their services. The two worked to link existing services and to fill any gaps. As examples, PCPL purchased the same resume software ONESTOP uses, and it adapted the content of ONESTOP's employability skills class to incorporate it into library computer classes. Both PCPL and ONESTOP recruited additional computer instructors as well as computer-savvy youth ages 16–21 to assist job seekers on a one-on-one basis at library branches.

Job Help includes multiple components. Job Help Toolkit is a set of steps to help job seekers take a systematic approach to their job search. The steps suggested include opening a designated e-mail account for the job search, logging into the Arizona Career Information System and creating an "action plan," and participating in online self-assessments that help match skills with occupations. Mobile career centers provide laptops set up in designated meeting rooms specifically for use by dislocated and midlife workers. The mobile career center computers are different from the library's public-access computers, which have time limits and are not conducive for activities like workshops, building resumes, or conducting job searches, all of which require a great deal of time. Drop In Job Help is also available at branch libraries; a computer instructor can answer questions on a wide variety of topics such as online job searching, resume writing, and e-mail accounts.

PARTNERS AND FUNDING To create and implement Job Help, PCPL partners with the Pima County ONESTOP Career Center, a program of the Pima County Department of Community and Economic Development. The program is funded by local Workforce Investment Act funds administered by Pima County and by state and federal discretionary grants. PCPL is a division of county government funded by the Pima County Board of Supervisors.

Jobs 2011: Back to Work
Fairfield Public Library, Fairfield, Connecticut
www.fairfieldpubliclibrary.org

WHAT This special series of programs for anyone who is unemployed included several activities geared to midlife adults, such as Fired! and Over 50—How to Overcome the Greatest Challenge in Job Search. The comprehensive nature of Jobs 2011, its targeted activities for 50+ adults, its use of professional volunteers from the community, and its networking component make it an excellent example of job and career support for midlife adults.

GOAL To provide out-of-work individuals with assistance and support while they seek a new job or career path.

FEATURES Jobs 2011 offers a wide variety of program formats and topics, ranging from interactive workshops on job interview techniques to expert presentations on managing stress and social media marketing to one-on-one job counseling. Each program includes a half-hour before the session to allow for individual networking, and there are special sessions such as a "Business Networking Meet and Greet" where employers and potential job candidates can learn about one another.

In addition to its formal job and career assistance programs, the Fairfield Public Library sponsors a weekly job networking group at the Main Library and an online group on LinkedIn.com, the Fairfield Public Library Networking Group.

Jobs 2011 won the 2010 Connecticut Award for Excellence in Public Service.

PARTNERS AND FUNDING Jobs 2011 is developed and supported by the library but is made possible through the in-kind donations of time by local experts in such areas as employment law, patents, QuikBooks, and women's careers.

> The over-50 age group now represents a significantly higher percentage (30%) of those unemployed over one year than for any other younger segment. Presenters . . . will discuss why there is such a strong job bias in this country and provide a clearly defined plan to help job seekers find their next job in the shortest time possible including the nine best ways to overcome age discrimination, how to make your age an asset, and the five keys to networking success.
>
> —Fired! and Over 50
> program description

LEARN
Five Library Districts, Michigan

WHAT LEARN was a free online program providing university-level e-learning and career rebranding courses for unemployed and underemployed Michigan baby boomers that was available in five library systems in Michigan. The project was an unusual partnership involving both for-profit and non-for-profit partners with the common goal of helping Michigan's unemployed midlife workers prepare for jobs that would be more secure in a changing economy.

GOAL To prepare more than 100,000 unemployed Michiganders to reenter the workforce in a new career.

FEATURES LEARN career rebranding courses focused on the following industries: health care, government and nonprofit, emerging technologies, and entrepreneurship. Offered free for out-of-work midlife adults, LEARN was the product of the Maria Madeline Project of Lathrup Village. LEARN courses were accessed online at participating public libraries in southeast Michigan: Ann Arbor District Library, Dearborn Library, Dearborn Heights Library, Grosse Pointe Public Library, and Salem-South Lyon Library.

LEARN online instructors prepared out-of-work older adults whose manufacturing jobs had ceased to exist for careers in the new economy. The courses were developed by Lynn Wooton of the University of Michigan's Ross School of Business in collaboration with the Maria Madeline Project. According to Wooten, "As the economy really moves off of a manufacturing economy to a service and knowledge economy, what are the skills the baby boomers need? What has changed? How do you think of your career if you've been laid off from a place like Ford or General Motors?"

LEARN was designed to provide a bridge between a former career and a new one, helping unemployed and underemployed older workers navigate their new career. It provided details on specific jobs and the criteria needed to seek employment successfully in various new industries. LEARN classes also included lessons on basic and intermediate computer skills, and on how to develop and maintain a positive attitude in a time of work transition. Each LEARN course included both an online instructor-led and online independent study portion.

PARTNERS AND FUNDING Five libraries in southeast Michigan partnered with the Maria Madeline Project to offer midlife patrons access to the LEARN software. The program was a collaboration between presenting library systems, the University of Michigan's Ross School of Business, the Maria Madeline Project of Lathrup Village, Inc., in Southfield, Michigan, and WJBK Detroit. The Ross School of Business was the academic partner and WJBK was the broadcast partner. LEARN was developed by the Maria Madeline Project, which offered resources free to public libraries.

The Ann Arbor District Library welcomes the opportunity to partner with LEARN as a workforce development resource in order to better serve the unique needs of individuals seeking new career paths in our community. The growing curriculum of LEARN, and its ease of accessibility through aadl.org and other community partners, lends a refreshing approach to what can oftentimes be a very daunting experience, to change careers.

—Terry Soave, manager, Outreach and Neighborhood Services, Ann Arbor District Library, 2010

Reinvent Yourself 55+ Job Program
Dayton Metro Public Library, Dayton, Ohio
www.daytonmetrolibrary.org

WHAT This five-week program assisted older adults with professional skills assessment, job search strategies, and skills development. The program was developed in response to the number of job losses in Dayton, where many 50+ adults, the fastest-growing demographic group, require help to enter or reenter the job market successfully.

GOAL To help midlife workers plan and search for jobs in Dayton.

FEATURES The Reinvent Yourself program was developed after staff participation in special training for work with midlife adults.[1] One key administrator was a Libraries for the Future Lifelong Access Libraries Fellow in 2008, and the outreach manager was in the Western IMLS Fellowship program in 2010. They organized the boomer advisory group that helped to develop Reinvent Yourself.

Reinvent Yourself offered a comprehensive approach to career assessment and preparation for reentering the job market, offering participants the opportunity to "examine your personality and strengths, where you've been and where you want to be." The program included a Meyers-Briggs assessment, skills and aptitude tests, and traditional resume and interviewing techniques. The classes were led by a career specialist from Sinclair Community College, supported by librarians who provided instruction on accessing library resources to help with job searching. To support instruction, the library acquired new materials for the job development collection, including audiobooks, DVDs, downloadable media, and new resume software.

Reinvent Yourself was widely advertised and very well received, with nearly seven hundred people attending the first fifty classes. However, despite high demand, the library has lost key staff and has not been able to continue the full program. Midlife adults are served by other offerings through the library's job center.

PARTNERS AND FUNDING There were no formal partners associated with Reinvent Yourself, which was fully developed and supported by the library.

Note

1. For more program details and discussion, see *Midlife Re-Careering Case Overview*, Shaping Outcomes, www.shapingoutcomes.org/course/cases/Midlife%20Case%20Final.pdf.

Take Charge! Career/Life Planning after 50
Westchester Library System, Tarrytown, New York
www.westchesterlibraries.org

WHAT This series of specialized workshops, called "Career Development Seminars," is led by trained professionals and offered at three of the Westchester Library System's (WLS) member libraries.

GOAL To assist 50+ participants to plan or manage their careers.

FEATURES The Take Charge! workshops are offered through the library's Career and Educational Counseling Service. They consist of eight weekly sessions offered several times throughout the year at member libraries. The workshops cover how to assess yourself and get a clear direction for the next stage of your career; gain access to a variety of informational resources; explore new ways of working in a high-tech world; and rediscover learning and explore volunteer and leisure options.

A second WLS Career Development Seminar, "Managing Your Career in Changing Time," also attracts midlife individuals who are considering work options after 50. Topics include "Explore Career Alternatives" and "Evaluating Your Skills, Interests and Personality."

The workshops are offered at two branches of the Yonkers Public Library (www.ypl.org) and at the Mount Vernon Public Library (www.mountvernonpublic library.org).

To complement the Career Development Seminars, WLS offers individual workshops on resume development, interviewing, job searching, and more at county libraries. In addition, it offers free one-to-one job counseling at scheduled times at member libraries.

WLS also offers online resources for all adults pursuing a career change, interested in an educational opportunity, or looking for a new job, such as WLS Career and Educational Counseling Service and Job and Career Accelerator (from Learning Express). Some member libraries conduct classes to instruct cardholders how to use these tools. The Mamaroneck class, "Take a Job Journey," guides users through the many resources available to those looking for work.

PARTNERS AND FUNDING WLS Career and Educational Counseling Service staff develop and implement the Take Charge! workshops. For particular workshops requiring specialists, they contract with career development professionals as presenters. Funding is provided by the New York State Library, a unit of the Department of Education/State University of New York.

Transition Yourself

Port Townsend Public Library, Port Townsend, Washington
http://ptpubliclibrary.org

WHAT This multifaceted program undertaken by the Port Townsend Public Library helps residents who are looking for work or changing careers. The program includes workshops for job seekers, the Transition Yourself Networking Group, staff training, and collection development. Although the program is not restricted to midlife adults, it serves many adults in their late forties, fifties, and even sixties who are unemployed because of the economic downturn or changes in their industry or profession.

> A lot of people coming to see us were highly skilled and were good workers who had always held a job. . . . They were dumped out of a job. They're in their late 40s and 50s. How do you get a job again? . . . People need to start thinking differently about how they are going to support themselves in this economy.
>
> —Susan Wilson, Transition Yourself coordinator

Transition Yourself demonstrates how a library can design a program in support of all unemployed workers that also responds to the special needs of midlife workers. It also shows how an institution can integrate multiple services, moving beyond provision of information to offer self-assessment tools, peer networking, and communications.

GOAL To help people who are unemployed emphasize their strengths and prepare themselves for a changing job market.

FEATURES Port Townsend's Transition Yourself initiative provides resources for job search and business information through expanded collections, including a variety of resources for those who are trying to figure out how to support themselves through hard times. It also provides training to strengthen staff capacities to help people who are searching for jobs or preparing for different careers.

Workshops for job seekers are the centerpiece of Transition Yourself. These consist of four consecutive two-hour workshops exploring the psychological aspects of job loss, how to find a job in tough times, and how to make the transition back to work or into self-employment. Workshop topics include skills assessment and resume building; emotional and financial aspects of job loss and where to obtain support; branding statements for job seekers and how to prepare for interviews; marketing strategies and networking; and how to evaluate your progress.

Workshop participants are invited to join a Transition Yourself Google Group to sustain information exchange. In addition, the library invites job seekers to become part of a Transition Yourself Network Group, which is facilitated by a coordinator and provides a mechanism to continue idea sharing and group discussion.

Along with the workshops and meetings, the library has added more than five hundred books, CDs, and DVDs on the topic of employment and career change and has a page on its website devoted to career transition.

PARTNERS AND FUNDING The library collaborates with other organizations helping job seekers, including WorkSource, Olympic Community Action Council, Jefferson County Chamber of Commerce, Jefferson County Library, and Washington State University Team Jefferson. Transition Yourself has received two years of grant support from the Office of the Secretary of State, Washington State Library as part of the Renew Washington Project, which is funded by the Bill and Melinda Gates Foundation and the IMLS.

Wisdom at Work
Portland Public Library, Portland, Maine
www.portlandlibrary.com

WHAT The Wisdom at Work program is a series of free workshops, geared in part to midlife adults, that help participants gain insight into many aspects of their current job or job search and make their work life more satisfying.

GOAL To help participants develop strategies for making the most of their time at work.

FEATURES Wisdom at Work consists of one-hour noontime sessions—brown bag workshops—presented weekly by specialists in diverse aspects of employment and career development. The series has been running since 2010. The first year's series included the following topics:

- It's All about Meaning: Career Transitions in Your Second Half of Life
- Boost Your Emotional Intelligence to Attract Success

- Five Real-World Strategies to Find a Meaningful Job
- Your Job Doesn't Have to Be Perfect for Life to Be Good

During the second series, June 2011, additional topics were offered, including these:

- Is Your Resume Working for You?
- How to Make a Professional Impact
- Take Your Values to Work

PARTNERS AND FUNDING The workshops are sponsored cooperatively with expert presenters from two local job counseling services.

COMMUNITY ENGAGEMENT PROGRAMS

Community Conversations Project
Lee County Library System, Fort Myers, Florida
http://library.leegov.com

WHAT This grant-funded initiative involves developing a volunteer corps to provide library programs for seniors who have difficulty using a library. The majority of volunteers are 50+ adults seeking to make a meaningful contribution to their community. With a thorough recruitment process to ensure a good match between volunteers and the program, in-depth training, and clear expectations for the volunteers, the Community Conversations Project offers a model structure for libraries seeking to deploy volunteers to carry out a special outreach program for frail elderly.

GOAL To "make a difference in the lives of older adults in our community . . . by exposing elders to stimulating ideas and thoughtful discussion," said Kathy Mayo, project coordinator.

FEATURES Community Conversations Project trains a group of volunteers to provide library programs for seniors at assisted living facilities, adult day-care programs, and congregate meal sites. Library staff state explicitly the qualities they seek when recruiting volunteers for the project, such as "friendly, outgoing personalities; experience facilitating group discussions or are willing to learn;

and a love of reading and a desire to share that enthusiasm." The volunteer commitment is explicit as well, including eight hours per month after the initial training. Volunteers work in teams of two and lead monthly activities with older adults at three or four sites.

Lee County's volunteer training for Community Conversations cover

- Understanding the aging process and working with older adults
- Facilitating group discussions
- Leading book and short story discussion groups
- Facilitating reminiscence-based activities
- Conducting adult storytelling sessions
- Developing thematic programs using library materials

In addition to preparing the Community Conversations volunteers, the library has hosted an invitational workshop on reminiscence-based programming for library staff and senior service providers.

PARTNERS AND FUNDING The many residential facilities visited by the volunteers are project partners. The Community Conversations Project was funded by an LSTA grant through the Florida State Library.

Creating Civic Engagement through Library Volunteers
Tualatin Public Library, Tualatin, Oregon
www.ci.tualatin.or.us/departments/communityservices/library

WHAT This yearlong project was designed to restart the library's volunteer program by recruiting and empowering experienced boomer volunteers and emerging Gen Y volunteers. The project emphasized building library capacity to recruit, assign, work with, and empower volunteers.

Creating Civic Engagement is an instructive project for other libraries exploring ways to mobilize midlife adults as volunteers. By emphasizing staff training the project addressed a fundamental challenge facing any library looking to revamp its volunteer program. In addition, the staff training and project design reflected library leaders' awareness of national trends in volunteerism and how these are affecting the expectations and behaviors of boomer volunteers.

GOAL To revitalize the library's volunteer program, to provide volunteers with a variety of positions that met their interests and skills, and to develop stronger library capacity to meet the rising expectations and increasing diversity of its clientele.

FEATURES Creating Civic Engagement started with an investigation of best practices for a growing volunteer program. Staff, volunteers, and outside experts conducted an internal environmental scan and surveyed current volunteers regarding ways to retain and engage volunteers. The survey measured staff and volunteer responses to such statements as "Employees have been trained to work with volunteers and to understand the needs and motivations of volunteers" and "The climate within our organization is conducive to productive volunteer involvement."

Staff training was organized to occur quarterly, focusing on specific aspects of working with volunteers, such as "meaningful delegation" and cultural competency. Informal staff training was also provided in monthly staff meetings. Anticipating additional volunteers, the library even made changes to a workroom to better accommodate the physical needs of volunteers.

Development of volunteer trainers was a key component of Creating Civic Engagement. This involved formation of an advisory group of volunteers and development of a train-the-trainer program. Tualatin adapted a curriculum used by Hands on Greater Portland (www.handsonportland.org) and also drew on the Points of Light Foundation (www.pointsoflight.org) volunteer service manual. Together with staff, volunteer trainers attended a series of trainings on learning styles, intergenerational communication, effective presentations, and coaching.

Parallel to the training component of the project, organizers identified ongoing tasks that could be delegated to trained volunteers, including tasks that require skills not possessed by library staff. They also designed volunteer options that took into account volunteers' needs for flexible scheduling and limited-term projects.

The final phase of the project included a variety of communications mechanisms to inform community members about the volunteer opportunities at the library and to recruit and retain new volunteers. Staff and newly trained volunteers visited target groups to talk about the library and volunteer opportunities and encourage participation in the library's growing volunteer program. A volunteer newsletter was developed to enable greater information sharing among volunteers and between volunteers and staff.

Certain kinds of volunteer projects helped in building a larger boomer volunteer base, including a monthly "spruce up the library" project that people with diverse skills could participate in and see quick results.

As a result of the project, 627 adults volunteered 10,127 hours at the Tualatin Library in a twelve-month period spanning 2010 and 2011. Volunteers and staff were again surveyed near the end of the project to identify changes in perceptions of the volunteer program. The changes in responses to these statements from the initial survey revealed the successes of the program in changing attitudes.[1]

PARTNERS AND FUNDING As a result of Creating Civic Engagement, the library developed working relationships with a variety of civic groups, educational institutions, and other organizations that share an interest in community building. The project was funded through an LSTA grant administered by the Oregon State Library.

Note

1. See a State of Oregon evaluation of the project, *Oregon State Library Services and Technology Act Grant Peer Evaluation*, January, 2011, at www.oregon.gov/OSL/LD/LSTA/2010/10-14-4peval.pdf?ga=t.

Volunteer Engagement and VolunteerMatch
San José Public Library, San José, California
www.sjpl.org

WHAT In this ongoing initiative, the San José Public Library is transforming its use of volunteers as a way of enhancing library services. With an emphasis on engaging adults interested in high-impact tasks, and on system-wide training of staff to work with volunteers, San José's project is instructive for other libraries looking to revitalize their volunteer program.

GOAL To build the capacity of the library by creating and supporting volunteer programs that are attractive to high impact volunteers.

FEATURES San José Public Library has a long tradition of giving San José residents opportunities to give back to their community through volunteerism. However, like many other libraries, its use of volunteers has until recently emphasized traditional tasks such as book tidying and clerical support. Only a limited number of volunteers worked independently on special projects aligned with their skills, experiences, and schedules.

Recognizing the need to rethink their use of volunteers, San José participated in the first round of the California State Library's Transforming Life After 50

As with many nonprofit and government entities, the Library's volunteer program has been predominantly focused on traditional volunteer roles and management. Volunteers are given specific tasks to complete, told exactly how the task should be accomplished, and expected to commit to ongoing service. Today's adult volunteers are looking for a different type of experience. They want to use their skills and know-how, they want their service to make an impact, and they want flexible scheduling that fits with their busy lifestyles.

For instance, instead of cleaning library books every Tuesday at 10:00 am, today's volunteer may want to focus on a one-time only project such as developing a training curriculum for technology mentors. These high impact volunteers do not replicate staff roles. They bring additional skills and expertise from which the Library can benefit. . . . These volunteers also expand the Library's circle of influence, as they tend to be connected in the community, and willing to engage their contacts with their volunteer efforts and the Library.

—Report on Library Volunteer Engagement Program to Neighborhood Services Education Committee

(www.transforminglifeafter50.org) grants to organize self-directed groups of volunteer boomers to plan and conduct new and innovative adult library programs.

In 2008, San José was selected as one of six pilot library systems to take part in Get Involved: Powered by Your Library (see below). Through Get Involved, a ten-member team of library staff and volunteers received training on volunteer engagement from national experts.

As part of Get Involved, the library received a Community Leader Premium Service Account with VolunteerMatch for each of its branches, enabling them to access an online service that helps match volunteers with opportunities in their community. The library implemented Volunteer Engagement and VolunteerMatch system-wide, and staff received substantial training on working with high-impact volunteers and using VolunteerMatch.

VolunteerMatch has been used to recruit volunteers for specific branch-based and system-wide opportunities. Over 1,200 volunteer referrals have been received for positions ranging from technology mentor to photographer to adult literacy tutor, the vast majority from qualified candidates for the specific positions.

The library is still looking ahead: "The initiative helped us lay a strong foundation for the transition to a volunteer engagement model. Our goal moving forward is to sustain and grow the program in the years ahead."

PARTNERS AND FUNDING The California State Library supported San Jose's Volunteer Engagement and work with VolunteerMatch through a series of federal LSTA grants as well as technical assistance provided by state library staff and consultants.

Get Involved: Powered by Your Library
California State Library / VolunteerMatch, Statewide Program
www.library.ca.gov/lds/getinvolved.html

WHAT Get Involved, a joint initiative of the California State Library (CSL) and VolunteerMatch (www.volunteermatch.org), is the largest web-based network of community volunteers created to promote midlife adult civic engagement through libraries. The statewide program provides resources to enable local libraries across California to think beyond their traditional use of volunteers (such as book menders and shelvers) to engaging baby boomers and the generations that follow in high-skilled/high-impact volunteerism (like graphic designers, event planners, literacy tutors, and computer coaches).

This is the first time a state library has collaborated with VolunteerMatch, and thus Get Involved stands out as an important national experiment in how and whether libraries can help convert 50+ adults' skills and experience into social capital.[1]

GOAL To expand the visibility and contributions of experienced and skilled volunteers through public libraries and to raise librarians' awareness of how volunteer engagement can benefit the library as well as the community. According to Carla Lehn, CSL Get Involved project director, "while we are building high value volunteer experiences, we are expanding the community's engagement in and support for their public library."

FEATURES Get Involved is an outgrowth of CSL's ongoing initiative Transforming Life After 50 (www.transforminglifeafter50.org), which emphasizes the potential for libraries to help midlife and older adults apply their experience and talents to solve community problems. The initial training helped libraries to consider the distinctions between traditional volunteer approaches and high-impact volunteering. A website was established that archives much of that training, together with examples of best practices that libraries are using to engage and support skilled volunteers more effectively.

The CSL-VolunteerMatch partnership, started in mid-2009, helps turn library websites into volunteer recruitment engines. Any library jurisdiction in California may receive a free upgraded membership in VolunteerMatch that enables them to use VolunteerMatch to match the experience and talents of

> Americans of all ages are more interested than ever in giving back, so the challenge is for institutions to create engaging and interesting ways to get involved. . . . We're delighted that California's libraries share our commitment to unlocking the potential of new generations of citizens to serve their communities.
>
> —Greg Baldwin, president of VolunteerMatch, announcing Get Involved launch

potential volunteers to the needs of the library and the community. By posting a specially branded widget on their websites, libraries can drive potential volunteers (through their zip code) to a branded "hub" site that aggregates library volunteer opportunities, literacy volunteer opportunities, and general volunteer opportunities within a twenty-mile radius of the zip code entered.

Libraries seeking higher levels of participation in Get Involved applied to attend one of two two-day institutes, one held May 2009 and one in February 2010. Travel, meals, and training materials were covered by CSL, with the stipulation that more than one librarian per library attend. Forty-six libraries attended the two-day program, designed to enhance participants' capacities to recruit volunteers, increase visibility of the volunteer opportunities they list on VolunteerMatch, and build stronger relationships with their own volunteers.

Beyond the institutes, twelve libraries received six months of hands-on training and coaching, a pilot group in 2008/9 and a second group in 2009/10. Several of these libraries are profiled in this chapter.

Get Involved is operated by a senior member of the state library staff who coordinates with a peer at VolunteerMatch. As of March 2011, 80 percent of

Selected Get Involved Programs

Monterey Public Library
Benefiting from its original Transforming Life After 50 grant and subsequent participation in Get Involved, Monterey Public Library has become a leader in addressing boomer volunteer issues in the broader community. Library staff have convened a working group of community partners to survey local agencies to assess the state of volunteer opportunities; conducted two boomer volunteer focus groups to explore needs for recruitment, recognition, and retention; organized a volunteer agency forum to share survey and focus group findings; hosted a one-day volunteer training summit for local agencies and organizations on best practices for engaging boomer volunteers; and offered VolunterMatch for local residents. The library also developed a collection of library materials on volunteering, designed a volunteer resources web page, and created a three-minute DVD on the project. (www.monterey .org/library/Home.aspx)

Roseville Public Library
Roseville Public Library participated in the initial Transforming Life After 50 initiative, enabling creation of a computer assistance program and enhancing of collections for 50+ adults. The library's participation in Get Involved revitalized its volunteer program and created five new volunteer-led services including a grant writer, computer literacy instructor, and storytime reader. Library staff recruited and trained twenty new high-level volunteers to

California libraries were participating at some level. Impact statistics indicate the following results:

- Participating libraries are generating an average of five hundred volunteer referrals per month; total referrals in the first eighteen months were 10,968.
- More than seven hundred volunteer opportunities have been posted on library accounts.
- In the second year of the program, CSL statistics showed a 10 percent increase in volunteer literacy tutors in libraries.

As California libraries adopt VolunteerMatch software and learn the benefits of helping older adults "give back," the initiative is influencing the course of adult services in California and beyond. Simultaneously, it is advancing libraries' concepts and practices around library volunteers and in many cases extending the capacity of participating libraries to serve their communities. The initiative is already having an impact at the local, state, and national levels and is being looked at as a model for other states.[2]

PARTNERS AND FUNDING Get Involved is a partnership between CSL and VolunteerMatch, a popular, national web-based volunteer network whose mission is "to strengthen communities by making it easier for good people and good

oversee the new volunteer services. Staff also developed volunteer training modules on leading a children's storytime and providing high-quality customer service. According to the library director, "library staff attitudes about volunteers were transformed by experiencing first hand the value of utilizing boomer volunteers in new high-level library roles that created services the library would not have been able to offer otherwise." (www.roseville .ca.us/library/default.asp)

Torrance Public Library
Torrance Public Library, one of the first pilot Get Involved libraries, used the coaching and training to create new volunteer job descriptions and retool existing library volunteer opportunities to better match the interests of baby boomers. Staff produced a new volunteer brochure and used Volunteer-Match to recruit volunteers. They also created two podcasts, on volunteering and careers in public service. Their success with the new tools, and the

fact that they were the first city department to create podcasts and blogs, has positioned them as the lead podcasting and blogging resources for the City of Torrance. The Get Involved grant also supported collection development focusing on the interests of boomers. (www .torranceca.gov/5465.htm) causes to connect." Funding for state-level administration and leadership is absorbed by CSL.

Notes

1. For more background, read Stephen Ristau, "Get Involved: Promoting Civic Engagement through California Public Libraries," *California State Library Foundation Bulletin* 97 (2010): 12–13, www.cslfdn.org/pdf/Bulletin97.pdf.

2. For examples of the work of specific libraries, view www.youtube.com/watch?v=LxZoX6 FWnlo&feature=related (on Monterey Public Library) and www.youtube.com/user/ getinvolvedcsl (on Mission Viejo Public Library).

Pathways to Engagement: Boomers Supporting a Caregiver Nation

Sarasota County Library System / Gulf Gate Public Library, Sarasota, Florida

http://suncat.co.sarasota.fl.us

WHAT Pathways to Engagement is a volunteer-driven program in which boomer volunteers trained by the Senior Friendship Centers (www.friendshipcenters .org) work with the Sarasota County Library System to provide information and support to caregivers. This initiative demonstrates how a library can enhance the work of a local agency by providing support for midlife volunteers and supplementary information services.

GOAL To engage boomer volunteers as active resources while improving the quality of life for caregivers and those they are caring for.

FEATURES Sarasota County's population is the oldest in the nation for its size, with more than 10 percent of the population over 85 (in 2010) and receiving some form of caregiver assistance. To address the need for caregiver support, the Pathways to Engagement program recruits and trains boomers as volunteers. Armed with computer-driven educational tools, the volunteers visit the Gulf Gates Public Library weekly to help caregivers assess their needs and access appropriate local services. The volunteers assume the role of caregiving "point persons," supplementing library information and expertise. Caregivers can share their concerns and raise questions; volunteers solve problems and make necessary referrals. The library provides space, staff, and support materials to supplement those of the Pathways to Engagement volunteers.

PARTNERS AND FUNDING Pathways to Engagement is a program of Senior Friendship Centers, a multifaceted aging services network that aims to "engage older adult volunteers in creating sustainable care giving resources." The library hosts and publicizes the program and provides additional information for caregivers as needed. The Senior Friendship Centers recruit, train and, coordinate the volunteers.

Prime Time Broward

Broward County Public Library, Fort Lauderdale, Florida

www.broward.org/Library/Pages/Default.aspx

WHAT Prime Time Broward is an intergenerational program that prepares older adult volunteers to read stories to disadvantaged children at federally funded day-care centers. Broward County Library offers numerous general volunteer opportunities; this program focuses on midlife and older adults as readers.

GOAL To engage older adults in a rewarding volunteer opportunity while increasing young children's exposure to literature and reading.

FEATURES The library recruits volunteers, prepares them to be effective storytellers, and organizes their visits to the child-care centers. The training involves a half-day workshop on how to present a successful story program for preschoolers and includes ways to stimulate young children's senses with puppets, hand stamps, and other methods during the story. Each volunteer is assigned for twenty weeks to a day-care center for 3–5-year-olds in their neighborhood.

PARTNERS AND FUNDING
The library partners with individual child-care centers to offer the volunteer reading program. Prime Time is sponsored in part by the Broward County Library Foundation.

> At Broward County Libraries, we value the knowledge and experience of our seniors and encourage you to check out the many exciting volunteer opportunities you can find here. It's a way for you to give back to your community—doing something fun and rewarding, and on a schedule that fits your lifestyle! A variety of volunteer opportunities exist.
>
> —Katy Mullon, Prime Time 2 coordinator

ReServe

Queens Library, Jamaica, New York

www.queenslibrary.org, www.reserveinc.org

WHAT Queens Library is partnering with ReServe to deploy continuing professionals 55 and older in positions throughout the library system that are relevant to their skills and interests. ReServe is a New York–based nonprofit that matches midlife adults with nonprofits and public agencies that can benefit from their experience and talents. Partnerships with ReServe have promise for libraries and library systems that could benefit from the organization's matchmaking expertise and its capacities to identify funds for stipends, as well as from the tangible assistance of the professionals who are ReServists.

> A lot of older workers have lost confidence because there is a lot of competition for jobs. . . . You have to project your experience, not your age, as a competitive advantage.
>
> —Sayyid Tirmizi, ReServist at Queens Library, ReServe news web page

GOAL To preserve and expand the library's community service programs by utilizing retired professionals. The program also provides the professionals with an opportunity to experiment with a new career in community service

FEATURES ReServe works with multiple agencies and retired professionals to develop short-term projects or longer-term commitments that meet both partners' needs. ReServists receive stipends for positions that are usually ten to twenty hours a week, in different categories of positions such as "Community Careers" or "Social Impact Initiatives." ReServists are paid a stipend and receive support from ReServe after training. The ReServe process involves careful screening of ReServist candidates and of potential agencies and assignments, to ensure successful matches.

In March 2010, ReServe received a multiyear grant to implement its program in branches across the Queens Library system. ReServists carry out a variety of important tasks at the Central Library and branch libraries: helping immigrants start new businesses; recruiting new adult literacy tutors; organizing cultural programming for homebound seniors who participate in lectures and discussions by telephone; creating Friends of the Library advisory councils to help with future fundraising; and leading adult literacy discussion groups for English language learners.

The ReServists' assignments vary depending on the needs of the branch and the background of the ReServist. For example, one ReServist, a former history professor, works as a job developer associate at the Central Library. His knowledge of five languages and professional background as an educator were good preparation for work in one of the most diverse neighborhoods in the country.

PARTNERS AND FUNDING A grant from the Charles H. Revson Foundation supports the Queens Library–ReServe partnership.

Senior Assistants
Brooklyn Public Library, Brooklyn, New York
www.brooklynpubliclibrary.org

WHAT Brooklyn Public Library's (BPL) Service to the Aging Department (see chapter 2) provides patrons 55 and older the opportunity to serve as paid senior assistants. The assistants organize programs and special events at neighborhood libraries and other locations throughout Brooklyn and provide an important liaison function between outreach locations and the central department.

GOAL To help the library fulfill its mission to enhance the lives of older adults throughout the borough of Brooklyn.

FEATURES Service to the Aging assigns each senior assistant to a senior center, nursing home, community center, or branch library. These assistants recommend programming relevant to constituents in those locations, and they also organize the programs, drawing on local resources to provide diverse arts, cultural, educational, and lifestyle activities. Some programs feature older adult performers or experts in topical subjects from the local neighborhoods. Senior assistants are paid as part-time workers.

> Senior Assistants are the Heart and Soul of Brooklyn Public Library's Service to the Aging Program.
> —**Service to the Aging web page, Brooklyn Public Library**

Although Brooklyn uses the term "seniors," many of the assistants are active midlife adults who do not fit the stereotype of dependent elders.

Brooklyn's engagement of 55+ adults to enhance services for elderly residents is an excellent means of addressing the needs of several generations of older adults. The work draws on senior assistants' unique skills for the benefit of their communities. The assistants gain the satisfaction of providing tangible and meaningful services while also receiving some income. For the library's Service to the Aging department there is also great benefit. The department can maintain closer connections to frail elderly who are unable to visit the library and can offer far more programming than would be possible with full-time staff.

PARTNERS AND FUNDING All of the senior centers, nursing homes, and community centers are institutional partners with the library, as are many of the local cultural groups that provide programs and events for patrons at these sites. The library's Service to the Aging department is partially funded by the New York State Coordinated Outreach Services Grant, the City of New York, and Con Edison. To make up the balance of funding needed to sustain the range and quality of Service to the Aging's major programs, the library also relies upon private sector support.

Volunteer Connections / Tempe Connections
Tempe Public Library / Friends of Tempe Public Library, Tempe, Arizona
www.tempe.gov/index.aspx?page=397, www.tempeconnections.org

WHAT Volunteer Connections information and counseling assists 50+ residents in finding ways to apply their experience and skills for community benefit. This was one of the first library-based volunteer matching programs in the country and as such has provided a model for other libraries and library-community collaborations. Program staff have documented volunteer placements resulting from the counseling program and maintained connections with those it assisted, building a record of what works and enabling organizers to continually refine the process.

Volunteer Connections is a core program of Tempe Connections (see chapter 2), a separate organization linked to and housed in the Tempe Public Library. It embodies the organization's commitment to building social capital by linking midlife adults with the organizations and issues in their communities that could benefit from their skills.

GOAL To match the talent we have in the community with the volunteer needs in the community.

FEATURES Volunteer Connections started in 2007, as Tempe Connections Talent Connection, with support from the Virginia G. Piper Charitable Trust. Initial organizers designed and tested the process for matching 50+ residents with service activities across the community—and the library. The program has evolved over the years while benefiting from participation in its operations by new volunteers. Today, a trained counselor works one-on-one with individuals interesting in community service, helping them assess their skills and find an appropriate organizational match.

Volunteer Connections maintains an up-list of volunteer positions with details on the kinds of skills and assistance sought by the community organization or agency. Tempe is home to a large college campus, Arizona State University, which produces a large crop of well-educated retirees every year from its faculty and staff. Nearby are high-tech firms such as Intel, Motorola, and Honeywell, which encourage their employees and retirees to volunteer. In its first two years of activity Tempe Connections tapped into those sources to match twenty-one experienced people with local volunteer projects. Examples include a former university manager who is now coordinating a continuing education program, building on her experience working with faculty and students and using contacts from her long career; and a retired executive from a high-tech company who is directing a team of volunteers who are videotaping interviews with 150 war veterans.

PARTNERS AND FUNDING Tempe Connections partners with the many organizations where volunteers have been placed, including Arizona Saves, City of Tempe Social Services Department, Experience Corps, and Tempe Community Action Agency. Tempe Connections itself is a community-wide endeavor involving more than twenty organizations.

Tempe Connections' Talent Connections, the forerunner of today's Volunteer Connections, was one of ten pilot projects funded in 2007 by the Virginia G. Piper Charitable Trust as part of its collaboration with RespectAbility, a program of the National Council on Aging, to launch a ten-site implementation of Maricopa Models of Significant Service.[1] The pilot projects each received $40,000 grants to implement experienced volunteer model programs. Over the two-year grant period, Tempe Connections and the other nonprofit sites worked together to share practices and learn from each other and from experts in the field. Subsequently, Tempe Connections, with support from the Friends of the Tempe Public Library, has continued and expanded the program.

Note

1. See *Helping Communities Solve Critical Social Problems by Engaging Adults 55+*, RespectAbility issue brief 3, March 2008, http://ncoaold.pub30.convio.net/news-ncoa -publications/publications/final-respectability-ib1.pdf.

IN BRIEF: WORK, CAREERS, AND COMMUNITY SERVICE

55+ Employment Workshops

Nassau County (New York) Libraries The Nassau Library System partnered with the Nassau County Department of Aging to offer workshops in member libraries designed to help mature workers enhance their job searches. The workshops, led by an employment specialist, helped job seekers define their work goals, improve their interviewing skills, and carry out more efficient job searches. (www.nassaulibrary.org)

Ace the Interview: Critical Skills for Midlife Jobseekers

Alameda County (California) Library / Newark Library Alameda County Library presented a program on interview techniques for midlife adults that focused on sending the right nonverbal messages, anticipating questions, creating essential examples, answering event-specific questions, and ending on a high note. The workshop was led by Eileen Williams, author of *Land the Job You Love: 10 Surefire Strategies.* (www.aclibrary.org)

A New Approach to Your Life and Work after 40

Hayward (California) Public Library As part of its Transforming Life After 50 programming, funded by the California State Library, Hayward offered a workshop with Craig Nathanson, a vocational coach and author of *Don't Just Retire and Die.* (www.library.hayward-ca.gov)

Job Hunting Ideas and Resources for Older Workers: Web Sites of the Week

Charleston County (South Carolina) Public Library Like many other libraries, Charleston County's periodically provides a special section of online resources to help meet the needs of older workers. (www.ccpl.org)

Job Seeking for the Mature Candidate

Charlotte Mecklenburg Public Library The library's job help center offers informative discussions led by a human resources specialist on the challenges unique to older job seekers. Topics include tips for resumes, interviewing, networking, and self-presentation. (www.cmlibrary.org/jobs)

Job Seeking over 50

Louisville (Kentucky) Free Public Library Louisville Library's Job Shop has many resources to assist older job seekers with their search, including staff to help navigate online applications and books such as *Finding a Job after 50, Resumes for the 50+ Job Hunter,* and *The Baby Boomers Guide to the New Workplace.* (http://lfpl.org/jobshop)

Mature Job Seekers: Hidden Jewels of the Job Market

Columbus area, Ohio This program was part of Any Age, Any Stage, a weeklong Central Ohio Library Collaboration offered in March 2011 that involved seven library systems in and around Columbus. The project provided regionally coordinated information and support for two categories of workers: first-time workers and experienced workers looking to change jobs or reenter the workforce. Two library systems offered specific activities for older workers: the

Old Worthington branch of the Worthington Library System offered "Encore Careers," and four branches of the Columbus Metropolitan System offered "Mature Job Seekers."

Over 50 and Out of Work

Cuyahoga County (Ohio) Public Library   The library's Career Center offers an "informative and motivational program designed for the over-50 job seeker." Participants learn how to increase marketability and success in today's job market. The library also provides an online guide: *Job Search Tips for Over 50 / Career Information Page.* (www.cuyahogalibrary.org)

ReVentures

Scottsdale (Arizona) Public Library   Scottsdale Library was a partner in a community collaborative, Boomerz, that was funded in 2006 as part of a larger initiative of the Virginia G. Piper Trust designed to create opportunities for baby boomers to maximize their contributions to society. The library created ReVentures to add high-value positions to its list of volunteer opportunities. Kathy Coster, ReVentures project manager and library manager for innovation stated, "We want people to use their life skills in productive and inspirational ways." As one example of a major ReVentures project, the library worked in 2007 with the Volunteer Center of Maricopa County to organize the "Vietnam Experience," collecting oral accounts of personal experiences from veterans of the Vietnam War and presenting a series of panel discussions and exhibits that told the story of the war from various points of view. ReVentures helped the library to integrate new kinds of volunteer activities into its overall volunteer structure, develop job positions for volunteers, and strengthen volunteer training, with an emphasis on utilizing the unique experiences and talents of 50+ volunteers. Today the Friends of the Scottsdale Library (http://scottsdalelibraryfriends.org) operates ReVentures, deploying volunteers for a range of functions from the Storytime Volunteer Corps to Library Advocates for Business, which uses volunteers to reach out to local businesses on behalf of library services. (http://library.scottsdaleaz.gov)

Service Opportunities after Reaching 55

Framingham (Massachusetts) Public Library   Framingham Public Library's Service Opportunities after Reaching 55 (SOAR) initiative provides midlife adults with more than one hundred opportunities for community service, including assisting parents and children through early literacy training, teaching entrepreneurship skills to prerelease inmates, and helping a shelter establish safety and support for adults and children fleeing violence. (www.framinghamlibrary.org)

CHAPTER 4

REFLECTIONS AND TRANSITIONS

Libraries have the potential to make the process of
re-imagining, revisioning and consciousness-raising possible.
People need to rethink what they can become.

—Mary Catherine Bateson, "Designs for Change" report on the National Library Leaders Forum, 2006

With more and more 50+ adults in the workforce, starting new businesses, returning to school, changing careers, caring for grandchildren or elderly parents, and challenging assumptions about health and mobility in their 60s, 70s, and 80s, our concepts and stereotypes about aging need to be rethought to reflect the realities of today. It is clear that a new life stage is emerging, a life stage that falls between full-time work or parenthood and, for some, the onset of frailty and dependency toward the end of life. It encompasses baby boomers as well as younger and older adults who are trying to envision "what's next?" It is not defined by chronological age as much as by an individual's physical and intellectual capacities and degree of engagement.

The new life stage is the subject of research and social commentary by professionals ranging from sociologists and economists to community planners, health care specialists, and business leaders. There are commentators, such as Marc Freedman, founder of Civic Ventures, who see midlife as a stage with enormous potential for individual and social renewal. Through a series of books, including *Prime Time* (PublicAffairs, 2002), *Encore Careers* (PublicAffairs, 2007), and *The Big Shift* (PublicAffairs, 2010), Freedman has promoted a redefinition of retirement and catalyzed the concept of second careers that combine individual purpose with high social value. There are others who approach midlife as a problem to be managed, offering how-to books with checklists and guidelines for retirement and life planning. There are also gurus offering advice on specific aspects of life change, including financial experts, life planning consultants, health and fitness proponents, and spiritual advisors. There is even a new genre of "Boomer Lit" emerging that speaks to the question of "what's next?" in the form of personal accounts of life transitions. Suzanne Braun Levine's, *Fifty Is the New Fifty* (Viking, 2009), is but one example of this genre.

TRENDS

The deluge of theory, advice, and personal examples about navigating midlife is relatively recent and so, even with the surge in awareness, there are still few roadmaps for transition. Adults approaching retirement, just retired, or facing new challenges and responsibilities in their midlife years do not have precedents to go on or clear steps for this next life stage. They are pioneers in midlife development, benefiting from longevity and health but facing unknowns in the social, personal, and economic spheres. They have little to guide them in planning their futures other than their own experiences and values. In this context, it is no wonder that midlife adults are grappling with a host of questions and options. For some, the questions revolve around *identity and purpose*. What are their values and how can they act on those values during their midlife years? Do they approach midlife as an opportunity to try out a new career or solve a social problem, or as a time to cultivate creative interests, hobbies, or intellectual pursuits? Do they see their lives becoming more static and constricted, or do they see possibilities for learning, adventure, and service? Is midlife a time to deepen their spiritual interests or to become more involved with civic affairs?

Other midlife adults have questions about *tangible aspects of midlife* and beyond. What are their economic assets and how can they ensure fiscal security in the future? Is a part-time job or second career necessary for their financial health, and if so do their skills and interests match the opportunities available? Is community service, paid or stipended, an option, and if so what are the avenues to find an appropriate service venue?

Midlife often triggers a desire to take stock of one's life. As they transition from one life phase to another, many adults focus on *heritage and legacy*: What is important about their lives, and how can they communicate their experiences and wisdom in ways that are meaningful for family and other generations? The concept of life review, coined by Robert Butler in his *Longevity Revolution* (PublicAffairs, 2008), is a process of thoughtful introspection that can be either oral or written. Life review is being widely adopted as a means of helping people come to grips with change while leaving a legacy for future generations.

For many the challenges of *caregiving* spark questions about responsibilities and capacities and drive midlife adults to seek information and community support. How can they redefine their relationships to their elderly parents, and how can they handle extended caregiving while navigating their own life changes?

These kinds of questions cannot be answered easily. They do not lend themselves to formulas or blueprints. There is no one-size-fits-all guide for midlife transitioning. These questions demand reflection and conversation. As described by anthropologist Mary Catherine Bateson, the transition from full-time parenting and work is a "punctuation point," a moment in the lifespan when focused attention and self-assessment can help define the future shape of one's life. Bateson and others liken this process to the consciousness raising that so many women participated in during the 1960s. She argues that older adults can benefit from reflection and discussion about the value of their experiences and skills. "To tap this potential, it is necessary to reimagine aging in order to break out of stereotypes and redefine the shape of a life. Libraries have the potential to make that possible, not just for the experts but for the older people themselves."[1]

Quality of Life: Life Review

Are you an older adult who believes lifelong learning keeps you young and relevant? There's a new class for you at Crowell Public Library. This free discussion group will meet weekly. . . . Get in on the ground floor of a very fulfilling journey. *Jump on a bandwagon that is active, interested and living longer with a positive attitude. Grab a cup of coffee and the hour will zip by!*

Program announcement, Crowell (California) Public Library

Unfortunately, there are no obvious places or formats for this kind of self-reflection and exchange. Some inquiry certainly can and does take place spontaneously, in settings such as coffee shops or fitness centers, but deep reflection and peer interaction of the sort recommended by Bateson benefit from facilitated conversations among peers in a neutral setting. Discovering What's Next, a Massachusetts nonprofit organized by midlife adults specifically to encourage such inquiry, identified the need for neutral settings:

We became aware that more and more local adults in their 50's and 60's, with high levels of experience and skills, were seeking ideas for how to be useful and productive following full time professional employment. . . . the group's founders started to experiment with programming that could offer examples of how individuals were making transitions—transitions from full-time to part-time work, from professional careers to creative work, from corporate life to non-profit service, etc. Through experimental programming, surveys and focus groups, DWN learned that advice, examples and dialogue about transitions were priorities for mid-life adults. They also learned that participants were seeking neutral, accessible locations for guidance and for conversations.[2]

The evolution of Discovering What's Next underscores the potential for libraries not only to offer a physical setting for questions and reflection about life transitions but even to be more intentional—to design programs that help guide the inquiry process and connect midlife adults with one another in helpful ways.

IMPLICATIONS FOR LIBRARIES

As the national movement for library services targeted to midlife adults takes hold, it is clear that some librarians recognize the questions and needs of individuals undergoing midlife transitions—needs to explore identity and purpose; to assess and express life experiences; to glean ideas and inspiration from peers; to learn about the practical steps required for transitioning to a new life stage; and, above all, to gain perspective as they grapple with life planning decisions for which they may feel unprepared. These needs are often more open-ended and less tangible than more specific information needs, requiring flexibility, imagination, and patron involvement for success.

In responding to these trends, several approaches are emerging that reflect new understanding by librarians regarding how to work effectively with midlife adults who are sorting out their past or exploring options for "what's next." For instance, more and more libraries have peer advisory groups that help plan programs, or they encourage boomers to work together to design their own programs. Memoir clubs or transition talks are examples of peer-led activities that support reflection and transition.

Community partnerships are another important ingredient for working with adults in transition. Librarians recognize that they do not have the expertise or internal resources to facilitate peer conversations on identity and "active wisdom" or to organize workshops on life planning. They also know that there are multiple community organizations with expertise that can complement library collections, spaces, and information. The majority of reflection and transition programs involve at least one partner.

Diversity is another characteristic of reflection and transitions programs. In responding to the questions and issues confronting midlife adults, librarians realize that a portfolio of programs is more appropriate than one-size-meets-all. The Multnomah County (Oregon) Public Library's Life by Design program, profiled below, exemplifies this expansive approach. During 2008/9, under the Life by Design umbrella, Multnomah Library offered multiple series as well as stand-alone programs that attracted individuals with different goals and needs as they planned for change:

- Perspectives on Positive Aging (series)
- Creating Connections and Community (series)
- Helping Your Aging Parents (series)
- Coffee and Conversation
- Books to Action (series)
- Spirituality and the Ageless Questions (series)
- Coffee for Caregivers (series)
- What's Next? Surviving Change (workshop)

What's Next? Surviving Change

Just laid off? Experiencing a major life change? The economy got you down? Newly single? This is your chance to start over! . . . Through lively discussion, exercises and reflection, this workshop will provide you with the tools and resources to find out where you want to be in your life and how to get there. Professional trainer and coach Mary Ellen Hoeh will help you identify at least one change you'd like to make and the steps to accomplish your goal.

—Life by Design program announcement, Multnomah County Public Library

Not all libraries interested in expanding services for midlife adults are in a position to offer such an extensive set of programs. However, numerous smaller libraries and individual librarians are experimenting with more limited approaches, some of which are profiled below. No matter the scope of the effort, it is clear that librarians are responding to the kinds of questions and issues concerning midlife adults outlined above. For instance, there are programs that help people in transition explore their changing identities and social purposes. The Hartford Public Library's Active Wisdom series exemplifies an open-ended, facilitated inquiry approach, and the Tempe Public Library's Transition Talks uses dialogue as a means of gaining self-awareness and exchanging ideas among other adults in transition.

With respect to programs that focus on the tangible aspects and challenges of life change, the Monterey Public Library's Boomer Education 101 program included the series Tough Topics, with topics such as "Caring for Yourself while Caring for Aging Parents," and the Pima County Library's Fit for Life 50+ programs deal with issues relating to work and postwork.

There are also numerous programs that offer midlife adults the opportunity to reflect on and communicate their life experiences and accomplishments. Whatever the program format—memoir writing, storytelling, digitally recorded interviewing, photojournalism, genealogy, or poetry—libraries are encouraging reflection and communication for the benefit of midlife adults, their families, and future generations. Programs include the national Veterans Oral History Program, which has engaged thousands in rethinking and recording their wartime experiences, and local projects such as Write Your Life memoir writing workshops at the Jericho (New York) Public Library.

Collectively, the reflection and transition programs taking place in libraries today reflect librarians' increasing understanding that libraries have a special role to play in helping midlife adults grapple with the uncertainties and options presented by a new life stage. No one type of program is dominant; libraries are experimenting with multiple approaches that match midlife adults' varied interests, experiences, and questions. Over time, as librarians and their midlife patrons refine and expand programming that supports life transitions, a clearer picture will emerge regarding best practices.

Notes

1. Mary Catherine Bateson, "Designs for Change: Libraries and Productive Aging. Report on the National Library Leaders Forum," cosponsored by Americans for Libraries Council and the Institute for Museum and Library Services, 2006, 22.

2. Discovering What's Next: Revitalizing Retirement (www.discoveringwhatsnext.org) is a community-based nonprofit organization located in Newton, Massachusetts, dedicated to "engaging midlife and older adults in the creative explorations of their next life stage." The quotation is from a 2009 interview with Carol Greenfield, founder of Discovering What's Next, in 2009, in Pauline Rothstein and Diantha D. Schull, eds., *Boomers and Beyond: Reconsidering the Role of the Library* (Chicago, American Library Association, 2010).

Bonus Years @ The Carnegie Speaker Series
Arizona State Library, Archives and Public Records / Carnegie Center Library, Phoenix, Arizona
www.lib.az.us

WHAT This series of presentations addressed "the next phase of life" for baby boomers and other active older adults. Bonus Years was organized by Arizona State Library, Archives and Public Records (ASLAPR) in 2006, during the first phase of the agency's initiative to position libraries as centers of information and education for Arizona's 50+ boomer population (see chapter 1).

GOAL To provide 50+ adults with information on options and issues relating to the "Bonus Years."

FEATURES Held in the landmark Carnegie Library on the grounds of the state capitol in Phoenix, Bonus Years drew its audience from state workers starting to plan for retirement or second careers and from downtown Phoenix workers and residents. The programs complemented other components of ASLAPR's 50+ initiative, which were primarily focused on training librarians to work with 50+ adults. Initial Bonus Years topics included healthy aging, lifelong learning, re-careering, and civic engagement. Each featured a national author or local expert, whose presentations were followed by dialogue with the audience.

> An increase in life expectancy and improved health for Americans are drastically changing the nature of aging and retirement. . . . What will you do with these Bonus Years? Is it time to start thinking about your transition plans?
>
> **—ASLAPR website**

In addition to the programs, ASLAPR prepared *Core Bibliography Information Guide for the Bonus Years* as an interactive website to which other librarians have added recommended titles in a variety of topical categories (www.lib.az.us/carnegie/bib/Default.aspx).

PARTNERS AND FUNDING ASLAPR staff organized and underwrote the programs without formal collaborators.

Boom Time at the Library:
Inspiration for Your Next 30 years
Louisville Free Public Library, Louisville, Kentucky
www.lfpl.org

WHAT This special series of programs for adults in their forties, fifties, and sixties provides, according to the program web page, "fresh perspectives and lively conversation" on how to "increase the odds for a healthy, active older age."

GOAL To provide information and inspiration for midlife adults considering making changes in their lives.

FEATURES The program includes lectures and panel discussions. Two Authors at the Library events kicked off the program in September 2011, featuring Laura L. Carstensen, author, psychologist, and founder of Stanford University's Longevity Center; and Marc Freedman, author and founder and CEO of Civic Ventures, a think tank on boomers.

After the two author events the library presented a three-part seminar with experts on life transitions and aging. Presenters included two physicians from the University of Louisville who discussed "Staying Healthy in the Long Run"; five career changers from local organizations and businesses in a conversation titled "Jumping the Tracks"; and a moderated discussion on "What's Next?"

Future programs will continue to combine expert advice and real people sharing experiences. Program coordinator Judy Richardson mentioned these for 2011 and 2012:

> **Fit: Your Body and What It's Telling You:** exercise physiology, activity, and nutrition

> **Sharp: Your Brain As It Ages:** the latest neurological science on driving, physical and mental activity, smoking, obesity, and diet

> **My Other Life:** testimonies regarding creative pursuits on the sidelines of busy work lives

> **What I Know Now:** life lessons from people over 75 about what they wish they had known at 45

No Act of Love Is Ever Wasted: taking care of ailing family members, with a panel of experts and family members

Are You Taking Too Many Drugs? the pros and cons of multiple drugs

Boom Time @ Work: strategies for staying "in the game and on top of your game" for those who continue working

PARTNERS AND FUNDING Boom Time at the Library was supported in part by the Louisville Free Public Library Foundation.

Conversation Salons
Allegheny County Library Association, Pittsburgh, Pennsylvania
www.aclalibraries.org

WHAT Facilitated, community-based discussion groups that meet regularly in local libraries. The discussions focus on dialogue and participation rather than presentation. Topics are determined by the participants themselves, and the discussions are led by participants.

GOAL To provide opportunities for nonprogrammed dialogues between neighbors on topics of mutual interest.

FEATURES Based on the French concept of the *salon*, the ACLA Conversation Salons were originally started by the Pittsburgh-based Elderhostel. When Elderhostel left the area, ACLA saw the opportunity for libraries to help sustain the programs. With the assistance of a volunteer with prior experience in organizing these salons, five ACLA member libraries initially offered the programs; there are now fourteen libraries offering Conversation Salons. They are held monthly. Topics are sometimes chosen in advance but more typically are selected spontaneously based on members' current interests and concerns. The emphasis is on the dialogue, not necessarily on a particular subject or theory. When a new group starts, it is facilitated by an ACLA staff

> This program is fantastic. Participants are dedicated to their group and are so appreciative of the opportunity for serious in-depth discussion. Once we work with the library to get a Salon up and running, the program runs on its own.
>
> —Charity Leonette, ACLA director of community partnerships

member, experienced volunteer, or librarian. Eventually the group identifies a participant who becomes the facilitator. One group is facilitated by a 92-year-old woman. ACLA hosts an annual luncheon for the Salon facilitators where they can exchange ideas and suggestions for topics.

Conversation Salons were originally developed for active older adults interested in intellectual stimulation. The ages of participants range from 50 to 95, with the majority in their sixties and seventies. ACLA encourages groups to bring in participants of other generations, having observed that the conversations have more varied perspectives when a wider age range is represented. Some libraries are experimenting with different time slots for the salons, hoping that evening programs, for instance, might attract more people who are still in the workforce.

PARTNERS AND FUNDING Member libraries support the peer-led Conversation Salons; no direct costs are incurred.

Discoveries in Aging:
What Boomers and Their Parents Need to Know
Chelmsford Public Library, Chelmsford, Massachusetts
www.chelmsfordlibrary.org

WHAT This program series on the physical, neurological, and social aspects of aging presents current research on aging and practical methods for mitigating the negative aspects of aging. The series is an instructive example of how a public library can help prepare midlife adults for their responsibilities as caregivers of their elderly parents while presenting practical information on ways to deal with the common changes of the aging process. In addition, the series demonstrates how an informational program—Mindful Listening—can be the catalyst for a one-day community event, a "Listening Day."

GOAL To inform baby boomers about new research on the aging process and the implications of this new research for them as well as for older generations.

FEATURES The first year of the program featured three presentations by local experts:

- Five Deciding Factors: A Guide to Navigating the Journey of Aging
- Which One of Us Is the Mother Now? Tales from the Nursing Home
- Caring Conversations: Talking with Aging Parents about Tough Subjects

The second program year, 2011, featured two presentations and a community event:

Staying Sharp: Brain Fitness for Boomers and Seniors: A neurotherapist and speech language pathologist provided key findings from recent brain research, including evidence for neuroplasticity, the ability to rejuvenate old brain cells and create new ones.

Mindful Listening: A neurotherapist presented a program on the neurophysiology of hearing and listening and highlighted the importance of listening for everyday communications and family relationships.

Listening Day: In conjunction with the national organization Story Corps (www.storycorps.org), the library led the community-wide Listening Day, in which individuals of all ages were encouraged to take one hour and listen carefully to another person, in a formal interview or informal listening session. The goal was to enhance community and family communications through listening.

PARTNERS AND FUNDING Discoveries in Aging was organized in collaboration with Chelmsford's Elder Services Departments and Healthy Chelmsford. Story Corps was an additional collaborator in 2011. The Friends of the Chelmsford Public Library supported Discoveries in Aging.

Fit for Life 50+
Pima County Public Library, Tucson, Arizona
www.library.pima.gov

WHAT Fit for Life 50+ brings a menu of opportunities to help midlife adults dealing with life changes. Programs include topics and activities ranging from financial literacy workshops and drawing classes to programs on postwork volunteerism.

GOAL To transform neighborhood libraries into "social centers for active living at age 50 and beyond, places where individuals can learn something new, connect with others, nurture artistic abilities, and share their talents and wisdom."

FEATURES A primary Fit for Life 50+ program series concerned issues of work and postwork identity. Led by specialists, the topic titles included "Planning at Midlife," "Entrepreneurship and Owning Your Own Business," "Employment at Midlife," "Financial Literacy at Midlife," and "Volunteering and Socializing." Some of the other series are Financial Fitness, Light Yoga, Art Workshops for Adults, Line Dancing, and Zuzi Dance Classes.

PARTNERS AND FUNDING *Fit for Life 50+* programs related to work and service were carried out in conjunction with Career Services Unlimited (www.eframing yourfuture.com). Other program partners include Wellness4Tucson, the Drawing Studio, and the Zuzi Dance Company.

Fit for Life 50+ programs were made possible by an LSTA grant administered by the Arizona Department of Library, Archives and Public records. The Friends of the Pima County Public Library have also supported the program.

Next Chapter Programs in Transition and Reinvention
New York Public Library, New York, New York

www.nypl.org

WHAT New York Public Library's Office of Outreach offered these special programs to target midlife and older active adults seeking options and ideas for their next phase of life. These programs are a component of the library's Next Chapter initiative (see chapter 2), which is a national model for the variety, quality, and reach of its offerings for midlife and older New Yorkers.

GOAL To stimulate individuals to challenge assumptions about aging and consider alternatives to traditional retirement.

FEATURES Through Next Chapter, the library has been offering a variety of programs on transition and reinvention since 2008. Programs take place at multiple locations: the Mid-Manhattan Library, the Steven R. Swartzman building, and branch libraries in the three New York City boroughs served by the library. All are promoted through social media vehicles, including the *Next Chapter* blog, and other library announcements. The programs, which are often presented in cooperation with other agencies or organizations, include author talks, lectures, and forums. The following 2010/11 examples suggest the range of topics and formats:

Yes, There Is Humor in Aging: an Evening of Laughs: with Mort Gerberg, longtime New Yorker cartoonist, who demonstrated the cartooning process and discussed his book *Last Laughs: Cartoons about Aging, Retirement and the Great Beyond*

Don't Retire, Re-invent: organized with the Transition Network, a New York–based organization of women who exchange ideas and strategies for productive aging

Changing Shoes: Getting Older—Not Old—With Style, Humor and Grace: presentation by author and TV personality Tina Sloan

The Age of Active Wisdom: with Mary Catherine Bateson, widely known anthropologist, discussing her book *Composing a Further Life*, a compilation of interviews with older adults who reflect on their age-related transitions

In Search of Purpose, Passion, and a Paycheck: Finding Work That Matters in the Second Half of Life: panel discussion featuring several recipients of the Purpose Prize who are creating new ways to solve social problems in their encore careers. This program, held in June 2011, was also the launch of Coming of Age New York City (www.comingofage.org/nyc), an initiative designed to help individuals 50+ connect and contribute to their communities

PARTNERS AND FUNDING According to Next Chapter organizer Brigid Cahalan, partnerships are the backbone of this programming. The author programs, for instance, often involve cooperation with a publisher. Don't Retire, Re-invent was presented in cooperation with the Transition Network (www.transition-network.org), and the May 2011 program In Search of Purpose, Passion and a Paycheck was a collaboration with Coming of Age New York City.

Although other components of the library's Next Chapter initiative are funded through specific grants, these programs are organized as part of the library's regular educational and outreach programs.

People & Stories / Gente y Cuentos

National Program

www.peopleandstories.org

WHAT A humanities program that creates "public grassroots connections to literature" by opening doors to new and imaginative landscapes. People & Stories involves groups of different ages and reading abilities in listening to and discussing literary works. One of the core programs, Senior Focus, engages midlife and older adults in conversations that spark creative and intellectual stimulation within a social context. The program takes place in varied community settings across the country, including libraries.

People & Stories was founded in 1972 in Cambridge, Massachusetts, as a program featuring stories and discussion in Spanish. English programming was added in 1986 when the program first received support from the New Jersey Council for the Humanities.

GOAL To engage participants in reflective dialogue and foster a discovery of the power of literature.

FEATURES People & Stories is a program without walls. The organization collaborates with different sites—such as alternative education programs, community centers, senior centers, and libraries—to provide reading materials, discussion leaders, evaluation procedures, and follow-up. Programs are conducted in English or Spanish, "using the reading and discussion of short stories to create a recreational, enjoyable and educational experience that is relevant to life." Fifteen to twenty people take part in each group, meeting for 90–120 minutes a week, for eight to ten weeks. Coordinators, who are specialists in literature and experienced discussion leaders, start each program by reading the story. They then facilitate a discussion aimed at eliciting reactions and dialogue among the participants.

> Through a democratic dialogue that is based on the strength of individual voices, participants discover their capacity for creative thinking, literary analysis, and problem solving. For seniors, the discussions provide opportunities to tap into their memories and share wisdom and knowledge acquired over a lifetime of experience.
>
> —People & Stories website

PARTNERS People & Stories collaborates with many local agencies to offer the discussion programs. More than twenty-five libraries are partners, including Gwinnett County (Georgia) Public Library, Princeton (New

Jersey) Public Library, San Francisco (California) Public, and Shelby County (Florida) Public Library.

Funding has come from the New Jersey Council for the Humanities and the National Endowment for the Arts. Local funders support the program in some locations. For instance, the Princeton Area Community Foundation provided funds to help bring People & Stories to Princeton.

Personal Stories of the Berkeley School Desegregation
Berkeley Public Library, Berkeley, California
http://berkeleypubliclibrary.org

WHAT Berkeley Public Library developed digital recordings of personal narratives about living through the desegregation of the Berkeley schools from 1964 to 1968. Because this was the largest city in the United States to desegregate its schools voluntarily, the Berkeley process had national as well as local significance. The individuals most directly affected by the desegregation process are now baby boomers, many with distinct memories of the community conflicts that took place. The project was undertaken as part of the California State Library's Transforming Life After 50 initiative (www.transforminglifeafter50.org).

GOAL To help the local community revisit, discuss, and reevaluate this pivotal period in the city's history and to increase baby boomers' knowledge and appreciation of the library.

FEATURES To carry out the personal stories project, the library recruited a corps of boomers who had attended Berkeley schools during desegregation. These individuals took part in three day-long workshops, led by the Center for Digital Storytelling (www.storycenter.org), on storytelling and digital technologies. They learned how to record their individual histories, including the integration of images and music. Each individual produced a brief digital movie based on his/her desegregation experience. These stories, now on DVD, are available as part of the library's circulating collection and also as downloadable movies on the library's website. Many of them can also be viewed on YouTube.

During a second phase of the project the stories were combined into a movie that was shown to the public and used as the basis for a public panel discussion. Since completing the project, the library has set up a volunteer-run digital storytelling workstation that will continue to gather stories on desegregation and other social and historical issues.

PARTNERS AND FUNDING To carry out the project, the Berkeley Public Library worked with the Center for Digital Storytelling, an international nonprofit that assists youth and adults in using digital media tools to create, record, and share meaningful stories from their lives. The library received a federal LSTA grant, administered through the California State Library, for the digital storytelling project.

Perspectives on Positive Aging / Life by Design @ your library
Multnomah County Library, Portland, Oregon
www.multcolib.org

WHAT Multnomah County's Central Library presented this monthly speaker series during 2009 and 2010 to explore diverse concepts and information concerning positive aging. Perspectives on Positive Aging was one of several program series offered as part of Multnomah County Library's Life by Design @ your library initiative and its overlapping Kaboom! project (see chapter 2).

GOAL To help baby boomers plan for new life phases and the challenges and opportunities for aging well.

FEATURES Speakers for Perspectives on Positive Aging were recruited from Portland institutions and organizations such as Tools for Diversity, Marlyhurst University, and the Institute on Aging at Portland State University. The series included topics such as the importance of community as we age; living more authentically as we age; creating a "portfolio life"; helping aging parents; phases of retirement; and combining work and care for an aging parent. Each program announcement included a recommended reading that was referenced by the speaker and included in the library's Life by Design Readers' Advisory.

PARTNERS AND FUNDING Life by Design NW (www.pcc.edu/climb/life) was a primary partner for all the library's Life by Design @ your library programs, including Perspectives on Aging. Life by Design NW helped to publicize the program and also helped to identify some of the presenters. As a result of this partnership, the library received funds from Atlantic Philanthropies to support a dedicated part-time staff member in outreach services who helped to plan and oversee Perspectives on Aging. Additional support was provided by an LSTA grant for the Kaboom! project, administered by the Oregon State Library.

Staying Put: A Retirement Alternative

Schlow Centre Region Library, State College, Pennsylvania

www.schlowlibrary.org

WHAT Schlow Centre Region Library developed this program to support local efforts to help midlife and older adults plan for aging in place. There are numerous national and local aging-in-place projects, reflecting the fact that midlife and older adults no longer assume that they will move to another part of the country or into an adult retirement community for their later years. Staying Put is an excellent example of how a local library can support individual and community planning regarding where and how aging people want to live.

GOAL To be a supportive member of the local aging-in-place movement and to showcase the library's informational services and meeting spaces for the benefit of a growing midlife and older population.

FEATURES Staying Put was launched at a library meeting in 2008 that brought community members together for a panel discussion about alternatives to residential retirement communities. Some one hundred people attended, many midlife adults along with older residents and their family members. Of these individuals, 40 percent had not previously visited the library. The meeting provided an opportunity to showcase library resources, including a new building with meeting space. That initial meeting helped launch a local aging-in-place group. Since then the library has continued to provide a neutral meeting space and information to support individual and group planning.

Staying Put was recognized by the Pennsylvania AARP as a winner of a 2009 Services to Older Adults Award.

PARTNERS AND FUNDING The library partnered with local citizens organizing an aging-in-place initiative. There was no special funding for this pro-

---

Staying Put: A Retirement Alternative

This program gives older adults in our community a focal point for discussing how and where they want to age. Most older adults would like to stay in their own homes. There were many suggestions about what the community could do to make this possible. . . . The children of many older adults attended to find ways to help their aging parents stay safely in their own homes.

—Schlow Centre Region Library website

gram, which is an extension of the library's normal use of facilities and informational resources.

The Living Room Series / A Free Series for Adults 50+
Santa Monica Public Library, Santa Monica, California
http://smpl.org

WHAT This series of educational seminars on key issues relevant to adults 50+ grew out of Santa Monica Public Library's 2009 participation in the California State Library's Transforming Life After 50 initiative. In 2011 the library joined with the community-wide Lifelong Learning Older Adult Task Force and the City of Santa Monica to expand the series.

GOAL To position the library as a center for information and education for midlife adults and to deepen ongoing collaboration with other providers of services to midlife adults.

FEATURES In 2009, Santa Monica Public Library launched the Living Room Project, presenting twenty-eight different educational and cultural programs for midlife adults on topics ranging from yoga to "Armchair African Safari." The library filmed three of the programs as webcasts and presented these on the library's website to extend outreach. In addition, the Older Adult Advisory Board was formed and has helped to continue development of the project. The support base was later expanded to include the City of Santa Monica.

Seminars offered in 2011 reflect the library's ongoing commitment to help midlife adults explore transition issues such as these:

> **The New Retirement: Women in Transition:** led by a national expert on retirement and life planning

> **Managing the Emotional Chaos and Crises of Caregiving:** the variety of emotions and crises faced by caregivers of adults with dementia or physical health challenges, and ways to ensure caregiver wellness

> **Who Will I Be When I Grow Up?** an interactive workshop, led by a faculty member from the College of Santa Monica, that assists participants in exploring purpose, creativity, and joy in later life as a way to express a unique living legacy

PARTNERS AND FUNDING The library's two key program partners are the Older Adults Task Force (www.smgov.net/Portals/Seniors/content.aspx?id=24892), a consortium of more than thirty-five local organizations that are part of Santa Monica's Lifelong Learning Community Project, and the City of Santa Monica's 50+ and Senior Programs (www.smgov.net/portals/seniors).

The City of Santa Monica, the Older Adults Task Force, and the Friends of the Santa Monica Public Library (www.friendsofsmpl.org) are primary program sponsors. Additional support is provided by Emeritus College, Commission for the Senior Community, Sunrise Assisted Living, UCLA Health System, and Brookdale Senior Living.

The Next Chapter: Designing Your Ideal Life
Monterey Public Library, Monterey, California
www.monterey.org/library/Home.aspx

WHAT This lecture series for adults in the second half of life on such topics as health and well-being, "following one's spirit," and planning for transition is an outgrowth of programming started in 2009 through support from the California State Library's Transforming Life After 50 program.

GOAL To inspire and inform midlife adults.

FEATURES The 2011 lecture series included the following presentations and a daylong workshop:

- Wellness and Healing
- Ways to Live a Rich Life Using Imagination and Creativity
- Moving Out of Pain with the Feldenkrais Method
- The Future of Mental Health Care
- An Integrative Approach to Insomnia
- Life Mapping (daylong workshop)

PARTNERS AND FUNDING The Next Chapter: Designing an Ideal Life is presented by the library with support from the Friends of the Monterey Public Library (www.mplfriends.com) and the Monterey Public Library Endowment Committee.

Transition Talks: Prepare for the Next Chapter of Life

Tempe Public Library / Tempe Connections, Tempe, Arizona

www.tempe.gov/index.aspx?page=397, http://tempeconnections.org

WHAT These conversations on life changes are offered through Tempe Public Library by Tempe Connections, a library-based community service program that provides adults with opportunities to discover new purpose through access to learning programs and volunteer participation (see chapter 2).

GOAL To foster awareness and reflection concerning life decisions and life changes that affect baby boomers and other active older adults.

FEATURES Since 2007, Tempe Connections has been offering its Transition Talks for the many 50+ residents of Tempe who are planning or adjusting to life after full-time paid work. These conversations, organized in thematic series, provide a chance for participants to explore approaches to handling change with subject experts and peers. They emphasize talk as a means of gaining self-awareness and exchanging ideas. Sample topics include the following:

> **Retirement Transition Talks:** featured three "successful professionals who have made the leap and are enjoying active lifestyles full of fun and fulfillment." Panelists shared their personal experiences, tips, and techniques for maintaining social connections, engaging in the community, and finding meaning in a postcareer life.

> **Health and Wellness Transition Talks:** featured a physician who specializes in naturopathic medicine, discussing food as medicine and secrets to keeping your brain fit and young.

> **The Search for Meaning:** Connecting to the Spiritual Riches within You: Transition Talks series based on the book *Transforming Fate into Destiny*, which explores thoughts and ideas that stimulate personal spiritual growth.

PARTNERS AND FUNDING Tempe Connections involves partnerships between the City of Tempe and public library and more than two dozen community organizations and educational institutions, some of which are partners in Transition Talks. Tempe Connections programs, including Transition Talks, are supported by the Friends of the Tempe Public Library and by community donations.

Veterans History Project
National Program
www.loc.gov/folklife/vets

WHAT The Veterans History Project is a national initiative of the American Folklife Center at the Library of Congress. The project aims to collect and preserve audio- and videotaped oral histories along with documentary materials such as letters, diaries, maps, and photographs of America's war veterans and those who served in support of them. The project covers veterans of all twentieth-century wars and the wars in Iraq and Afghanistan. Many libraries are partnering with the Library of Congress as official repositories for the Veterans History Project as well as conducting their own local veterans history projects.

The Veterans History Project directly benefits the many midlife adults who are veterans, whether they served in the Korean War, the Vietnam War, or more recent wars. The project honors their service and preserves the story of their participation in these wars for future generations. The project also benefits the many midlife volunteers who are the backbone of the local documentation projects; it gives them meaningful roles as trainers, interviewers, project organizers and, in effect, community archivists. Local veterans history projects would not be implemented without these adults' participation and commitment.

GOAL To recognize and record the contributions of the nation's veterans and to encourage Americans to play personal roles in preserving the nation's history by collecting firsthand accounts of those who defended the United States during wartime.

FEATURES The libraries that are official Library of Congress partners are responsible for identifying and recruiting interviewees, recording their stories, operating the camera equipment, processing the sessions, processing the audio or video recordings, and sending duplicate copies of recordings and documentary materials to the Library of Congress for inclusion in their archives and national database. Some library partners carry out the work with staff; others recruit and train volunteers. Just as many of the individuals who are interviewed are midlife adults, so also are many of the volunteers. In Tempe, Arizona, for instance, the Tempe Connections program for boomers at the Tempe Public Library carries out a veterans history project with its midlife volunteers.

Although the emphasis in the national Veterans History Project is on veterans who served overseas, some of the local library projects include individuals who served on the "home front." The Fairhope (Alabama) Public Library de-

Sample Veterans History Project Sites

Fairhope (Alabama) Public Library:
www.fairhopelibrary.org

Flagler County (Florida) Public Library:
www.flaglercounty.org/
index.aspx?NID=112

Frederick County (Maryland) Libraries:
www.fcpl.org/index.php

Indian Prairie (Illinois) Public Library:
www.indianprairielibrary.org

Lehigh Valley (Pennsylvania) Veterans
History Project Roundtable:
www.lvveteranshistory.org

Melrose Park (Illinois) Public Library:
www.melroseparklibrary.org

Nashville (Tennessee) Public Library:
www.library.nashville.org

Niles (Illinois) Public Library District:
www.nileslibrary.org

Public Library of Cincinnati and Hamilton (Ohio) County:
www.cincinnatilibrary.org

Riverside (California) Public Library:
www.riversideca.gov/library

Roanoke (Virginia) Public Libraries:
www.roanokeva.gov/WebMgmt/
ywbase61b.nsf/DocName/$library

Tempe Connections at Tempe
(Arizona) Public Library:
www.tempeconnections.org

Timberland (Washington)
Regional Library: www.trlib.org

cided to expand the parameters of the project to include those who were on the home front during the major wars, such as war industry workers, USO workers, flight instructors and medical volunteers. Many of those who supported various wars from home and who are now midlife and older adults have wartime memories and stories that complement other veterans' accounts of their military experiences.

In Roanoke, Virginia, and in some other public libraries the Veterans History Project is carried out as an intergenerational activity. In Roanoke, the Gail Borden Public Library partnered with the local Elgin Academy to pair eighth-grade students as interviewers with World War II, Korean, and Vietnam veterans.

Some of the libraries participating in this national program organize local events that feature veterans and showcase stories from the project. On occasion local libraries partner with local museums or historical societies to carry out their veterans history project and to host special events with or for local veterans. The Tempe Connections project, for instance, partnered with the Tempe Historical Museum to offer an open house for veterans, veterans groups, and veterans' family members to learn about the project and view related exhibits.

Most of the official Veterans History Project partners maintain websites with information on the project and a database of locally recorded interviews and documentary materials. Some include videostreamed versions of selected interviews, thus honoring the veterans who are interviewed and reinforcing understanding of midlife adults and older adults as essential sources of community memory.

PARTNERS AND FUNDING All of the local libraries carrying out official Veterans History Projects are affiliates, or partners, with the Library of Congress. Many libraries work with local schools, community colleges, veterans organizations, historical societies, and museums to implement their projects and communicate the results. Some library projects are funded by their library Friends groups or local businesses.

When Did I Get Old? Reflections on Aging Today
Monroe County Public Library, Bloomington, Indiana
www.monroe.lib.in.us

WHAT These screenings of feature films and documentaries showcasing older adults were one component of Monroe County Library's participation in Bloomington's First Annual Creative Aging Festival, held in May 2011.[1]

GOAL The festival's purpose is to promote intergenerational understanding and to highlight the value of creative engagement for adult health and well-being.

FEATURES The Monroe County Library was a key collaborator in the Creative Aging Festival, which brought together multiple organizations and agencies under the leadership of the Center on Aging and Community at Indiana University's Institute on Disability and Community (www.iidc.indiana.edu). The library's Reflections on Aging Today film screenings took place throughout the monthlong festival. The first film, *When Did I Get Old?* was cosponsored by the Center on Aging and Community, whose director appears in the film. Other films in the series were *Young at Heart* and *Sunset Story*. The library prepared a list of additional films about experiences of aging for public distribution.

In addition to the film screenings the library hosted "Seeing between the Lines," a photography exhibit of intergenerational images, a panel discussion titled "Aging in Place: Making Homes and Our Community Elder-Friendly," and another panel discussion featuring older members of local activist and community organizations discussing ways to connect a new generation with civically engaged elders.

PARTNERS AND FUNDING Organization of the film showings and other library events were carried out in partnership with the Center on Aging and Community at Indiana University and numerous local organizations that took part in festival planning and implementation. The festival was cosponsored by the City of Bloomington and the Center on Aging and Community.

Note

1. See the festival brochure at http://bloomington.in.gov/media/media/application/pdf/8685.pdf.

Workshops on Aging / LiveWires
Reading Public Library, Reading, Massachusetts
www.readingpl.org

WHAT Reading Public Library has been a leader in providing enriched programming for active older adults, designed for and with patrons, through its ongoing LiveWires programming (see chapter 2). Two in-depth workshops on aging complemented other activities, offering participants the opportunity to reflect on what is important in their lives and consider what kind of legacy they would like to leave future generations.

GOAL To introduce older adult patrons to theories and activities regarding purpose and legacy in "the Second Half of Life."

> Having been able to offer these two workshops, in addition to our other programming, allowed the Reading Public Library to demonstrate to our constituents the commitment we have to continuing and expanding upon our services to active older adults.
>
> —Reading Public Library, Final Report on the Workshops on Aging, 2009

FEATURES LiveWires, an interdisciplinary series of presentations developed with and for active older adult patrons, is the centerpiece program for older adults at Reading Library. Program topics are recommended by program participants. In 2009, with special funding from the Northern Massachusetts Regional Library System as a Lifelong Access Center of Excellence, Reading was able to offer several in-depth workshops on aging.

Living on Purpose in the Second Half of Life was a three-hour workshop led by a psychotherapist and certified life coach specializing in older adults. The workshop used self-discovery exercises and readings and presented goal-setting tools and practical resources to help participants focus on what is important in their lives.

Living Your Legacy, a two-and-a-half-hour experiential workshop, looked at some of the ways people might share stories and enliven their lives by creating today what they want to be remembered for tomorrow. The program topic was determined based on the interest of participants in the first workshop.

PARTNERS AND FUNDING Reading received special funds for the workshops from the Northern Massachusetts Regional Library System (NMRLS) in recognition of Reading Library's enriched programming for active older adults. NMRLS, which has since been discontinued, received its funding through an award from Libraries for the Future as a Lifelong Access Libraries Center of Excellence. The Workshops on Aging were held under the aegis of LiveWires, which is supported by the Friends of the Reading Public Library.

Writing for the Future
Santa Monica Public Library, Santa Monica, California
www.smpl.org

WHAT Many libraries offer memoir writing workshops, memoir clubs, or other programs to encourage reflection through writing. Writing for the Future, a writing workshop series for 50+ adults at the Santa Monica Library, was similar to other programs, with a teacher, assignments, and a focus on leaving a legacy for future generations. At the same time, a complementary program, Listening to Your Voice with Poetry of Memoirs, offered an opportunity for older adults and others to consider memoir writing from a theoretical point of view and to reflect on the process as well as engage in it.

GOAL To help those who want to write about their lives for future generations.

FEATURES Writing for the Future was a three-session workshop led by a retired English professor. Simple writing assignments were intended to help participants "give family and friends a glimpse into their experiences and personalities."

In a separate program, Listening to Your Voice with a Poetry of Memoirs, the library collaborated with the Senior Arts Foundation (www.seniorartsfoundation .org) and the City of Santa Monica to host a forum to "help you to find your inner voice through words." Members of several local older adult poetry workshops recited poetry, followed by a panel discussion on poetry, writing, and aging. The panel was moderated by a professor of psychiatry at UCLA and included an educator, a marriage and family therapist, and a Manhattan Beach poet, who explored ways poetry can provide a creative outlet for personal history.

PARTNERS AND FUNDING

Writing for the Future was a program of the Santa Monica Library; no special funding was involved. The forum was organized in collaboration with the Senior Arts Foundation and the City of Santa Monica.

IN BRIEF: REFLECTIONS AND TRANSITIONS

Adults in Transition

Sturgis (Massachusetts) Library In 2008 the Sturgis Library's annual literature discussion program was dedicated to the theme "Adults in Transition." Staff expanded the circulating collection of books and audiobooks to include the transition theme and other issues of interest to midlife adults. The program was supported with grants from the Friends of the Sturgis Library and the Massachusetts Humanities Foundation. (www.sturgislibrary.org)

Aging and Spirituality: My Neighbor's Faith

Alameda County Library, Fremont, California Aging and Spirituality was a discussion series cosponsored by the Alameda County Library and the Stanford Geriatric Education Center, with funding from the U.S. Department of Health and Human Services and the Tri-City Elder Coalition. (www.aclibrary.org)

Boomers and Beyond: Creating the Life You Love

Case Memorial Library, Orange, Connecticut Case Memorial Library partnered with Orange Community Services to offer an interactive workshop, led by a life coach, that explored choices and opportunities for individuals and couples already retired or approaching retirement. (www.orange.lioninc.org)

Connecting with Your Inner Self

Lyndhurst (New Jersey) Public Library This continuous monthly program at Lyndhurst Public Library is geared for those 50+ years old. The purpose is "to stimulate discussion about topics such as fears, aging, changing obstacles into opportunities, dealing with problems optimistically and appreciating where you are in life." (www.lyndhurstlibrary.org)

Conversations about Aging: A Book Discussion

Converse Free Library, Lyme, New Hampshire Converse Free Library organized a five-week book discussion series advertised as follows: "The senior years, like each of life's chapters, present their own issues. Whether you are approaching these years or are 'there,' conversations with others can be helpful, offering new perspectives and a common experience." The first book discussed was *The Art of Aging,* by Sherman Nuland. (www.lymenhlibrary.org)

Encore Reading Club

Grand Rapids (Michigan) Public Library Through a partnership with Grand Rapids Community College's Older Learner Center, Grand Rapids Public Library is offering an opportunity to explore topics affecting today's aging society. The 90-minute discussions are led by topical specialists. The primary text is *Longevity Rules: How to Age Well into the Future.* (www.grpl.org)

Memoir Writing for Older Adults

Oakmont (Pennsylvania) Carnegie Library The six-week creative writing class offered by Oakmont Carnegie Library is geared toward people who want to write about their lives. A local resident and former journalist leads the class. The program announcement states: "Whether it is stories of your life you'd like to save in writing or tales for your grandchildren, this class is for you." (www.oakmontlibrary.org)

Quality of Life: Life Review

Crowell Public Library, San Marino, California Crowell Public Library offered this interactive class on approaches to improving the quality of life fall 2011. The class covered such issues as the importance of social connections, having a positive attitude, personal independence, and being realistic and resilient. (http://sanmarinopl.org)

The Human Condition and the Realities of Aging

Fairfield (Connecticut) Public Library In June and July 2010, Fairfield Public Library presented an exhibition of woodcuts by artist Donald Axelrod on the theme of aging. Stephen Jones, director of the Center for Healthy Aging at Greenwich Hospital, presented a special lecture in conjunction with the exhibition on Alzheimer's disease and research. (www.fairfieldpublic library.org)

Widowhood: The Journey Continues

Middle Country (New York) Public Library Middle Country offers monthly meetings that provide emotional and informational support for those adjusting to life after the death of a spouse/partner. The majority of participants are midlife or older adults who are moving from a couple's identity to rediscover themselves and learn the roles of a new life. (www.mcpl.lib.ny.us)

Write Your Life

Jericho (New York) Public Library Jericho Library offered an eight-session workshop during fall 2011 designed to encourage 50+ amateur writers to write their memoirs. The workshop was presented with Taprock Workshops and Journal, an organization that promotes writing by 50+ adults. (www.jericholibrary.org)

Write Your Own Memoirs Workshop

Ocean City (New Jersey) Library According to the Ocean City Library, Write Your Own Memoirs "will teach you how to turn your seemingly ordinary life into a creative work. Participants decide on the scope of their memoir and organize memories of relationships and events. When completed, a lovingly written memoir is a special gift to pass on to loved ones. It is also a tribute to oneself, an acknowledgment that our experiences and opinions are unique and important." (http://home.oceancitylibrary.org)

CHAPTER 5

HEALTH AND WELLNESS

The library can become the place people think about immediately when they wake up and wish to get a good brain health workout. In short, the library becomes a health center geared towards brain health with opportunities and stimuli for all age groups, particularly for boomers.

—Paul Nussbaum, clinical neuropsychologist

ealth information is said to be the highest-ranking subject area request in public libraries across the United States. Some health information specialists interpret this trend as a result of the number of older adults who are suddenly facing health issues as they hit their fifties and sixties. Others believe it is because of the expanding number of people in their eighties, nineties, or older and an indication of caregivers' needs for information. Yet others see the demand as a result of limitations on the time that physicians can spend with patients, or limited access to health professionals for many people. Librarians see the rise in requests for health information as a result of the massive amount of health information online, much of it hard to verify, hard to interpret by a layperson, or hard to access for those not computer literate. Whatever the reason, it is clear that libraries are key sources of information on health and wellness in every size and type of community, especially those with high concentrations of 50+ adults. Increasingly, through programming, libraries are also becoming centers for health education.

TRENDS

Depending on the health profiles of their communities, librarians are encountering requests from 50+ adults that cover a wide range of health and wellness content areas, from disease management, disease prevention, and caregiving to public health issues, insurance coverage, and nutrition. There is interest in obesity and weight reduction, environmental pollutants affecting health, lifestyle changes to improve individual or family health, and alternative medicine. These issues are important for all adults, but they are especially relevant to those undergoing midlife transitions or caring for older family members. In general, the concerns associated with aging that prompt library inquiries fall into the following broad categories:

Disease and infirmity prevention. With the larger number of people who are 50+, it is not surprising that there is expanding demand for information on the diseases and other problems especially associated with aging. For all too many individuals, the library is the primary source of information on particular illnesses. They may be seeking information about the illness itself, trying to understand a diagnosis or gauge the severity of their condition, or looking for advice on how to manage their disease and what to expect from their medical providers. Heart health, memory problems, and Alzheimer's disease, as well as cancer and bone health, are high on the list of concerns. People want facts to help them assess the risk factors. They may also be seeking the latest studies of new medicines and therapies, new treatments in trial, recommendations for ways to avoid risks or prevent recurrence, or access to databases such as those of the National Institutes of Health and local social service agencies. In addition, they may need to share their questions and concerns with peers.

Medical services and benefits. With ever more attention to the structure and solvency of the nation's Medicare services, librarians across the country are striving to keep up with requests for information on federal and state policies and issues of coverage. They are also striving to help people identify or interpret other kinds of coverage for which they may be eligible or find online or in-person sources of assistance in applying for coverage.

Brain health. Recent research on cognitive changes that occur during aging is a high-interest content area that has emerged over the past decade. With the increase in scholarship on older adult capacities with respect to memory, decision making, creative expression, and analytical thinking, libraries have become key points of access to information on brain health. This topic is especially relevant to the question of libraries' roles in advancing positive aging. Some experts see an opportunity for libraries to provide significant support in ongoing intellectual acuity and activity through varied opportunities for learning, creativity, and social exchange.

Personal health management. For all too many individuals, the library is the only access point for online information on particular illnesses. They may be seeking information about the illness itself, trying to understand a diagnosis, or attempting to gauge the severity of their condition. They may also be seeking the latest studies of new medicines and therapies, new treatments in trial, or access to databases such as those of the National Institutes of Health and local social service agencies. Or they may be looking for advice on how to manage their disease and what to expect from their medical providers.

Public health issues. Health is not just a personal matter. It is also a major social and economic issue, affecting the overall health of the society and each local community. Whether it is food safety, flu shots, or the availability of public transportation, midlifers recognize that public health issues have both individual and community implications.

Caregiving. Caregiver services are aspects of health services that are especially relevant to 50+ adults. The number of family caregivers in this country is rising, and the majority of them are midlife adults. (Some studies indicate that a high proportion of family caregivers are women baby boomers.) Many caregivers are responsible for elderly parents or infirm spouses, but other generations often require care as well. The Pew Research Center reports that the number of grandparents serving as primary caregivers for their grandchildren increased 8 percent between 2000 and 2008, to 2.6 million.[1] The challenges to this "Sandwich Generation" are real. Midlife adults caring for younger or older relatives find that caregiving can be physically, emotionally, and economically draining. They require information, assistance, and moral support.

These content categories are by no means comprehensive. Mental health and spirituality and health are just two additional topics that could be listed. However, these six categories mentioned above suggest the range of health content areas to consider in terms of collection development, reference assistance, and programming for midlife adults.

In addition to the content areas of interest to midlife adults, there are other issues that may be equally important in considering how to strengthen libraries' as centers of 50+ health information and health education. In what formats should health information be conveyed? Is health literacy an issue for the target population? What are the technology competencies of those seeking health information? Do some 50+ adults learn best from one another?

Raw data and scholarly references may be eagerly sought by some midlife adults but highly inappropriate for others. Many may have difficulty accessing online health information because of basic e-literacy issues. Some may have difficulty with reference assistance or programming because of language barriers. Others may benefit more from health education in the form of expert presentations than from raw data, and still others may be seeking information from peers in support groups or social networks online. It is not surprising that librarians who work with 50+ adults are experimenting with varied approaches to convey information and provide health education.

IMPLICATIONS FOR LIBRARIES

Aside from issues of content and format, the growth in demand for health information from 50+ adults presents numerous challenges to the library community. Until relatively recently, most librarians, other than certified medical librarians, were hesitant to provide health information or to even guide patrons to different sources. The received wisdom was that librarians needed to be careful about influencing an individual's choices with respect to disease management, selection of a health professional, or health and wellness in general. However, with the recent explosion of health sources on the Internet, and the general increase in demand for assistance, librarians are starting to recognize that health literacy is an important service goal and that local librarians should be able to help patrons. The National Network of Libraries of Medicine (www.nnlm.gov), the National Institute for Aging (www.nia.nih.gov), and some state libraries are developing workshops and tools to help improve librarians' capacities to respond to the new demands, efforts that can benefit 50+ patrons.[2]

Health literacy:
The degree to which individuals have the capacity to obtain, process, and understand basic health information and services needed to make appropriate health decisions.
—National Network of Libraries of Medicine, Healthy People 2010

With more and more health information online, the problem of e-literacy is a baseline hurdle in the provision of health information services. The capacity to access and identify credible information is key to becoming health literate today. Some libraries are offering special classes to help older adults learn to access health information online. At the same time, librarians are teaching patrons to recognize and interpret authentic scientific and medical sources.

Another challenge is the need to ensure that relevant health information is available in languages and formats appropriate to the individuals in a particular community. This implies the necessity of carrying out needs assessments, surveying potential patron groups, and building relationships with others in the community who can help overcome barriers of language or cultural tradition. Libraries serving multiple language groups, such as New York's Queens Library, provide exceptional examples of partnerships and programs to ensure that health information and health programming are accessible to all residents.

In addition to the baseline challenge of ensuring that older adults have access to relevant, understandable information, librarians face the challenge that information, in and of itself, may not be enough. For librarians and others who work with 50+ adults, participatory programming and health education may be equally important. If, for instance, obesity is a public health issue in a given community, the library can provide leadership by organizing walking groups or cooking classes. If there are many caregivers in the library's service area, it may be far more important to provide a neutral, accessible setting for group exchange than to offer online manuals or printed resources. If heart health is a prevalent concern, the library can provide access to experts through face-to-face presentations or question-and-answer sessions. Certainly, libraries cannot attempt to carry out multiple programs alone. However, they can work with other organizations in their communities, from hospitals to recreation specialists, to carry out joint programming that leverages library-based information for the benefit of baby boomers and other older adults.

Caregiving is one facet of health information that public libraries are especially well positioned to provide. They can marshal the kinds of information required by caregivers and make it accessible in multiple formats; organize fairs and networking programs to connect caregivers with peers and community services; and offer programs for caregivers that enrich their lives, reduce isolation, and help ensure their own health and quality of life. The following examples suggest the range of ways that libraries are supporting caregivers, many of them 50+ adults who find themselves taking on the role of caregiver.

As the following examples reveal, there is no one formula for addressing the challenges of health services for the diverse needs of our aging population. Building librarians' capacities to help older adults access health information; providing information in diverse media, formats, and languages; and, above all, helping patrons interpret and use that information through varied programs—all of these approaches must be part of the portfolio for a 50+ library.

Notes

1. Gretchen Livingston and Kim Parker, "Since the Start of the Great Recession, More Children Raised by Grandparents," Pew Research Center, September 9, 2010, www.pew socialtrends.org/2010/09/09/since-the-start-of-the-great-recession-more-children -raised-by-grandparents.

2. See National Network of Libraries of Medicine, "Health Literacy," http://nnlm.gov/outreach/consumer/hlthlit.html; and Centers for Disease Control and Prevention, *Improving Health Literacy for Older Adults: Expert Panel Report 2009*, U.S. Department of Health and Human Services, 2009, www.cdc.gov/healthliteracy/pdf/olderadults.pdf.

> Just as you make plans to secure your financial future, building a plan for your wellness can help ensure that you maintain your most important asset of all: your health and vitality. . . . folks at midlife (50–75) can make investments in health and wellness that provide significant improvements to their longevity and vitality.
>
> —Age Well, Be Well program announcement, Newton Free Library website

Age Well, Be Well
Newton Free Library, Newton, Massachusetts
www.newtonfreelibrary.net

WHAT Newton offered this three-part series on the aging process for those ages 50–75 in winter 2010/11. The program combined information on an array of issues, including findings from recent research on aging, with practical suggestions for incorporating changes in behavior and lifestyle that can improve well-being during aging.

GOAL To dispel myths about aging, present the latest research on key aspects of the aging process, and offer concrete steps that can contribute to longevity, vitality, and an improved quality of life.

FEATURES This three-part series was led by a longtime geriatric nurse practitioner known for her innovative approaches to health support for midlife and older adults. Topics included the following:

Understanding the Aging Process and Why Some People Live Longer: reviews of the latest research on longevity enhancement

Add Years to Your Life and Life to Your Years: ways to identify risks and modify risks and challenges to our health and well-being

Myths and Misconceptions about Aging, or Why You Just Might Want to Live to Be 100: various myths and truths about aging and practical suggestions for improving health and well-being during midlife and beyond

PARTNERS AND FUNDING The program was cosponsored by the library, City of Newton Department of Senior Services, and Newton at Home (www.newtonathome.org).

The Brain Fitness Project

Metropolitan Library Association, Minneapolis, Minnesota

www.melsa.org

WHAT This multifaceted project on brain health, offered at twenty-three MELSA member libraries in the Twin Cities metropolitan area (see chapter 2), provides special programs, services, and information to help individuals maintain brain-healthy lifestyles. The project combines workshops, Brain Fitness Stations, and resource materials. With twenty-three Brain Fitness sites across the metropolitan area, the project is reaching a large and varied audience, especially midlife adults, with an important message about the value of physical and intellection stimulation throughout the life span.

GOAL To inform residents of the Minneapolis/St. Paul area about activities that promote healthier brains and may help lower the risk of developing Alzheimer's disease.

FEATURES Recognizing the importance of brain health for an aging population, MELSA teamed up with the local Alzheimer's Association to provide programs

Selected MELSA Brain Fitness Sites

Brain Fitness Stations, Ramsay County Libraries

Brain Fitness Stations are located in two Ramsay County libraries. According to the library's website, when people think about staying fit, they generally think from the neck down. But the health of your brain plays a critical role in almost everything you do: thinking, feeling, remembering, working, playing—even sleeping. (www.rclreads.org)

Maintain Your Brain: How to Live a Brain-Healthy Lifestyle, Hennepin County Library

Seven Hennepin County libraries, including the main library, are offering the Brain Fitness work-shops. They are marketed as part of the library's overall Age Well, Live Smart initiative, which includes other programs for older adults such as Laughter Yoga and First Pages: Start Your Memoir—For Writers 55 and Older. (www.hclib.org)

Maintain Your Brain Workshop, Anoka County Library

The Anoka County Library is offering Maintain Your Brain Workshops in two libraries, using the following announcement: "Learn about the four pillars of health: mental stimulation, physical activity, nutrition, and stress reduction. Also, learn how the brain works and changes with age, how the heart and brain are connected, and how social connections and emotional health affect the brain." (www.anoka.lib.mn.us)

Maintain Your Brain Workshop, Dakota County Library

Three Dakota County libraries are offering Brain Workshops as part of Know the Secrets to a Long Life, the county library's overall Healthy Living in Minnesota, Minnesota Mosaic Winter 2011. Other comple-mentary programs include Wellness for Everyone and sessions on yoga, pilates, and karate; creativity and aging; and computer heath resources. (www.dakotacounty.us/library)

and information that focus on what people can do to keep their brains stimulated and active as they age while reducing the factors that contribute to Alzheimer's disease. All participating libraries offer three primary program components:

Maintain Your Brain Workshops that provide firsthand information from experts and practice activities to stimulate ongoing brain development.

- The Brain: how the brain works and changes with age
- The Body: how the heart and brain are connected
- The Person: how social connections and emotional health affect your health

Brain Fitness Stations, where individuals find educational books and activities and games designed to stimulate the brain and keep it healthy. The focus is on the four "pillars of brain health": mental stimulation, physical activity, nutrition, and stress reduction.

An extensive list of recommended resources on brain health, both national and local, that pertain to brain health and Alzheimer's disease.

In addition to these components, some MELSA libraries are offering additional activities to reinforce the concepts and recommendations regarding brain health. Member libraries have found strong public interest in all facets of the Brain Fitness project.

PARTNERS AND FUNDING The Brain Fitness Project is a partnership of MELSA, the Minnesota–North Dakota chapter of the Alzheimer's Association, and the host libraries. The project is supported by an LSTA grant administered in Minnesota by the Minnesota Department of Education.

Brain Health and Fitness Fairs
New York Public Library, New York, New York
www.nypl.org

WHAT Special presentations, films, and resource fairs that help promote understanding of cognitive and physical fitness were offered under the umbrella of Next Chapter, New York Public Library's initiative to provide midlife New

Yorkers with opportunities for learning, civic engagement, and creative expression (see chapter 2).

GOAL To focus attention on recent research about brain health and to promote fitness through health-oriented recreational activities.

FEATURES The library offered two programs on brain health in 2009:

- Practical Advice to Keep Your Brain Sharp, led by Alvaro Fernandez of SharpBrains, featured recent scientific studies on older adult brain development and offered recommendations for making informed decisions about cognitive fitness.
- Film screenings and discussions focused on Alzheimer's disease presented evidence that engaging in mentally stimulating activities through education, jobs, and leisure lowers the probability of developing Alzheimer's symptoms.

In 2009/10 the library presented four Fitness Fairs at key branch libraries in Staten Island, the Bronx, and Manhattan. The fairs introduced 50+ New Yorkers to free and low-cost fitness opportunities to become more active and physically fit while having fun. More than a dozen organizations sent representatives to the fairs to distribute literature, give presentations on activities in the metropolitan area, and invite participation, including the Outdoors Club, Shorewalkers, Appalachian Mountain Club, Urban Park Rangers, Bike New York, and Transportation Alternatives.

PARTNERS AND FUNDING The presentation on brain fitness was cosponsored with SharpBrains (www.sharpbrains.com); the Alzheimer's screenings and discussions were cosponsored with the New York Chapter of the Alzheimer's Association. The Fitness Fairs included participants from more than a dozen local organizations. No direct grant support was involved.

CLIC-on-Health
Rochester Regional Library Council, Rochester, New York
http://cliconhealth.org

WHAT CLIC-on-Health is a collaboration of hospitals and public and school libraries in the Rochester, New York, region that provides public access to high-quality health care information and resources, including a special component designed to benefit older adults. The program is unusual in the number and type of library organizations that make up the collaborative, cutting across public, academic, and medical library boundaries. It is also unusual in its combination of public access components and professional development targeted to both librarians and community groups seeking to help older adults.

GOAL To ensure that residents of the Rochester area have access to the latest unbiased information they need to make wise lifestyle and health care choices, and to build the capacity of local librarians to help older adults search for reliable information.

FEATURES CLIC-on-Health operates under the leadership of the Rochester Regional Library Council, with an advisory committee of fifteen area librarians. The collaboration includes the following elements:

- A "one-stop shopping" portal providing up-to-date, reliable information on health issues and medical treatments, with links to sources that comply with the HON (Health on the Net Foundation, www.hon.ch) guidelines for authoritative content, authoritative websites and RSS feeds that range from NIHSeniorHealth (http://nihseniorhealth.gov) to NOAH (New York Online Access to Health, www.noah-health.org), which features easy-to-search health information and support groups in English and Spanish and maintains a special section on aging.
- The Senior Health Project, which trains local librarians and community groups in the use of health information on the Internet. This training builds the capacity of local information providers to help seniors use the computer and Internet to find trustworthy online sources of medical information.
- Information on medical and health care providers in the Rochester region, through links to cooperating websites.

PARTNERS AND FUNDING Eight different libraries and library systems make up the collaboration, ranging from the E. G. Miner Library of the University of Rochester Medical Center (www.urmc.rochester.edu/hslt/miner) to the Henrietta Public Library (www.hpl.org). In addition, the staff of the community groups that receive training tend to collaborate with participating library staff, creating a stronger overall regional information and support network. The collaborating institutions contribute staff time to make the project possible.

Cooking It Up! Hartford Health and History

Hartford Public Library / History Center, Hartford, CT

http://www.hhc.hplct.org

WHAT Workshops at Hartford Public Library on culinary traditions, nutrition, and neighborhood history combine "good food, good health and fond memories and feature Hartford restaurants." Cooking It Up! is a novel approach to promoting greater awareness of nutrition as a key factor in good health. By exploring nutrition through the lens of social history, the program involves and educates midlife adults while drawing on their memories and traditions to provide documentation that will become part of the library's History Center collection. The program is an instructive example of promoting wellness while drawing on community traditions.

GOAL To promote awareness of healthy nutritional practices while documenting Hartford's varied food cultures and specialty restaurants, and to expand the library's historical collections through the focus on Hartford food.

FEATURES Cooking It Up! offers midlife adults the opportunity to participate in a series of twelve cooking workshops with chefs from local restaurants representing diverse cultural traditions. The chefs prepare well-known recipes from the restaurant kitchens while a nutritionist provides commentary, making suggestions on how to modify recipes for better health. Attendees are encouraged to bring in their family recipes for the nutritionist to recommend ingredient substitutions to make them healthier while keeping their traditional flavors. A moderator hosts the workshops, working with the chef, nutritionist, and audience to facilitate discussion about variations on the recipes and preparation of healthy dishes.

When the dishes are ready, they are shared by all. Copies of the recipes, before and after, are on the library's website and will be cumulated in book form. The workshops are being taped and made available as videos and podcasts. The audiotapes and corresponding materials are being entered into the Hartford History Center's special collection as a unique collection of Hartford restaurant and neighborhood history.

The Cooking It Up! workshops, taking place during fall of 2011 and spring 2012, are moderated by a former host of Connecticut Public Television who engages participants in discussion of the Hartford food and dining landscape, both historically and today. The workshops are being filmed before a live audience by Hartford Access Television in the library's cooking demonstration kitchen.

PARTNERS AND FUNDING Partners in Cooking It Up! include Healthy Hartford (Health and Human Services), Health and Human Services Senior Services Division, Hartford Food System, Lincoln Culinary Institute, Hartford Access Television, and the local restaurants whose chefs and recipes are featured. Funding is through an LSTA grant administered by the Connecticut State Library.

---

eHILL (Electronic Health Information for Lifelong Learners)
Prince George's County Memorial Library System, Hyattsville, / College of Information Studies, University of Maryland, College Park, Maryland
www.pgcmls.info, http://ischool.umd.edu

WHAT This series of research and implementation projects, carried out under the leadership of Dr. Bo Xie of the University of Maryland College of Information Studies in collaboration with the Prince George's County Memorial Library System, focused on methods for meeting older adults' needs for accessible, authoritative, and relevant health information. With a content focus on health, the projects also were geared to build understanding of older adult learning through technology.

Individually and as a group, the eHILL projects make strong contributions to the literature on libraries, technology training, and health informatics. They also have practical implications for public libraries trying to build older adults' capacities to access specific types of electronic information, particularly health information.

GOAL To test and measure different approaches for enabling older adults to access and understand web-based health information.

FEATURES The genesis of these projects was academic research, but their implementation has had beneficial impacts on participants and on the local library. Prince George's County Library has been a close partner in these projects, facilitating recruitment of participants and logistics for the computer training and programming. Under the umbrella title eHILL, the projects included the following:

Public library computer training. This innovative project developed and evaluated a public library computer training program to teach older adults (131 adults, age 54–89) to access and use high-quality Internet health information. Key findings related to participants' perceptions of the computer training and the information available from two NIH websites (NIHSeniorHealth.gov and Medlineplus.gov). As a result of the project, many participants started using these online resources to find high-quality health and medical information and, further, to guide their decision making on health or medicine. Participants' computer interest and efficacy also increased and computer anxiety decreased over the course of the training.[1]

Peer computer training. The project involved design of a high-quality Internet-based health information program for older adults of diverse backgrounds. Core components were the incorporation of a cadre of committed, older adult volunteers who helped design the curriculum and then served as peer trainers, teaching other senior volunteers how to access, assess, and use a broad range of online resources. The project developed curricula, procedures, and other guides for use by libraries nationwide.

Collaborative learning. This 2009/10 project developed and tested collaborative learning as a method for promoting older adults' (172 adults) e-health literacy, or the ability to access and use high-quality health information through electronic sources. Assessment of their experiences and gains in knowledge and skills provided evidence that collaborative learning can be an effective method for improving older adults' e-literacy in informal learning settings such as the public library.[2]

Over the course of the eHILL projects, researchers and support personnel trained more than 550 older adults, and results from earlier stages of the project have been published in top LIS journals.[3]

PARTNERS AND FUNDING Over a period of five years the work led by professor Xie has involved multiple institutional collaborators including the Prince George's County Memorial Library System, the National Institute on Aging and the National Library of Medicine of the National Institutes of Health, and the Library and Information Science academic program at the University of Maryland.

The eHILL projects have been funded by a variety of sources including the University of Maryland College Park and federal funds from the National Library of Medicine, National Institutes of Health, Department of Health and Human Services, under contract with the University of Maryland Baltimore, and through IMLS.

Notes

1. Bo Xie and Julie M. Bugg, "Public Library Computer Training for Older Adults to Access High-Quality Internet Health Information," www.ncbi.nlm.nih.gov/pmc/articles/PMC2818317/?tool=pubmed.

2. Bo Xie, "Older Adults, e-Health Literacy, and Collaborative Learning: An Experimental Study," *Journal of the American Society for Information Science and Technology* 62, no. 5 (2011): 933–46.

3. Summaries of these publications can be accessed through Xie's website: http://terpconnect.umd.edu/~boxie.

Go4Life / American Library Association
National Program
www.ala.org, www.nia.nih.gov/Go4Life

WHAT This national public-private campaign encourages physical activity for older adults. For librarians who are trying to improve the quality of life for 50+ adults, the Go4Life website, with its rich array of informational and motivational resources, can complement other health information services and programs.

GOAL To provide older adults with resources they can use to incorporate exercise and physical activity into their lives.

FEATURES In October 2011, ALA announced that it would join a national coalition of public agencies and private sponsors to help inform and motivate older adults regarding the importance of regular, sustained exercise. ALA's participation in the federal campaign involves offering Go4Life resources such as free guides and DVDs to attendees at its two primary professional conferences in 2012. By providing these resources to librarians and encouraging them to make them available in local libraries, ALA is assisting efforts to motivate the growing number of older people to start exercising—and keep exercising—to improve their health and achieve a better quality of life.

The Go4Life campaign is based on research showing that physical activity and regular, sustained exercise can help people stay healthy and independent and prevent some of the chronic conditions associated with aging. According to Richard J. Hodes, director of the National Institute on Aging, "You're never too old to exercise. . . . This new campaign reaches out to older people who traditionally have not embraced exercise and shows them how to start exercising safely and keep going."

The primary feature of Go4Life is an interactive website that provides information on the benefits of physical activities for individuals and families, health care professionals, and organizations. Contents include success stories, exercises, and free materials to encourage regular, sustained exercise.

Many organizations are participating in the campaign, incorporating Go4Life into their health and wellness activities; disseminating campaign web links and materials to their members, employees, or customers; and sponsoring exercise events for older adults.

PARTNERS AND FUNDING Go4Life is spearheaded by the National Institute on Aging and the National Institutes of Health. A wide array of public and private organizations are partners in the campaign. The informational resources distributed by ALA to libraries are provided by the Go4Life campaign sponsors.

GrandFamily Resource Centers
South Carolina State Library

www.statelibrary.sc.gov/grandfamily-resource-centers

WHAT The GrandFamily Resource Centers are community locations—local libraries—that house resources for grandparents who are raising their grandchildren. The local centers are partnered with the State Library of South Carolina, which offers a model that is "more than simply a collection of books or other items" and includes "a kind of personal support and programs that a library can offer as well as information." The South Carolina model offers an instructive example of how a library or library system can create a place that informs and supports midlife adults caring for their grandchildren.

GOAL As noted on the South Carolina State Library website, "It is not just a collection, it is a center. It provides assistance to guide grandparents toward resources and also hosts support groups. The goal is to provide one place that can provide information to assist the grandparent who is "parenting again."

FEATURES The State Library of South Carolina has taken a leadership role in helping to address a growing problem in the state and across the nation: the rising number of children living in grandparent-headed households. This problem affects all races, ages, and income levels. To assist grandparents raising grand-children, the state library has created a model for GrandFamily Resource Centers adopted by many libraries in the state. Features include a resource collection, "Grandparents Chair" (a chair and quiet place for a grandparent to sit with a child), signage and marketing materials, volunteer training, support groups, and library support. The state library assists with setting up the collections and training for libraries that want to open a Resource Center.

PARTNERS AND FUNDING The local GrandFamily Resource Centers are partnerships between the State Library of South Carolina (the funding agency) and local libraries. Participating community libraries include Edgefield Public Library, Greenwood Public Library, Florence Public Library, and Cherokee Public Library. In many communities with Resource Centers, the library works with other community agencies that serve grandparents and other caregivers.

Head to Toe: A Health Care Series for Older Adults
New Haven Free Public Library, New Haven, Connecticut
www.cityofnewhaven.com/library

WHAT This series of health care presentations for older adults was offered under the aegis of the New Haven Free Public Library's 50+ Transition Center (see chapter 2). The Head to Toe program was unusual for its comprehensiveness. Instead of one or two topical programs, the series offered a complete tour of the main parts of the body and related health issues.

GOAL To inform older adults about a variety of health concerns they will face as they age.

FEATURES The series consisted of presentations by local experts on health issues and aging. The six programs were held at the same time each week. Presentation titles included "Head: Use It or Lose It!," "Stomach: How We Feed It; How We Abuse It," and "Managing Your Own Care."

PARTNERS AND FUNDING Head to Toe was presented in partnership with East Rock Village (www.eastrockvillage.org). There was no dedicated funding for this collaboration; each partner helped with logistics and marketing, and the experts did not charge for their presentations—an excellent approach to collaboration for public benefit.

Healthy Aging / National Network of Libraries of Medicine

National Program

http://nnlm.gov/training/healthyaging

WHAT Healthy Aging is a training program of the National Network of Libraries of Medicine (NN/LM), which is a network of primary access libraries, resource libraries, and regional libraries that are part of the U.S. National Library of Medicine (www.nlm.nih.gov), which serves all health professionals and the public. Established as the Regional Medical Library Program over forty years ago, that network has grown, with participating libraries now providing links to vital information for hospital managers, dentists, nurses, pharmacists, social workers, medical librarians, and physicians in all specialties. The network office is located at the National Library of Medicine.

NN/LM provides an essential, important national infrastructure to ensure that health professionals and members of the general public have access to reliable, up-to-date, unbiased health information. For 50+ adults, for whom health information can become important on a daily basis, this infrastructure is especially important. Through its Healthy Aging training program, and

Selected NN/LM Grant-Funded Projects

Holyoke (Massachusetts) Consumer Health Library
Holyoke Public Library is one of six partners in this initiative to support and enhance access to reliable health information. The project aims to reach older adults along with low-income Spanish-speaking consumers, teens, women seeking health care, and the general public. Project partners created a network of consumer health stations in Holyoke, with staff trained in the use of National Library of Medicine health databases and approaches for conducting outreach.

James Herbert White Library, Mississippi Valley State University
In partnership with Golden Age and the Boys and Girls Club of the Mississippi Delta, the MVSU library established a program to train youth and senior adults in locating and using electronic health information, including National Library of Medicine databases and resources. The goal was to promote and give access to reliable electronic health resources to seniors and youth in the underserved rural communities of Leflore County. (www.mvsu.edu)

Missoula (Montana) Public Library and Maureen and Mike Mansfield Library, University of Montana
The Health Info to Go! project involved a mobile reference system promoting access to health information resources for the baby boomer generation. Missoula Public Library's refurbished bookmobile is its transportation unit. Visitors are also informed of resources available in the state of Montana through the MedlinePlusGo Local Montana website. (www.missoula publiclibrary.org, www.lib.umt.edu)

Wicomico (Maryland) Public Library
Wicomico Library partnered with the Peninsula Regional Medical Center and the Wicomico County Health Department to enhance older adults' access to electronic health information by developing the Life Options Community. The library created an area especially for seniors where they attend instructional classes on electronic health information, use the resources on their own, and have continuing access to the technology, staff assistance, and peer support in a familiar and comfortable environment. (www.wicomicolibrary.org)

through grant programs, NN/LM enables professionals in many local institutions, including libraries, to help 50+ adults find relevant information through high-quality sources in a timely way. Through its grants, member libraries' outreach, training, and health information promotions, NN/LM provides unique and comprehensive services that benefit older adults.

GOAL The goal of Health Aging training is to assist librarians to help their older adult patrons find heath information. The overall NN/LM goal is to provide health sciences information to medical professionals and other members of the health professions.

FEATURES NN/LM is organized around Regional Medical Libraries (RMLs) that coordinate health sciences information services regionally. Each region has a consumer health librarian on staff. The RMLs collaborate with state libraries, regional and county library systems, and individual libraries to carry out their mission. NN/LM activities and services relevant to public libraries include professional development, administration of federal grants for projects that increase public access to health information, and promotion of libraries' health information resources. Within each of these service areas NN/LM and its regional RML have been instrumental in advancing older adult access to health information.

Professional development. NN/LM develops curriculums for the use of RMLs in training librarians at collaborating libraries and other health agencies. One workshop curriculum created recently, Healthy Aging at Your Library: Connecting Older Adults to Health Information, is available to RMLs training public librarians throughout the country via http://nnlm.gov/training/healthy aging.

As one example of regionalized training to increase the capacities of local libraries to work with older adults, in 2008 the Montana RML worked closely with the Montana State Library to offer Healthy Aging at Your Library, which reached more than seventy librarians in the state. The training was part of a larger initiative, Montana Baby Boomers Get Fit at the Library (see below) to market libraries' health information services for older adults. In addition to the basic curriculum covering health reference issues, topical subject area sources, and special health concerns of older adults, the workshop includes suggestions for health education programs on topics such as Wii Fit tournaments, avoiding health fraud, complementary and alternative medicine, and legal issues regarding health.

Grants. The National Library of Medicine provides grants to libraries, health services organizations, and other health-related institutions for collaborative projects that increase public access to and use of libraries' health information. These grants, some of which aim to improve older adult access to online health and wellness information, are administered by NN/LM.

Promotion of RML visibility. Through promotional endeavors planned to increase network member visibility at both state and community levels, NN/LM aims to increase the general public's awareness and use of online health information resources and to reach health professionals with little or no previous contact with medical librarians. Montana Baby Boomers Get Fit at the Library (see below) is an excellent example of a coordinated, nationally supported effort to market regional libraries' health information services for older adults.

PARTNERS AND FUNDING Depending on the region or project, an RML works with local partners such as health departments, library systems, hospitals, businesses and corporations, government agencies, and non-profits. NN/LM is funded through the National Library of Medicine, which receives annualized support through the federal government.

Just for the Health of It!
East Brunswick Public Library, East Brunswick, New Jersey
www.ebpl.org

WHAT This consumer health initiative involves development of health-related collections, programs, and spaces for the boomer generation and their elders. All elements of the project were based on community surveys and medical specialists' input. Just for the Health of It exemplifies appropriate methods for gaining community feedback before designing a program. The comprehensiveness of the program and the library's effort to make health information a library-wide priority are both exemplary.

GOAL To meet the growing need for simplified, high-quality health information by baby boomers and other older adults.

FEATURES In 2009 the New Jersey State Library offered a competitive grants program titled Senior Spaces for libraries planning programs, services, and spaces dedicated to the interests of the state's growing baby boomers and elderly population (see chapter 12). The grants were administered by New Jersey's IN-FOLINK, the Eastern Regional Library Cooperative.

The East Brunswick Public Library was the only one of the Senior Space libraries to focus on health. Just for the Health of It involved multiple components:[1]

- A telephone poll of at least four hundred residents ages 60–85 living in East Brunswick to ascertain their major concerns and information needs in regards to health and wellness
- Use of poll results to identify areas of concern to be addressed immediately by the purchase of additional materials for the library's collections
- Consultation with a local doctor familiar with health concerns and local disease patterns
- Programs tailored to local issues and targeted for the 50+ age group
- Development of a separate but integrated space in the library where the boomer generation and their elders meet and comfortably access health information in every format

The library also created its special health collection by integrating newer books from the general collection and adding circulating and reference works, particularly for health conditions and diseases identified as the most prevalent by the consulting physician. Health reference librarians assisted with the selection of websites and collection materials. The health collection headings were designed to avoid medical jargon, such as "Healthful Aging," "Staying Fit," "Living with Diabetes," "Your Cancer Toolkit," "Heart Health," and "Emotional Wellness."

A specially designed health computer with access to licensed databases and links to authoritative Internet sources adds to the library's dedicated space. In addition, there is a custom research service for patrons who are not comfortable performing their own research, in the form of a medical search request form available online and in paper form. Librarians are available to research any health topic submitted by patrons and can send personalized packets on demand. The health

Just for the Health of It

Did you know that librarians can research any health topic and send you a packet of information that is personalized just for you? We have books, articles, databases, and DVDs that we can deliver to you in a timely manner. And best of all, we're free to all East Brunswick residents and library card holders.

—East Brunswick Public Library website

computer offers links to high-quality medical information in several languages through Medline (www.nlm.nih.gov/medlineplus) and other specialized websites.

As part of the marketing of Just for the Health of It, project staff reached out to several area hospitals to inform them about the library as a health information resource. They also trained library staff on health information search strategies, with an emphasis on how to assist residents in finding relevant health information.

As a result of the project, East Brunswick Public Library is one of the few public libraries accepted into the National Network of Libraries of Medicine for the Middle Atlantic Region (www.nnlm.gov/mar) and is recognized for providing customized medical research for 50+ consumers who need to overcome language barriers or special needs.

PARTNERS AND FUNDING The East Brunswick Public Library received critical assistance from librarians at the Health Sciences Library Association of New Jersey (www.hslanj.org), the MD Anderson Cancer Institute in Houston (www.mdanderson.org), and a local physician who acted as advisor to the project. Just for the Health of It was one of three projects funded through New Jersey's INFOLINK with an LSTA grant from the New Jersey State Library.

Note

1. For more details, see www.seniorspaces.pbworks.com/w/page/15791752/EAST
   -BRUNSWICK-PL.

Montana Baby Boomers Get Fit at the Library
Montana State Library / National Network of Libraries of Medicine, Statewide Program
www.msl.mt.gov/WhatsYourStory

WHAT A major, multipart health literacy and health information marketing initiative, during 2005–2008, consisted of programming, professional development, and communications aimed at Montana's growing population of older adults. The project was a joint effort of the Montana State Library (MSL) and the Regional Medical Library (RML), a member of the National Network of Libraries of Medicine (NN/LM, http://nnlm.gov/pnr).

The Montana project may be unique as a statewide initiative to promote the health of 50+ adults using libraries and media outreach. It was unusual for its combination of public programming, marketing, and training for librarians and members of the public, and for the range of multisector collaborators. In addition, the project had numerous documented impacts, such as building contact between health professionals and medical librarians and increased public awareness of NN/LM. It is an instructive example for other states.

GOAL To promote baby boomers' awareness of public libraries as sources of health information and to build Montana librarians' capacities to meet boomers' health information needs.

FEATURES Montana Baby Boomers Get Fit at the Library was part of a larger marketing campaign—What's Your Story? Find It at the Library—to help Montana libraries promote their varied services to the public. The campaign targeted one key audience annually; in 2005 it targeted the state's growing population of baby boomers and other older adults. In 2006/7 the focus was on health. Throughout the project there was NN/LM training for public library staff. Key project components included the following.

Marketing. MLS staff, working closely with RML and NN/LM staff, developed an entirely new set of tools and materials for libraries to use in their promotional efforts. These marketing and programming materials included programming suggestions and guides, tips on collaboration within communities, how-to guides on everything from writing a press release to controlling interviews, as well as customizable TV and radio ads, bookmarks, posters, business cards, and other promotional items. TV and radio public service announcements were distributed to and extensively broadcast statewide, emphasizing cable channels watched by baby boomers. The marketing support materials reinforced the broadcast ads and announcements, the health fairs, and the health information trainings, making the overall promotional effort exceptionally strategic.

The results of the broadcast marketing were readily apparent. In the month after the project ran its first ad, there was a 73 percent increase in the use of statewide health databases over the previous month. Over 2008 there was a 68 percent total increase in health database use over 2007. According to the final RML and NN/LM report on the project, these increases could not be attributed to any other factor.[1]

Health information training. Montana RML staff and MSL staff offered a series of trainings for public librarians on how to help older adults find authentic health information online. Training materials, including a primer developed by RML, were distributed to every public library in Montana and are available online.

Health fairs. More than thirty public libraries across the state hosted health fairs in April 2008. Some of the fairs involved a series of events related to health and highlighting the library's collections, capped with an actual health fair with multiple vendors. Other libraries hosted a presentation on accessing reliable health information online, and others participated in existing community health fairs for the first time. The Montana AARP distributed information on the health fairs to their 100,000+ Montana members. The Montana Medical Association promoted the health fairs, and Montana NN/LM members, including staff at hospital libraries, collaborated in the development and implementation of many of the fairs.

To promote the health fairs and the idea of using libraries and statewide health databases as resources for health information, MSL paid for a month-long sponsorship on the two NPR stations in Montana. These stations reach nearly every citizen in Montana, in large cities and remote rural areas. A special ad and public service announcements, developed with the assistance of RML and NN/LM, ran more than 2,800 times on cable channels favored by baby boomers, including Discovery channels, History Channel, ESPN-2, Lifetime, TNT, CNN, the Weather Channel, the Food Network, and the Home and Garden Network. Health fairs were promoted through NPR Montana. As noted above, the results of the marketing efforts paid off in increased public use of statewide health databases.

PARTNERS AND FUNDING Led by MSL and RML, the project involved Montana's hospitals and hospital libraries as well as Montana public libraries, Montana AARP, statewide radio and TV stations, and the Montana Medical Association.

Different parts of the project received different sources of support. The marketing efforts were enabled through support from cable companies and local broadcasters. RML supported development of the ads and many of the training and other publicity materials. MSL sponsored promotion of the health fairs on NPR Montana. LSTA monies, administered by MSL, supported the printing and distribution of training materials for public librarians. Other sources of financial assistance were the Montana Library Association (www.mtlib.org), a local bank, and some broadcast stations.

Note

1. "Montana Baby Boomers Get Fit at the Library," http://nnlm.gov/pnr/funding/reports/MT_State_Library_Health_Fair_SummaryFinalReport.pdf.

Put Life Back in Your Life! and Senior Health Series

Whitehall Library, Pittsburgh, Pennsylvania

www.whitehallpubliclibrary.org

WHAT Two health-related program series for older adults, one on chronic health problems and one on strategies for healthy living, resulted from the opening of the library's Second Chapter Café, a dedicated space for baby boomers and other aging adults to connect and to learn. The café was funded through Senior Spaces, a grant program of the Pennsylvania Office of Commonwealth Libraries.

GOAL To improve the health of aging residents and to expand use of the library by 50+ adults.

FEATURES Put Life Back in Your Life! a workshop series, dealt with chronic problems such as diabetes, high blood pressure, arthritis, and heart disease. The Senior Health Series presented experts discussing the importance of healthy living during midlife and beyond. It offered attendees a chance to obtain free medical information from health care professionals and receive related educational materials provided by the library. Topics included nutrition, fitness, disease prevention, and stress reduction.

PARTNERS AND FUNDING Put Life Back in Your Life! was made possible through a partnership between the Pennsylvania Department of Aging, Allegheny County Health Department of Human Services, United Way of Allegheny County, and Vintage, Inc. The Senior Health Series was made possible through collaboration with the University of Pittsburgh. The Second Chapter Café received initial funding from the Office of Commonwealth Libraries through the Senior Spaces grant initiative. Both health-related programs were supported by the library as part of its programming for the café.

Stay Well Exercise Program for Older Adults

New York Public Library / Queens Library, Jamaica, New York

www.nypl.org, www.queenslibrary.org

WHAT In a collaboration between the library systems and the New York City Department of Aging (www.nyc.gov/html/dfta/html/home/home.shtml), the

Stay Well health promotion program for adults 60 and older utilizes trained midlife volunteer coordinators. It provides a substantive civic engagement opportunity for older adults while meeting their health education needs. It is an excellent example of interagency cooperation in an urban setting and reflects the trend for libraries to provide participatory health promotion activities as well as health and wellness information. Stay Well also exemplifies the trend for libraries to engage midlife volunteers to carry out community programming that would otherwise not be possible.

GOAL To encourage older adults to follow healthier lifestyles and to promote use of libraries' health and wellness resources. It is also designed to leverage the energy and commitment of midlife adults whose engagement as volunteers makes the program possible.

FEATURES The Stay Well program introduces participants to special exercise, relaxation techniques, and the benefits of good nutrition. Each of the exercises, such as those for flexibility or cardiovascular health, can be adapted to different skill levels. The program also includes discussion groups, blood pressure monitoring, and walking clubs. Midlife adults are recruited by the host library and trained to lead the health promotion activities. Two volunteers are required for each session. New York City's Department of Aging health promotion staff provide on-site training and all necessary equipment to implement and maintain Stay Well activities. To initiate the program, the host library system offers a demonstration session class for branch library directors and adult services coordinators. Branch libraries that opt to host the program are responsible for recruiting local volunteers to run the program, coordinating training of volunteers with the Department of Aging, and promoting the program locally.

Stay Well is offered at ten New York Public Library branches. The program is an important component of the library's overall Next Chapter initiative and it complements other health promotion initiatives, including four health fairs organized by the library in 2010.

Like the New York Public Library program, Stay Well at Queens Library engages volunteers as key partners in health programming for peers and older adults. It is offered at three libraries in the Queens system.

PARTNERS AND FUNDING Stay Well was developed by the New York City Department of Aging and implemented in partnership with libraries and other community agencies. Other than for cooperative planning and management, no special funding was involved in implementing this program. It grew out of the participating agencies' mutual commitment to promote the health of the city's 50+ residents.

IN BRIEF: HEALTH AND WELLNESS

Arizona Cancer Center Lecture Series

Oro Valley (Arizona) Public Library Oro Valley Library partnered with the Arizona Cancer Center, a National Cancer Institute at the University of Arizona Health Sciences Library in Tucson, to offer a four-part lecture series by experts on the latest discoveries in cancer prevention, diagnosis, and treatment. The majority of participants were 50+ adults. (www.orovalleylib.com)

Back to Basics Nutrition for Boomers

Denton (Texas) Public Library Through a partnership with Better Living for Texans, a division of Texas AgriLIFE Extension Service, the City of Denton's library is offering a class covering food safety procedures, food resource management, how to read labels, and up-to-date nutrition information. The classes are interactive, with food demonstrations. At the end of the three weeks, participants receive a certificate of completion, handouts, and recipes. (www.cityofdenton.com)

Benefits CheckUp

Skokie (Ohio) Public Library Many libraries offer Benefits CheckUp, a tool created by the National Council on the Aging for locating government programs for seniors. The Skokie Library, in partnership with CJE SeniorLife, supported by the Jewish United Fund/Jewish Federation, offers Benefits CheckUp for adults age 60 and older. Participants have the opportunity to find out about their eligibility for Medicare, energy assistance, prescription drugs, property tax assistance, food stamps, Medicare D subsidy, subsidized housing, and social security. Trained staff assist with the inquiry process. (www.skokielibrary.info)

Boomers and Benefits

Lexington (Kentucky) Public Library, Beaumont Branch The library hosted representatives from the Bluegrass State Health Insurance Program to educate aging residents about Medicare benefits. Topics included Medicare Parts A, B, C, and D; Medigap insurance; and programs to help with out-of-pocket costs. Similar to many other programs around the country, this seminar was geared toward baby boomers new to Medicare, but it was also open to all. (www.lexpublib.org)

Brain Fitness

Santa Monica (California) Public Library The Brain Fitness workshop at the Santa Monica Library teaches participants how to strengthen their brains and improve their focus and concentration, including current information on nutrition and other strategies for cognitive improvement. Led by a brain fitness/memory enhancement teacher, the workshop includes an interactive demonstration of scientifically designed and tested exercises. (http://smpl.org)

Building Brain Power

Hartford (Connecticut) Public Library In 2007, through a partnership with the Think Well Center, the Hartford Library offered two series of weekly workshops to "build your brain power with activities and exercises to increase concentration, memory, reasoning, and/or speed of processing skills." The exercises included puzzles, mind maps, and journaling. The programs were offered at three branches and the main library. (www.hplct.org)

Do You Take Care of a Person with a Memory Problem? (Program in Mandarin Chinese)

Queens (New York) Library Through a collaboration with the Alzheimer's Association, New York City chapter, Queens Library is offering caregivers a monthly support group in Mandarin Chinese. The group provides a secure and safe place for participants to share experiences and enables them to review the unique challenges that caregivers face in caring for a person with Alzheimer's disease or any of the other dementias. (www.queenslibrary.org)

Fabulously Fit Seniors

Cuyahoga County (Ohio) Public Library Among its programs for older adults, the Cuyahoga County Library offers a program consisting of an hour of low-impact aerobics and chair exercise. In addition, participants learn how to make homemade weights using kitchen items. The library also offers other health and fitness programs, including presentations on osteoporosis prevention and management and free blood pressure screenings. (www.cuyahogalibrary.org)

Feed Your Brain

Palo Alto (California) City Library The Palo Alto City Library used grant funds from California's Transforming Life After 50 initiative to organize five lunchtime programs that featured experts on brain fitness and healthy aging from Stanford University's Medical Center. Local restaurants partnered to provide free, healthy refreshments. A blog was started and podcasts of the brain fitness programs were created to expand access. The program was targeted to boomers who work in Palo Alto but live elsewhere. Funds also enabled expansion of the library's collections and software related to brain health. (www.cityofpaloalto.org/depts/lib/default.asp)

Food for Thought

San Diego (California) Public Library The San Diego Library partners with a local senior nutrition provider to offer Food for Thought, in which older adults take part in physical activities and receive a nutritious meal. The library also provides space for events at which older adults can bring in their medications for review by a pharmacist to identify medication-related problems and reduce medicine waste. Midlife adults take advantage of the program, along with those considered seniors. (www.sandiego.gov/public-library)

Harmony, Mind, Body, Spirit

Upper St. Clair Township Library and South Park Township Library, Pennsylvania Harmony, Mind, Body, Spirit provides local residents with integrated holistic approaches to lifestyle choices affecting health and aging. The project involves building complementary collections of print and nonprint materials at both libraries and offering a parallel joint series of programs. Topics include acupuncture, holistic reflexology, stress management and mindfulness, and yoga workshops. Funds are provided by the Friends of the two library organizations and through the LSTA. (www.twpusc.org/library, http://southparklibrary.org)

Life Long Health & Fitness Health Fair

Port Washington (New York) Public Library Port Washington Public Library sponsors an annual Life Long Health & Fitness Health Fair for "Boomers and Beyond." Attendees are invited to follow "Sherlock Healthy" as he travels through the library discovering clues for lifelong healthy habits. There are prizes and clues for a long and fit life provided by many local health and fitness experts in dentistry, yoga, dance, posture, nutrition, and memory—and a walking challenge. In 2009 the library also offered weekly Exercise for Over 50 classes, which were so popular that tickets were distributed via a lottery. (www.pwpl.org)

Mental Fitness and Memory

Alameda County (California) Library Hope Levy, a lifelong learning specialist on the faculty of the Older Adult Learning Department at the College of San Francisco, offered a series on mental fitness in early 2011 at the Alameda library. Presentation titles included "Why Lifestyle Factors Make a Difference?"; "When Should I Worry?"; and "What Can I Do?" (www.aclibrary.org)

Put Life Back in Your Life!

Whitehall Public Library, Pittsburgh, Pennsylvania In spring 2011, as part of the opening of its Second Chapter Café, funded by the Pennsylvania Office of Commonwealth Libraries, the Whitehall Public Library offered a six-week series for adults 60 and older on chronic health conditions such as diabetes, high blood pressure, arthritis, and heart disease. Local partners included the United Way of Allegheny County, Pennsylvania Department of Aging, and Allegheny County Department of Health and Human Services, and Vintage, Inc. (www.whitehallpubliclibrary.org)

Senior Health Fair

Greensboro (South Carolina) Public Library The Greensboro Library annual Health Fair enables older adults to connect with community resources and learn about organizations that can help them achieve independent and healthy lifestyles. Free screenings and massages are included. Twenty-four community organizations sponsor and take part in the fair. (http://greensboro-nc.gov/index.aspx?page=780)

Senior Health NIA Toolkit

National Training Program To expand older adults' capacities to search for and find reliable health information online, the National Institute on Aging has developed a free training curriculum for librarians and others who teach and work with older adults. The toolkit includes a 9-minute introductory video and nine individual training modules with printable handouts for attendees. Many public libraries include this toolkit in their expanded health information collections. (www.nia.nih.gov)

Transforming Life After 50

Orange County (California) Public Libraries As part of the California State Library's Transforming Live After 50 initiative, the Orange County Library System designed programming to address boomer health issues such as nutrition and lifestyle choices. Information packets on twelve major health concerns of boomers were created and distributed to all branch libraries. Library staff also offered a "walk and learn" event with the County Parks department. (http://egov.ocgov.com/ocgov/OC%20Public%20Libraries)

Wii Sports Resort

West Babylon (New York) Public Library West Babylon is using the new Wii Motion Plus accessory to promote older adult activity. There are regular two-hour programs. The library encourages participants to "try all 12 Wii sports, and learn to play with even more precision." (http://wbab.suffolk.lib.ny.us)

Wise Walk

Allegheny County (Pennsylvania) Library Association In 2008 the Allegheny County Library Association in partnership with AARP, the Highmark PALS (People Able to Lend Support) Program, and member libraries invited 50+ adults to take a Wise Walk, a free ten-week walking program. Designed to offer a weekly exercise and social experience, Wise Walk has grown to include twenty-four library walking groups and received the AARP Library Services for Older Adults Award in 2009. Walkers receive a pedometer, walking guide, T-shirt, and healthy snack. (www.aclalibraries.org)

Yoga for Older Adults

Kansas City (Missouri) Public Library As part of Kansas City's Yoga Month in 2008, the library offered yoga classes for older adults, designed "to inspire a healthy lifestyle." Other public libraries throughout the country offer yoga classes, some for adults in general and a few especially for older adults. (www.kclibrary.org)

IN BRIEF: CAREGIVING

Caregiver Information Fairs

Libraries across the country organize informational events and fairs, enabling caregivers to learn about local services and support agencies. Examples can be found at Fayetteville (Arkansas) Public Library (www.faylib.org), Geneva (New York) Public Library (www.geneva publiclibrary.net), and Middletown Township (New Jersey) Library (www.mtpl.org).

Caregiver Resource Center

Somers (New York) Library Somers is one of five Caregiver Resource Centers in Westchester County. Each center houses a collection of information and materials for caregivers of older adults as well as older adults caring for children under age 18. The collection includes books, DVDs and videos, pamphlets, and reading and resource lists. (www.somerslibrary.org)

Caregiver Resource Centers

Peoria (Illinois) Public Library Through the State of Illinois Department of Aging, seven Peoria libraries and twenty-five other libraries in six west-central Illinois counties participate in the state's Caregiver Support program. These Resource Centers help caregivers locate such services as counseling, housekeeping assistance, financial and legal services, case management help, and assistive devices. (www.state.il.us/aging/1caregivers/crc.htm)

Caregiver Resource Information Series

Grand Rapids (Michigan) Public Library Grand Rapids Library offers a series of programs on caregiving, carried out in partnership with the Caregiver Resource Network (CRN). Topics included "Stress Management for Family Caregivers" and "Mental Health Issues for Family Caregivers." During November 2011, National Family Caregivers Month, the library partnered with CRN again to offer The Art of Caregiving, an event focused on how to incorporate creative therapies into the caregiving process. (www.grpl.org)

Caregiver Support Group

Northland (Pennsylvania) Public Library In conjunction with the Pittsburgh Caregiver Support Network, the Northland Library hosts a support group where participants can share stories, learning about caregiving resources, and reduce the isolation and stress of caregiving. (www.northlandlibrary.org)

Caregiver Support Panel

Prosser Public Library, Bloomfield, Connecticut In partnership with the Bloomfield Senior Center, Prosser Library hosted a forum for caregivers from Greater Hartford, featuring a variety of experts including a librarian. They discussed services and options available locally and the special challenges facing caregivers of individuals with dementia, Alzheimer's, and other chronic problems. The library is the recipient of a grant from the Family Caregiving 101 website, funded by the National Family Caregivers Association and the National Alliance for Caregiving, through which the library works with a clinical social worker to host a weekly family caregivers support group. (www.prosserlibrary.info)

Caregiver Workshops

West Los Angeles (California) Regional Branch Library The library featured a series of workshops in early 2012 designed to support caregivers. Facilitated by a representative of the Department of Aging, the series covered varied topics such as learning to deal with dementia and creating positive interactions. (www.lapl.org/branches/Branch.php?bID=27)

Conversation and Coffee for Caregivers

Multnomah County (Oregon) Public Library During November 2011, Family Caregivers Month, Multnomah County Library offered a series of facilitated discussions about practical, spiritual, and emotional aspects of caregiving. Participants learned about resources to help navigate medical, legal, respite, and insurance issues. The series was cosponsored by Multnomah County Aging and Disability Services' Family Caregiver Support Program and was made possible in part by Life by Design NW (www.pcc.edu/climb/life/) and federal funding through an LSTA grant administered by the Oregon State Library. (www.multcolib.org)

GrandKits: A Day of Fun in a Big Blue Bag

Delaware County (Pennsylvania) Library System In 2004 the Delaware County Library System received an LSTA grant through the Office of Commonwealth Libraries to compile three hundred GrandKits for distribution to its twenty-eight member libraries. These sets of educational materials provide grandparent caregivers with educational toys, books, games, and activity ideas for use with children age 3–11. They are organized around themes such as bugs, kitchen chemistry, music, and gardening. (www.delcolibraries.org)

Grandparents Raising Grandchildren Resource Centers

Dallas (Texas) Public Library According to the Dallas County KinCare Network, there are 64,000 grandparent-headed households in Dallas County. In 2006, in partnership with the KinCare Network and the City of Dallas Office of Senior Affairs, the Dallas Library created the first branch library Resource Center in the Audelia Road Branch. The centers are designed to provide grandparents with financial, social, health, and legal informational resources. A total of five centers are now open, and the library is seeking sponsorship for others. Each center includes a collection of books on parenting, computer resources, grandparents rights, kinship care issues, and picture books on topics that relate to grandparents as caregivers. Three centers also offer support groups. All centers include a "Grandparents' Chair," to "symbolize the library's commitment to grandparents." (www.dallaslibrary2.org/kincare)

Prepared Caregiving for the Elderly

Fargo (South Dakota) Public Library Fargo Public Library offered a series of programs on how to be prepared caregivers for aging adults in collaboration with the local Family Caregiver support program. Topics included elder law and online resources for caregivers. (www.cityof fargo.com/CityInfo/Departments/Library)

CHAPTER 6

INFORMATION TECHNOLOGY AND SOCIAL MEDIA

It's a perfect storm of demographics and technology.

—Molly Baker, "The New Retirement," *Wall Street Journal*

nformation technology—in the form of printed books, microfilm readers, Kurzweil readers, CDs, audiobooks, e-readers, and stationary or laptop computers—is ubiquitous in the library. It advances the mission of the library to provide access to the record of human expression. Availability, however, does not ensure access. Therefore, it is no surprise that training in the use of the newest such technologies has become a central feature of library services. However, until recently, the special training needs of midlife adults have not been a professional concern. With the aging of America and growth in the number of people age 50+ who are seeking jobs, volunteer opportunities, and learning and social connections, greater consideration must be given to *how* these individuals learn, *what* is motivating them to learn, and *what their skills levels are* in relation to other generations.

TRENDS

The shift from print to electronic communications has affected 50+ generations and individuals differently. No service provider can make assumptions about

[159]

the levels of patrons' or clients' skills, whether they are dealing with a CEO on the verge of retirement, a 50+ immigrant seeking a job, a small business owner in her sixties, or a grandparent in his eighties.

Whatever their skill level or background, 50+ adults want and need computer skills to stay in the workforce, communicate with family and friends, participate in financial transactions, keep up with the latest health information, or take advantage of online travel or shopping information. These needs are reflected in the large number of older adults who line up for computer classes at community centers, community colleges, workforce development agencies, and libraries. Some librarians report that all the introductory and advanced classes they can offer are usually filled to capacity, with the majority of students being midlife adults. For librarians considering how best to respond to this phenomenon, the following trends may inform their planning.

GENERATIONAL DIVIDES

The so-called generational divide that is applied to different age groups' participation in digital environments is often defined in terms of age. The assumption is that tweens and teens are immersed in social media and far ahead of their grandparents, who may use e-mail at most. There is, however, growing evidence that the divides are not so much in terms of skill levels as in terms of the devices used, the approaches to social media, and the online content sought.

The relationship between 50+ adults and new information technologies is changing so rapidly that generational behaviors documented as recently as 2009 are now outdated. The Pew Internet Project, for instance, reported that as of December 2009 only 16 percent of adults 65+ were going online wirelessly using a laptop or handheld device. This contrasted with 55 percent of all adults who were connected to the Internet wirelessly. Pew researchers stated that "older Internet users (over 65) are also likely to stay in the shallow end of the Internet activities pool: email and search. A few pioneers have jumped into the social media deep end, but these seniors are the exception, not the rule."[1]

By August 2011, Mary Madden, senior research specialist at Pew had reported these numbers:

- Between April 2009 and May 2010, social networking use among Internet users ages 50–64 grew by 88 percent—from 25 to 47 percent.
- During the same period, use among those age 65+ grew 100 percent—from 13 to 26 percent.
- By comparison, social networking use among users ages 18–29 grew by 13 percent—from 76 to 86 percent.

- Among adults age 65 and older, 13 percent log on to social networking sites on a typical day, compared with just 4 percent who did so in 2009.

In her report "Older Adults and Social Media," Madden writes: "Young adults continue to be the heaviest users of social media, but their growth pales in comparison with recent gains made by older users. . . . Email is still the primary way that older users maintain contact with friends, families and colleagues, but many older users now rely on social network platforms to help manage their daily communications."[2]

In spite of the surprisingly rapid adoption of new technologies by 50+ adults, including those 65 and over, there continue to be wide deviations in whether and how individuals go online. People encounter computers and other digital communications in different ways and at different times. Baby boomers, for instance, run the gamut from early adopters who started using computers in their teens or twenties and have kept up with the evolution of new technologies, including social media, to those who have elementary familiarity, at best, with new hardware, gadgets, or software. More and more are able to handle applications for jobs, mortgages, or benefits online, to search for health information, or even to join Facebook—and, yet, some still are not. Although there is a phenomenon known as "Boomer Social Media Mavens," most boomers fall somewhere in the middle of the skills spectrum.[3]

For those who are active and in their seventies or eighties, the picture is even more uneven. As documented by the Pew Project, many are highly motivated, learning to use the Internet for shopping and travel information and even for communicating via social media. But there continue to be more in this age group who are simply not familiar with computers and have not found it necessary or possible to enter the online world.

BEYOND BASICS

Building on the issues outlined above, it is especially important for libraries to understand that many midlife adults, especially the younger baby boomers, are not computer novices. They are intensive users of these new technologies. They are highly aware of the pace of technological change and the need to keep up with new developments in order to function in the workplace, communicate effectively with younger colleagues and family members, and participate in community activities. They are looking to learn about technological trends and the newest apps, how to select the right smartphone or e-reader, or how to use advanced Excel and photo editing software. Some of these computer-literate midlife adults may no longer be working, and thus, though they may have time to go online, they may not have opportunities to sharpen their skills and keep up-to-date.

For these advanced users the challenge is not how to handle the technology itself but how to access and manipulate particular content most effectively. They are not looking for one-size-fits-all classes but, rather, for opportunities to advance their expertise in a particular area such as small business development or financial planning. To the extent possible, options should be provided. Intensive instruction in particular software may be the answer for some; informal opportunities to exchange information and ideas with peers may be the answer for others. In fact, the evolution of computer clubs and other networking groups for computer enthusiasts reflects in part the need of 50+ computer experts to keep their skills up-to-date.

ADULT LEARNING

As new communications and information technologies emerge that can help promote positive aging, there has been relatively little interaction between academic researchers and institutional practitioners regarding the most effective designs for technology training. Many institutions that offer computer classes, even those that target 50+ adults and have a wide array of topics, do not necessarily factor in the best approaches for teaching midlife adults as opposed to young people or even younger adults. They may not be aware of new research about adult learning. In fact, there is a burgeoning field of research focused on adult learning and on older adult cognitive development, some of which can be effectively applied by libraries as they work with midlife adults.

Over the past two decades there has been extensive research on adult learning and older adult cognitive development, leading to new theories of adult learning including andragogy, as in the tradition of Malcolm Knowles; David Kolb's theory of experiential learning; Philip Candy's discussions of self-directed learning (SDL); Robert Kegan's constructive development theory; Jack Mezirow's theory of transformative learning; and, most recently, Ellie Drago-Severson's framework of "pillar practices" for supporting adult development.[4]

Two examples illustrate the value of adult learning research for development of computer and software training programs for midlife adults. One is the national OASIS Connections Technology Training Program, profiled in this chapter, developed by the OASIS Institute for national application in community settings, including libraries. The program design is informed by new research on older adult learning. The curriculum emphasizes hands-on active learning, including practice examples relevant to older learners, step-by-step procedures, screen illustrations, and adequate time for skill practice and positive reinforcement.

An evaluation of the OASIS program, including a control group that had not received training, was carried out by the Center on Aging at the University of Miami Miller School of Medicine. Individuals who had received training showed significant progress in the use of computers, computer knowledge, Internet knowledge, computer skills, and satisfaction. According to Sara Czaja, principal investigator for the study and codirector of the Center on Aging:

> Learning to use new technologies can be challenging for many older people. . . . There are cognitive changes that may make it difficult for older adults to engage in new learning. Some older adults may also experience anxiety in new learning situations or have doubts about their ability to learn something new. This does not mean that older adults are unable to learn to use new technologies or are "technophobic," but rather that training programs must be tailored to their needs.[5]

A second example is a project titled Electronic Health Information for Lifelong Learners (eHILL) that is based on research by Bo Xie of the University of Maryland College of Information Studies and carried out at the Prince George's County Library in Maryland. Although health information was the focus of inquiry for the participants (see chapter 5), the purpose of the investigation was to develop and test educational approaches for training older adults to use computer technology to meet their information needs. Through three related projects researchers documented several factors that promote older adult e-literacy, including the value of informal learning settings in promoting learning and the efficacy of peer learning (building on social interdependence theory) and collaborative learning.[6]

In another study, of older adults and social media, Xie and her colleagues worked intensively with ten older adults to explore participants' perceptions and preferences for learning strategies. Three key findings are important to the design of technology training for midlife adults: introducing the concepts before introducing the functions, responding to participants' privacy concerns, and making social media personally relevant.[7]

As new research points the way toward more efficient approaches for technology learning, it is incumbent upon library leaders and librarians to take these findings into account:

> Public libraries, in their role as providers of equal information access for all citizens, must work to ensure that the computer training they provide meets the formal and informal needs of older adults.

The trust that patrons have for public libraries, the ability of librarians to provide assistance, and the atmosphere of information access and exchange fostered within libraries combine to make them an ideal environment in which to provide computer training programs that focus on both the educational and social aspects of computer training for older adults. The interactive nature of public libraries might also encourage computer-savvy older adults to take leadership roles in helping others in the training programs.[8]

PEER SKILLS TRANSFER

In response to the growth in demand by midlife adults for computer instruction, there is a growing phenomenon of peer training. Given the number of boomers who are tech-savvy and are looking for volunteer or stipended community work, there is a natural opportunity to mobilize these individuals to help meet their peers' needs for technology instruction. The importance of this trend is reinforced by Xie's research that shows the value of peer training and by other research that indicates that boomers benefit from opportunities to share their unique skills and experience with others. The OASIS Connections program mentioned above is one example of peer learning that takes place in many community settings, including libraries.

IMPLICATIONS FOR LIBRARIES

There is no question that libraries, even the smallest and most remote, are offering technology training for midlife adults. Training is ubiquitous in libraries, and midlife adults are taking part. The challenge, then, is to offer the kind of training that aligns with older learners and matches different categories of 50+ adults. To plan 50+ information technology and social media services, libraries need to consider these kinds of questions: Is the training age-inclusive or age-targeted? Volunteer led or peer led? Does the content match documented interests and skill levels? Are all the classes introductory or do they include topics for advanced learners? Are the teaching approaches formal or informal? Do they involve collaboration with other agencies? What is the learning environment—informal, formal, on-site, or in a mobile space? Is self-teaching software used as a stand-alone or as a complement to face-to-face instruction? And, above all, how can the library develop and redevelop its staff capacities to provide the appropriate training?

As the following examples make clear, at this time there is no clear model and no simple set of answers to these questions. Library responses run the gamut, from the provision of Generations on Line software for self-paced instruction in the library to robust training and informational programs such as New York Public Library's program Becoming an Age-Friendly Library: Enhancing Technology Services to Older Adults.

With respect to the question of age-inclusive versus separate offerings, the majority of libraries offer computer training for adults but with no particular age groups designated. If they do provide training for designated adult age groups, they tend to use the terms "adults" and "seniors," without reference to boomers, 50+, or midlife adults. The latter are assumed to be part of one of the other two large categories rather than an audience category of their own. This is the case, oddly enough, even where some libraries offer other specifically targeted and titled 50+ programs.

Whatever the label given and whatever the target audience, typical offerings veer on the side of the basics. Although some libraries may include classes or workshops for experts as well as novices, most are simply trying to accommodate the many beginners that continue to come forward. For instructional personnel, libraries are using a combination of library staff, outside instructors (some paid), trained volunteers, and peers who offer to lead workshops. As can be seen in the following examples and in chapter 10, on intergenerational programs, some libraries are also relying on paid or unpaid teen helpers.

With respect to the content of library offerings, the majority of libraries offer basic computer use training and generic "search" instruction rather than thematic instruction. There are some exceptions, such as the libraries working with the National Network of Libraries of Medicine to offer workshops on identifying and retrieving health information. Others work with local manpower or workforce development agencies to train patrons in online job search strategies or industry research, and some teach how to use genealogy resources such as Ancestry.com and HeritageQuestOnline.com. Many focus their technology training on increasing participants' abilities to access library or community information resources. As libraries move beyond the basics, they are finding that midlife patrons are ready for more topical or specialized classes, and even that some patrons are ready and willing to lead these classes themselves.

Whatever their approach to technology training for 50+ adults, few libraries have taken into account the trends outlined above. For instance, few have carried out the research necessary to document the technology skill levels and interests of 50+ adults in their communities. One exception is the Paul Pratt Library in Cohasset, Massachusetts, which investigated midlife adults in their community, including offering an online skills assessment test. As a result, the Pratt Library is one of the very few libraries, outside of the large urban libraries and suburban systems, to develop a robust series of topical offerings for midlife adults that goes much beyond the basics. With LSTA funding through the Massachusetts Board of Library Commissioners, Pratt Library offered twenty-two different classes and programs over a ten-month period, including presentations on technology trends, how to set up a Facebook page, and how to create a "Twitter Strategy" (see profile below).

Across the library landscape, even with a multiplicity of technology training programs that could benefit midlife adults, there are almost none that visibly integrate new findings on adult learning into their class and workshop designs. Key exceptions are the academically oriented projects being carried out by Xie and the OASIS Connections training approach. It is telling that the latter program, although offered in libraries, was not developed by the library community. Whether the problem is a lack of awareness of new research on older adult learning, a lack of resources, or a lack of infrastructure for bringing academics and practitioners together, the absence of evidence-based programming is a critical blank on the library landscape. With acknowledged growth in demand, and demographic indicators that demand will increase, library leaders must become more versed in adult learning environments and the teaching and learning approaches that are most effective for building 50+ adults' capacities to take part in digital environments.

Finally, concerning the use of peers for 50+ technology training, there is evidence of increased awareness and interest on the part of librarians. Multnomah County (Oregon) Public Library's Cyber Seniors program, described below, involves trained 50+ assistants. Recruiting and preparing computer-savvy midlife adults may be a key strategy for meeting growing demand.

The rapid growth of technology training in libraries reflects the societal shift from print to digital communications. As discussed above, this shift is affecting 50+ adults rapidly and in different ways. Librarians cannot make assumptions about what motivates midlife adults to attend computer classes, what skill levels they have, what learning styles are most effective, and whether and how they can help one another participate more effectively in digital environments. In fact, they can make few assumptions in such a dynamic environment. They can, however, attempt to keep up with older adults' increasingly rapid adoption of new technologies, the wide differences between individual capacities within age groups, and the reality that comfort levels and skill levels vary widely within and between different older generations. It is clear that in the realm of technology training there is no one "best practice," no one size that fits all.

Notes

1. Susannah Fox, "Four in Ten Seniors Go Online," Pew Internet and American Life Project, January 13, 2010, www.pewinternet.org/Commentary/2010/January/38-of -adults-age-65-go-online.aspx.

2. Mary Madden, "Older Adults and Social Media," Pew Internet and American Life Project, August 27, 2010, www.pewinternet.org/Reports/2010/Older-Adults-and-Social -Media.aspx.

3. Lori Bitter, "Baby Boomers Emerging as the New Social Media Mavens," CNBC Guest Blog, March 4, 2010, www.cnbc.com/id/35318009/Bitter_Baby_Boomers_Emerging _as_the_New_Social_Media_Mavens.

4. Malcolm Knowles, *The Modern Practice of Adult Education: From Pedagogy to Andragogy* (River Grove, IL: Follett, 1980; David A. Kolb, *Experiential Learning: Experience as the Source of Learning and Development* (Upper Saddle River, NJ: Prentice-Hall, 1983); Philip C. Candy, *Self-Direction for Lifelong Learning* (San Francisco: Jossey-Bass, 1991); Robert Kegan, *In Over Our Heads* (Cambridge, MA: Harvard University Press, 1994, and *The Evolving Self: Problem and Process in Human Development* (Cambridge, MA: Harvard University Press, 1982); Jack Mezirow, *Learning as Transformation: Critical Perspectives on a Theory in Progress* (San Francisco: Jossey-Bass, 2000; Eleanor, Drago-Severson, *Leading Adult Learning: Supporting Adult Development in Our Schools* (Thousand Oaks, CA: Corwin Press, 2009), *Becoming Adult Learners* (New York: Teachers College Press, 2004), and "Library Leadership for Mature Adult Learners in a Changing World: The Importance of Attending to Developmental Diversity," in *Boomers and Beyond: Reconsidering the Role of Libraries*, ed. Pauline Rothstein and Diantha D. Schull, 23–46 (Chicago: American Library Association, 2010).

5. OASIS, "Research Shows Connections Curriculum Succeeds in Teaching Computer Skills to Older Adults," access via www.oasisnet.org.

6. Bo Xie, "Older Adults, E-Health Literacy, and Collaborative Learning: An Experimental Study," *Journal of the American Society for Information Science and Technology* 62, no. 5 (2011): 933–46, http://terpconnect.umd.edu/~boxie/XIE_01192011_JASIST _accepted.pdf.

7. Bo Xie, I. Watkins, J. Golbeck, and M. Huang, "Understanding and Changing Older Adults' Perceptions and Learning of Social Media," *Educational Gerontology* 38, no. 4 (2012): 282–96; for draft version, see http://terpconnect.umd.edu/~boxie/EduGeron _OlderAdults_and_SocialMedia_accepted.pdf.

8. Bo Xie and Paul T. Jaeger, "Computer Training Programs for Older Adults at the Public Library," *Public Libraries* 47, no. 5 (2008): 52.

Becoming an Age-Friendly Library:
Enhancing Technology Services to Older Adults

New York Public Library, Next Chapter, New York, New York

www.nypl.org

WHAT Becoming an Age-Friendly Library is a two-year project that helps adults 60 and older become familiar with new technologies through hands-on training and informational programs. The project is an important component of New York Public Library's (NYPL) overall Next Chapter initiative (see chapter 2), and it complements two current New York City "age-friendly" initiatives: A City for All Ages, and Age-Friendly New York City, a project of the City of New York and the New York Academy of Medicine.

Becoming an Age-Friendly Library stands out as an urban library model for scope and depth in technology-related programming. It not only includes substantive computer training for adults in diverse neighborhoods but also offers presentations for members of the public and librarians that promote broader understanding of computers and digital environments.

GOAL To build the capacities of older New Yorkers to participate in digital environments.

FEATURES NYPL's initiative involves classes at branch libraries in all three boroughs served by the library. Eight twenty-session computer classes are being offered through a partnership with the organization Older Adult Technology Services (OATS, www.oats.org). One of the sessions is offered in Spanish. Classes cover basic online communication techniques plus half-day workshops on health, Internet safety, and workforce skills. Other project components include technology-related lectures by OATS staff for librarians as well as members of the general public at eleven locations to make them more comfortable with digital environments, social networking, computer selection, and purchase; computer training for NYPL librarians by OATS staff; a series of branch library presentations by author Abby Stokes titled "Demystifying Computers"; and design of web access and guides for older adults on the NYPL website to help them with reserves, renewals, and computer appointments.

PARTNERS AND FUNDING NYPL's instructional partner for Becoming an Age-Friendly Library, OATS, specializes in preparing adults to become engaged in digital environments through high-touch hands-on training. The initiative is supported by an LSTA grant administered by the New York State Department of Education's Office of Library Development.

Cyber Seniors
Multnomah County Library, Portland, Oregon
www.multcolib.org

WHAT Cyber Seniors trains older Portland area residents to use computers comfortably, with a focus on library resources. It also trains volunteers to function as instructors and assistants, many of whom are themselves midlife adults. As a complement to other Multnomah County Library efforts to encourage civic engagement, specifically through the Life by Design @ your library program (see chapter 2), Cyber Seniors is an excellent example of library volunteering as an important form of civic engagement.

GOAL To assist older adults who are interested in learning the "very basics" of how to use a computer, search the Internet, and use e-mail.

FEATURES The program consists of three classes that introduce participants to computers and help them learn to use the library's online catalog, surf the Internet, and sign up for free e-mail. Each session consists of one hour of instruction and one hour of practice. The volunteer instructors are trained to follow the library's prescribed curriculum.

In addition to the in-person session at the library, two online tutorials, "Computer Basics" and "Internet Basics," are available, along with a class schedule, registration information, and other links of interest to seniors.

PARTNERS AND FUNDING The opportunity to volunteer as a Cyber Senior instructor is marketed through the library's ongoing partnership with Life by Design NW (www.pcc.edu/climb/life). The program is supported through the library's regular budget.

eTrain and Aging Well in Jefferson County

Jefferson County Public Library, Lakewood, Colorado

http://jefferson.lib.co.us

WHAT Jefferson County's mobile computer training lab provides access to computer training for midlife and older adults at sites throughout the county. The training lab was created in collaboration with the Jefferson County Workforce Center (www.jeffcoworkforce.org) and is designed to better prepare the older citizens of Jefferson County for job readiness. Although the project does not focus on services at the library, the target audience is midlife adults who can benefit from gaining the skills required to become employed or reemployed. The eTrain program builds a connection with these adults, many of whom eventually come to the library for further information and assistance.

GOAL To reach older adults who have been out of the job and volunteer search market and to assist them in gaining the computer skills they need to identify and qualify for opportunities.

FEATURES The eTrain is an innovative mobile computer training lab with eight computer workstations and a trained instructor from the library on board. It offers on-site two-hour classes in computer basics and Internet job and volunteer search skills.

The eTrain has been featured on Colorado Public Radio in the program "Libraries As Job Centers" (see www.cpr.org/article/Libraries_As_Job_Centers).

PARTNERS AND FUNDING The library is partnering with the Jefferson County Department of Human Services and the Aging Well in Jefferson County project (www.co.jefferson.co.us) and is also reaching out to local community groups and faith-based organizations to make sure that midlife adults who could benefit from the program are made aware of the training and the eTrain schedule. The project is supported by a grant from the Rose Community Foundation with a matching in-kind contribution from the library.

Generations on Line
National Program
www.generationsonline.com

WHAT Special software designed for older adults has been developed by Generations on Line (GoL), a national nonprofit devoted to Internet literacy and access for older adults. GoL is used in more than 1,300 facilities in the United States and Canada, including libraries. As a self-teaching tool, GoL software is an excellent option for older adults without prior Internet experience and without access to an instructor or workshop. It is also an option for libraries to enhance or replace computer training for midlife adults.

GOAL To enhance the quality of life for older people by promoting and assisting their use of Internet technology.

FEATURES Older adults use GoL applications for a wide variety of reasons: to acquire basic computer skills in order to join or rejoin the workforce, to communicate online, or simply to become comfortable with new communications technology. Libraries offering GoL vary in their approaches. Some use the software to complement classes or workshops or as the basis for small-group or one-on-one computer instruction. Others simply offer the service as a self-teaching resource. Libraries must subscribe to GoL in order to provide access to the software in the library; the software is not available to users remotely.

The GoL software uses familiar images and large-type instructions. With on-screen, step-by-step instruction it guides users through four basic Internet functions: simplified e-mail, including setting up a free e-mail account; memories—posted questions and answers in which supervised fourth-grade children ask seniors about their memories; Internet searching in thirty-six languages; and links to other websites relevant to old-

Sample Libraries Offering Generations on Line

Alameda County (California) Library: www.aclibrary.org

Atlantic City (New Jersey) Free Public Library: http://acfpl.org

Dayton Metro (Ohio) Library: www.daytonmetrolibrary.org

Florence-Lauderdale (Alabama) Public Library: www.flpl.org

Free Library of Philadelphia: www.freelibrary.org

Lincolnwood Public (Illinois) Library: www.lincolnwoodlibrary.org

Mid-Hudson (New York) Library System: http://midhudson.org

White County (Tennessee) Public Library: www.wtclibrary.org

er adults, including Social Security and Medicare, veterans affairs, newspapers around the world, and various health portals.

In 2002, GoL won the MindAlert Award for innovation in older adult learning from the American Society on Aging and the MetLife Foundation.

PARTNERS AND FUNDING Libraries that offer GoL software often partner with a local business, human resources or manpower development agency, or department on aging to underwrite the GoL subscription and market the service to older adults. For example, the White County Public Library in Cookeville, Tennessee, partners with the Upper Cumberland Human Resources Agency and Senior Service America; the Florence-Lauderdale Public Library in Florence, Alabama, partners with the Northwest Alabama Council of Local Governments; the Lincolnwood (Illinois) Library received an initial grant from the Chicago Community Trust to acquire access to GoL.

Mac and Windy Get Married: Bringing Library Technology Instruction into the 21st Century

Julia Hull District Library, Stillman Valley, Illinois

www.juliahull.org

WHAT This project provided technical and creative programming for older adults and senior citizens using MacBook laptop computers installed with both Windows and Leopard software. The project was unusual in its use of Mac/Windows combined instruction, the range of course offered, and its focus on older adults in a small, rural community. Mac and Windy Get Married proved highly successful, accounting for increases in program and general attendance and positioning the library as a central source of technology instruction for older adults.[1]

GOAL To educate older adults and senior citizens about current trends in computer technologies, including software programs and laptop hardware.

FEATURES The Mac and Windy Get Married project evolved from the library's recognition that within its patron base 54 percent of cardholders were 50+, and that these patrons did not have easy access to free computer training. Library staff sought a means of providing these residents high-quality instruction. By acquiring MacBooks dual-booted with Mac and Windows operating systems, the library was able to enhance its technology instruction program. In addition to sixteen MacBook computers, grant funds underwrote acquisition of software, a special projector and a digital projector, a mobile projector cart, a portable pull-up screen, and a laptop storage-charger cart. Using the new equipment, library staff provided instructional sessions on the basics—laptop use, operating system variances, office applications, web and catalog searching—as well as more creative activities such as home movie design, music composition, and maintenance of wireless technologies.

Through course surveys and statistical analysis of attendance and circulation during the grant period, the library was able to document success in meeting project objectives, including enabling participants to gain confidence in using computers and in becoming more active users of library services. Since the 2009 grant, the library has leveraged its investment in the new equipment by expanding its computer instruction to meet the needs of other groups in the community, such as teens (scrapbooking), Girls Scouts and Boys Scouts (badges for computer skills), and job seekers. The library has also continued to offer computer instruction for older adults and seniors.

PARTNERS AND FUNDING The Mac and Windy Get Married project was supported by an LSTA grant administered by the State Library of Illinois. The grant was matched by contributions from the Friends of the Library and the Stillman Valley Lion's Club.

Note

1. For more on Mac and Wendy Get Married, see "Library Spotlight: Julia Hull District Library, April 27, 2010, WebJunction, http://webjunctionworks.org/il/blog/index.php/category/standouts.

OASIS Connections Technology Training Program
National Program
www.oasisnet.org

WHAT Connections is a national technology training program designed for people age 50+ that is offered in public libraries and other community locations. The program was developed by the education organization OASIS, a national nonprofit that aims to enrich the lives of mature adults by "engaging them in lifelong learning and service programs so they can learn, lead and contribute in their communities."

OASIS volunteers are themselves 50+ adults. As class instructors they provide models for active engagement through teaching and learning.

GOAL To build older adults' skills and confidence in using computers in their personal lives and at work; to provide technology training in underserved neighborhoods through partnerships; and to provide necessary training for older adults who want to get back to work.

FEATURES The OASIS Connections program is an evidence-based technology training program developed by the OASIS Institute.[1] The curriculum provides participants with basic computer skills along with skills in Internet searching; using MSWord, Excel, and PowerPoint; creating resumes and doing job searches online; and using social media. The course development is informed by research on adult learning and emphasizes hands-on active learning, relevant activities, step-by-step procedures, screen illustrations, and time for skill practice and positive reinforcement. A recent study by the University of Miami School of Medicine documented the impact of the introductory Connections courses in terms of their effectiveness helping older adults develop computer skills.

Connections classes are offered by OASIS through more than ninety partners. Aside from public libraries, these include YMCAs, senior centers, churches, and retirement housing centers. OASIS provides support for partners through instructor training, marketing tools, implementation guidance, and evaluations. By partnering with OASIS libraries can augment their own technology training programs with special classes geared to 50+ adults and, in so doing, position themselves as technology learning centers for midlife adults.

PARTNERS AND FUNDING Libraries partner with their local OASIS offices to offer the Connections workshops, which are developed and coordinated by the national OASIS headquarters. Volunteer training and support are provided by the local OASIS organization with additional support from the national headquarters through a grant from

Sample Libraries Offering OASIS Connections

Albany (New York) Public Library: **www.albanypubliclibrary.org**

Broward County (Florida) Library, Hollywood Branch: **www.broward. org/Library/LocationsHours/ Branches/Pages/HO.aspx**

Dallas (Texas) Public Library, Hampton Illinois and Pleasant Grove Branches: **http://dallaslibrary2.org**

Donald W. Reynolds Library, Baxter County (Arkansas): **www.baxtercountylibrary.org**

Pima County (Arizona) Public Library: **www.library.pima.gov**

Sacramento (California) Public Library: **www.saclibrary.org**

AT&T. Some library Connections sites have special funding to help support implementation and marketing of the program. The Pima County (Arizona) Library, for instance, receives support from the Friends of the Pima County Library.

Note

1. OASIS, "Research Shows Connections Curriculum Succeeds in Teaching Computer Skills to Older Adults," access via www.oasisnet.org.

Senior Computer Classes
District of Columbia Public Library, Washington, D.C.
www.dclibrary.org

WHAT A pilot project and follow-up initiative provided free computer classes for 55+ adults. The 2009 pilot took place at two library branches: Woodridge and Francis A. Gregory. Byte Back computers (www.byteback.org), a nonprofit that provides computers to low-income communities, delivered training in basic computer literacy to 468 older adults living in two of the District of Columbia's most economically distressed wards. The pilot was so successful that it led to a second phase involving 1,600 people in seven branch libraries supported by a federal Broadband Technology Opportunities Program stimulus grant.

GOAL To "transform a person with no interest in or knowledge of computers and broadband into a lifelong, effective broadband user."[1]

FEATURES The Senior Computer Classes were divided into two modules. The first module introduced participants to computer basics such as accessing the Internet, establishing an e-mail account, creating and saving documents, and basic searching strategies. The second section included file management, communicating via e-mail, downloading documents, Internet safety, and identifying health and financial services resources. A special website featuring relevant content was created to help participants become comfortable searching the Internet.

> The seniors are serious students. They bring their eagerness and willingness to master PC 1 and PC II for beginners. The students practice exercises in typing tutorials, learn PC terminology and word processing, create e-mails and even spreadsheets.
>
> —Woodridge Branch Library website

Participants were highly engaged in the classes, and instructors reported high attendance rates. At the end of the program participants received a free refurbished computer, with software, from First Time Computer, an organization that trains at-risk youth to refurbish computers, and two years of free broadband access via Cricket Communications.

The pilot programs were so successful that the library developed a two-year initiative with six partners to work with 1,600 District residents to provide broadband education, skills training, educational and appropriate content, a computer and broadband connections in the home, and ongoing support.

The District of Columbia Public Library won a 2011 Urban Libraries Council award for its pilot Senior Computer Classes.

PARTNERS AND FUNDING The library partnered primarily with Byte Back, First Time Computers, and Cricket Communications for the pilot program. Additional partners for the expanded initiative include the D.C. Office of the Chief Technology Officer and One Economy (www.one-economy.com).

The pilot project was funded by a grant from the Holden Bequest, a gift given to the D.C. Public Library to benefit the Woodridge and Francis A. Gregory neighborhood libraries. The current expanded initiative is supported through a $1.5 million federal Broadband Technology Opportunities grant for Sustainable Broadband in the District.

Note

1. "Sustainable Broadband," BROADBANDUSA, www.dclibrary.org/broadbandusa.

Senior Tech Day
Hennepin County Library, Rogers Library, Minneapolis, Minnesota
www.hclib.org

WHAT Rogers Library held this special event for adults 55 and older that connected them with new technologies through demonstrations and assistance in using electronic devices from young tech-savvy people.

GOAL To help older adults learn what is new in technology and gain confidence in using different types of devices.

FEATURES The hands-on event featured demonstrations of five devices: MP3 players, digital cameras, cell phones, high-definition TVs, and laptop computers.

Best Buy provided sample devices and assistance from several young associates who worked one-on-one with the participants. Participants learned how to download e-books and music from the Hennepin County Library catalog onto MP3 players. Attendees could sign up for a free e-mail account and try out the electronic fitness games, Wii Bowling and Wii Fit. Wii bowlers received "I Bowled Them Over at the Rogers Library" stickers as a reminder of the introduction to virtual sports. Attendees were also invited to bring in their own devices to learn how to use their features, and many took advantage of this opportunity to learn to use their equipment more effectively.

In addition to Senior Tech Day, Hennepin County Library offers programs to help build older adults' capacities to use new technologies, including Senior Surf Day, Digital Photography, and Individual Computer Tutoring. In recognition of Senior Tech Day, the Friends of the Rogers Library, the primary program sponsor, was awarded the Minnesota Association of Library Friends' Evy Nordley Award in 2008.

PARTNERS AND FUNDING The local Best Buy, located near the Rogers Library, collaborated with the Friends of the Rogers Library in presenting and funding the event.

Tech Teens / Gadget Coaching
Sno-Isle Libraries, Snohomish and Island Counties, Washington
www.sno-isle.org

WHAT Through Tech Teens, young volunteers help older adults learn to use computers and other digital communications devices. As with other projects involving teens as computer mentors, the Tech Teens program benefits the teen "teachers" as well as the older participants. The adults gain the skills necessary to communicate with family or colleagues or to undertake new job functions, while the teens gain experience in intergenerational interaction, learn to transmit their skills for the benefit of others, and fulfill school requirements for community services.

GOAL To build older adults' capacities for online communications while providing teenage tutors with opportunities to gain social skills and community service experience.

FEATURES Starting in 2002, Sno-Isle Libraries recognized the need to reach out to older adults who were uncertain about how to use computers or did not own one. To address this problem, library staff created Tech Teens, recruiting tech-savvy teens willing to answer questions and help adults learn to use new technologies. For group training they used a new computer area in the Mount Lake Terrace Library equipped with special training equipment. The 90-minute classes were offered monthly, with teens available to help with a range of questions and skill levels. While one student trainer directed the lesson, assistants helped individual users at their terminals. Within five years more than three hundred older adults had taken advantage of the new service, gaining computer literacy from local students. Some of the older adult "students" were participating in order to update their skills for new jobs.

More recently, the library has offered weekly Gadget Coaching, in which tech-savvy teen volunteers are available to assist older residents with questions about their cell phones, MP3 players, laptops, and other handheld devices.

PARTNERS AND FUNDING There were no specific project partners. Tech Teens was started with a small grant from the Greater Everett Community Foundation (www.greatereverettcf.org).

The Next Chapter: Lifelong Learning
Paul Pratt Memorial Library, Cohasset, Massachusetts
www.cohassetlibrary.org

> If not now, when? You can begin your creative work today!
> —Gene Cohen, Paul Pratt Memorial Library website

WHAT This series of computer and writing workshops for 50+ adults was offered from October 2010 through June 2011. As part of Pratt Library's effort to widen offerings for active midlife adults, the series included topics for computer novices and for those wishing to deepen their skills in particular social media. The series was not limited to online communications; it also included workshops on memoir writing and fiction writing.

The Next Chapter is an excellent example of how a library can meet the diverse technology needs of midlife adults, ranging from beginners to those interested in technological trends and design. The project also stands out for its use of a technology skills assessment test for potential students.

GOAL To position participants to engage in current computer and social networking Internet tools so that they can fully participate in a networked world.

FEATURES There were twenty-two different Next Chapter workshops, taught by professionals, covering everything from "Basic Computer Skills" and "Internet Research" to "Blogging for Business," "Creating an Effective Twitter Strategy," and "PC Troubleshooting." To help participants gauge their skills level before registering for a workshop, the library offered a skills test: "Public libraries have become centers for productive aging, lifelong learning and civic engagement. We have designed a program that will position older citizens to engage in social media for work, volunteering and personal lives. Challenge yourself by completing our '11 by 11' skills test."

PARTNERS AND FUNDING The Social Service League of Cohasset assisted with marketing the program and funding. The workshops were also funded by an LSTA grant administered by the Massachusetts Board of Library Commissioners. The local Goodwin Graphics also supported Next Chapter.

IN-BRIEF: TECHNOLOGY PROGRAMS AND SERVICES

55+ Computer Series
Pikes Peak (Colorado) Library The Cheyenne Mountain Branch and Penrose Library offer special computer classes for older adult computer novices to help them learn basic word processing skills. (http://ppld.org)

Basics for Adults and Seniors
Charlotte Mecklenburg Library, Charlotte, North Carolina The Charlotte Mecklenburg Library offers a series of five classes that provide beginners with the basic skills they "need to get around in Windows using a mouse." The series includes "Computer Basics for Seniors and the Absolute Beginner" as well as instruction on how to use a simple word processing program, how to create and edit images, and an introduction to the Internet. (www.cmlibrary.org)

Ebooks for Your Kindle
Bloomfield Township (Michigan) Public Library A "Boomers and Beyond" class at Bloomfield Township Library teaches how to get free e-books through the library. Participants bring their devices to the class. They must be able to use their e-reader before attending the class and should have downloaded at least one book through Amazon. (www.btpl.org/adult-services/boomers-and-beyond)

Facebook Set-Up for Seniors @ Libraries
Fort Bend (Texas) County Libraries In June 2011, Fort Bend offered a special program at three branches to help older adults learn more about social networking and Facebook. Participants were required to have a personal e-mail account and a basic working knowledge of computers. (www.fortbend.lib.tx.us)

Facebook / Twitter for Seniors

Torrance (California) Public Library This class at Torrance Public Library aims to help older adults "bridge the generation gap and get up to speed with Facebook and Twitter!" Topics include learning how to connect with friends and family, play games, adjust privacy settings, use instant messaging functions, and more. (www.torranceca.gov/Library)

Intermediate Computers for Senior Adults

Dallas (Texas) Public Library This Dallas Library monthly class for non-beginners features a new topic each time. Class size is limited for in-depth instruction. (www.dallaslibrary2.org)

Older Adult Computer Classes

Palatine (Illinois) Public Library The Palatine Library offers courses that are progressive; participants are expected to take the full series, which cover use of a mouse, searching on the Internet, and using e-mail. (www.palatinelibrary.org)

Open House

Whitehall Library, Pittsburgh, Pennsylvania This regular Saturday afternoon program invites older adults to stop by the library café and ask local teenagers general technology questions and explore the e-readers and iPads that can be checked out from the library. (http//whitehall publiclibrary.org)

Romance after 50—Taking It Online!

Wilmette (Illinois) Library A June 2011 program guided participants through the dating game, with an emphasis on online sites. The workshop included creating a profile as well as learning about safety issues. (www.wilmette.lib.il.us)

Seniors in the Driver's Seat

Clinton Essex Franklin Library System, New York With the goal of "helping older adults embrace technologies to become fluent E-Citizens," the Clinton Essex Franklin Library System developed programs to build adults' comfort level with computers. Among the activities was a pairing of a senior with a young adult "to expand their familiarity with computer applications and environments." (www.cefls.org)

Silver Scholars Computer Classes for Boomers and Beyond

Jefferson Hills (Pennsylvania) Public Library The Silver Scholars computer classes are specifically designed for 50+ individuals, but all are invited. The classes are "fun and interactive." They cover the basics as well as such topics as digital cameras and Excel. Each topic consists of two two-hour sessions. Classes are limited to ten students. (www.jeffersonhillslibrary.org)

Wii Programming for Aging and Older Adults

Mohawk Valley (New York) Library System In an effort to "extend library services to the community in new ways," the Mohawk Valley libraries are using new technology to build intergenerational library-sponsored activities for seniors. Introducing sports programs in the Wii format has the added benefit of providing physical exercise and social interaction for older adults throughout Fulton, Montgomery, Schoharie, and Schenectady counties. (www.mvls.info)

CHAPTER 7

CREATIVITY

Poetry has been a pretty good workout. . . . Being a poet
has made me a pretty spry old man.

—Samuel Menasha, Creativity and Aging in America conference

With the aging of the baby boomer generation and the increase in the number of healthy and vital 50+ adults, new views of aging are emerging. The prevailing view as a time of decline and deficit is giving way to a picture of a time ripe with opportunities for personal growth, intellectual challenge, community participation, and creative expression. This view, termed "positive aging," suggests the need for institutions such as libraries to rethink traditional older adult programming and to experiment with approaches that foster learning and participation.

TRENDS

"Being a poet has made me a spry old man" expresses the essence of recent research on aging and the arts that documents both cognitive and physical benefits of creative pursuits in the later years. Experiments are showing that structured engagement with the arts provides "a good workout" and has multiple positive effects on older adults. As a result of growth in the field of creative aging, more and more aging specialists are encouraging arts participation.

One of the most influential studies on the effects of arts participation was carried out by Dr. Gene Cohen, former director of the Center on Aging, Health and the Humanities at George Washington University. Cohen examined whether and how continuous learning, especially participatory arts programs, has a positive influence on the well-being of older adults. His 2006 landmark report *The Creativity and Aging Study: The Impact of Professionally Conducted Cultural Programs on Older Adults* affirmed that structured arts education has positive social, psychological, and cognitive impacts as well as physical benefits.[1] A particularly important finding was that sequential arts learning programs foster mastery and promote social engagement—two key ingredients for positive aging. The study confirmed what arts educators and practitioners have observed anecdotally; namely, the arts are good for you.

> Lifelong learning in the arts educates and engages older adults as teachers, learners, and as creators, thereby contributing to individual, community, and public life.
>
> —National Endowment for the Arts conference

Cohen's work complements other current research on the plasticity of the adult brain and the potentials for older adult learning. There is a growing body of evidence that the human brain is not static, even in the older years. It is continually responsive to input, and activities that engage both sides of the brain—such as memory work, creative expression, learning new routines, movements, and ways of seeing—seem to have physiological as well as psychological benefits during the aging process. It is not surprising, then, that arts programs, especially participatory programs, seem to be beneficial during aging.

The particular art form does not seem to make a difference as much as the regularity of the activity, the degree to which it stimulates motion and expression, and the extent to which it involves social interaction.

As a result of the new research, some gerontologists and advocates of positive aging are seeking methods for engaging more older adults in structured arts activities. They are encouraging arts educators to work more seriously with aging adults, revitalizing aging services and senior centers through arts programming, and identifying public spaces such as libraries that offer natural opportunities for creative aging programs.

Several organizations are leaders in arts education for elders. The National Center for Creative Aging (www.creativeaging.org) is dedicated to fostering understanding of the vital relationship between creative expression and healthy aging and has promoted the field through advocacy efforts. The National Endowment for the Arts has encouraged arts education for older adults and in 2007 compiled instructive examples in *Creativity and Aging: Best Practices*.[2] The New York State Council on the Arts recently expanded its arts education guidelines beyond the K–12 sector to include "lifelong learning." Lifetime Arts, a national organization based in Westchester, New York (see profile below), is the only group to focus on libraries as a venue for creative aging. Lifetime Arts has developed multiyear demonstration projects with the Westchester Library System, the New York Public Library, and the Brooklyn Public Library and is expanding these to other libraries across the country.

As new practices fostered by these groups evolve and become more visible, they are providing new evidence for analysis by researchers on aging and the arts. Thus there is a dynamic relationship between research and practice in the emerging field of creative aging. Libraries that are involved in creative aging are also contributing to the field.

IMPLICATIONS FOR LIBRARIES

For libraries, the connection with creative aging seems a natural. Most libraries have collections that provide access to artistic expression in different disciplines, formats, and cultural traditions, and most offer some form of arts programming for adults. These range from the New York Public Library's Library of the Performing Arts, with its specialized collections, galleries, and performance spaces, to the Portland (Maine) Public Library, with ongoing community arts programming. Some libraries, such as the Nashville (Tennessee) Public Library and the Newton (Massachusetts) Public Library, partner with orchestras or other performance groups to provide regular concerts. Some feature displays or demonstrations on the book arts, many have rotating exhibits of local artists, and others organize tours to museums or galleries. All across the country, libraries have adopted the practice of "lending" passes for local museums. In addition, many libraries, such as the Brooklyn Public Library, include arts activities in their outreach to senior centers, community centers, assisted living residences, and nursing homes.

> Adults can and should be active learners and creators into their older years.
>
> —Robert Butler,
> The Longevity Revolution

It is clear from the scope of library-based arts programming for adults taking place today that the question is not *whether* to offer arts programs for 50+ adults but *how*. Do current programs reflect basic principles of creative aging, or are they simply forms of entertainment? Do they encourage structured learning, social engagement, and participation? Do they involve arts educators who can enable mastery of a new skill? Do they recognize and present creative work by older adults?

Unfortunately, with the exception of some literary programs, memoir workshops, and occasional visual classes, libraries emphasize access to the arts rather than creation and expression. No matter the quality, the performances, readings, exhibitions, or demonstrations are primarily passive experiences that do not encourage active participation.

To take full advantage of the library as a center for creative expression and to support positive aging in their communities effectively, librarians must shift their perspective about older adults. They must see them as creators as well as consumers. They must recognize that film screenings and trips to local museums are not, by themselves, sufficient to promote positive aging. They must involve constituents in selecting programs and designing participatory activities. They must abandon the notion that they can "provide" all the programs and instead form partnerships with arts educators and cultural institutions. Finally, they must retool spaces and collections to support active arts education.

Considering these challenges and opportunities, the fact that so many libraries are already providing arts programming in one form or another is a plus. In many libraries there are assets to build on such as space, cooperative colleagues, community partners, and related collections. Nevertheless, these assets must be reexamined through the lens of creative aging. How can they be utilized to support active engagement in the arts by 50+ adults?

The following profiles of creative aging programs show how libraries are starting to make the shift from entertainment to engagement, from access to participation. They suggest the possibilities for more intentional programming that can transform libraries into centers for creative aging.

Notes

1. Gene Cohen, *The Creativity and Aging Study: The Impact of Professionally Conducted Cultural Programs on Older Adults*, Final report, April 2006, www.arts.gov/resources/accessibility/CnA-Rep4-30-06.pdf.

2. Jessica E. Thomas and Katie Lyles, eds., *Creativity and Aging: Best Practices*, National Endowment for the Arts, January 207, www.nea.gov/resources/accessibility/BestPractices.pdf.

Art of Aging

Hennepin County Library, Minneapolis, Minnesota

www.hclib.org

WHAT This exhibit of works by four women artists from the Minneapolis area, ages 65–80, features their creative and personal responses to the experience of growing old. The exhibit was on view for three months in 2010 in the Cargill Hall Gallery of the Central Library.[1] It was accompanied by public programs on arts and aging at two Hennepin County libraries: Central and Southdale. The complementary programming expanded the exhibit experience by engaging participants in a community inquiry on the meaning and representation of aging in our society.

GOAL To present "a visual discourse on aging."

FEATURES Art of Aging showcased talented aging artists while focusing attention on the range of emotions experienced as one grows old. Working in a variety of media—glass, photography, sculpture, and charcoal and pastel drawings—the four artists communicated insights about ageism, identity, and other experiences of aging.

The artwork on display provided a catalyst for multiple public programs on the theme of arts and aging, including an artist panel, readings, and a performing artists showcase featuring storytelling and classical singing. Twin Cities Public Television worked with the artists to document and discuss their work and its relationship to aging and creativity. The video biographies of the artists were part of the exhibit at the library and were also expanded into a 30-minute program broadcast during the period of the exhibition.

PARTNERS AND FUNDING The Art of Aging was a collaboration between the Hennepin County Library and the Minnesota Creative Arts and Aging Network (www.mncaan.net). Twin Cities Public Television participated as a broadcast partner. The exhibit and programs were supported in part by the State of Minnesota's Arts and Cultural Heritage Fund, with additional funding provided by the Metropolitan Regional Arts Council (www.mrac.org).

Note

1. Details of the program are archived at "Art of Aging Exhibit and Programs Begin June 10 at Hennepin County Library," www.hclib.org/pub/info/newsroom/?ID=306.

Arts and Archives: Master Classes in Arts and Humanities
Hartford Public Library, Hartford, Connecticut
www.hplct.org

WHAT For this series of in-depth instructional arts and humanities workshops for midlife adults, the Hartford Public Library recruited highly skilled arts educators, provided a supportive environment, and recognized the participants, as artists, in a culminating exhibition. In addition, the teaching artists all used artifacts and documents from the library's Hartford Collection as resource materials for the classes, enriching the arts instruction with social and historical context. The series is an exemplary model for participatory arts instruction that reflects an understanding of the importance of arts education for positive aging.

> Arts and Archives participants are rediscovering their creative side. These classes are much more than your usual "arts and crafts" sessions, and they don't just fill time with busy work. We hire master artists to lead each class, and each brings a lifetime of sophistication and skill. Attendees grow to treasure the opportunity to work alongside these artists and connect with them on a deep level.
>
> —Brenda Miller, director, Hartford History Center

GOAL To provide attendees "opportunities to be creative, develop their artistic skills, and hone their critical thinking" and to build awareness and use of the library's Hartford Collection as source material for artistic expression.

FEATURES Arts and Archives consisted of seven modules, or workshop series, focused on different media or heritage-themed topics. In the first series, held September–November 2010, sculpture, pen-and-ink drawings, and mixed media were covered. Beginning February 2011, the program focused on music appreciation with an emphasis on jazz and blues. In March four workshops were held on memoir writing. Poetry and photography finished the series, in April and May 2011.

Each of the workshop modules was taught by a professional artist with experience in arts education. The classes were designed to provide intellectual stimulation along with hands-on instruction. Instructional enhancements included a tour of Hartford's public art by the sculptor/instructor and exposure to the library's history collections. Each module included a seminar incorporating artifacts, images, and personal narratives from the collections of the Hartford History Center.

The series culminated in an exhibition of work by workshop participants in the library's gallery. Titled "Arts and Archives on the ARTWALK: The Intersection of History and Art," the exhibit was on display during July and August 2011. The opening reception featured a talk about aging and creativity by cultural anthropologist Mary Catherine Bateson.

Arts and Archives classes were well received, with waiting lists for each workshop series. According to program coordinators, many participants were new library users. The classes attracted considerable media attention, including an October 2010 broadcast by WBS in Hartford on its *Better Connecticut* show.

Hartford Public Library was awarded an Urban Libraries Council ULC 2011 Innovations Initiative for Arts and Archives in the Innovation Category of Education. "Older adults in Hartford discovered (or re-discovered) and expressed their creativity and developed artistic and critical thinking skills in an information-rich library setting. . . . By exploring creative expression through the lens of community history, this program offers an exceptionally dynamic way to involve and educate adults while also connecting them to Hartford's richly diverse heritage."[1]

FUNDING AND PARTNERS The Master Classes in Arts and Humanities were supported, in part, by an LSTA grant administered by the Connecticut Division of Library Development.

Note

1. "Arts and Archives: Master Classes in the Fine Arts and the Humanities," Urban Libraries Council, 2011, http://urbanlibraries.org/displaycommon.cfm?an=1&sub articlenbr=751.

Art for Life Residencies
Metropolitan Library Association, Minneapolis, Minnesota
http://melsa.org

WHAT This participatory arts program by the Metropolitan Library Association (MELSA; see chapter 2) emphasizes the creative capacities of older adults and builds stronger relationships between teaching artists, adult-care centers, and public libraries. Arts for Life Residencies is the only program profiled in this chapter that does not fully take place in a library. It is included as an example of how libraries can strengthen their outreach to adult-care centers while promoting librarians' understanding of the importance of participatory arts for positive aging.

GOAL To provide opportunities for high-quality arts instruction for underserved older adults in the Twin Cities and to connect them with nearby library resources.

FEATURES Teaching artists trained by the Minnesota Creative Arts and Aging Network (www.mncaan.net) work for three days at the centers, providing in-depth instruction in a particular art form. The instruction is based on the concept of the older artist and his or her life experiences as sources for artistic expression. The instructors help participants gain artistic skills in one of ten artistic disciplines ranging from songwriting, dance, and storytelling to creative writing, ceramics, painting, and collage. In one neighborhood participants paid "Homage to the Library" through creative movement. The artwork produced is exhibited or performed at a local library, a community center, or other public venue. Through the exhibits the artists' works and the lives on which they are based are recognized as community assets.

The adult centers are usually located near a library recommended by a MEL-SA library member that already has an outreach relationship with the center or a desire to establish a relationship. Librarians from these libraries take part in the program, informing participants about the library's services and arts resources.

The Minnesota Creative Arts and Aging Network provides training for the artists, volunteers, local librarians, and adult-care center staff regarding the benefits of creativity in later life. The training is especially valuable to teaching artists, many of whom have limited experience working with older adults.

PARTNERS AND FUNDING Art for Life Residencies is a joint project of MELSA and the Minnesota Creative Arts and Aging Network and involves local libraries and adult-care centers in twenty-four Twin Cities neighborhoods. Support derives from the Minnesota Legacy Amendment Arts and Cultural Heritage Fund, which enables MELSA to develop cultural programs and partnerships with and for member libraries serving audiences in the Twin Cities.

Art Workshops for Adults
Pima County Public Library, Tucson, Arizona
www.library.pima.gov

WHAT Art Workshops for Adults, presented at fifteen branches of the Pima County Library over the course of 2011/12, introduce participants to drawing from observation and creating handmade books. The program is offered in conjunction with The Drawing Studio (TDS, www.thedrawingstudio.org), known for its teaching programs in which practicing artists work with older adults in varied community settings. The Art Workshops are part of the Pima County Public Library's ongoing Fit for Life 50+ program. By teaming up with The Drawing Studio, the library is enabling midlife adults in Tucson to take part in a substantive visual learning experience.

GOAL To transform neighborhood libraries into "social centers for active living at age 50 and beyond, places where individuals can learn something new, connect with others, nurture artistic abilities, and share their talents and wisdom."

FEATURES Fifteen local libraries in the Pima County system are hosting Art Workshops for Adults, most of them offering the full sequence of eight 90-minute sessions. The workshop series is organized around the same components used by The Drawing Studio in its Outreach Art Tutoring for Seniors (OATS) program, including practicing drawing skills to create interesting compositions and creating handmade books that combine words, drawings, photos, and collage.[1] The program announcement states: "Instructors emphasize that the practice of art is a lifelong exploration."

PARTNERS AND FUNDING The workshops involve a partnership between the Pima County Public Library's Fitness for Life 50+ program and The Drawing Studio's OATS program. The programs have complementary purposes and through collaboration the two organizations are leveraging each others' assets for the benefit of midlife and older adults in Tucson.

Support for Art Workshops for Adults is provided by the Friends of the Pima County Public Library. In addition to the library's funds, The Drawing Studio receives grants from local foundations that help ensure free participation in the workshops. Initial funding for the overall Fitness for Life 50+ program was provided through an LSTA grant administered by the Arizona State Library, Archives and Public Record.

Note

    1. For more information, see "Outreach Art Tutoring for Seniors (OATS)," The Drawing Studio, www.thedrawingstudio.org/programs_seniors.html.

Celebrate Arts and Aging / Creative Conversations
Free Library of Philadelphia, Philadelphia, Pennsylvania
www.freelibrary.org

WHAT This exhibition of works by older artists and a panel discussion on aging and creativity were organized to coincide with the citywide Celebrate the Arts and Aging Festival in May 2011. The project provided a showcase for the artists and stimulated community dialogue about the links between aging and the arts.

GOAL To highlight the talent and creativity of older Philadelphians.

FEATURES The month-long exhibit included artworks by artists age 55 and above, both professional artists and those who took up art in their later years. The exhibit was organized by the Philadelphia Corporation for the Aging (www .pcacares.org) in honor of Older Americans Month. For the opening of the exhibition, the library's Central Senior Services Department organized a "Creative Conversation" that featured experts discussing the links between aging and the creative process.

PARTNERS AND FUNDING Project partners were the Philadelphia Corporation for the Aging and the Creative Arts and Aging Network. The citywide festival was sponsored by a large number of corporations, local businesses, and agencies.

Creative Aging in Our Communities: The Libraries Project
National Program
http://lifetimearts.org

WHAT This model for helping public libraries provide effective, high-quality instructional arts programs for their active older adult populations was developed by Lifetime Arts, a national organization that "exists at the intersection of aging and the arts." First demonstrated at libraries in the Westchester County (New York) Library System, Creative Aging in Our Communities has now been implemented in library systems in New York City and will soon be expanding to libraries throughout New York State and nationwide (see In-Brief).

The Lifetime Arts model for library-based creative aging programs reflects the organization's commitment to building collaboration between teaching artists and public librarians to implement and sustain professionally conducted, free arts programs for older adults. It also reflects Lifetime Arts' recognition of the potential for public libraries to engage older adults in varied forms of creative expression. Through its involvement with the national community of teaching artists and arts education organizations, Lifetime Arts has brought libraries into the national discussion about creativity and aging and is helping reposition libraries as key centers for creative aging.

GOAL To help public libraries respond to the growing demand for high-quality programming for an aging population and to enhance the quality of life for active older adults through participatory arts programming.

FEATURES Lifetime Arts works cooperatively in specific communities to apply the Creative Aging in Our Communities model, which involves a partnership between Lifetime Arts and a library system. Individual libraries within the system are given the opportunity to apply for competitive grants of up to $5,000, which must be developed by the library in partnership with a local teaching artist. Libraries approved for the grants partner with teaching artists to design and deliver programs that engage older adults in participatory, sequential, socially interactive art making. The grants to libraries cover the costs of engaging the teaching artists and implementing and marketing the proposed program series.

All arts disciplines (visual, performing, and literary arts) are supported through the Creative Aging in Our Communities model, and all local programs culminate in a public exhibition or performance. Programs target high-functioning, older adults including baby boomers and active members of older generations. Participants in current programs range in age from 54 to 95.

Lifetime Arts' role is to work with the local system to administer the programs, provide technical assistance to the program sites, and evaluate the programs.

> The Westchester Libraries Project provided older adults with a unique outlet to express themselves artistically in the comfort of their local library. It was wonderful to witness the creative energy at each participating library.
>
> —**Terry Kirchner, executive director, Westchester Library System**

Lifetime Arts also provides professional development for participating librarians, covering administrative, programmatic, and funding practices that can lead to institutionalizing and sustaining robust creative aging programs.

Lifetime Arts has carried out two yearlong phases of Creative Aging in Our Communities at thirteen libraries in the Westchester County Library System, the most recent being 2009/10. That work will continue in 2012. Lifetime Arts has also led a yearlong pilot project at six libraries in the New York Public Library System. That project is being repeated and expanded to thirty-four locations in Brooklyn, Queens, Staten Island, and Manhattan. Planning is also under way for expansion of the program to libraries across New York State and in other states.

PARTNERS AND FUNDING Lifetime Arts' funding has derived primarily from private foundations, including the Fan Fox and Leslie R. Samuels Foundation, the Helen Andrus Benedict Foundation, and the New York State Council on the Arts. Starting in 2012, with support from the IMLS, Lifetime Arts will expand Creative Aging in Our Communities to rural and suburban library systems in New York State. In addition, funding from the Metlife Foundation will enable expansion in 2012 to Miami, Dallas, and Boston.

IN-BRIEF: LIFETIME ARTS SITES, NEW YORK

Creative Aging in Our Communities
Westchester Libraries Over the course of two funding phases, 2009 and 2010, more than three hundred older adults took part in seventeen sequential instructional Lifetime Arts workshop series at thirteen libraries across Westchester County. The libraries applied to take part in the program and received grants of between $2,500 and $4,000. They worked with local teaching artists to design and provide arts classes relevant to local adults' learning interests. Participants from 60 to 95 years old danced, painted, wrote memoirs, and made collages, murals, and ceramic tiles. A culminating exhibition and performance celebrated the skills acquired and the art works produced. Funding was provided by the Helen Andrus Benedict Foundation.

Creative Aging in Our Communities
New York City Libraries Lifetime Arts worked with the New York Public Library in 2010 to test the Creative Aging in Our Communities model in community libraries in Staten Island, the Bronx, and Manhattan. Libraries interested in participating were matched with teaching artists with whom they designed an instructional program relevant to their communities. Through a competitive grants process six libraries were selected to carry out the free instructional arts programs, including promoting them to the active older adults in their service areas. A wide variety of art forms were employed in the local programs. The project was evaluated by the Fordham University's Ravazzin Center on Aging. Based on positive results, the Fan Fox and Leslie R. Samuels Foundation provided a second round of funding, enabling project expansion

to thirty libraries in 2011, including libraries in the Brooklyn Public Library system. Hundreds of New Yorkers from four of the city's five boroughs will be able to take advantage of high-quality arts instruction in their neighborhoods.

Creative Cabaret Project: One Dance at a Time

Mount Vernon Public Library Working and learning together at the library, Mt. Vernon's older adult participants scripted, staged, and performed a musical based on their collective interests and skills. With instruction in a variety of art forms, everyone played a part in the production. (www.mountvernonpubliclibrary.org)

The Drawing Experience

Somers Public Library Building on successful watercolor and acrylic painting workshops, this series of nine instructional sessions at the library in Somers taught participants basic drawing techniques with a thematic focus on the town of Somers. Workshops were enhanced with art history discussions and local sketching excursions in collaboration with the Somers Historical Society. (www.somerslibrary.org)

Life Maps

Countee Cullen Branch, Manhattan Focusing on line, texture, point of view, and color, participants at the Countee Cullen branch examined a variety of maps and the work of map artists such as Romare Bearden. Using new understanding of the principles of art and design, and new skills in the use of basic collage vocabularies, materials, tools, and techniques, they created their own life map collages. (www.nypl.org/locations/countee-cullen)

LiveStories: A Personal Journey through Memoir and Performance

Grand Central Library, Manhattan Through memoir writing and performance, participants at the Grand Central branch reflected on their lives, found ways to express their unique personal voices, and learned skills for documenting and sharing their experiences with others. They were introduced to the work of established writers working in the area of memoir, including Edwidge Danticant and Spalding Gray. The series culminated in a live collaborative performance of original written work by members of the workshop. (www.nypl.org/locations/grand-central)

Memoir Tiles

Chappaqua Library Participants in this interdisciplinary project at Chappaqua Library wrote memoir "snapshots" and converted them into sketches and then into sculpted, glazed ceramic tiles. The written memoir snapshots have been compiled into a book with photos of the corresponding tiles. The tiles will be added to a frieze on the exterior of the library. (www.chappaqualibrary.org)

Roaring Chorus Workshops for Older Staten Island Adults

West New Brighton Library Branch, Staten Island At the West New Brighton branch, forty-two older adults received sequential, skill-based music instruction focused on vocal training, introduction to basic harmony and music theory, basic ear training, and chorus singing. The repertoire focused on popular music of the twentieth century, including works by Gershwin, Porter, and Mancini. (www.nypl.org/locations/west-new-brighton)

Sanctuary for Creativity

Riverfront Branch, Yonkers Public Library The Riverfront branch created a Sanctuary for Creativity, an environment within the library for older adults to express themselves through the arts. Participants in this eight-week workshop interpreted their unique life stories through mixed media collage, incorporating both words and imagery. (www.ypl.org/riverfront)

Seniors Come Out Swinging

Grinton I. Will Branch, Yonkers Public Library Two simultaneous workshop series were offered at the Will branch, each geared to engage participants in a final public performance. One workshop was in ballroom dance and one in visual arts, where participants designed, painted, and installed a stage set and program for the culminating dance performance at the library. Participants selected one of the two series and met twice weekly. All participants took part in the final performance, as dancers or as contributors to the stage design. (www.ypl.org/grinton)

Sing for Life, Sing for Joy

Baychester Branch, Bronx A ten-session choral program responded to the interests of older adult residents of Co-op City, one of the city's largest concentrations of seniors. The program focused on a capella singing to encourage vocal improvement and to help build a sense of community. Participants learned about vocal and performance techniques, music theory, improvisation, and composition while enjoying music making and exploring folk music and spirituals. (www.nypl.org/locations/baychester)

Creativity and Aging Forums

Metropolitan Library Services Association, Minneapolis, Minnesota

www.melsa.org

WHAT Despite the growth of instructional arts programs that engage older adults and promote positive aging, there is a dearth of opportunities for librarians to learn about the new research on which these types of programs are based. These forums offered librarians from the Metropolitan Library Services Association's (MELSA) Twin Cities service area an opportunity to learn about recent research and its implications for practice from one of the leading national experts on arts and aging, Susan Pearlstein, founder of Elders Share the Arts (www.estanyc .org) and the National Center for Creative Aging (www.creativeaging.org). The forums also welcomed other service professionals into the conversation and provided access to research information for members of the general public.

GOAL To promote awareness of new research on the benefits of the arts for positive aging.

FEATURES Creativity and Aging consisted of two presentations, one for librarians and health services professionals and one for members of the public. More than one hundred individuals attended the public program. Held at Hennepin County Library, the programs were scheduled to complement the Art of Aging exhibit (see above) on display during the summer of 2010.

In both forums, Pearlstein examined the connections between daily life and creative aging, focusing on arts and lifelong learning, arts and community engagement, and the use of arts in social service and health care settings. She drew from her work at the Center on Aging, Health, and Humanities at George Washington University, including the landmark research by Dr. Gene Cohen, to talk about the positive benefits of engaging in arts and cultural programs, such as improvement of the immune system, fostering a sense of mastery and control, and improvement in social engagement.[1]

Pearlstein also offered recommendations for continuing innovations in the fields of arts and aging in the coming decades. The interactive sessions engaged people in discussions about the types of art and creativity that influenced their lives.

PARTNERS AND FUNDING The Creativity and Aging forums were organized by MELSA in collaboration with the Vital Aging Network (www.vital-aging-network.org) and the Hennepin County Library. MELSA's 50+ Services Committee helped to organize and market the forum for professionals. Minnesota's Arts and Cultural Heritage Fund supported the two forums through monies allocated for MELSA and its cultural partnerships.

Note

1. See Gene Cohen, *The Mature Mind: The Positive Power of the Aging Brain* (New York: Basic Books, 2006).

Senior Art Exhibit
Hammond Public Library, Hammond, Indiana
www.hammond.lib.in.us

WHAT Hammond Public Library puts on an annual juried exhibition of artworks by artists age 55 and above. Although many libraries showcase local artists as part of their community arts activities, there are few occasions when they feature work by older artists. This library's unusual effort to shine a light on midlife and older artists demonstrates a means by which libraries can celebrate lifelong creativity and promote positive aging.

GOAL To showcase works by 50+ artists.

FEATURES The Hammond Library's annual Senior Art Exhibit started in 1994. Until then, the library had featured local artists' throughout the year. The library director at the time, Arthur Myers, became concerned about the lack of older artists included in the displays. In 2000 he established a partnership with the then Northern Indiana Art Association (NIAA) to exhibit works at both the Main Library and NIAA's Hammond location, Substation No. 9. With the exception of several years when the exhibit was suspended, it has been continuous.

> There are a lot of good older artists out there. It's competitive, and it's growing.
>
> —Betty DeLink, artist showing at the 2010 Senior Art Exhibit, Hammond Public Library

According to display curator Scott Kingry, both the quality and quantity of the art submitted for the Senior Art Exhibit have increased each year. Artists are allowed two possible entries in a variety of media. The greatest growth has come since 2009, a reflection of the increase in older adults in the region and the state.

PARTNERS AND FUNDING The library exhibit is a partnership with the NIAA. For the past three years, as the project has grown, the Friends of the Hammond Public Library has provided support to cover exhibit expenses and an opening reception.

Story Circle / Elders Share the Arts
Brooklyn Public Library, Brooklyn, New York
www.brooklynpubliclibrary.org, www.estanyc.org

WHAT In partnership with the Brooklyn-based Elders Share the Arts (ESTA), Brooklyn Public Library's Services to the Aging Department offers Story Circle, a series of reminiscence-based storytelling workshops. Story Circle offers low-income midlife and older adults the opportunity to create photos and books that reflect personal stories and memories. The program demonstrates the value of the ESTA approach and how it can be incorporated in a library setting. It also reflects Brooklyn Public Library's commitment to participatory arts programming for older adults.

GOAL To provide elders with opportunities to find their stories, develop a voice, hear the stories of the group, and reflect on commonalities and differences.

FEATURES Story Circle is conducted by ESTA in local branches of the Brooklyn Public Library. The programs are led by professional artists who are also arts educators trained in ESTA's method, combining oral history and art. Older adults are matched with a writer who helps shape their oral reminiscences. Programs move from the oral to the written and involve public readings, presentations, and bookmaking. The branch libraries provide collection resources to support and enhance program activities.

The Story Circle method aims to foster both creative expression and social interaction. Participants build skills in creative writing and photography throughout the program while improving self-esteem, speaking and singing skills, posture, breath support, and relaxation techniques. Story Circle culminates in a community celebration and presentation of participants' work in an extended exhibit.

PARTNERS AND FUNDING Story Circle is offered though a partnership between the library's Services to the Aging Department and ESTA, a Brooklyn-based organization that specializes in intergenerational arts programs that bring together the old and young through a unique synthesis of oral history and arts called "Living History Arts." ESTA provides a broad range of arts programming—creative writing, storytelling, visual arts, theater—for older adults at varied community sites, including libraries.

Story Circle is currently funded by the Metlife Foundation. Brooklyn Public Library provides staff support, space, and publicity for the program.

IN-BRIEF: 50+ CREATIVITY AROUND THE COUNTRY

Creativity: Aging and Professional Success

Free Library of Philadelphia, Central Senior Services The Free Library's Central Senior Services offers regular forums on topics of interest to midlife and older active adults. This conversation in February 2011 focused on American cultural icons who "found success late in life." The program moderator asked "What did they have in common and how did they do it?" (www.freelibrary.org)

"It's a Wonderful Life" Live Radio Play

Boulder (Colorado) Public Library Boulder's Society for Creative Aging produces an annual fall performance at the Boulder Public Library, using the talents of both their older members and others in the community. Another sponsor has been the Boulder International Fringe Festival. (www.s4ca.org/Home.html) Live at the Library

Live at the Library

Anoka County (Minnesota) Library All eight branches of the Anoka County Library participate in an annual Live at the Library day, which showcases "some of the great talent and cultural resources in the county." More than thirty performing and visual artists, many of them midlife adults, share their talents with the community. Performances include folk music, pottery, quilting, and Ukrainian egg decorating. (www.anoka.lib.mn.us)

Owl: Older Writers Laboratory

San Francisco (California) Public Library San Francisco Public has hosted this special "laboratory" for older poets for many years. Participants join together regularly to share their work at the library. (www.sfpl.org)

Stagebridge Theater Company

San Francisco (California) Public Library The Stagebridge Company, made up of actors ages 50–90, is dedicated to narrowing the gap between generations and presenting positive images of older adults via theater arts classes, workshops, healthy-aging programs, and public performances. As part of the San Francisco Public Library's WiseUp! Learn and Live Well at Any Age program, the company presented a sampler of it performances for midlife adults attending the class "Staying Engaged for a Lifetime." (www.sfpl.org)

STARS: Senior Theatre Acting Repertory

The Queens (New York) Library hosts weekly workshops for older adults interested in performing theatrical works. The most recent series was in fall 2011. (www.queenslibrary.org)

CHAPTER 8

INFORMATION AND COMMUNITY CONNECTIONS

As aging baby boomers make the transition to retirement, they need sources for life direction and social connections.

—Marc Freedman, president, Civic Ventures

s individuals in midlife shed old responsibilities, assume new ones, and transition to and through one or two new life stages, they go through a process of self-discovery and usually explore multiple pathways. To do so, they require information, ideas, connections, and models—exactly the resources libraries are in the business to provide. Libraries have a unique opportunity to offer a hub, both physical and virtual, where midlife adults can find what they need to navigate personal, economic, and social transitions.

TRENDS

When midlife adults turn 45, then 50, 55, and so on, many start to come to grips with the fact that their lives may be significantly longer than they had ever dreamed, and that they will be healthier and more active through their seventies and even eighties than previous generations. In all likelihood they will experience several decades of "bonus years," years for which they are unprepared. This relatively recent demographic phenomenon, resulting from increased longevity, is adding years to the middle of the lifespan, after full-time parenting or work but before the frailty or disability of elderhood.

Faced with these realities, how are midlife adults responding? How are they planning for their bonus years? How are they revising plans for "retirement" to take into account their interests, talents, financial resources, and personal responsibilities?

Above all, midlife adults are seeking information, lots of information, to help them make decisions about next steps. They are seeking ideas and models for how other people are living their bonus years. And, too, they are seeking opportunities to explore their options with others facing the same realities and choices.

In this Information Age there is a dizzying array of sources, both traditional sources such as books and newer sources such as e-books, virtual information centers, and blogs. Midlife adults have many information options and seem to be taking advantage of them all. For some, the traditional formats such as printed books, magazines, and face-to-face conversations are still preferred. In fact, publishers are responding to the coming of age of baby boomers and the phenomenon of the bonus years with a raft of new publications—publications on brain fitness and retirement budgeting as well as stories of midlife crises and tips for choosing second careers. There are workbooks for life planning, magazines on style and health, and guides to eating, relocating, caregiving, and grandparenting.

Ironically, although these types of publications are expanding, it is not easy to find them. Whether readers search Amazon.com or at their public library, informational sources on midlife or the bonus years are distributed across subject areas, from autobiography to accounting to caregiving. There is, as yet, no consistently adopted subject category equivalent to teen lit for what might be called "midlife lit."

In addition to books and periodicals, face-to-face contact with experts or trusted individuals continues to be an important source of information for those moving into their "third age." They are turning to different people sources for information on educational opportunities, volunteering, starting a business, or insurance options. These sources range from trusted peers with experience and contacts to college advisors, employment counselors, accounting specialists, and service agency staff. There is even a profession known as life planning (aka life coaching, life mapping) that is becoming more established with the aging of baby boomers.

Just as with published information sources, sources of personal advice are widely scattered with little collective visibility. Access is random at best. Even the purveyors of life planning services operate independently, and there is no primary information hub on their qualifications and whereabouts. Local senior centers may have much information relevant to midlife transitions, but a majority of midlife adults do not identify with the term "senior" and avoid senior centers, even those that are updating their services to appeal to a younger crowd. There is no one community location, no one-stop place for questions and conversations on the concerns of 50+ adults.

Beyond traditional information sources, there is a wide new world of virtual information and "community" for 50+ adults: websites, podcasts, YouTube presentations, blogs, online forums, Twitter conversations, and other forms of social media. These seem to be proliferating as fast as boomers turn 65. They range from Baby Boomer Lifeboat (www.babyboomerlifeboat .com), a website that provides "Tips for Comfortably Retiring on a Limited Income," to Life Over 50 (www .life-over-50.com), a more personally designed website organized around "Family, Home and Gardening, Tech and Finance, Travel, Health." Life Over 50 even offers online dancing lessons.

Some online information sources are developed by actual organizations that promote meet-ups, conferences, and face-to-face communications to reinforce a sense of community and foster shared interests. The Transition Network (www.thetransitionnetwork.org), for example, is a virtual and actual national network of professional women who share experiences of life transitions. Whether they are commercially motivated or organized from a nonprofit perspective, these digital sources and places both complement and substitute for traditional information sources.

One of the largest sources of online information for 50+ adults is Eons (www.eons.com), a social network and information portal organized around "Fun, Love,

Don't despair if you are a Boomer, or a Silent, or a Greatest— the public library is with you every step of the way. Chances are you grew up going to your public library. But people have changed; they take advantage of the myriad options now available for getting information and spending leisure time. And libraries have changed; the passing of the card catalog since the 1980s has left some bereft of a lifelong friend. Libraries throughout the U.S. constantly retool to meet the needs of library users and, as librarians, we welcome the 50+ population, in its millions of manifestations, through our physical and virtual doors.

—Brigid Cahalan,
Next Chapter blog,
New York Public Library

Money, Body, Goals, Obits, and Lifemaps." Eons states that it is "the online community for Boomers" and features cRanking, the "first age-relevant search engine." The increase in the number of advertisers joining Eons demonstrates the extent to which businesses increasingly see 50+ adults as an important consumer market.

IMPLICATIONS FOR LIBRARIES

In this busy information environment, with so many sources and options, access to relevant and trustworthy information on life transitions seems increasingly difficult. Seeking information and connections to guide their next steps, midlife adults are confronted with a dizzying array of sources with agendas and biases that may not be in their best interests. Although this is a challenge for the public, herein lies an opportunity for libraries, which are uniquely equipped as trustworthy hubs for the provision of information in both traditional and emerging formats. In fact, if only through their information services, libraries have the potential to become essential centers for midlife inquiry, discovery, and planning.

Most midlife adults are familiar with the library as a source of information in traditional formats: print materials, subject guides, information and referral services ("I&R"), and directories of community resources. In addition, some libraries have augmented community referral services by organizing fairs or expositions that directly link midlife adults to opportunities for work, community service, or education, as well as sources for improved health and fitness. The traditional information sources and services still exist, although many are duplicated or adapted to an online environment. At the same time, traditional sources are now enhanced by digital sources and new communications technologies, including but not limited to web pages, blogs and online forums with experts or peers, matching services (for volunteering or dating), podcasts and audiotapes, community services directories, guides to local and national lifelong learning opportunities, and social media. From books to blogs, from fairs to Facebook, libraries offer an unparalleled array of resources for informing and connecting 50+ individuals and helping them navigate their transition to new life stages.

The fact that libraries are organized to promote access to all sources, for people of all ages and backgrounds, underscores their potential to become information hubs for 50+ adults. Yet not all libraries are ready to make the changes required to fulfill this potential. Many librarians still cling to outdated stereotypes of seniors as infirm, isolated, and dependent. Their attitudes and practices do not take into account the bonus years and the vitality and diversity of baby boomers and other active older adults. Most do not distinguish between seniors and 50+ adults, or even between adults and 50+ adults, in terms of their collections, readers' advisories, blogs, directories, expositions, or, especially, library websites. Most still use "seniors" as an umbrella term for all older adults, and very few have a place on their home pages that welcomes 50+ adults as a key population group.

Unless and until more libraries change the prevailing paradigm for organizing and identifying older adult services, libraries' information assets will be invisible and libraries' potential as sources for midlife development will be unrealized.

The challenge for librarians is to make sure that the information they have is relevant *and visible* to midlife information seekers. If midlife adults do not know that the library can point them to training or retraining opportunities, suggest credible websites for research on health or financial issues, provide access to specialized business or professional databases, or help them set up a Facebook account—then all the collecting, training, organizing, investing, and digitizing libraries are doing will be in vain.

Despite the predominance of outdated terms and practices, some libraries are on the way to fulfilling their potential as information hubs for 50+ adults. They are proving that their long-respected expertise in information services can benefit their midlife patrons, and they are offering a visible, trusted, physical, and virtual space for information exchange between peers.

As the following examples make clear, some libraries are making changes in their terminology, the structure of their websites, the scope of their information services, and their uses of social media. In so doing they are starting to position themselves as essential sources for midlife adults. From New York Public Library's *Next Chapter* blog to Torrance Public Library's LINK web pages, there are examples of library experiments emerging that can be adapted by other institutions. Although these experiments are works in progress that are constantly subject to updating and refinement, they offer instructive models for other libraries working to strengthen their 50+ information services.

50 Plus

Daniel Boone Regional Library, Columbia, Missouri

www.dbrl.org/reference/subject-guides/50-plus

WHAT A subject guide and resources directory.

CONTENT 50 Plus is a thorough and clearly organized directory of information sources, community agencies, and other resources that reflects a conscious emphasis on midlife adults. Two features stand out: the Live & Learn section is particularly substantive, including local, national, and international learning resources; and the Featured Articles on topics relevant to midlife adults are well selected and updated often.

The 50 Plus directory offers these categories:

- Directory of County Services
- References on Elder Law and Estate Planning; Health, Eldercare and Support Groups; Live & Learn; Social Activities, Networks and Organizations; Put Your Experience to Work; Retirement; Transportation; and Volunteering
- Other Helpful Websites
- Featured Articles

50 Plus

Thomas Crane Public Library, Quincy, Massachusetts

https://thomascranelibrary.org/50plus

WHAT 50 Plus is an online resource center for midlife and older adults coupled with occasional programming targeted to this age group. It evolved from Next Chapter, Rewriting Midlife and Beyond, a project developed as part of a training and start-up grant provided jointly by the Massachusetts Board of Library Commissioners and Libraries for the Future using LSTA funds. Funding enabled the library to create the online directory, which is now sustained as part of core library offerings for midlife adults.

CONTENT The 50 Plus site is designed to "connect 50+ adults to essential information in print and online, to connect them to community organizations and other resources, and to alert them to programs in the library and in the community." It is organized around life planning, money management, and wellness, three key concepts that emerged during the two-year Next Chapter project. The site provides an annotated list of community organizations and services relevant to midlife issues. Although not listed on the library website home page, the 50 Plus site can be accessed through a search tool.

Adults 50+ @ the Library
Pierce County Library, Pierce County, Washington
www.piercecountylibrary.org/services/adults-50

WHAT An online directory of services, informational sources, and events.

CONTENT The site is clearly focused on 50+ adults, providing a comprehensive portal to library activities and community learning opportunities, with information on periodicals, book recommendations, classes, special events, e-services, and other services "useful for active older adults." The activities listed include those for general adult audiences. By highlighting these on the 55+ site, the library indicates that participation by midlife adults is welcome and appropriate. The list of links to lifelong learning resources in the Seattle area is especially thorough. In addition, the list of book recommendations—"Adults 50+ Book List"—is one of only a handful around the country that provide guidance on reading resources for midlife adults.

50+ and Older Adults
DeKalb Public Library
www.dkpl.org/seniors/seniors.html

WHAT A web page that offers an overview of activities, services, and informational materials relevant to boomers and other older adults.

CONTENT The DeKalb Library uses the web page to draw 50+ adults' attention to particular subject categories and collections, such as travel books and travel logs on DVD, genealogy resources, and magazines on photography, where to retire, and more. Readers are invited to check the library calendar to learn about book clubs in which they might participate. In addition, the web page includes links to national or local organizations with information on the categories Health and Fitness, Personal Money and Finance, Fun and Travel, and Local Links. By listing subject categories that could interest midlife adults, the web page enhances access to relevant sources.

The Art of Living: Age 50 and Beyond
Toledo Lucas County Library, Toledo Ohio
http://database.toledolibrary.org/senior

WHAT A web page that directs older adults to library resources and other useful links.

CONTENT In addition to an overview of library collections, services and events, The Art of Living pages include links to community resources and information on travel and entertainment, health and wellness, financial and legal issues, and education and jobs.

The library's home page has a tab titled "Seniors," but the actual web page to which the tab leads indicates a broader reach and the inclusion of information relevant to midlife adults. This approach is not uncommon, thanks to a lack of standardized terminology for 50+ adults, but it can be confusing for those browsing home page topics for information relevant to midlife.

Baby Boomer Resources
Tompkins County Public Library, Ithaca, New York
http://tcpl.libguides/com/boomers

WHAT An online guide to materials that can be useful to baby boomers seeking information about life transitions.

CONTENT The Baby Boomer Resource guide includes listings of books and DVDs, databases, local organizations, magazines, and other guides. It includes a link to an excellent booklist that could be helpful to other libraries trying to build a collection to support 50+ services.

Fifty-Five +

Cincinnati-Hamilton County Library, Cincinnati, Ohio

www.cincinnatilibrary.org/fiftyfiveplus

WHAT A special website for 55+ adults, inaugurated in 2010, that helps the library "continue to meet the changing needs of the community." Although the site is titled "Fifty-Five +," it offers services and resources relevant to both mid-life adults and homebound older adults.

CONTENT Fifty-Five + is organized around selected resources from the library's collection and the web. Categories include Book Discussion Groups, Caregiving, Grandparents, Health and Wellness, Getting Started in Genealogy, Retirement, and Technology.

Fifty-Five + is highly visible on the library's home page, with the same prominence given to sections on teens and children. Its title and placement, as well as the diverse content, are clear signals that the library is trying to broaden its definition of older adults and provide information for everyone 55 and over.

In the KNOW 55+

Tulsa City-County Library, Tulsa, Oklahoma

www.tulsalibrary.org/55plus

WHAT A special section of the Tulsa City-County Library's web page that offers information for midlife adults. Like many other such sites, it also includes information for seniors.

CONTENT In the KNOW 55+ is organized into six sections: Use the Library; Travel and Leisure; Community Resources; Health, Wellness and Caregiving; Legal Issues; and Computer and Technology. The listings for each of these categories include library materials as well as local and national organizations.

The website has a regular feature for 55+ adults called "In the Spotlight." During July and August 2011, the featured service was the library's Job Lab, where in a dedicated space adults and anyone else can update their resumes, search for jobs online, or explore a new career. This feature is an effective way of promoting specific library services and encouraging visits to the library.

Lifelong Learners
Oak Bluff Public Library, Vineyard Haven, Massachusetts
www.oakbluffslibrary.org/lifelong_learners.shtml

WHAT A web page that offers information on library programs and community resources of interest to 50+ adults.

CONTENT The Lifelong Learners web page developed out of a program series called Illuminations for Lifelong Learning that was funded by the Massachusetts Board of Library Commissioners through its Equal Access Libraries–Lifelong Access training and grants program with Libraries for the Future (see chapter 1). The web page content includes information on library collections—Books and More—and library events as well as community and web resources on finances, health, work and activism, home and garden, local history, and technology.

The May 2012 web page features an online survey being used to collect feedback from the community about the Illuminations for Lifelong Learning program and to help plan future 50+ programs and services. The site encourages patron input and indicates continuing commitment to programming relevant to midlife adults. It is an excellent means of building closer relationships with viewers and helping them understand that they have an opportunity to help shape library services.

Lifelong Information, Networks, and Knowledge
Torrance Public Library, Torrance, California
http://www.torranceca.gov/Library/18147.htm

WHAT Web pages accessed via the Torrance Public Library's website that increase midlife adults' access to the educational, informational, cultural, and recreational opportunities in the region.

CONTENT Lifelong Information, Networks, and Knowledge (LINK) includes three major features:

- *LINK Logs* is a blog created by the Torrance Public Library staff for communication with library patrons. Its purpose is to "connect Baby Boomers to the information and people that will help them achieve their life goals." Topics covered include finances, health, travel, and more, as well as community information and library services. *LINK Logs* is designed to be interactive; readers are encouraged to post ideas and communicate with others in an extended online community.

- Podcasts provide access to interviews with key local officials and volunteers as well as recordings of community meetings on topics relevant to boomers.
- Resources offer an annotated list of local, state, and national information sources on the following topics: Computers, Science and Information; Health, Sports and Fitness; Home Improvement; Reading; Religion; Retirement; Transportation; and Travel.

The content of the LINK pages as well as the prominently placed title of that section on the library's home page reflect a clear focus on baby boomers. LINK emerged from the LINK project undertaken in 2009, supported through an LSTA grant administered by the State Library of California through its Transforming Life After 50 initiative. The first phase of the project involved a community needs assessment to determine the information and services needs of midlife adults.

LINK is one of the best examples of a site designed specifically for 50+ adults. The library's home page offers a direct link to LINK through a button titled "LINK—Resources for Boomers." The variety of information formats enriches the site. And the Link Log blog consists of well-written and well-researched pieces on such topics as "Libraries and Technology."

Live Well, Age Smart: Senior Resource Guide
San Antonio Public Library, San Antonio, Texas
http://guides.mysapl.org/seniors

WHAT Live Well, Age Smart is the umbrella title for San Antonio Public Library's special programs for older adults. The online component, the Senior Resource Guide, provides information on library services, online sources, and local organizations for seniors. Although the title is "Senior Resource Guide," the target audience on the site is identified as "baby boomers and other older adults."

CONTENT The guide has information on a variety of resources including Live Well, Age Smart programs, favorite books, audiovisual materials, links to the library on social media sites, senior group magazines, and "Learning Activities for Baby Boomers and Beyond" (local lifelong learning and sports opportunities). Examples of the library's Live Well, Age Smart programs are "Sage-ing Circle," "Road Scholar/Elder Hostel Introduction," and "Tai Chi for Health."

Live Well, Age Smart is an example of a library website that is starting to make a distinction between baby boomers and seniors but continues to market its information services for both groups in the same way and the same place. In fact, the site uses "Seniors," "Senior Group," and "Baby Boomers and Beyond" for different categories of information, but without explaining the distinctions in audiences or services.

Live Well, Age Smart also exemplifies the fact that many libraries have developed resource guides and web pages specifically for older adults but do not promote them on their home pages. The only way to find Live Well, Age Smart is to encounter a program listing on the general library calendar; the only way to find the Senior Resource Guide is to go to the web page that lists all of the library's subject guides. Without visibility on the home page, the library's effort to organize and provide information for older adults is relatively invisible to the very people it could benefit.

One excellent feature of this web page is the inclusion of a photo and name of the staff member who prepared the online information. This personalizes the site and reduces the anonymity so characteristic of online guides.

Multnomah County Library Podcasts
Multnomah County Public Library, Portland, Oregon
http://multcolib.libsyn.com/category/Life%20by%20Design

WHAT For several years the Multnomah County Library, in partnership with Life by Design NW, has offered events "exploring Positive Aging and supporting the 50+ community" (see chapter 2). The resulting podcasts are available through the library's website, along with videotaped portraits of 50+ library volunteers.

CONTENT The Multnomah County Library Podcasts web page offers online access to events, interviews, and special recordings of expert presentations at the library. Gift People is a series of recorded conversations with four exemplary 50+ volunteers. They discuss their lives and interests and what motivates their commitment to civic engagement. Life by Design @ your library: Perspectives on Positive Aging documents events and materials under such titles as "Creating a Portfolio Life," "Taking Care of Your Aging Parent," "Living More Authentically as We Age," and "Taking Care of You: Powerful Tools for Caregivers."

The podcasts are an exceptional means for documenting and expanding public access to special presentations held at the library and also for signaling the library's ongoing commitment to the concerns of midlife adults. The Gift People section is especially effective, providing real-life models of individuals who have committed significant amounts of time to community service—through their library. The podcasts can be downloaded for personal computers or MP3 players. Partial support for the podcast program was provided through an LSTA grant through the Oregon State Library.

Next Chapter: Social Media and a 50+ Resource Fair
New York Public Library, New York, New York
www.nypl.org/blog, www.nypl.org/voices/blogs/blog-channels/next-chapter

WHAT The New York Public Library *Next Chapter* blog, along with its entries on Facebook and Twitter feed, shares news and views focusing on 50+ adults. They are designed to promote awareness of the library as a central information resource for midlife New Yorkers and to provide an online forum for topics of concerns to the 50+ population.

In addition to the blog, the library organized a 50+ Resource Fair for older adults in 2009. The blog, the fair, and uses of social media all reflect the library's commitment to informing and supporting midlife New Yorkers. They are key components of the library's overall Next Chapter initiative, which includes programs, collection development, and events (see chapter 2).

CONTENT The *Next Chapter* blog is part of an emerging genre of specialist-librarian blogs designed to illuminate collections and services. It consists of regular entries by older adult specialist Brigid Cahalan that include news of upcoming events, observations on pertinent issues such as volunteering or brain fitness, recommended books or other media sources, and reports on library programs or other events. A reader forum that includes readers, library patrons, and librarians helps build a community conversation. The related Facebook page and Twitter feed focus on specific, timely topics drawn from the blog.

The blog topics often relate to key national events or special Next Chapter programs at the library. Sample topics:

- Work to Be Done: Volunteering over 50 (January 21, 2009)
- Women Making History in the Second Half of Life (March 23, 2010)
- Aging Creatively at the New York Public Library (August 2, 2010)
- An Organization Is Born—Welcome, Coming of Age, NYC (July 25, 2011)

The *Next Chapter* blog is one of the library's featured blog channels and may be accessed via the Blogs/Blog channels links on the website.

The 50+ Resource Fair One was an initial event organized under the Next Chapter initiative. Held at the Mid-Manhattan Library, it featured seventeen organizations that focus on education and volunteering. Each organization sent literature and representatives to speak with individual participants about their interests in service work or educational programming.

Since September 2008, New York Public Library's *Next Chapter* blog has provided a national leadership example in both its positioning and its content. The Next Chapter initiative is listed on the library's website, and the blog channel has equal standing with others offered by the library. The quality and scope of the blog are exemplary. Other libraries will find much to inspire and to adapt.

Older Adult Resources
Preble County District Library, Eaton, Ohio
www.pcdl.lib.oh.us/seniors

WHAT A section of the Preble County District Library website that provides information on library services, community services and activities, and online resources for "older adults," which in this case includes both seniors and midlife adults.

CONTENT The Older Adult Resources website is organized around several categories of informational listings. Three categories concentrate on resources and services geared to seniors: Library Services, Community Services, and Nursing Homes. The remainder include information useful to midlife adults, including Learning and Education, Health and Wellness, Independent Living, Food and Recipes, Fun and Games, Travel, Computers and Internet, and Interesting Links.

This site is an example of a transitional online resource that combines information for seniors who are homebound, isolated, and in need of assistance with information appropriate for active "older adults" (midlife adults) who are seeking educational and travel opportunities and interesting forms of entertainment. Surprisingly, there is no link to information on work or community service. The Interesting Links and Fun and Games sections are unusual, bringing together an array of unexpected resources including websites on how to play Yahtzee and one titled "Set My Clock."

Refresh Your Life
Hayward Public Library, Hayward, California
www.library.hayward-ca.gov

WHAT Refresh Your Life was the title of a grant-funded project to "support people in middle life with programs, events, materials, etc." The project was carried out in two phases, 2008/9 and 2009/10, under the auspices of the California State Library's Transforming Life After 50 initiative.[1] In addition to programming, the project included a blog, also titled *Refresh Your Life*, that continued beyond the grant project, with a focus on health and wellness.

CONTENT The original Refresh Your Life project started with a community survey to determine the needs and interests of midlife residents. Based on responses to the survey, the library organized nineteen programs on a wide variety of topics; titles included "A New Approach to Your Life and Work after 40," "Investor Education," and "Caring for Your Parents." More than a third of program participants were new to the library.

The *Refresh Your Life* blog, started in September 2008, was designed as a "a place to share thoughts and ideas about how we are refreshing our lives as well as to discuss ways the Hayward Public Library can support people in middle life." Trudy Toll, adult reference librarian, wrote periodic entries over the two years of the project on a variety of topics, some of which were directly relevant to the Refresh Your Life programs and some on other topics relevant to midlife adults. *Refresh Your Life* was an unusually comprehensive blog that addressed multiple issues important to adults going through midlife transitions. The personal tone, the quality of the writing, and the creativity in putting together the entries made this a superior example of a new genre: the library-based midlife blog.

Note

1 For the program's introduction, see www.refreshyourlife.wordpress.com/2008/09.

Senior Centered

Lake Villa District Library, Lake Villa, Illinois

http://test.lvdl.org/Seniors/tabid/273

WHAT Senior Centered is an informational page on the Lake Villa District Library website that focuses on midlife adults including active "seniors." It is a primary component of the library's Positively Senior: Cultivating an Optimistic Outlook on Aging project, funded by a 2007 LSTA grant through the State Library of Illinois.

> ### Cultivating an Optimistic Outlook on Aging
>
> How do you grow older gracefully in a youth-obsessed culture? Resolve to live your life to the fullest! Let the Lake Villa District Library help you get the most out of each day.
>
> —Lake Villa District Library, Positively Senior web page

CONTENT Senior Centered is organized around broad categories of information, with titles such as "Keep Fit," "Share Your Skills," and "Get Out and About." The web page is designed to provide information and links to library and community resources that promote positive aging. According to reference librarian Suzanne Neumann, "the Lake Villa District Library wants to encourage seniors in our district to view the aging process as one of enrichment rather than solely of decline."

Although the website is titled "Senior Centered," the tone and content are directed to active, independent 50+ residents. The organization of the page, with broad categories of information at a glance, offers an effective alternative to a simple listing of resources. Unfortunately, the library's home page has no obvious link to Senior Centered.

Take the H.E.L.M. Boomers

Seminole County Library, Casselberry, Florida

www.seminolecountyfl.gov/libraries/adultservices/boomers

WHAT A website with information on print and online resources relevant to baby boomers and other older adults.

CONTENT The website is organized around four primary topics, each with subtopics:

Health. Diseases and Conditions, Emotional and Mental Health, Finding Care, Getting Older, and Staying Healthy

Enrichment. Activities and Events, Social Networking, Travel, Volunteering

Learning. Cultural Opportunities, Lifelong Learning, Local Classes and Activities, Reading Groups

Money. Legal Planning, Personal Finance, Real Estate, Retirement Planning, Starting a Business

The library includes "Boomers" as a key population category on the home page, along with "Kids," "Teens," and the library catalog. "Boomers" takes a patron directly to the Take the H.E.L.M. page. Although the directory is less extensive than some others, Take the H.E.L.M. Boomers is a solid overview of relevant sources and organizations for local boomers.

Wise Up! / Resource Fair for Older Adults
San Francisco Public Library, San Francisco, California
http://sfpl.org

WHAT The Wise Up! Resource Fair, held in May 2011, encouraged "learning and living well at any age." The fair offered attendees the chance to learn about services, programs, and volunteer opportunities offered by numerous San Francisco institutions. For some attendees the Resource Fair was also an opportunity to sign up as a volunteer.

CONTENT The Resource Fair for Older Adults included organizational representatives from medical and financial institutions, educational organizations, environmental groups, and cultural organizations including the Community Music Center, Episcopal Community Services, Institute on Aging, San Francisco environmental groups, and Osher Lifelong Learning Institute.

The fair was part of a larger initiative, Wise Up! cosponsored with the Stanford University School of Medicine, San Francisco Department of Aging and Adult Services, and City College of San Francisco. Wise Up! includes programs on topics such as mental health and creative writing.

By bringing together a wide variety of community organizations in a match-making environment, the San Francisco Public Library reinforced the library's identity as a central information resource for midlife adults.

IN-BRIEF: INFORMATION AND CONNECTIONS

55+
Evansville Vanderburgh (Indiana) Public Library 55+ is organized around eight categories of information: Use the Library, Computers and Email, Family History, Financial and Legal, Free Time, Health, Local and Indiana Resources, and Reading and Listening. (www.evpl.org/seniors)

55+—Explore New Beginnings
San Mateo (California) County Library 55+ is a special section of the library's website that offers information for midlife adults on events, books and other collections, local organizations, volunteer opportunities, and other recommended resources. The site is exceptionally well designed, with a mix of images and text. Each month there are special features, such as Pacifica and Coastside Stories and Computer Classes @ your Library. 55+ is listed on the library's home page along with Adults, Teens, and other key age groups. (www.smcl.org/content/55)

Adult 50+ Resources
Calcasieu Parish Public Library, Lake Charles, Louisiana This online directory is organized around these categories: Services; Local Information; Education, Employment and Family; Computer Classes; Government, Financial and Legal; Health and Insurance; Recreation, Leisure and Travel. (http://calcasieulibrary.org/adult55)

Boomers and Beyond . . .
Lower Merion (Pennsylvania) Library System A guide to library resources, online information, and community services. The site features different organizations with in-depth descriptions, such as the International Volunteer Programs Association. (www.lmls.org/boomer.html)

KBOOM: Keep Boomers Options Open and Manageable
Apache Junction (Arizona) Public Library This web page for midlife adults includes links to local and national organization websites in the following categories: Business, Investment and Finance; Travel; Resources; Employment and Careers; Volunteering; Health and Medicine; and Life Skills. The library received an LSTA grant in 2007 to outfit two new library spaces—an outdoor multimedia area and a discussion room for programming—to help meet the information and programming needs of community members age 45 or older. (www.ajpl.org/kboom.html#websites)

More to Explore 50+
King County (Washington) Library System This web page titled "50+" highlights programs and resources in the library, online and in the community, organized in three sections: Programs and Events, Resources, and Accessibility (outreach services for homebound). The site is not

just for midlife adults, and it does not offer extensive listings of community resources. However, it includes descriptions of upcoming programs and events that are varied enough to be relevant to 50+ residents. (www.kcls.org/50plus)

Senior Central

Washoe County Library, Reno, Nevada Washoe County provides substantial information for older adults, including midlife adults, on its Senior Central web page. The directory is organized around Book Reviews and Book Clubs, Computers and Internet, Heath and Fitness, Travel and Leisure, and Lifescapes (a Washoe County program). The directory is well linked on the library's home page. (www.washoecounty.us/library/seniors.html)

The Plus Side of Life for People 50 and Up

Cobleigh (Vermont) Public Library A web page that "invites viewers to travel on," with resources about business, health, books, resources, and fun. (http://cobleighlibrary.org/main/?page_id=97)

CHAPTER 9

LIFELONG LEARNING

As adults 55 and over work to make sense of their options, opportunities and future directions, libraries will necessarily play key roles for continuing learners.

—**Ellie Drago-Severson, in *Library Leaders for Mature Adult Learners in a Changing World***

Major changes are taking place in American education today, with a new emphasis on learning across the life course. In this dynamic environment, libraries are well positioned to become centers for older adult learning. Libraries and learning are synonymous in the public mind. Most libraries include learning as part of their mission statements, their collections and services exist to support learning, and most currently offer some form of adult learning programs along with "enrichment opportunities" for seniors.

Still, the potential of the library as a center for 50+ learning is unrealized. Some experimental activities are in place, but relatively few librarians, as yet, are focusing specifically on midlife adult learning. Even those experimenting with new approaches lack theoretical grounding in older adult learning or a framework for practice. In the context of an aging society, libraries have an opportunity to fulfill their missions to advance community learning more effectively if they are more intentional about meeting the needs of baby boomers and other active older adults.

TRENDS

In recent years there has been a growing national discussion about lifelong learning, prompted in part by demographic changes, including the coming of age of the first baby boomers and evidence of an increase in human life expectancy. Robert Butler, who coined the term "ageism," discussed the need to revamp our institutions and practices in such fundamental areas as education:

> With the Longevity Revolution, the world enters a new and unprecedented stage of human development—the impact of which has been made greater because of its rapidity. . . . Many of our economic, political ethical, health, and other institutions, such as education and work life, have been rendered obsolete by the added years of life for so many citizens.[1]

With extended lifespans there is increased attention to learning as a means of ensuring intellectual acuity and vitality during the third and fourth phases of the lengthening life course. New research is providing evidence that learning continues through all phases of the life span, and with positive mental, physical, and physiological consequences. Research is also provoking greater understanding of the human brain and cognitive capacities of older adults, helping to dispel some of the myths surrounding aging and fueling interest in learning for "brain fitness" in the later years. There is a burgeoning body of literature on the benefits of intellectual and mental stimulation for positive aging, including Gene Cohen's landmark study "Creativity and Aging: The Impact of Professionally Conducted Cultural Programs on Older Adults," which documents the positive impacts of structured arts education programs for older adults.[2]

New research in the field of education, and theories such as multiple intelligences and different "ways of knowing," have also fueled interest in lifelong learning. Theoretical developments have helped build appreciation for the different ways adults learn, including informal learning, peer learning, experiential learning, and free-choice or self-directed learning. At the same time, the current pace of technological change is a major driver of change in the educational environment. Older adults, as well as young people, now have an expanded array of tools, approaches, and environments for learning, all of which are influencing approaches to learning across the lifespan.

The new focus on lifelong learning is having a profound impact on American institutions and educational practices. To cite just a few changes, afterschool learning and free-choice learning are becoming more common, with community-based institutions such as libraries taking on educational roles heretofore relegated to schools and families. "Adult education," which at one time carried a connotation of remedial learning, is now understood as an umbrella for all sorts of learning opportunities, from literacy and e-literacy to certificate programs in nursing and courses in marketing, acting, engineering, or software programming. Adults of all ages are continuously learning how to use new technologies and are retooling their skills for new jobs and careers.

Lifelong learning has taken center stage in the cultural arena as well. In 2001 the IMLS defined its mission as creating and sustaining "a nation of learners." In her opening remarks for the 2006 Designs for Change: Libraries and Productive Aging symposium cosponsored by IMLS and Libraries for the Future, then acting director Mary Chute stated:

> Libraries and museums should be leaders in fostering vibrant learning communities, with learning defined broadly to embrace "what we do to make sense of the world." Such learning occurs at school but also out of school, and it includes everyone, especially the great number and diversity of adults who are approaching traditional retirement age, whether or not they are actually retiring. Time spent now, "planning and thinking strategically about how to engage with active productive older adults," is a necessary investment for the continued vitality of our communities and our institutions.[3]

Baby boomers are spurring these trends as they seek to sharpen old skills or develop new ones for a twenty-first-century economy. In the process of starting new businesses, pursuing long-postponed intellectual or artistic interests, or preparing for an entirely new life stage, they are seeking out new formal and informal learning opportunities. In fact, the market for older adult learning is such that community colleges and universities are opening their doors to students in their fifties and sixties, creating satellite campuses, flexible schedules, and special tracks or cohort groups to attract older adults. In so doing they are discovering new revenue streams. The number of college students ages 40–64 has jumped by almost 20 percent to nearly 2 million in the past decade. Returning to Learning at the College of St. Catherine's in St. Paul, Minnesota, and the Plus 50 Initiative conducted by the American Association of Community Colleges are but two examples of the innovative programs to engage the 50+ learners who are cropping up at campuses around the country. Other institutions of higher education are creating lifelong learning institutes or learning-in-retirement programs. These usually exist as parallel entities on campuses with their own administrative units and their own faculty, often drawn from peers or retired local educators. Campus-based programs often partner with community agencies to offer access to classes and study groups at community locations, including libraries.

> It is clear that libraries can and do play a vital role in meeting the substantive lifelong learning needs of adults—especially those in this important age bracket, with so much wisdom to offer and so much to achieve. . . . In our work with adults and libraries, we have learned that there is a pressing need to better understand how to support adult learning and development. One compelling reason to attend to ways of knowing is that in any library community, adults will make sense of their experiences in developmentally different ways.
>
> —E. Drago-Severson and J. Blum, in *Library Leadership for Mature Adult Learners in a Changing World*

IMPLICATIONS FOR LIBRARIES

With the growing interest in informal as well as formal adult learning, the public library has important roles to play. One of these roles is as a *gateway to learning*, in which the library offers information on learning opportunities in the community, books and resources for self-directed learning, and access to online learning. The gateway role is not new. Reference assistance, in its most basic form, is a means of fulfilling the gateway role. Assistance in identifying useful information on the Internet, the provision of spaces for other institutions' educational programs, and hosting of mentoring and counseling activities across the lifespan are also part of this function. With the increased number of baby boomer patrons, libraries are extending these functions, such as hosting Elderhostel "Ambassadors" who introduce patrons to travel and learning opportunities through Elderhostel and its new "Road Scholar" programs,[4] or offering adult students the opportunity to take GED exams or tests for other certification programs at the library. An increasing number of libraries are creating robust websites with information on learning opportunities for mature adults.

Beyond functioning as a bridge to learning, some librarians are also taking more active roles in fulfilling libraries' potential as *centers for lifelong learning*. These librarians see the importance of moving beyond information services and community connections to offer on-site educational programs relevant to the needs, backgrounds, and interests of midlife adults. They see the possibilities for helping prepare midlife adults for new kinds of work or service, and they see the value of the library as a community setting in which different kinds of learning can occur. As a result, these librarians are providing 50+ adults with a wide variety of learning services, including options in subject matter, medium, expertise available, and program structure. They offer many instructive examples, from traditional program formats such as topical book clubs, language instruction, and weekly film programs to less traditional activities such as intergenerational nature hikes, formal college-level instruction, and peer-led "community conversations" on public affairs.

Because of their variety and scope, today's lifelong learning programs for midlife adults belie labeling or easy categorization. But to capture the variety of models that are evolving, it is helpful to organize them into three broad categories: informal learning, reading and viewing, and academic learning.

> Lifelong learning now means actively learning longer for Missouri's up-and-coming Baby Boomer generation. Libraries everywhere are recognizing the tremendous impact they can have on this growing user audience: Missouri's 65 and above population is projected to increase 15% by 2010. You can't afford not to engage the interests and support of this significant user audience by developing and expanding programming for older adults.
>
> **—Ann Roberts, older adult services coordinator, Missouri State Library**

INFORMAL LEARNING

Informal learning activities for midlife adults are by far the most numerous and most varied of all the types of lifelong learning programs taking place in libraries. Topics vary from philosophy and local history to yoga, language instruction, world affairs, and sustainable gardening. Formats vary as well, including clubs, workshops, performances, demonstrations, and tours. Along with their variety, some current informal learning programs for 50+ adults reflect a new level of awareness on the part of librarians regarding these key principles of adult learning:

- Organizing learning in groups, and including a social component
- Offering opportunities for individual expression and group dialogue
- Introducing program participants to complementary library resources for further independent learning
- Providing options in program formats and schedules

Training to support these new efforts is not systematic or widely available to librarians. Some librarians have, however, benefited from professional development opportunities covering life transitions and principles of adult learning, most notably the California State Library's Transforming Life After 50 initiative, Libraries for the Future's Lifelong Access Institutes, and the Western States IMLS Fellowships. Librarians who attended these trainings are currently leading the field by introducing new 50+ learning services in their libraries and applying older learning concepts such as organizing peer advisory groups, hosting peer-led discussion programs, and combining learning with social interaction.

With the emergence of informal learning programs specifically targeted to 50+ adults, a new program genre is emerging, a genre that can be termed "the Library Experience." Library experience programs typically involve presentations on varied topics, offered on a regular schedule, that include opportunities for group learning *and* social exchange. These are typically designed with input from peer advisors and reflect organizers' efforts to move beyond one-time programming to a sustainable structure for ongoing 50+ programming. Examples of library experience programs include Reading (Massachusetts) Public Library's LiveWires: Coffee and More program and the Lunch and Learn initiative at the Russell Library in Middletown, Connecticut, which are profiled below. These kinds of projects reflect midlife adults' affinities for group learning, another older adult learning principle affirmed by experts and practitioners.

Library experience activities are so widespread and so successful that it is possible to imagine that they could evolve as a core infrastructure for 50+ learning services. Some are already spawning complementary programs. For instance, Reading Library's monthly LiveWires initiative inspired LiveWires Presents, a series of evening presentations on special topics. More specialized activities, including formal classes, thematic reading programs, or intergenerational activities, may then be added to create a full menu for midlife adults.

LEARNING THROUGH READING AND VIEWING

Reading is the ultimate "free-choice" learning experience—reading alone, in groups, or online. The range of reading opportunities, reading-related resources, and reading encouragement activities available to adults at and through libraries is enormous. Even today, with libraries equipped as community information centers with a constantly changing array of learning technologies besides books, reading, in whatever medium, is at the core of the library experience. Whether the "text" is a film, an audio recording, an electronically transmitted text, or a physical book, the library promotes reading, viewing, and listening for learning in many forms. Most libraries offer some or all of the following:

- Collections of books, CDs, DVDs, tapes, and other forms of text for use in the library or at home for learning and enrichment
- Reader's advisories and book lists, both in print and online

- Book clubs and kits to support formation of book clubs
- Reading groups, based on particular themes, genres, or participant choices
- Scholar- or specialist-led reading and discussion programs
- Author talks or readings
- One Book, One Community programs, which involve people of all ages
- Book-related radio programs, videotapes, and web-based presentations
- Book festivals

In even the smallest libraries, these types of collections and services are available to adults of all ages, offering midlife adults a rich array of learning possibilities where there may be no targeted programs to their age group. Indeed, many reading and viewing programs for general adult audiences attract high numbers of midlife adults, despite the lack of targeted marketing or special scheduling. For instance, Karen Hansen at the Evanston (Illinois) Public Library, a co-organizer of "Ulysses, Mission Impossible" (see below), said when interviewed that she never "intended the program especially for 50+ adults, however, they make up by far the majority of participants."

Librarians across the country report that midlife adults fill up their discussion programs on "Great Books," author talks by politicians or public figures, history book clubs, and opportunities to read or work on projects involving gardening or the environment. As a result, some librarians believe that the key to serving midlife adults through collections and reading-related programming is not so much a matter of offering age-specific content as it is of offering a wide enough array of the themes and types of programs that appeal to 50+ adults.

> As stewards of lifelong learning, libraries are well-positioned to become cornerstone institutions for mid-life adults . . . IF they can also appeal to them with new, intriguing, and flexible approaches to learning.
>
> —Transforming Life After 50, California State Library website, www.transforming lifeafter50.org/midlife-trends/lifelong-learning

Even as librarians see more midlife adults filling up their adult reading and viewing programs, they are also beginning to organize and market activities specifically for midlife adults. Some series focus on a particular theme of interest to older adults. A program genre emerging as a result of the 50+ service movement is called "Books-to-Action" (see below), pioneered by the Multnomah (Oregon) County Library System. Books-to-Action involves reading and discussion around a text concerned with a particular social issue, accompanied by a service project at a local organization relevant to the issue. The approach fulfills two complementary goals: to provide a stimulating group reading and learning experience, and to expose midlife patrons to local issues and organizations that could benefit from their skills and experience.

ACADEMIC LEARNING

The third common approach to lifelong learning for 50+ adults is academic learning—learning that is structured, purposeful, has academic leadership or facilitation, and may lead to mastery or recognition in the form of a degree or certificate. Although there are far fewer academic learning programs in libraries than other forms of lifelong learning, they reflect the national trend for older adults to pursue long-delayed or new educational interests, to master a skill, or to prepare for a new career.

A key feature of academic learning programs in libraries is collaboration with a local institution of higher learning such as a community college, college, university, or local learning-in-retirement program. These collaborations benefit both partners as well as the class attendees. For colleges and universities that do not have a community location accessible for older adult learners, collaboration with the local library helps them gain visibility and recruit students. In addition, by offering faculty-led classes in public libraries, they can fulfill institutional goals for community service. Partnerships with academia benefit the libraries as well. Libraries do not have "faculty" per se to cover all topics of potential interest to older adults and do not have the academic standing to grant certificates or degrees. Having formal classes available to patrons enables librarians to offer midlife adults a greater range of learning options, introduce the students to library resources, and encourage ongoing use of the library for other forms of learning and life development. The partnerships emerging between libraries and some of the Osher Lifelong Learning Institutes (see below) exemplify how academic and public libraries can collaborate to expand lifelong learning for 50+ students.

Collaboration between academic institutions and public libraries obviously benefits participants. For many older adult learners, returning to a formal classroom or campus can be intimidating. By attending classes at the library they can refamiliarize themselves with academia while benefiting from peer support and a community setting with resources to support their learning. In addition, for many older adults the fees for courses at a college or university or for a membership-based learning-in-retirement program may be beyond reach. Most academic learning programs in libraries do not involve a fee and thus are accessible to a wider number of individuals.

Given the number of midlife adults who are seeking formal learning opportunities, it is likely that partnerships between libraries and academic institutions will increase in the coming years. Some of the examples described below suggest the potential for more libraries to incorporate academic learning programs into their service plan for 50+ adults.

Within one library or library system the three types of lifelong learning—informal learning, reading and viewing, and academic partnerships—may coexist, or they may overlap with other categories of programming, such as health or creativity. As librarians learn more about their midlife constituents and these constituents become more involved in libraries, learning programs are constantly evolving. With overall growth in demand for lifelong learning for 50+ adults, it is obvious that libraries are well positioned to carve out a special niche as *the* community center for midlife learning.

Notes

1. Robert Butler, *The Longevity Revolution* (New York: PublicAffairs, 2008), 17.

2. For a final report, see www.nea.gov/resources/accessibility/CnA-Rep4-30-06.pdf.

3. Mary Chute, *Designs for Change: Libraries and Productive Aging*, Libraries for the Future and Institute for Museum and Library Services, 2005, www.imls.gov/assets/1/AssetManager/DesignsforChange.pdf, page 11.

4. Louisville (Kentucky) Public Library, the Richland (South Carolina) Public Library, and Patchoque-Medford (New York) Library are examples of libraries that have hosted introductory programs for Elderhostel or its new Road Scholar Program.

LIFELONG LEARNING THROUGH INFORMAL LEARNING

Get PLUGGED In @ The Robbins
Robbins Library, Arlington, Massachusetts
www.robbinslibrary.org

WHAT This new initiative at Robbins Library, established in 2011, strengthened programs and services for adults 50–70 years of age. Get Plugged In was typical of a new genre of programming for midlife adults—library experience programs—which combine information, education, social exchange, and service opportunities.

GOAL To "energize Arlington's active adults. Engage them. Excite them. And electrify them."

FEATURES According to Arlington's 2009 census, adults 50–70 were at that time more than 25 percent of the population. Get Plugged In was designed to "to assist the target group in their desire to remain active, involved and intellectually stimulated." Planning for Get Plugged In reflected an important principle of older adult education: involvement of peers. A survey and focus groups of patrons and potential program participants helped inform early planning, and a peer advisory committee assisted library staff to determine monthly program topics, evaluate the programs, and extend outreach to the target group.[1]

Get Plugged In focused on three areas: programs, the library collections, and the library website. Among the program topics were Web 2.0, volunteer opportunities, retirement planning, healthy living, and careers after 50. A kickoff event in March 2011 featured a presentation titled "Your Next Chapter: Possibilities and Challenges for the Second Half of Life."

PARTNERS AND FUNDING Get Plugged in was funded by a grant from the IMLS through the LSTA administered by the Massachusetts Board of Library Commissioners. The grant was one of several 2011 MBLC grants under its current Next Chapter initiative.

Note

1. See the Robbins survey at http://surveymonkey.com/s/RobbinsActiveAdultsSurvey.

Great Decisions
National Program of the Foreign Policy Association
www.fpa.org

WHAT Great Decisions is a framework for foreign policy discussions led by scholars and public experts that take place in libraries and other community institutions. It is the flagship program of the national Foreign Policy Association. Although Great Decisions is not designed specifically for 50+ adults, libraries report that many, if not most, of those who take part are midlife or older adults.

GOAL To provide a proven framework for responding to 50+ patrons' interests in national and international affairs and their needs for social and intellectual exchange.

FEATURES The eight-week program offers participants an opportunity to discuss issues of concern to U.S. policymakers today that are foreign policy challenges of tomorrow. Each year a Foreign Policy Association editorial board selects eight pressing issues that are the basis for a briefing book, TV programs, and online resources. Topics for 2010 included "Rebuilding Haiti" and "US National Security." Presenting libraries may choose to offer all eight topics each year or may offer a shorter series. Local policy experts and scholars are usually recruited to make introductory remarks and lead the discussions, which are preceded by a 30-minute DVD produced by the Foreign Policy Association. In addition, briefing books are available at presenting libraries.

PARTNERS AND FUNDING Libraries often choose to work with another community organization in presenting Great Decisions events. Local chapters of the League of Women Voters or community colleges are typical partners. Costs depend on whether or not the public policy experts who lead the discussions require fees and transportation expenses. Underwriting is not usually necessary, although some programs are supported by library Friends groups.

Sample 2010/2011 Great Decisions Sites

Batavia, Geneva, and St. Charles (Illinois) Public Libraries
"To stimulate discussion of foreign policy issues," the libraries jointly offered three of the Great Decisions topics. They rotated locations for each program and encouraged participants to attend all three. Presenting librarians moderated the programs. (www.bataviapublic library.org; www.geneva.lib .il.us/; www.stcharleslibrary.org)

Carver County (Minnesota) Library, Chanhassen Library
The Friends of the Chanhassen Library sponsored the Great Decisions Discussions, organized locally by the Minnesota International Center. Discussion leaders included professors from the Uni-

versity of Minnesota and Carleton College. (www.carverlib.org)

Jacksonville (Florida) Public Library
Great Decisions is sponsored locally by the World Affairs Council–Jacksonville. The library offers the series annually and engages professors from local universities to lead the discussions. (http://jpl.coj.net)

Kitsap (Washington) Regional Library
The library partnered with the Bainbridge Island Arts and Humanities County. Participants were invited to "spend Saturday mornings at the Bainbridge Island branch for coffee, pastries, and a stimulating discussion on foreign affairs." (www.krl.org)

Oro Valley (Arizona) Public Library
Librarians or participants led the discussions, using Foreign Policy Association briefing books. (www.orovalleylib.com/ Page185.aspx)

Pioneer Library System, Oklahoma
The library recruited University of Oklahoma professors and a retired ambassador to lead the discussions. (www.pioneer.lib.ok.us)

Williamsburg (Virginia) Regional Library
The library partnered with the League of Women Voters of the Williamsburg area. Policymakers were recruited as discussion leaders from Washington, D.C., and New York City. (www.wrl.org)

Keeping Current with the World around Us
Hamilton-Wenham Public Library, South Hamilton, Massachusetts
www.hwlibrary.org

WHAT This series of current events presentations for baby boomers grew out of community needs assessments carried out in 2007/8. The positive response to the programs underscores the value of involving 50+ patrons in program development.

GOAL To offer programs and collections that match the needs and interests of the community's older adult patrons.

FEATURES In 2007, staff from the Hamilton-Wenham Library took part in an Equal Access training and grant program provided by the Massachusetts Library Commission and Libraries for the Future. In implementing this project the library focused on programming for 50+ adults and carried out a survey of baby boomers in its service area. The staff learned that travel, local history, and current events were the topics of highest interest. The resulting Keeping Current series featured speakers, films, and discussions about contemporary issues and events such as pension fraud, the global economy, and where our food comes from. Each of the evening programs featured a well-known specialist, author, or film maker who engaged in discussion with the audiences after the presentations.

Keeping Current was an extension of prior programs developed by the library in 2006 to meet older adult interests, including drawing classes and the Self-Published Authors Fair.

PARTNERS AND FUNDING In 2008 the Hamilton-Wenham Library received a grant from the Northern Massachusetts Regional Library System to cover program expenses and collection development related to the Keeping Current topics. Programming was also supported by the Friends of the Hamilton-Wenham Public Library.

Learning for a Lifetime
Chelmsford Public Library, Chelmsford, Massachusetts
www.chelmsfordlibrary.org

WHAT 50+ adults get the chance to learn about "weighty topics" and engage in serious discussion with experts and peers in this weekly program series, which is carried out in partnership with the local Learning in Retirement Association (LIRA).

GOAL To provide older adults with regular opportunities to deepen their knowledge of domestic and international affairs.

FEATURES Learning for a Lifetime topics are selected by the library and LIRA, based on patron suggestions and current issues. Scholars are recruited from colleges and universities in the region to lecture. Each lecture is followed by a time for questions and dialogue. The series was launched in 2010 with an overview and discussion of lifelong learning. As the first program announcement put it,

> It's a way to enhance and enrich our "After-50" years, making them the very best years of our lives. Thanks to a vast array of opportunities available in the lifelong learning world today, older adults now have the chance to make their later years far more exciting than they ever dreamed possible. Incorporating lifelong learning keeps our minds more stimulated, our bodies more active and our spirits more fulfilled.

The series is continuing in 2011/12 with a variety of current affairs topics. According to Kathy Cryan-Hicks, assistant director for community relations and programming, "people are looking for challenging programs that keep them connected with what's going on in the world and prompt them to think and talk."

PARTNERS AND FUNDING The Chelmsford LIRA helps select the topics and market the program. Learning for a Lifetime is sponsored by the Chelmsford Friends of the Library.

Lifelong Learning Institute
Winter Park Public Library, Winter Park, Florida
www.wppl.org

WHAT The Lifelong Learning Institute, the adult education department of the Winter Park Library, is a separate entity that offers educational and cultural programs to members on a fee basis. The Institute coexists with the library and is self-supporting. This unusual arrangement is one of a handful of situations where public libraries offer programming on a membership fee basis; it may be the single instance of a library that is doing so specifically for older adults. The Institute is also unusual in terms of the extent of its educational offerings.

GOAL To provide meaningful, high-quality learning opportunities in a relaxed, nonthreatening environment.

FEATURES With a long tradition of learning programs for adults, the library institutionalized and expanded its class offerings in 2002 in the form of the Institute, which has a specific mission: to support adult learning independent of a formal educational environment. The Institute is based on a philosophy of "participant-centered adult learning" whereby adults may engage in personal development and enrichment, engage in continuous learning through training and development, and learn how to better access information in an electronic age.

The Institute's program offerings are diverse, ranging from how-to courses and practical workshops to courses and seminars on art, literature, health and wellness, history, and public affairs. Most are led by local professionals, authors, or topical specialists; some are facilitated by library staff. Sample topics include:

> **Cinemagic: Seeing Movies through Mystical Eyes,** a six-part series of feature-length film viewings and discussions that "explore the filmmaker's use of color, light, sound and story to communicate wisdom, truth and sociopolitical subjects"
>
> **Musical Sundays,** a regular series of live concerts at the library
>
> **Health and Wellness,** a seven-part series on such topics as laughter and Qigong I
>
> **Creating Spaces That Support You,** on home and landscape design principles

PARTNERS AND FUNDING Institute programs are usually organized by the library, but some special events involve a partner or sponsors such as the Rollins College Office of Student Leadership and Service, Orange County Commission on Aging, City of Winter Park, Central Florida Library Cooperative, Winter Park Historical Association, and Orange TV/Vision TV. The Winter Park Health Foundation was instrumental in making the Institute possible through its financial support. Membership fees cover Institute expenses.

LiveWires: Lifelong Learning at the Library

Reading Public Library, Reading, MA

www.readingpl.org

WHAT LiveWires is informal learning programs developed with and for active older adults. This was one of the first educational enrichment programs in the country targeted for "boomers and beyond" and has provided a model for library experience programs, a new genre of library programs that offer varied interdisciplinary learning activities for midlife adults.

GOAL To provide educational programs for "persons in midlife and beyond to introduce them to different ways of thinking about midlife and retirement." The program has evolved to meet a broad range of learning needs and interests of active older adult patrons.

FEATURES LiveWires is the centerpiece program for older adults at the Reading Library. The program has different strands, with several programs monthly, except in the summer when there is one program each month.

LiveWires Coffee and More is the core LiveWires program. These are regular midmorning presentations, usually including a formal talk by a specialist or author followed by discussion. Topics are recommended by program participants. They have included a viewing and discussion of the PBS documentary *The Open Road*, which examines the obstacles and issues associated with the aging of America; a talk by a local author on the art

> LiveWires is a program for people who never want to stop learning. Join us for a stimulating lifelong learning series!
>
> —2009 LiveWires brochure

and craft of writing; a program on legal issues for "boomers and beyond"; and a talk by the author of *Bald as a Bean* on "how to live gracefully with what life hands you."

Coffee and More is a social program where librarians present new books and resources for active older adults. The social component has allowed attendees to make new friends and form groups that continue outside of the library.

Film discussions are another popular strand of LiveWires programming, consisting of facilitated discussions following film screenings. Some films focus on aging, such as *Nobody's Fool*, and others, such as *Notes on a Scandal*, examine topics of friendship, relationships, and unexpected life adventures.

Special events, called LiveWires Presents, are evening programs featuring experts on a wide range of topics, with such titles as "Lighthouses Far and Near" and "Sports History of Boston." Offering these programs in the evening allows the library to meet the lifelong learning needs of older adults who work during the day.

LiveWires exemplifies key principles of older adult programming: involvement of peers in program design and implementation; attention to location, amenities, and schedule; a mixed portfolio of topics and activities; and a combination of educational content and social interaction.

PARTNERS AND FUNDING LiveWires is developed with a group of library patrons who are advisors to the library. The program is supported by the Friends of the Reading Public Library and other local sponsors. Initial support was provided by an LSTA grant from the IMLS, administered by the Massachusetts Board of Library Commissioners. Since 2006 the program has been sustained with small grants and local support.

Meet, Learn and Discover Series
Norfolk Public Library, Norfolk, Virginia
www.npl.lib.va.us

WHAT The Meet, Learn and Discover (MLD) series is a partnership between the Norfolk Public Library and AARP Virginia that offers midlife adults the opportunity to come together once a month to hear a topical presentation and meet other people. MLD also involves a joint website on topics relevant to Norfolk's older adults.

MLD is one of the few instances of a sustained, programmatic partnership between a library and a state AARP office. The assets of the local library and the local AARP are brought together for the benefit of the region's older adults, and AARP members are exposed to library resources. In addition, the program features two key principles for effective older adult learning: interdisciplinary content, and a balance between learning and social interaction.

GOAL To help people 50+ improve the quality of their lives by learning new things, discovering new ideas, and meeting new people.

FEATURES MLD involves weekly evening presentations at the Mary D. Pretlow Branch Library in Norfolk. Some programs draw as many as one hundred people. A core group comes to almost every program, and additional participants come in for specific topics. The topics range from travel to workshops on tracing the history of your house. They are selected with input from participants.

The Pretlow branch and Norfolk's collaboration with Virginia's AARP office emerged from Age in America (www.reimaginingageproject.org/projects.cfm), a national initiative in which the Norfolk Public Library was one of three libraries testing new approaches for community programming and community around age and aging. In 2011, Norfolk received the Virginia Public Library Directors Award for Outstanding Program for Seniors award for MLD.

PARTNERS AND FUNDING AARP Virginia is cosponsor of MLD. AARP is involved with program development and has provided speakers for the MLD programs. MLD was initially developed with funding from Libraries for the Future, a former national library advocacy organization that initiated Age in America, a demonstration project supported by the IMLS.

Programs for Older Adults / Lunch and Learn

Russell Library, Middletown, Connecticut

www.russelllibrary.org

WHAT Russell Library offers a variety of informal learning programs targeted to active older adults. In their interdisciplinary approach, use of peers for expert presentations, and combination of education and social exchange, these programs exemplify the emerging genre of library experience programs.

GOAL To position the library as a destination for mobile older adults by providing an array of opportunities for free-choice learning and social interaction.

FEATURES For several years Russell Library has been strengthening its services to older adults through expanded programming. Staff have reached out to local experts, many of whom are 50+ themselves, to engage them as presenters and help strengthen older residents' use of the library as an educational and social resource. With grant funds the library has been able to experiment with approaches and topics. Current programs include the following:

- Lunch and Learn is an informal midday series on topics such as travel, history, and health. Participants bring their own meals, and the library provides drinks and desserts.

- Evening programs on special topics are offered. As one example, the library hosted a spring 2011 lecture, "Close to the Epicenter: A Professor's Perspective on Recent Events in Japan," by a professor from nearby Wesleyan University.
- Other program formats—film discussions, one-time workshops, daytime book discussions, and group activities such as "Russell Writers"— provide a rich menu of activities for midlife patrons. In addition, they are encouraged to participate in regular adult classes such as "Using Social Media" or "Small Business Development."

To develop these activities the library created a new part-time older adult specialist position as well as a multistaff Older Adult Team. With initial funding for the specialist position, the library has now been able to incorporate the position in its regular budget.

PARTNERS AND FUNDING There are no formal partners for this program. The library received a two-year $20,000 LSTA grant, administered by the Connecticut State Library, to carry out initial program expansion to reach more midlife adults. Another small LSTA grant and a grant of $4,800 from the local community foundation have also helped to strengthen 50+ programming.

The Boomers: Reflecting, Learning, Sharing
Athens Regional Library System, Athens, Georgia
www.clarke.public.lib.ga.us

WHAT A project developed jointly by the Athens Regional Library System and the Lyndon House Arts Center offers opportunities for lifelong learning and community engagement for midlife adults. As a relatively new initiative, with implementation starting only in mid-2011, the evolution of the project will be instructive for other libraries committed to involving their 50+ patrons in program planning and execution. The Boomers project will also be instructive as a model for a library–arts center collaboration.

GOAL To "engage and encourage Active Boomers in the Athens area" and to "develop a Best Practices service model for public libraries and museums around the country."

FEATURES The Boomers emphasizes activities developed by and for peers, with multiple strands of programming intended to reinforce one another. Monthly Community Snapshots is a program series featuring presentations by local midlife adults on issues of community concern or topics on which they have personal knowledge or professional expertise. The snapshots are available live on the new program's website—www.boomers inathens.org. The website also has discussion forums, a photo gallery, and an events calendar. An annual event is hosted by the two program partners; special exhibitions are featured at the Lyndon House Arts Center.

PARTNERS AND FUNDING The program is a partnership between the library and the Lyndon House Arts Center, which encourages residents to "appreciate the arts and to develop their creative talents." The new program is supported by a grant from the IMLS.

> The Athens Regional Library and Lyndon House Arts Center have partnered to develop a new service model for older adults. Thanks to a grant from IMLS, we will have cutting edge technology at our fingertips to help us explore new programs and new ways to deliver them to our diverse Boomer population. We hope to develop a stronger sense of community—to discover what we have in common and to celebrate our individuality. Our goal is to engage and encourage active Boomers in the Athens area.
>
> —Boomers program website

World at Your Door
Free Library of Philadelphia, Philadelphia, Pennsylvania
www.freelibrary.org

WHAT World at Your Door is a series of public affairs presentations featuring area diplomats who offer insights on the foreign policy priorities of their nations. The series complements other programs provided by the library's Central Senior Services that are more locally or personally oriented (see chapter 2).

GOAL To increase participants' understanding of the global community.

FEATURES During spring 2011, the library offered presentations by area diplomats representing Canada, Jamaica, Poland, Chile, Haiti, and Israel. The program offered an opportunity for Philadelphia's midlife adults to gain firsthand knowledge of global events and relationships. Each diplomat provided his or her perspective on the current international scene and addressed issues of jobs, resources, and influence through the lens of their particular nations. The series was organized and led by the library's Central Senior Services but was open to people of all ages.

PARTNERS AND FUNDING Local consulates of each of the countries represented in the program cooperated in the program planning. The series was carried out with support from Central Senior Services' primary funders, the Christian R. and Mary F. Lindback Foundation.

LIFELONG LEARNING THROUGH READING AND VIEWING

Books-to-Action / Life by Design @ your library
Multnomah County Library, Portland, Oregon
www.multcolib.org

WHAT The unusual Books-to-Action program combines reading, discussion, and action, offering 50+ adults a chance to "engage both body and mind." It involves a series of readings and discussions for midlife adults on books about major social issues followed up by responses to these issues by individuals and communities. The series also engages participants in one-day service projects in which they are exposed to opportunities for practical work in the community—"in their backyard."

The program was well received in Portland, by participants and by the agencies they became involved with as volunteers. The format has also captured the attention of other librarians experimenting with ways to engage midlife adults in both reading and community service. At least two libraries are currently running similar programs: Hayward Public Library in California and Boise Public Library in Idaho.

GOAL To deepen understanding about social issues and civic engagement in Portland through common reading, discussion, and service activities.

FEATURES Books-to-Action was one of several programs offered by Multnomah County Library's outreach services as part of Life by Design @ your library, a two-year partnership with the local coalition Life by Design NW (www.pcc.edu/climb/life). The series was coorganized by the library and Hands on Greater Portland (www.handsonportland.org).

Each Books-to-Action event was hosted by a different local library. The readings and complementary service projects included the following:

> *Life Is So Good*, by George Dawson and Richard Glaubman. This memoir of a manual laborer who learns to read at age 98 was linked to an adult literacy service project at the library's Title Wave Used Bookstore.

> *Half the Sky: Turning Oppression into Opportunity for Women Worldwide*, by Nicholas D. Kristof and Sheryl WuDunn. This depiction of the oppression of women in the developing world was paired with a service project at Jean's Place, a transitional housing program for adult, single, homeless women.

> *Bowling Alone: The Collapse and Revival of American Community*, by Robert Putnam. This examination of how we have become increasingly disconnected from family, friends, neighbors, and even our democratic structures provided the basis for volunteers to assist at Zenger Farm, a working urban farm and a center for environmental education and community events.

As a result of Books-to-Action, some participants have become regular volunteers at the community agencies they learned about in the program. In addition, the series introduced participants to the library, each project partner, and Hands on Greater Portland.

PARTNERS AND FUNDING Through its overall partnership with Life by Design NW, Multnomah County established the partnership with Hands on Greater Portland to design and implement Books-to-Action. Multnomah County's Life by Design @ your library initiative was initially supported through a grant to Life by Design NW from Atlantic Philanthropies and subsequently through a two-year LSTA demonstration project, Kaboom! administered by the Oregon State Library.

Books to Action . . . Learn, Talk, Do
Boise Public Library, Boise, Idaho
www.boisepubliclibrary.org

WHAT This project was a book discussion on a text with a social purpose theme and a companion service project. The success of the first program in Boise, in 2011, has led to planning for a similar program in 2012. The Boise project was initiated as a result of a local librarian's participation in the Western States IMLS Fellowship, where she learned about the Books-to-Action project carried out at the Multnomah County Library in Portland, Oregon (see above).

GOAL To provide a vehicle for midlife adults interested in volunteering to "try on" different organizations to see if they fit their interests, and to augment the role of the library as a safe place for the open exchange of ideas about local and global issues.

FEATURES The text selected for the Boise program, *Half the Sky: Turning Oppression into Opportunity for Women Worldwide*, by Nicholas D. Kristof and Sheryl WuDunn, led to a partnership with the Boise Women's and Children's Alliance, whose mission is to provide safety, healing, and freedom to victims of domestic abuse and sexual assault. As a result of the program, three participants have become regular volunteers for the organization. The target audience for Books-to-Action, midlife adults, includes full-time, part-time, and laid-off workers, retirees, and at-home caregivers. To make the program accessible to as many people as possible, the library scheduled each book discussion twice: two different locations, one weekday, one weekend, one during the day, and one in the evening.

PARTNERS AND FUNDING The inaugural Books-to-Action program was sponsored by the library itself. Beyond the costs of the extra sets of books (which were then rolled over into the library's "Books for Book Clubs" set), there were few expenses. The Boise Women's and Children's Alliance was the key partner.

Community Cinema / Club Book
Metropolitan Library Association, Minneapolis-St. Paul, Minnesota
www.melsa.org

WHAT These two Metropolitan Library Association (MELSA) programs (see chapter 2) offer 50+ adults opportunities for cultural enrichment and learning. Although neither program is limited to 50+ adults, they are both designed to benefit midlife adults as well as younger adults and "seniors," and they have both attracted high numbers of 50+ residents. They are excellent examples of carefully designed adult programming with high value for 50+ adults.

GOAL To "establish area libraries as vital, vibrant centers of cultural programming and exchange."

FEATURES Since 2008, as a result of Minnesota voters' approval of the Arts and Cultural Heritage Fund (ACHF), MELSA's cultural programs have increased considerably. As MELSA and its member libraries have offered more programs, they have also designed and marketed them to encourage participation by 50+ residents. Two key strands of region-wide ACHF-funded adult programming developed by MELSA, one involving a partnership with the Library Foundation of Hennepin County, have attracted large numbers of 50+ adults.

Community Cinema offers film screenings in local libraries of films from the award-winning PBS series Independent Lens as part of its national engagement program. Each program pairs an independent film with a panel discussion featuring local experts and community leaders, moderated by hosts from Twins Cities Public Television.

Club Book, which is coordinated with the Library Foundation of Hennepin County, brings best-selling and award-winning national and regional authors to library communities across the metropolitan area. The writers discuss their books and some also do readings. Nine libraries and library systems are participating in the two-year Club Book, from Stillwater to Minnetonka and St. Paul.

PARTNERS AND FUNDING Community Cinema screenings and discussions are presented in partnership with Twins Cities Public Television and the Independent Television Service. Club Book is presented in partnership with the Library Foundation of Hennepin County. Both are made possible by Minnesota's ACHF, which supports cultural programming and partnerships across the state. Club Book receives substantial in-kind support from Minnesota Public Radio and other key local businesses.

Great Books

Great Books Foundation, National Program

www.greatbooks.org

WHAT Great Books is a text-based method of learning that features discussion about some of the world's great literature. Developed by the Great Books Foundation, the Great Books program discussions take place in colleges, schools, community organizations, and libraries. Many libraries that offer Great Books as an adult reading and discussion program find that midlife adults constitute a high percentage of participants.

Sample Great Books Library Sites

Cumberland County (North Carolina) Public Library
www.cumberland.lib.nc.us

Douglas County (Arizona) Libraries
http://douglascountylibraries.org

Gail Borden Public Library District, Elgin, Illinois
www.gailborden.info/m

Keene (New Hampshire) Public Library
http://keenepubliclibrary.org

Richland County (South Carolina) Public Library
www.richland.lib.sc.us

San Francisco (California) Public Library
http://sfpl.org

SouthShore Regional Library, Ruskin, Florida
www.hcplc.org/hcplc/locations/sho

Springfield (New Jersey) Free Public Library
www.springfieldpublic library.com/joomla15

GOAL To "foster communities of readers who value intellectual growth and civic discourse among friends."

FEATURES Great Books is a national program that engages adults of all ages in "Shared Inquiry" discussions in which readers "collaborate to explore ideas and experiences drawn from literary selections." The "great books" on which the discussions are based include classic and contemporary writings from around the world and across the disciplines. Libraries that offer Great Books may select books in a particular discipline, category, or theme. The Oak Lawn (Illinois) Library website, for instance, states that its Great Books Group meets "to discuss and interpret significant works of fiction, philosophy, political science, poetry and drama."

Some libraries use anthologies of readings published by the Great Books Foundation, such as its Great Conversations series. Most have the anthology available for checkout and for purchase. Many reading selections are also online or in other anthologies.

Great Books discussion leaders may be librarians, local participants with experience in facilitating book discussions, literature scholars, or individuals who have received training in the "Shared Inquiry" method from the Great Books Foundation.

PARTNERS AND FUNDING Local libraries often partner with other organizations, such as a local or regional Great Books council, to offer the Great Books program. They often receive support from their local Great Books Council or Friends group.

Literary Speed Dating for Boomers
San Francisco Public Library, San Francisco, California
http://sfpl.org

WHAT This San Francisco adaptation of typical speed dating methods uses brief book discussions as a vehicle for bringing singles together.

GOAL To provide single baby boomers with the chance to meet like-minded people in the context of a literary conversation.

FEATURES San Francisco Public Library has developed an innovative way to attract boomers who are looking for partners and are also interested in literature. The dating events are aimed particularly at baby boomers, although all ages are welcome. Program organizers recognized that some boomers feel too mature for discos and other kinds of meeting places. They also recognized that many boomer-age adults enjoy reading and sharing their ideas about books with others. The program that resulted is organized for two different audiences: one evening is for LGBT (same gender) dating and the other for straight dating (opposite gender).

Participants are encouraged to bring their favorite book to the sessions.

> In classic speed dating style, you will have five minutes to talk with every participant about your favorite, most loathsome, perplexing or intriguing book and have the opportunity to potentially meet your next sweetheart. Due to space limitations, each event is limited to 36 participants.
>
> **—Speed dating program announcement, San Francisco Public Library website**

PARTNERS AND FUNDING The program does not involve institutional partners. The library supports the Literary Speed Dating program through its regular budget for adult programs.

PALS Book Clubs

Allegheny County Library Association / PALS, Pittsburgh, Pennsylvania
www.aclalibraries.org

WHAT These are monthly reading and discussion programs for Medicare-eligible adults, held in local libraries, senior centers, and high rises. This long-running program is an excellent example of how one program can both serve and engage 50+ adults while utilizing the skills and experience of other 50+ adults as program assistants.

GOAL To provide a literary challenge and social interaction for participants while offering service opportunities for older adults in Pittsburgh.

FEATURES The Allegheny County Library Association's (ACLA) long-standing commitment to providing services for midlife and older folks (see chapter 2) is exemplified by the PALS Book Clubs, which have been operating continuously for more than ten years. Originally launched in two locations, these clubs are now in twenty-two libraries. They are operated collaboratively by ACLA and the PALS (People Able to Lend Support) program, a volunteer service credit program available through Highmark Senior Markets that offers in-home services and activities clubs for older residents of the Pittsburgh area. Older adult PALS volunteers support fellow members by providing help with routine activities or assisting with a book club.

ACLA works collaboratively with the Highmark PALS program to organize the book clubs and distribute the books to participating facilities, including libraries. Club members make book selection suggestions each year; ACLA determines the final choices based on what books are available in large print and audio. Club sizes vary, with most ten to twelve individuals. The discussions are facilitated by library staff, local program staff, and peer volunteers. When the clubs are started, a librarian models how to lead book discussions.

Each year PALS Book Club members are invited to an ACLA annual author luncheon featuring a local author. Club readers also participate in ACLA's annual One Book, One Community program (see chapter 10), and members are the first to read the book selected for the year.

Building on the success of the PALS Book Clubs, ACLA and the Highmark PALS program are currently sponsoring three pilot Intergenerational PALS Book Clubs, with the expectation that these will be expanded. The success of these book clubs also helped stimulate development of ACLA's Wise Walk (see chapter 5). More than sixty PALS Book Clubs are hosted in seventeen Pennsylvania counties, including Allegheny. In 2004 this program was the winner of the Pennsylvania AARP Library Services to Older Adults award.

PARTNERS AND FUNDING The project is a collaboration between ACLA and the Highmark PALS program, a volunteer initiative created by Highmark, a Pittsburgh-based health insurance company. The Highmark PALS program has also developed other library collaborations in Pennsylvania and West Virginia. Highmark and ACLA jointly sponsor the PALS Books Clubs.

Mission Impossible
Evanston Public Library, Evanston, Illinois
www.epl.org

WHAT In this program, yearlong discussions of major literary classics take place at Evanston Public Library. The 2010–11 text was James Joyce's *Ulysses*; the 2011–12 text was Tolstoy's *War and Peace*. According to program organizers, the majority of participants are 50+, many of them new to the library.

GOAL To "create a community of readers who encourage one another as they participate in a literary journey."

FEATURES The concept behind the Mission Impossible programs is that some readers, even serious readers, need support and encouragement to finish some of the more complex literary classics. Two adult librarians at Evanston Library developed the concept after polling their colleagues and finding that there were quite a few "Great Books" that people had tried to read but never finished. They decided that people might find it easier to complete these works if they could read them in groups with other readers.

The first Mission Impossible text was *Ulysses*, a text of approximately 265,000 words. The librarians expected to attract approximately twenty people and were astonished when 120 registered. Nearly half of the original 120 stayed through the entire project. The reading and discussion groups met on alternate months. At several points during the year there were special events to enrich the discussions. A well-known Joyce scholar from Northwestern University spoke at the opening program and also led participants through the especially difficult "Circe" chapter.

The *Ulysses* readers formed into six discussion groups, led by four staff members and two community volunteers. The groups read the same assignments on the same schedule, and some organized their discussions around prepared questions. However, the groups had different approaches to the discussions and each formed their own identity. One group named itself "Baby Bloomers" after the book's main character, Leo Bloom.

Ulysses, Mission Impossible, was so well received that the library repeated the process with *War and Peace*. The first meeting for *War and Peace* brought in 160 people; additional reading groups were created to accommodate them. According to Karen Hansen, one of the key program organizers, "Mission Impossible was never intended especially for midlife adults. However, by far the majority of participants are 50+. They seem to crave something challenging to read and the chance to talk about the book in an intimate setting."

PARTNERS AND FUNDING There are no institutional partners involved in the program. The specialist scholars who have spoken to the Mission Impossible groups donated their time, and the library provided the books.

LIFELONG LEARNING THROUGH ACADEMIC PARTNERSHIPS

Academic Connections: Learn for the Love of Learning
Tempe Connections / Osher Lifelong Learning Institute, Tempe, Arizona
www.tempeconnections.org, http://lifelonglearning.asu.edu

WHAT Tempe Public Library offers these academic programs for 50+ audiences, primarily short courses, through Tempe Connections. The variety and depth of offerings make Academic Connections more substantive than many other library-academia partnerships for lifelong learning.

GOAL To provide Tempe boomers and other active older adults opportunities for intellectual stimulation and exposure to a wide range of topics.

FEATURES Tempe Connections, housed at the Tempe Public Library, is a non-profit community-led organization that offers a wide array of programs and services for 50+ adults, including options for volunteering, informal learning programs, seminars in life planning, and the Tempe Connections Café, a space for social exchange.

Through Academic Connections, Tempe Connections partners with the Osher Lifelong Learning Institute, Arizona State University chapter, one of a network of university-affiliated Institutes across the country. Osher Institutes provide varied academic experiences including short courses, lectures, and workshops. The college-level courses enable older adults to expand their knowledge while meeting new friends and forming new social networks. The Tempe Connections courses are primarily led by Arizona State retired faculty, community college professors, and other professionals.

Academic Connections classes take place at Tempe Public Library and are open to community residents and members of the general public. There is a registration fee of $35 for each semester that includes an Osher Lifelong Learning Institute membership. Maximum class size is twenty-two. Tempe residents are given preference for registration.

> I've worked most my life with younger people. Now my students are in their 50s through their 80s. I've begun to appreciate how wonderful people my own age really are. They're often more interested and engaged than younger students.
>
> —Pam Eck, volunteer coordinator, Academic Connections program

Academic Connections participants have a wide array of educational options. Three or four courses are available at any one time in the following subject areas: science, history and political science, literature, and film history. Courses range from eight to eleven sessions. Courses offered since 2009 include "The First 100 years of Quantum Physics"; "Annie Dillard, Nature Writer Extraordinaire"; "Hybrid Contemporary Poetry"; "Reflections on Diversity and Change in Arizona History: 1930–Present"; and "A Director Who Defined Film: Akira Kurosawa."

PARTNERS AND FUNDING Tempe Connections partners with the Osher Lifelong Learning Institute and the Center for Continued Learning of the Emeritus College, both at Arizona State University. It is supported by the Friends of the Tempe Public Library and community donations.

Academy for Lifelong Learning
Saratoga Springs Public Library, Saratoga Springs, New York
www.sspl.org, www8.esc.edu/esconline/across_esc/alretire.nsf/home.html

WHAT Academic classes are offered at the Sarasota Springs Public Library through a partnership with Empire State College of the State University of New York and the Elderhostel Institute Network (www.roadscholar.org/ein/intro.asp). The Academy for Lifelong Learning (A.L.L.) brings together the multiple resources of these partners, including access to faculty members, to offer university-level classes for motivated older adults.

The arrangement between A.L.L. and the Saratoga library reflects the growth in membership-based continuing education programs and the potential for libraries to be *the* centers where learning takes place.

GOAL To provide older adults with opportunities to engage in college-level courses taught by faculty from nearby academic institutions.

FEATURES A.L.L. is a nonprofit membership-driven organization "of mature adults who share a love of participatory learning." Members pay an annual fee, which qualifies them to take up to three classes per semester and to participate in special-interest group activities outside the classes. A.L.L. has no space of its own. Saratoga Springs Library is one of five institutions and organizations that host A.L.L. classes.

The library is one of the preferred locations for A.L.L. classes. Participants take advantage of the library's collections to carry out their studies and use the spaces to continue their group learning. They also benefit from the library's accessibility and identity as a neutral ground.

A.L.L. members meet with instructors for eight to eleven sessions. Class members are organized into "study groups," with no more than ten individuals per group. In fall 2011, topics offered at the library were "How to Read Faulkner"; "French for Complete Beginners"; and "Why So Many Love Jane Austen: A Collaborative Reading."

A.L.L. faculty are drawn from the many institutions of higher education in the area as well as local retired faculty.

PARTNERS AND FUNDING The partners are Empire State College, the Elderhostel Institute Network, and Saratoga Springs Public Library. A.L.L. memberships cover faculty compensation, the key program expense.

Allegheny County Faculty
Allegheny County Library Association, Pittsburgh, Pennsylvania
www.aclalibraries.org

WHAT The ACLA Faculty is a group of librarians who share their expertise with students in local lifelong learning programs. This initiative may be unique as an organized effort to ensure that academic programs taking place outside of libraries benefit from the expertise of librarians at local libraries.

GOAL To enrich the learning and reading experiences of lifelong learners through exposure to the resources of local libraries and the knowledge and skills of local librarians.

FEATURES The Allegheny County Library Association (ACLA) has a strong record of supporting lifelong learning (see chapter 2). With more and more older adults engaging in lifelong learning programs at local universities and other educational organization, ACLA Faculty was organized to help these students take advantage of local libraries to meet their learning goals. Starting with an initial presentation at the Osher Lifelong Learning Institute (OLLI) at Carnegie Mellon University in 2005, the ACLA Faculty have been invited to present each fall at the OLLI at the University of Pittsburgh as well as at Pittsburgh Oasis, the local affiliate of this national education organization for 50+ learners. In some cases ACLA Faculty members present one session in a larger series. At the invitation of the University of Pittsburgh, OLLI faculty members have provided a full series. Presentation titles have include "Why We Read What We Read: A Sampling of Genres for Your Pleasure!"; "A Surprising Community Asset: What You May Not Know about the New Public Library"; and "Expand Your Genres: A Sampling for Your Reading Pleasure!"

PARTNERS AND FUNDING ACLA Faculty partners with Pittsburgh OASIS and the OLLIs at the University of Pittsburgh and Carnegie Mellon University to enrich their lifelong learning offerings. There is no dedicated funding for the ACLA Faculty presentations.

Brown Bag Lunch and Learn
Multnomah County Public Library / Portland Community College, Portland, Oregon
www.multcolib.org

WHAT Brown Bag Lunch and Learn is a free series of presentations on a wide range of topics related to professional skills. The series stands out for its multi-year collaboration with a community college, the range of topics, and the availability of the programs as live podcasts.

GOAL To help adults in Portland develop and increase professional skills.

FEATURES Since March 2008, Multnomah County Library and Portland Community College have worked together to present the Lunch and Learn programs. Although they are marketed as general adult programs, they have enriched the library's special initiatives for baby boomers such as Kaboom! (see chapter 2), they were listed as part of the overall Life by Design initiative—which focuses on baby boomers and other active older adults—and a high percentage of those who attend the events *are* midlife adults. Program titles vary widely, including "Leading through Service"; "Meaningful Work"; "Moving through Transitions"; and "Stress Rescue."

The programs are held at the central library. Podcasts of the programs are available through the library's website.

PARTNERS AND FUNDING The program is a joint effort of Multnomah County Library and Portland Community College's Community Education office. The two partners have jointly covered incidental costs associated with the program. Presenters' fees are covered by Portland Community College.

Lifelong Learners @ the Library
Champaign Public Library / Parkland College, Champaign, Illinois
www.champaign.org, www2.parkland.edu/communityed

WHAT A collaboration between Champaign Public Library and Parkland College's Lifelong Learners program provides monthly programs on topics of interest to older adult learners. Library patrons gain access to instructors and other expertise at the college, and the library's position as a destination for lifelong learning is reinforced.

GOAL To engage the community in learning.

FEATURES Lifelong Learners @ the Library is a morning program held once a month at the library. It is designed to widen older adult access to the learning resources at Parkland College and to provide an opportunity for intellectual and social exchange. Each hour-long presentation or facilitated discussion is followed by refreshments and an opportunity for socializing. Some presentations involve field trips. The topics reflect the range of programs offered by the college's Lifelong Learners program, including a presentation on the history of rural cemeteries and a discussion of dowsing.

PARTNERS AND FUNDING Parkland College's Continuing Education program, Lifelong Learners, collaborates with the Champaign Public Library to present the series. The two partners share incidental expenses associated with the series.

Lifelong Learning Series

Framingham Public Library / Framingham University's Division of Graduate and Continuing Education, Framingham, Massachusetts

www.framinghamlibrary.org, www.framingham.edu

WHAT A ten-session series offered jointly by Framingham Public Library and Framingham State University Division of Graduate and Continuing Education brings serious and entertaining programming to residents while introducing them to the learning resources at both partner institutions.

GOAL To provide Framingham 55+ residents an opportunity to take part in Framingham State University's continuing education program and to widen awareness of the lifelong learning resources at the library.

FEATURES The Lifelong Learning Series consists of ten presentations, five offered at the library and five at the university. Both institutions market the series and recruit participants. Unlike some university-library partnerships, all presentations in Framingham are by university faculty. Sample topic titles are "Billy Budd by Herman Melville: An Unforgettable Tale of Good and Evil"; "James Dean at 80"; "Dreams Denied, Hopes Abandoned: Russia since the Fall of the USSR"; and "Why Can't the English . . . : An Encounter with My Fair Lady."

PARTNERS AND FUNDERS The library partners with Framingham State University's Division of Graduate and Continuing Education. A grant from MetroWest Community Health Care Foundation made this lifelong learning collaboration possible.

Mental Aerobics

**San Francisco Public Library / City College of San Francisco,
San Francisco, California**
www.spl.org, www.ccsf.edu/olad

WHAT The Older Adults Department of the City College of San Francisco offers this free weekly mental health exercise class for older adults, including baby boomers, in association with the Access Services Department of San Francisco Public Library.

The library's collaboration with the City College of San Francisco is unusual in several ways. First, it is a semester-long series of programs that take place at the main library rather than on the college campus, thereby extending access to public participants who might not attend a campus offering. Second, it combines information on the latest research on brain health with practical approaches to maintaining active mental health. Third, it is structured as a drop-in program as well as a series for regular participants.

GOAL To help older adults maintain and improve cognitive vitality and memory.

FEATURES Mental Aerobics is offered weekly at the library's Civic Center main branch over a period of five months. The library announcement included the following:

> The old saying "use it or lose it" applies as much to the brain as it does to any other muscle in the body. In this very social class, Hope Levy, a member of City College's Older Adults Department since 2003, will lead attendees through fun, challenging and creative brain exercises designed to maintain and improve cognitive vitality and memory. Levy will present ways of conquering everyday memory challenges, such as remembering names and "tip-of-the-tongue syndrome." She will also discuss the latest news on mental fitness. The class is appropriate for first-timers as well as those who have previously attended a memory and mental fitness program.

Library patrons can take one class, the entire series, or pick and choose from among the classes.

PARTNERS AND FUNDING The library partners with the Older Adult Department of the City College of San Francisco.

Osher Lifelong Learning Institute

National Program

www.osherfoundation.org

WHAT In programs of the Osher Lifelong Learning Institute branches (OLLIs), university-based communities of older adults engage socially and intellectually with peers as teachers and learners. The OLLIs largely take their cues from participating adults. Partnerships between OLLIs and libraries offer a means of extending the university offerings to broader public audiences while providing a structure and support for older adult learners and teachers.

GOAL To meet the needs and interests of older learners who want to learn for personal fulfillment.

FEATURES

The OLLIs were established by philanthropist Bernard Osher, who believed that many older adults could benefit from teaching as well as continuing to learn. Today there are 117 institutes, each operating independently, with members

Selected OLLI-Library Partnerships

Crowell Library, San Marino, California
In a partnership with the UCLA OLLI, Crowell Library offered three OLLI classes, including "Aging as Exemplified in Drama." The library's announcement read: "Over 50 and seeking intellectual, cultural or social experiences? Eager to stay informed or master new skills? Have a desire to meet others with similar interests? If you live in the San Marino area, you're in luck: UCLA extension is coming to the Crowell Public Library. and provides opportunities to learn and to socialize." (www.sanmarinopl.org)

Hennepin County (Minnesota) Library
Partnering with the University of Minnesota OLLI, Hennepin Library offered Books You Don't Have Time to Read. The announcement for the program read: "Hear a University of Minnesota OLLI member present a book that tackles a challenging subject of the day. Then discuss the issues involved." (www.hclib.org)

Southbury (Connecticut) Public Library
In 2011, Southbury Public Library offered a four-part holistic lifestyle course in concert with the University of Connecticut–Waterbury OLLI. Each meeting of The Holistic Lifestyle: Contemporary Science Discovers Ancient Wisdom explored "a scientifically proven, simple and natural method of achieving optimum health," such as "Sleep and Your Health and Bacteria—Friend or Foe." (www.southburylibrary.org)

State Library of Missouri
Lifelong Learning for Older Adults University was offered by the state library and the University of Missouri–Columbia OLLI. With the goal of offering "quality education programming for older adults in rural Missouri," the state library purchased OLLI courses for transmission via videoconference to libraries around the state. Preference was given to small and rural libraries with limited programming options. (www.sos.mo.gov)

who enjoy learning and spending time with like-minded individuals. Members, who pay a fee for participation, elect from an array of courses and activities, many led by peers. Drawing upon their local professional and artistic communities, each institute offers courses in a wide variety of subject areas, taught by working, or retired but active, professionals. Courses usually last from four to eight weeks and include topics ranging from politics and science to visual arts, theater, history, music, and gardening. Activities beyond the classroom include special-interest groups, hiking, biking, field trips, and national and international educational tours. Most courses are designed to facilitate learning, encourage discussion, and provide opportunities to socialize.

The OLLI National Resource Center disseminates information to local institutes on effective educational programming for older learners, provides information and connections via a website, publishes a national research journal, organizes an annual conference, and carries out other strategies for OLLIs.

Public libraries are excellent locations for lifelong learning opportunities. Lifelong learning gives a sense of meaning to life, helps establish connections with others and increases cognitive vitality. Keep in mind the importance of a regular time each week, or month; lack of structure is one challenge when one retires; having something to do on a regular basis— e.g., every Tuesday morning—will give people something to structure the rest of their week around.

—Sara Sokoloff, director, Osher Lifelong Learning Institute, Brandeis University

As the OLLIs have become established in their communities, some have started to build partnerships with local libraries, offering peer- or scholar-led classes at libraries or collaborating in special events. For libraries, the OLLI partnerships expand lifelong learning offerings to patrons and bring the library's learning resources to the attention of OLLI members. For OLLIs, the partnerships provide a community location, accessible to members, and opportunities to become more visible to a wide range of potential participants.

Each OLLI–public library partnership is designed differently, depending on members' interests and the two institutions' goals. The OLLI at the University of Arizona is partnering with the Tempe Public Library's Tempe Connections (see chapter 9) to provide a robust array of workshops, lectures, events, and travel. This partnership contrasts with those in which a local OLLI works with a local library to offer one course or special event or, as in the case of Missouri, where the state library has contracted with the OLLI at the University of Missouri to make available videotaped presentations of OLLI courses at libraries throughout the state.

The library-OLLI collaborations are relatively new. As they evolve, both libraries and OLLI organizers will be able to assess what kinds of interactions are most effective to advance their mutual goals of supporting older adult learning and connections for mature adults.

In at least one instance, the academic library associated with an OLLI—that at the University of Illinois—has taken a role in local implementation, offering special privileges to OLLI members, leading classes on preservation and historical topics, and building a closer relationship between participants and the academic library. It is likely that there will be more integration of university library and OLLI functions as this model becomes better known to other OLLIs.

PARTNERS AND FUNDING Partnerships are between local OLLIs and libraries and do not usually involve special funding.

IN-BRIEF: LEARNING

Adult Education Expo

Chelmsford (Massachusetts) Public Library The Adult Education Expo was an opportunity for local educators to promote their courses to adults. Many 50+ residents interested in academic learning took advantage of the chance to learn about local opportunities. Chelmsford also has a substantial online "Adult Education Subject Guide," which includes library resources as well as links to the educational resources in the region. (www.chelmsfordlibrary.org)

Baby Boomer Series

Milanof-Schock Library, Mount Joy, Pennsylvania The Baby Boomer series at Milanof-Schock Library consisted of six informal learning programs to "educate, entertain and enrich our older adult patrons." Some topics were based on patron suggestions; all involved a partner agency or expert. Topic titles included "New Career Options" (partnered with Lancaster Office of Aging); "Retiring: Thriving—Not Just Surviving" (a local geriatric psychiatrist); and "Elderhostel: Adventures in Lifelong Learning" (Lancaster Elderhostel Ambassador). (www.lancaster.lib.pa.us)

Discussion Forums for 50+ Patrons

Andrew Bayne Memorial Library, Pittsburgh, Pennsylvania These forums are one component of the library's overall effort to become a center for older adult exchange and learning. They include a monthly fiction book discussion, a mystery book discussion, and a weekly movie discussion. The sessions are moderated by staff members. Members of the group help select titles of the movies, which often tie in with book selections. (www.baynelibrary.org)

Encore! 55 and Better!

Musser Library, Muscatine, Iowa This series of informal learning programs consists of two parallel strands: monthly educational presentations and weekly computer classes. Encore! responds to a surge in the number of older adults living in the region and offers an example of how a library can brand itself as a destination for 50+ adults with relatively few resources. (www.musserpubliclibrary.org)

Independent Lens / ITVS Community Cinema

Saratoga Springs (New York) Public Library The library partners with the Independent Television Service Community Cinema to present Independent Lens documentaries. The screenings attract numerous 50+ adults along with general adult audiences. (www.sspl.org)

Learn at the Library

Washington County (Minnesota) Library This monthly series of educational and enrichment "mini-classes" is held annually from October through May. Topics focus on a skill that could improve the quality of participants' lives or challenge them to pursue further study. The classes are not limited to midlife adults, but they make up the majority of participants. (www.co.washington.mn.us/info_for_residents/library)

Lecture Series

Sarasota County (Florida) Libraries The library offers weekly opportunities for viewing filmed or videotaped lectures by college professors. Some presentations are one-time lectures and others are a series, similar to a class, on such topics as the history of impressionism. Midlife adults are a majority of the audience for these academic screenings. (http://suncat.co.sarasota.fl.us)

Never Too Late Group

Boston (Massachusetts) Public Library This series of weekly informal learning programs for 60+ adults is said to be the longest-existing library-sponsored program for older adults in the country. Although the program is labeled for "seniors," many midlife adults are regular participants. Never Too Late runs from September to June each year, offering a variety of subjects and formats including lectures, documentary and feature films, videos, concerts, and readings. (www.bpl.org)

Unraveled Crafters

Fargo (South Dakota) Public Library The Unraveled Crafters group is similar to many programs around the country that encourage people who engage in crafts activities to work on projects at the local library, where they can learn from others while taking part in informal discussions. Although such programs are not typically targeted to a particular age group, they attract high proportions of 50+ adults. (www.cityoffargo.com/CityInfo/Departments/Library)

Young at Heart

Mengle Memorial Library, Brockway, Pennsylvania Young at Heart is a weekly informal learning program that includes lectures, painting classes, and public affairs discussions designed to help keep active older adults "abreast of contemporary issues, cultural opportunities and technological advancements." The library's goal is to be seen as a community focal point "and not merely the traditional purveyor of print and non-print resources." The project earned the 2010 Pennsylvania AARP Library Services for Older Adults Award. (http://menglelibrary.org)

CHAPTER 10

INTERGENERATIONAL PROGRAMS AND SERVICES

Intergenerational programming is defined by programs, policies and practices that increase cooperation, interaction and exchange between people of different generations, allowing them to share talents and resources and support each other in relationships that benefit both individuals and their community.

—Generations United International Conference, 2009

The public library is inherently intergenerational. Although this characteristic is usually subsumed in mission language that refers to "lifelong learning" and "patrons of all ages," the intergenerational aspect of the library is one of its core qualities. This quality has heightened value in the context of an aging America, when more intentional cross-generational contact can help breach generational divides and benefit all citizens.

TRENDS

Many organizations, institutions, and policymakers advocate programs that bring individuals from different generations together to work on mutually beneficial activities. They share the conviction that such programs are beneficial to the program participants, who contribute to and learn from each other, and to the communities of which they are a part. Whether the context is a family, an institution, or a neighborhood, the process of becoming familiar with individuals of another generation, and developing trusting relationships, helps eliminate stereotypes that one generation may have about another and prompts new perspectives on different life stages.

For many intergenerational advocates, the primary motivation is to combat ageism and to prepare young people for their own aging. The late Dr. Gene Cohen, a leading advocate for cross-age interaction, encouraged librarians to be more intentional in shaping activities to bring generations together in order to counteract societal trends toward ageism. Cohen worked with the Association for Library Services to Children to develop *Books for Children Portraying Aging and Older Characters in a Positive Light.*

Another advocate of intergenerational programs, Ann Gale, of Chicago's Department of Aging, also argues for such activities as an antidote to ageism:

> Today's children will enjoy an unprecedented longevity. Many will live for 80 or more years. When they are 65, about 20 percent of the population will be 65 or older. So it is essential for children to develop positive attitudes toward older people, toward aging, and toward planning for their long lives. Interaction with older people helps children understand the different roles we accept as we age and grow personally and professionally. . . . Children can become more responsible citizens through programs that help them recognize the value of older persons; encourage them to plan for a long life; and allow them to share experiences with older persons who are not relatives and may be from different cultures.[1]

Beyond the need to combat ageism, there are other reasons to bring different generations together. For instance, it is now widely accepted that children and youth benefit from regular exposure to older adults, through tutoring, mentoring, and other skills-oriented activities. Among the research findings confirming these benefits was a major 1995 study of the national mentoring program Big Brothers, Big Sisters, carried about by Public/Private Ventures. The evaluation showed, among other things, that substantially fewer youth in the program were likely to initiate alcohol or drug use during the program, that academic behaviors and performance were superior to those in the control group, and that the quality of participants' relationships with their parents was also better.[2] Subsequent studies, such as an analysis of the national tutoring program Experience Corps, have shown that similar programs contribute positively to participating students' achievements.[3]

One result of the growing consensus on the benefits of intergenerational contact for young people is the growth in mentoring and tutoring programs, particularly in urban areas. Many corporations and service organizations have enlisted workers and volunteers in tutoring and mentoring projects that involve regular one-on-one contact between an adult and the mentee.

For some years the field of intergenerational programming has been dominated by the assumption that benefits accrue mainly to the young people in the relationship. However, recent research is indicating equally strong benefits for the older adult participants—the mentors, tutors, storytellers, chess partners, and master gardeners. New studies of the process of aging document the importance of social contact, physical activity, intellectual challenge, and assistance to others in mitigating the changes that come with aging. It is not surprising that intergenerational programs, which usually involve all of these, have positive effects on the psychological outlook and physical condition of older participants.[4] As a result of such findings, attention is now being paid to the quality of the intergenerational experience for the older participants as much as for the younger ones.

Intergenerational programs do not always involve older adults and youth. "Intergenerational" can mean book discussions involving three or four adult generations, midlife adults interviewing elderly veterans, family literacy programs serving multiple generations, activities for grandparents and grandchildren, and teenagers teaching baby boomers how to use digital cameras. These multigeneration approaches are a natural result of the demographic changes taking place today, especially the fact that, "in the United States, we are, on average, living 30 years longer than we did in the 19th century, 20 years longer since World War II."[5]

With these variations in the motivation for intergenerational programs and the ages of participants, it is no wonder that there are many different types of program models. For the purposes of description, these fall into one of five broad categories

> **Learning programs** usually involve drawing on the experience and skills of older adults to help young people gain a particular skill or improve their academic performance. Sometimes both children and adults learn together, as in family literacy programs, musical workshops, art classes, or health-related programs.

> **Recreational programs** range from father-son sports to chess clubs, nature walks, poetry slams, and, most recently, video or digital gaming.

> **Cultural and historical transmission programs** engage older adults as sources of memory, stories, specific skills, and cultural traditions.

Projects to address social problems, such as adult mentors for youth "at-risk" of dropping out of high school, for teen parents, or for homeless youth, also include programs that address the social isolation of homebound elderly.

Practical, problem-oriented activities might address intergenerational gardening or cleanup projects, document community environmental assets or hazards, or involve planning some aspect of community infrastructure such as transportation or parks.

IMPLICATIONS FOR LIBRARIES

As an inherently intergenerational space, libraries are especially well equipped to fulfill Generations United's definition of intergenerational programming, with its emphasis on opportunities for different generations to learn about one another and to build relationships (see epigraph). (Generations United is the premier national organization advocating intergenerational programs and defining best practices.) Many libraries do recognize their own value in this regard, and all across the country, in all types of libraries, there are cross-age activities. These are usually concentrated in the learning, recreational, and cultural and historical transmission categories, such as literacy tutoring and afterschool homework assistance for young people, storytelling for children, and volunteer outreach to preschools or nursing homes. Some libraries make a point of inviting people of all ages to participate in chess clubs, knitting classes, or even art classes, and a few organize book discussions for multiple generations. Many libraries also lead or take part in community reading programs such as One Book, One Community, which bring generations and groups together around a common text.

Despite the number of cross-age programs in libraries, they are usually focused on the benefits to the younger generation. Responsibility for these programs is usually assigned to children's or teen librarians, and efforts to target midlife adults as key participants are relatively few and far between. With some exceptions, programming is not necessarily consciously focused on the reciprocal benefits to the older participants. The value of developing more strategic intergenerational activities that also promote positive aging is just beginning to be recognized by the library community.

With the recent advent of the national movement to expand library-based activities for midlife adults, some librarians are including intergenerational programs in their plans. Building on aging research that documents the benefits of social and intellectual stimulation for older adults, the new programs are organized as much from the perspective of the older adult as from that of the younger participants. The Allegheny County (Pennsylvania) Library Association, for instance, which has had a sustained focus on older adult programming, is now developing a concept for an "Intergenerational Academy" and is experimenting with intergenerational art projects and book discussions on the basis that they contribute to positive aging. Allegheny County aims to move from one-time projects to an ongoing portfolio of intergenerational activities beneficial to participants of all ages.

As libraries begin to organize intergenerational activities from the perspective of 50+ adults, they are also looking for ways to help midlife adults interact with both young and older generations. The Lee County (Florida) Library, for instance, has organized Community Conversations, in which midlife adults take leading roles in outreach to frail elderly (see chapter 3).

As libraries are faced with high baby boomer demand for assistance in using new communications technologies, they are turning to younger people for help. They are instituting "tech tutor" programs in which young people, either teens or college students, assist older adults in learning how to carry out basic computer functions and use digital cameras and social media tools. These activities empower young people as teachers and empower older adults as participants in networked communications. They also help participants build new understandings of one another. One example of "tech transfer" is New Haven (Connecticut) Free Public Library's Technology across Generations project, in which Yale students work one-on-one with older adults to help them improve their skills in digital communications (see chapter 6).

Another type of activity that is growing in libraries involves multigenerational civic engagement projects. These include community gardens or community cookbooks but also library murals or community history projects designed by participants of a variety of ages.

One of the newest and fastest-growing programming trends in libraries is intergenerational gaming, consistent with a general trend in libraries to adopt video games and Wii. For instance, nearly eight hundred libraries participated in ALA's National Gaming Day @ your library event in November 2011. Although there is no scholarly consensus, some recent studies document benefits for young people in the use of certain kinds of games, including digital games, especially for literacy and learning.[6] Similarly, new research by specialists on brain health and aging sees physiological benefits of interactive and intergenerational gaming for older adults.[7] As gaming of all kinds becomes more prominent in libraries, it will undoubtedly be used as a strategy to promote intergenerational contact in the same way that a book discussion might do. Minds @ Play, developed by the Tigard (Oregon) Public Library, and the Intergenerational Gaming offered by the Fayetteville (New York) Public Library are harbingers of other projects involving multiple generations that benefit 50+ adults and their younger team members.

The following examples suggest the range of library-based intergenerational opportunities open to 50+ adults. As in other categories of 50+ services discussed in this volume, some of the programs are labeled for "seniors" rather than midlife adults, though in reality they involve or even focus on midlife adults.

Notes

1. See synopsis of Ann Gale, "Longer Lives: Children Learn about Changing Roles. Education Goals," at Intergenerational Initiative, Southern Illinois University Carbondale, http://iii.siuc.edu/Publications/ed/three.html.

2. Joseph P. Tierney and Jean Baldwin Grossman, with Nancy L. Resch, *Making a Difference: An Impact Study of Big Brothers Big Sisters* (Public Private Ventures, reissue 2000 [1995]), http://ppv.org/ppv/publications/assets/111_publication.pdf.

3. G. W. Rebok et al., "Short-Term Impact of Experience Corps® Participation on Children and Schools: Results from a Pilot Randomized Trial," *Journal of Urban Health* 81, no. 1 (2004); abstract at www.ncbi.nlm.nih.gov/pubmed/15047787.

4. S. R. Zedlewski and S. G. Schaner, "Older Adults Engaged as Volunteers," Washington, DC: Urban Institute, *The Retirement Project: Perspectives on Productive Aging*, no. 5 (May 2006), www.urban.org/UploadedPDF/311325_older_volunteers.pdf.

5. Mary Catherine Bateson, *Composing a Further Life: The Age of Active Wisdom* (Tantor Media, 2010).

6. James Paul Gee, *What Video Games Have to Teach Us about Learning and Literacy* (New York: Palgrave Macmillan, 2003.

7. Sarah Francis and Laura Sternweis, "Older Iowans Are Living (Well through) Intergenerational Fitness and Exercise—LIFE," Iowa State University Extension and Outreach, March 29, 2012, www.extension.iastate.edu/article/older-iowans-living-intergenerational-fitness-exercise.

Across the Age Divide

Queens Library, Jamaica, New York

www.queenslibrary.org

WHAT This intergenerational oral history project involves teens and older adults in two neighborhood branches of Queens Library—Bayside and Ozone Park—plus two local schools and the Long Island division of Queens Central Library. The project was a first for the branches involved, and it offers a model for bringing generations and institutions together around a shared community history.

GOAL "To highlight the importance of older adults as sources of community memory and to give both age groups a chance to come together and discover (or rediscover) that our similarities are far more important than our differences."

> [Across the Age Divide] gives the students a chance to bring history alive and to improve their writing skills at the same time. For the older adults, it's an opportunity to remember their own lives and engage with people younger than themselves.
>
> —**Queens Library newsletter**

FEATURES Across the Age Divide was developed in two phases. The initial phase involved elementary school students interviewing 50+ adults at a community center; the second phase brought together students from an elementary school and a high school with older adults from a senior center. The students interviewed the informants in pairs, using questions concerning work, neighborhood, friends, and family. High school students also filmed the interviews to create a short documentary on Ozone Park.

The interviews, which were written up by students in Q&A form, are the basis for booklets on the two projects that are available at the schools and are now part of the collections of the two branch libraries as well as the Long Island division at the Queens Central Library.

PARTNERS AND FUNDING The library's outreach services division organized the collaboration between the schools and senior centers in the two communities. Teachers in the participating schools helped recruit the students. The Long Island Division provided advice on documentation. The project was carried out without special funding.

". . . Age"
Hartford Public Library, Hartford, Connecticut
www.hplct.org

WHAT This intergenerational history and arts program on the themes of age and aging was cosponsored by the History Center of the Hartford Public Library and the Amistad Center for Art and Culture at the Wadsworth Atheneum in 2008/9. It was one element of a larger national demonstration project, Age in America, that involved libraries, museums, and community cultural organizations in Norfolk, Virginia, and Long Island, New York.

". . . Age" was the first ever collaboration between the library's History Center and the museum's Amistad Center, and it provided an effective vehicle for both institutions to showcase aspects of their collections relating to age. The collaboration extended to numerous other cultural organizations, each engaging their constituencies in the ". . . Age" theme. In fact, the number of project participants and community organizations involved in the project prompted a wide variety of intergenerational and cultural activities, helping promote discussion and reflection about the changing roles of older adults in Hartford and across the nation.

> [This project] made me appreciate people older than me . . . what they have experienced that I haven't. I used to brush this off. I listen more to stories now. I also realize what I can contribute. Kids are the ones who know about technology. If knowledge of the past can be linked with tech knowledge, we have one big archive of information.
>
> —Amistad Center Teen Advisory Group member

GOAL To promote public awareness of aging as a historical and cultural phenomenon and to engage community members, including 50+ adults, in creative interpretations of age and aging in Hartford.

FEATURES ". . . Age" included multiple initiatives undertaken by partner organizations, which collectively contributed to wider awareness of the aging theme. The original plan was to explore aging through art, history, and language, which the project did do in full measure. However, as the project evolved it became evident that intergenerational communication was a key element.

The central feature of ". . . Age" was a public art installation of large banners depicting a series of objects and images from the collections of the History Center or the Amistad Center. Related activities included the following:

- Teens from the Amistad Center's Teen Advisory Group selected artifacts or images from the two partners' collections and named each artifact with an "age" word—*message, courage, vintage, bondage, voyage*—expressing their personal responses. For each artifact and the "age" word assigned to it, a teen and an older adult from the community gave their personal oral responses. These were filmed in interviews conducted by the Amistad curator and a *Hartford Courant* columnist. The videos were included in the eventual History Center exhibit.
- Poets affiliated with nearby Hill-Stead Museum created verbal images of one of the key artifacts or images in the form of an audio recording and transcripts of oral responses to that item. The resulting poems were featured in the Museum's 2009 Poetry Festival.
- The Hartford School of Art received the images, interviews, and poetry with which student and adult artists worked together to create banners for the public art exhibit, each featuring an "age" word plus excerpts from the artifact image and language from the poetry.
- A culminating event drew the public, staff of partnering organizations, and contributing poets, artists, teens, and adults to an intergenerational poetry presentation, exhibition opening, and project reception at the History Center.
- The *Hog River Journal* (subsequently renamed *Connecticut Explored*) dedicated its Summer 2009 issue to themes of aging viewed through a historical lens, including ". . . Age" and "Can You See What I See? It's Stories That Surround Me!" by Brenda Miller, director of the History Center.

PARTNERS AND FUNDING The two primary ". . . Age" partners were the History Center of the Hartford Public Library and the Amistad Center for Art & Culture (www.amistadartandculture.org) at the Wadsworth Atheneum Museum of Art (www.thewadsworth.org). Other partners included the Hartford Art School at University of Hartford (www.hartfordartschool.org), the Hill-Stead Museum in Farmington (www.hillstead.org), and the statewide *Hog River Journal*.

The History Center and the Amistad Center jointly received a grant to carry out ". . . Age" from the Re-Imagining Age project, which was funded to carry out Age in America through a national demonstration grant from the IMLS. Each local partner contributed staff time, materials, and other in-kind resources.

Create Together: Intergenerational Art Program / ACLA Intergenerational Academy

Allegheny County Library Association, Pittsburgh, Pennsylvania
www.aclalibraries.org

WHAT Create Together is a six-week program of visual arts instruction for 50+ adults and children in third through sixth grade. Offered since 2006, the program has been so well received that the Allegheny County Library Association (ACLA) has developed the Intergenerational Academy, a summer program offering intergenerational instruction in other disciplines, as well as yoga, at member libraries. By creating the Academy, ACLA is moving from one-time projects to a more systemic, long-term approach to intergenerational programming. ACLA staff are deeply committed to intergenerational activities, resulting in innovative offerings that benefit county residents of multiple ages while attracting 50+ residents to local libraries. ACLA is a national leader with respect to library-based intergenerational activities that include 50+ adults (see chapter 2).

GOAL To facilitate intergenerational communication through use of the library as a space for cross-age arts instruction and creative expression.

FEATURES ACLA has long-standing experience with intergenerational programming and has encouraged member libraries to experiment with different program formats. In 2002 it sponsored a training workshop, "How to Develop Intergenerational Programs," in partnership with Generations Together, a research and advocacy institute at the University of Pittsburgh. In 2004 it provided scholarships to several librarians, including its current community partnerships coordinator, to take part in Generations Together's International Intergenerational Training Institute hosted in Pittsburgh. After this experience ACLA piloted an intergenerational visual arts instruction series at the Andrew Bayne Memorial Library in Bellevue. The program has been operating for four summers and has proven highly successful in terms of sustained participation and student enthusiasm.

The program model ACLA developed involves a partnership with a local arts education organization, the Brew House Association, which recruits and helps prepare the arts instructors. The classes include five or six 50+ adults and a similar number of children from third to sixth grade. Each week a different medium is taught. According to the project director, the arts instructors report that they are learning themselves, having had experience in teaching one age group or another but not the experience of working with both groups together.

Given the enthusiasm of both program participants and arts instructors, ACLA is now expanding the concept to create the ACLA Intergenerational Academy, designed to offer different instructional series in member libraries. Subjects for the summer and fall of 2011, the first year, were writing, health and yoga, music, and art. The Academy will also include the monthly Intergenerational PALS Book Clubs hosted at additional libraries as well as a pilot program of an Intergenerational Conversation Salon and Wise Walk.

ACLA staff see many possibilities for cross-age creative activities. Charity Leonette, community partnerships coordinator, believes that libraries need to be more intentional about intergenerational contact and collaboration: "There are so many programming possibilities with the arts. Librarians can experiment with formats that facilitate substantive contact and communication between different generations."

PARTNERS AND FUNDING ACLA consulted originally with the Valley Care Association, a local service organization for seniors and families that shared its intergenerational art program and exhibit through schools, and Generations Together at the University of Pittsburgh, which helped to launch the program with its intergenerational expertise. The current partner is the Brew House Association, a Pittsburgh arts organization. Yoga in Schools (yogainschools.org) was a new partner for 2011.

Initial funding for Creating Together originated from the Americans for Libraries Council, which recognized ACLA as a Lifelong Access Center of Excellence and Innovation in 2006. ACLA is now pursuing additional grant funding.

Grandparents and Books
Los Angeles Public Library, Los Angeles, California
www.lapl.org

WHAT Grandparents and Books (GAB) is a citywide, intergenerational reading enrichment program made possible by 50+ volunteers. It is nationally known as a proven approach for library systems to increase reading enrichment through coordinated training and support of older adults. The program's Dialogic Reading method provides a framework for the volunteers to use in working with their reading partners. The consistency and continuity of the program and the quality of the volunteer training are unusual, as are the numbers of children and volunteers who have benefited from the program over the years.

Similar to other intergenerational projects that engage older adult volunteers to work with young people, GAB could also be categorized as a model for civic engagement (see chapter 3).

GOAL To increase children's literacy and comprehension skills.

FEATURES Los Angeles Public Library recruits and trains GAB volunteers to read aloud and perform book-centered activities with children at the library after school and on weekends. All volunteers make a six-month commitment to read with children at the library at least two hours per week.

GAB has been operating for twenty years, during which time library staff have trained thousands of volunteers. The program is one of a few public library programs in the country that uses the Dialogic Reading method, which emphasizes discussions and open-ended questioning during a reading. The method also includes narrative and choral reading, repetition, and multisensory activities. Sponsors support the costs of training workshops and annual purchases of new books.

PARTNERS AND FUNDING GAB is supported by the Kenneth T. and Eileen L. Norris Foundation, Dan Murphy Foundation, Carrie Estelle Doheny Foundation, Frances and Benjamin Benenson Foundation, and William H. Hannon Foundation.

Intergenerational Gaming
Fayetteville Free Library, Syracuse, New York
http://fflib.org

WHAT This intergenerational game program, started in 2008, involves people ages 5 to 95. The program is unusual in the extent to which it is integrated throughout the library. In developing the program, the Fayetteville Free Library has benefited from the involvement of experts at the Syracuse University School of Library and Information Services, who have created a Game Lab at the university.

GOAL To promote literacy skills, strategic thinking, and analysis, and to help people of different ages to come together and interact, creating a community among library patrons.

FEATURES The program was started as an intergenerational event to which the library invited families, senior citizens from local residential facilities, adult patrons, and teens. According to Monica Kuryla, director of virtual and innovation services at the Fayetteville Library, "people of all ages would come in and they would teach each other and play together. It was really exciting." Since then the library has developed a collaborative relationship with Scott Nicholson, a Syracuse University School of Library and Information Services professor, who has helped students at the "ISchool" create the Game Lab. With Professor Nicholson's advice the library has built a collection of board and video games capable of being played anywhere in the library from a portable gaming cart. The cart carries four flat-screen TVs, two Xbox 360 Kinects, and two Wiis.

Gaming is integrated throughout the library, and children, families, teens, and 50+ adults are encouraged to learn how to play and enjoy the games. The gaming program is guided by a committee that includes Nicholson and a Game Lab colleague, students, clerks, and librarians.

The library is currently raising funds to create a "Fab Lab" that will provide community access to new, innovative creativity tools like 3D printers. The Fab Lab will promote collaboration and "making." It will also promote exchange of knowledge and skills across generations. The library's executive director, Sue Considine stated, "Our philosophy is that libraries exist to provide access to opportunities for people to come together to learn, discuss, discover, test, create."

PARTNERS AND FUNDING The library's Intergenerational Gaming program has benefited from a working relationship with the Game Lab, a project of the Syracuse University School of Library and Information Science. Local business sponsors have helped the library acquire gaming materials.

Intergenerational Poetry Slam / Books-to-Action
Hayward Public Library, Hayward, California
www.library.hayward-ca.gov

WHAT Hayward's annual intergenerational poetry workshop and intergenerational poetry slams have all involved many 50+ adults. The library also developed a special Books-to-Action series for boomers that involved an intergenerational community gardening day in 2011.

GOAL To stimulate cross-generation communication while engaging midlife adults in activities that meet their needs for creative expression, learning, and civic involvement.

FEATURES Both the projects outlined here were initiated as a result of the California State Library's Transforming Life After 50 initiative (www.transforming lifeafter50.org), which prompted Hayward staff to recognize that the library could be instrumental in engaging midlife adults more substantively in the life of the community. Intergenerational programs were seen as a strategy for engagement.

The poetry workshops and slams were carried out in conjunction with the 2011 Big Read, an inherently intergenerational community reading program. High school students, 50+ adults, and others in the community took part in the workshops and culminating event.

Hayward's Books-to-Action program was modeled on a similar project developed by the Multnomah County Public Library (see chapter 2) in which 50+ participants read a book about a social issue, discuss its local implications, and then take part in a community service project where they can make an immediate difference in addressing a related problem. In 2011, Hayward selected the book *Farm City: The Education of an Urban Farmer*, by Novella Carpenter. Participants in the *Farm City* discussions took part in an intergenerational community garden work day at a local middle school.

PARTNERS AND FUNDING The poetry workshops and slam, as part of the 2011 Big Read, involved partnerships with the National Endowment for the Arts and Arts Midwest. In addition, there were many local partners including the local high schools. Books-to-Action partners included the Chabot College Book Club, Project EAT, Alameda County Office of Education, and American Association of University Women Hayward/Castro Valley branch.

Funding for the workshops and slam derived from an LSTA grant administered by the California State Library and from the Eureka! Statewide Leadership program (www.eurekaleadership.org). Hayward's Books-to-Action was also supported by LSTA funding from the California State Library as well as by the Friends of the Hayward Public Library and the Chabot College Foundation.

Long Island Grows Up

Middle Country Public Library / Long Island Museum, Centereach, New York

www.mcpl.lib.ny.us, www.longislandmuseum.org

WHAT A collaborative intergenerational project carried out during 2008/9 by Middle Country Public Library, in partnership with Long Island Museum, involved oral history interviews of older adult residents concerning their memories of growing up on Long Island. The project complemented an exhibition titled "Growing Up on Long Island" organized by the museum. It was one of three local projects that formed Age in America, a national demonstration of the potential for library-museum collaboration around the theme of "age" and "aging" in America.

The collaborative nature of the project was unusual, as were the integration of the intergenerational interviews in the museum exhibit and the inclusion of museum exhibit "memories" in the library's local history archive. Both institutions' collections and audiences benefited from the oral history process. Beyond the teens and the older adults they interviewed, the project reached diverse multigenerational audiences, and the interviews are still available online. In addition, Long Island Grows Up added a new dimension to the library's WISE program, which provides information and activities for seniors.

GOAL To prompt young people's awareness of older adults as important sources of experience and information on local history and social change, to stimulate cross-generational dialogues about the process of growing up, to add a personal dimension to the Long Island museum exhibition, and to expand the library's local history archive.

FEATURES During planning for the museum exhibit, the library's teen advisory group conducted a series of oral history interviews with older adults, some of whom were actually grandparents of the young people. The general theme of the recorded conversations was "Growing Up on Long Island," with questions designed to elicit memories regarding specific topics such as games, school, and becoming an adult. The museum exhibit included three TV-DVD installations playing these interviews, which were placed in different sections of the exhibit and on the project website. The full recordings are now available as part of the library's local history collection.

In addition to the oral histories, special events at the library targeted families and older adults, including intergenerational book talks, films, and a tour of historic sites. The Middle Country Reads project (www.middlecountryreads .org), an intergenerational community-wide reading program, provided a book discussion, films, and social events that brought generations together to enjoy stories, music, dance, and crafts from other eras. More than three hundred people of many ages read the book selection for the year, *Wish You Well*, by David Baldacci. Several hundred additional people participated in programming related to the book, thus extending the intergenerational discussion about age and aging on Long Island.

The museum also carried out events that prompted "growing up" reminiscences from exhibition viewers. They engaged people in "memory" events whereby their recollections of childhood and their reactions to the exhibition were captured. Recorded memories from the exhibit now form part of the library's local history archive.

PARTNERS AND FUNDING The primary partners for Long Island Grows Up were the library and the Long Island Museum. The oral history project and related activities were based on the museum's "Growing Up on Long Island" exhibit, on display during spring and summer 2009. The library and museum reached out to many local and regional organizations to build awareness of the exhibition and the overall project, including Dowling College, senior centers, community centers, and other libraries.

Long Island Grows Up received a grant through the Age in America project, based on national funding from the IMLS. The Long Island Museum received exhibition support from Astoria Federal Savings Bank.

Oasis Reading Club
Pima County Public Library, Tucson, Arizona
www.library.pima.gov, www.oasisnet.org/Cities/West/TucsonAZ/Tutoring.aspx

WHAT This intergenerational reading skills tutoring program for elementary school students at El Rio Branch Library was operated by the library and OASIS volunteers trained by the Tucson OASIS Intergenerational Tutoring Program.

GOAL To build reading skills through "the power of writing" and the assistance of adult volunteers.

FEATURES The OASIS Reading Club involves hour-long tutoring sessions during which adults assist students in writing a journal. The philosophy behind the nine-week program is to increase reading skills through the interests of the child rather than by following the standard school model of completing a certain amount of material in a given period. Tutors try not to impose reading or writing as tasks to be performed and instead work with children to increase their love of reading and self-expression. Families are involved as well, with tutors encouraging parents to find ways to stimulate their children's independent reading and writing.

The El Rio Branch Library is housed at El Rio Neighborhood Center, which has helped facilitate identifying children and families interested in participating in the reading club. The library's project coordinator is responsible for pairing tutors and students; OASIS recruits the tutors. As in other OASIS programs, the tutors receive training before working with the children. OASIS has found that recruiting tutors is not difficult; tutors state that they enjoy the one-on-one sessions with children and see the work as a means of making a difference in their communities.

The program at El Rio Branch Library was so well received by family participants that it is being expanded to six additional branches in the county library system.

PARTNERS AND FUNDING The OASIS Reading Club project is a partnership between the Pima County Public Library, Tucson OASIS Intergenerational Tutoring Program, El Rio Neighborhood Center, and participating branch libraries. OASIS is a national program that promotes positive aging through learning, healthy programs, and volunteer engagement. The Tucson OASIS Intergenerational Tutoring Program has existed since 1981; the Reading Club is the first formal partnership with the public library, for which it provides tutor training and supplies.

One Book, One Philadelphia
Free Library of Philadelphia, Philadelphia, Pennsylvania
www.freelibrary.org

WHAT This city-wide initiative engages thousands of people, including many 50+ adults, in reading an annual selection and participating in complementary discussions, workshops, and programs. One of the largest and oldest One Book,

One Community initiatives in the country, One Book, One Philadelphia offers 50+ adults, along with people of all ages, a wide array of opportunities to engage with literature, history, and issues relevant to residents of Philadelphia today. Intergenerational discussion is an important feature of the program.

In 1998 the Seattle Public Library's Center for the Book initiated a One City, One Book program for the city of Seattle. The goal was to involve residents of all ages and backgrounds in a joint reading and discussion experience and to foster enjoyment of literature. The concept quickly took hold in the library community and beyond. Today there are more than four hundred localized book programs across the country, with titles such as "One City, One Book" or "One [City] Reads." These vary widely in scope and approach. In most locations the local library is the lead or a key partner. The majority of the reading programs involve complementary activities such as author talks, performances, read-a-thons, school-based activities, and exhibitions or movies on the themes of the book.

Like libraries, One Book, One Community programs are inherently intergenerational. In addition, they are often organized by 50+ adults and nearly all attract and benefit 50+ adults as readers and program participants. The examples featured throughout this chapter reflect the diversity of these programs and the extent to which they are strong additions to the portfolio of a "50+ Library."

GOAL To promote reading, literacy, library use, and community building by encouraging multigenerational residents of the entire greater Philadelphia area to read and discuss a single book.

Selected One Book, One Community Programs

One Book, One Community
Allegheny County Library Association, Pittsburgh, Pennsylvania
The Allegheny County library system (ACLA) was an early adoptee of the annual One Book, One Community concept. ACLA's approach is unusual, with its primary focus a particular theme rather than a book. The first project focused on racial tolerance, using Harper Lee's *To Kill a Mockingbird* as the common text. Through readings, discussions, and related programming, individuals throughout the county participated. Later themes have included environmental preservation, friendship

across the generations, and mental disability. ACLA has expanded the initiative each year, with multiple partners and related programs, and has made it a signature initiative. The goal is "to create the feeling of a county-wide book club, where residents of all ages and backgrounds read and discuss one book." All forty-five member libraries participate; ACLA provides kits for local book clubs, and numerous partners extend the reach of the program. (www.acla.org)

Arlington Reads
Arlington (Virginia) Public Library
For six years the library has

presented an annual community read to promote "intergenerational dialogue and the joy of reading." A county-wide initiative, Arlington Reads encourages residents of diverse generations to read one thought-provoking book each year. All residents are encouraged to participate in accompanying programs that stimulate further reflection and cross-generational discussion. Programs include film screenings, author talks, storytimes for young children, and panel discussions. Funded by the Friends of the Arlington Public Library, partners include the Arlington Teen Network Board, Starbucks Coffee

FEATURES Since its inception in 2002, the Free Library of Philadelphia has taken the lead in organizing One Book, One Philadelphia. All library departments and their patrons are involved, including the library's Central Senior Services. In fact, as a lifespan initiative, this program is important in linking older patrons with younger readers in the library and throughout the city.

Each year One Book, One Philadelphia organizes varied programs to enhance and extend the reading of the selected text, including performances, film screenings, workshops, author events, and activities designed for teens, children, and families. Many of the programs are intergenerational, and most of the book titles selected for the annual reading are intended to be read by mixed age groups.

PARTNERS AND FUNDING One Book, One Philadelphia is a joint project of the Mayor's Office and the Free Library of Philadelphia. For implementation, more than six hundred community partners were involved in the 2011 program, ranging from Temple University, the Rosenbach Museum and Library, and Thompson Reuters to local parks groups, churches, senior centers, theaters, book groups, and restaurants.

Among the many sponsors for the 2011 program were Walmart, Field Foundation, North American Beverage Company, WHYY, City Paper, and other professional and business sponsors. In addition, hundreds of community partners have developed programs and contributed resources to facilitate the success of the program.

Company, and Busboys and Poets. (http://library.arlingtonva.us)

One Book, One Community
Brown County Library,
Green Bay, Wisconsin
Green Bay's One Book, One Community initiative was organized by a coalition of agencies to "engage the community in dialog and foster page-turning togetherness." Brown County Library hosts many of the events. The program developed from a community-wide event focused on issues of diversity, and the texts have included Elie Wiesel's *Night* and Paul Fleischman's *Seedfolks.* Today, multiple partners are involved, from Brown County University of Wisconsin Extension and Green Bay Area Public Schools to the Volunteer Center of Brown County. (www.co.brown.wi.us/library)

Stanislaus Reads
Stanislaus County Library,
Modesto, California
To help address low literacy rates in the county, and to build interest in reading and literature, the County Library, County Office of Education, and other sponsors started a community-wide, intergenerational reading program with multiple events and book discussions at all library locations. This program was unusual in its effort to engage a wide variety of readers by selecting books with themes relevant to the local community (family and farming) and by using three books for three different reading levels. Complementary programs include Write Where You Are: A Memoir Writing Workshop, designed for all ages. Those who write in a language other than English are encouraged to participate. Stanislaus Reads illustrates how to adapt the One Book, One Community model for different communities and individuals with different reading capacities. (www.stanislauslibrary.org)

Senior Savvy

West Hartford Libraries, West Hartford, Connecticut

www.westhartfordlibrary.org

WHAT Teens at the West Hartford libraries worked one-on-one with older adults to help them gain basic computer skills, learn word processing, and become familiar with the Internet. In a town where adults over 65 are 20 percent of the population, this program provided a well-coordinated system for matching talented young people with older adults of different computer skill levels and a desire to improve their online communications.

GOAL To provide older adults with customized, individualized instruction, using the computer know-how of teens from the community. The program also encouraged cross-generational interaction and appreciation.

FEATURES West Hartford librarians developed Senior Savvy after noticing the high demand for computer instruction by older patrons but, at the same time, the limitations of group instruction. With project funding they were able to pay the teen tutors a stipend, hire a coordinator to recruit the teens and older adults and oversee the year-long program, and also purchase support materials.

Senior Savvy proved successful far beyond expectations. Teens were diligent in carrying out their one-hour sessions for up to six adults on Saturdays. They were able to respond to a wide variety of needs and questions from the older adults and to help them accomplish tasks they had been unable to do without the focused assistance. The teen services were considerable: during the year-long program twelve teen tutors helped 159 older adults in more than four hundred tutoring sessions. In addition, many of the teens and their older students took a personal interest in one another. Project director Doreen McCabe stated, "This intergenerational connection between the two groups has been a delight to watch and a real bonus to the program."

Unfortunately the project could not continue without dedicated funding, especially for the position of coordinator. Nevertheless, Senior Savvy provides an excellent model for intergenerational connections based on computer skills exchange.

PARTNERS AND FUNDING There were no formal partners for this project. The library received an LSTA grant through the Connecticut State Library's Division of Library Development

Socrates Café
National Program

www.philosopher.org/en/Socrates_Cafe.html

WHAT This model for community discussions involves people from different backgrounds and different generations who exchange ideas based on the "Socratic method."

GOAL To encourage philosophical discussions and to foster an understanding and respect for others' opinions.

FEATURES Socrates Café gatherings, which are usually coordinated by volunteers, take place around the world in public locations such as libraries. Those taking place in libraries in the United States engage individuals from different generations, including baby boomers, who enjoy the opportunity for free-form intellectual exchange. The groups are loosely based on a book, *Socrates Café*, by Christopher Phillips, who describes the approach as "making a more inclusive world" while engaging in the Socratic method of open deliberation.

There is no set curriculum for the Café discussion. Discussion topics are selected at the beginning of each session. At the Pikes Peak Library District, the "adult group discusses philosophy, religions, spirituality, and the common threads among humanity."

Discussion usually focus on a key question such as "What is a just war?" at the Largo (Florida) Library or "Are there any absolute truths?" at the Hennepin County (Minnesota) Library. According to the Socrates Café method, there are no right or wrong answers to topic questions. Participants are encouraged to listen to others' opinions and to express their own without concern about criticism. The method is intended to widen participants' understanding of an issue and to gain respect for multiple perspectives.

Sample Socrates Café Sites

Albright Memorial Library, Scranton, Pennsylvania
www.lclshome.org/albright

Boulder (Colorado) Public Library
http://boulderlibrary.org

Delaware County (Pennsylvania) Library / Marple Public Library
www.marplepubliclibrary.org

District of Columbia Public Library / Takoma Park Library
www.dclibrary.org/node/11315

Hennepin County (Minnesota) Library / Ridgedale Library
www.hclib.org

Largo (Florida) Library
www.largo.com

Indian Valley Library, Telford, Pennsylvania
www.ivpl.org/Joomla

Nordonia Hills (Ohio) Branch Library
www.akronlibrary.org/nordoniahills

Pikes Peak (Colorado) Library District
www.ppld.org

Libraries hosting a Socrates Café group may help publicize the sessions and provide complementary study materials. Some librarians moderate the face-to-face discussions and related online forums. The Socrates Café model is an example of programming that can be initiated by older adults themselves, with the library providing a comfortable, neutral environment and playing a supportive role.

PARTNERS AND FUNDING Socrates Café groups are usually independently organized in each community, with the library as a supporting partner. The discussions do not depend on external funding.

Sprouting Together

Altoona Area Public Library, Altoona, Pennsylvania

www.altoonalibrary.org

WHAT This program for grandparents and grandchildren ages 6–10 encouraged joint engagement in art projects, crafts, and games. The high level of interaction between the generations, a special focus on family stories, and the opportunity to create a scrapbook of memories demonstrate how the public library can deepen intergenerational communication between family members.

GOAL To promote interaction between grandparents and their grandchildren and strengthen the bonds between these generations.

FEATURES Grandparents and grandchildren were invited to the Altoona Area Public Library for a "celebration of two different generations" in spring 2008. Sprouting Together was held on Saturday mornings for two hours. Each session included different crafts and games. Focusing on family history in an interactive learning environment, participants worked on family tree art projects, discussed cultural and economic changes over the generations, used clothing to imagine different eras, and created scrapbooks with personal stories and family-related images.

One innovative aspect of the program was videos of the session on YouTube, which allowed participants to share the experience with family and friends outside the local area. The library received a 2008 AARP Library Services for Older Adults Award for the program.

PARTNERS AND FUNDING Sprouting Together did not involve specific partners. Funding was provided by the United Way of Blair County, Pennsylvania.

IN-BRIEF: INTERGENERATIONAL PROGRAMS

Arlington Voices: The Story of Our Lives

Robbins Library, Arlington, Massachusetts A weeklong oral history project, held June–July 2010, gave students in grades 4–8 tools for interviewing and creating public presentations. Guided by a professional storyteller, adults were interviewed by students who then created an evening program for the general public. The project reflects the value of older adults' experiences and memories and how different generations can learn about each other. (www .robbinslibrary.org)

Chess Club

Pima County Public Library, Quincie Douglas Branch, Tucson, Arizona All across the country libraries offer chess for both young people and older adults. The Pima County Club is totally intergenerational, with members from elementary school age to 50+ and older. All receive instruction and individual attention from an expert instructor, and games are played without regard to age. (www.library.pima.gov)

Hooks and Needles: Knit and Crochet

Fresno County (California) Public Library, Auberry Branch Many libraries offer classes and workshops on knitting, sewing, scrapbooking, or other crafts, and 50+ adults are taking advantage of these opportunities to mix creative activities with social interaction. Fresno Library encourages teens and adults to "join others to learn together how to knit or crochet." (www .fresnolibrary.org)

Intergenerational Book Club

Allegheny County Library Association, Pittsburgh, Pennsylvania A pilot project, held at the Carnegie Library in 2010, tested the concept of intergenerational book discussions designed to promote shared learning and exchange of opinions between two critical age groups. The Book Club brought older adults together with high school students to discuss three texts focused on social issues. It expanded on the library association's prior work to support book clubs that engage 50+ adults in stimulating discussion while fostering social interaction. (www.acla.org)

Intergenerational Poetry Night

Morrill Memorial Library, Norwood, Massachusetts In 2011, the annual intergenerational poetry evening at the library featured a poetry group known as PROPOPEs (Prose, Poetry and People), from the Norwood Senior Center, along with students from a local middle school. Participants were invited to read one or two poems of their own creation or by their favorite poets. The theme was "bright objects hypnotize the mind," from Elizabeth Bishop's poem "A Word with You." (http://norwoodlibrary.org)

Lasting Memories

Cuyahoga County Public Library, Fairview Park Branch, Parma, Ohio The Lasting Memories Oral History Project was designed to bring students and older adults together to discuss and preserve the personal and community history of Cuyahoga County residents. The program was organized in pairs made up of a student and an adult at least 50 years older. (www.cuyahoga.lib.oh.us)

Minds at Play

Tigard (Oregon) Public Library In 2010 the Tigard Public Library offered a yearlong gaming series for all ages, including "Boomers, Seniors and Teens." The two-part program emphasized twenty-first-century literacy and the role of the library as a community hub. The first series included board games and sports such as bowling, golf, and baseball that involved social components and light physical activity with the Wii gaming system. Older adults were invited, with teen volunteers and relatives assisting. The second series—twelve events—included games involving strategy, narrative, knowledge, and action such as board games and role-playing games. A Retrogaming program was included, where adults and teens could test their skills on '80s-era consoles and computer games. Minds at Play was funded by an LSTA grant administered by the Oregon State Library. (www.tigard-or.gov/library)

Spellbinders

Douglas County Libraries, Castle Rock, Colorado Spellbinders are volunteer storytellers, ages 50 and up, who relate stories to children in schools. The Douglas County chapter is a collaboration between local libraries and the Douglas County School District. The Douglas County Libraries literacy department recruits volunteers who want to share "their amazing stories with young people" and provides training and support. The program is an example of midlife adult civic engagement as well as a vehicle for intergenerational contact. (http://douglascounty libraries.org)

Take a Hike! An Intergenerational Walk in the Woods

Reading (Massachusetts) Public Library In August 2011 the Reading Public Library invited "all ages," including grandchildren, children, and friends of all ages to take a "reading walkabout." Two librarians led this nature hike, in which participants discovered "the flora and fauna of our community, with just a touch of history!" (www.readingpl.org)

Wii Sports for Seniors

Peters Township Public Library, McMurray, Pennsylvania Teen volunteers facilitate a Wii Sports for Seniors program for 90 minutes weekly. They use the Teen TV room, which is specially equipped with a TV, a Wii, and four X-Boxes. Some teens have taught older adults how to play sports using the Nintendo Wii and acted as personal trainers and cheerleaders for the older adult participants. Both the teens and their older students benefit from the program, which allows teens to contribute their skills and time and helps keeps the older adults fit and socially connected. (www.ptlibrary.org)

CHAPTER 11

FINANCIAL PLANNING AND BUSINESS DEVELOPMENT

The older you are, the more likely you are to be self-employed or a small-business. I don't think it's new, but I do think it's growing.

—Edward Rogoff, professor of entrepreneurship, Baruch College

For nearly two decades libraries have been expanding their business and financial planning services. Some have organized business development centers, providing one-stop business reference assistance, specialized collections, online databases, and workshops for small business owners. Others have focused on public programs and advisory services to increase residents' financial literacy and capacities for financial planning. With the aging of the U.S. population and substantial change in how 50+ adults choose to spend their time and support themselves, libraries' business and financial planning services are especially valuable. It is not surprising that librarians and workshop presenters report that older adults of all generations, from boomers to centenarians, are responding favorably to library offerings in business and finance. Still, given the growing number of midlife adults and their needs for assistance in examining options and planning for a new life stage, it would behoove libraries to be more intentional in developing programs for this age group.

TRENDS

Two national trends are driving development of financial planning and business development services for 50+ adults: a boom in the numbers of older adults who are self-employed or small business owners; and a growing need by older adults for assistance in acquiring basic skills in financial planning, financial management, and investing. These trends have spawned new reference services, expansion and marketing of print and online resources, and new partnerships with financial education and business development organizations.

SMALL BUSINESS OWNERSHIP AND ENTREPRENEURSHIP

The national discourse about aging and longevity tends to focus on the economics of aging and, specifically, on the potentially negative economic impact of increased numbers of older Americans. There is wide acceptance of the view that baby boomers, members of the "silent generation," and other older adults will collectively create an insupportable fiscal burden on the country. Will our current formulas for Social Security and Medicare be sustainable? Must we continue to raise the age at which people are allowed to retire with full benefits? Will an increased proportion of older adults mean a more sluggish economy and less entrepreneurial activity?

Unfortunately, this discussion rarely takes into account another important side of the aging equation, that is, the number of 50+ adults who are not only productive members of the workforce beyond the usual retirement years but are also managing, creating, and expanding businesses. Baby boomers are becoming business owners faster than any other cohort. According to the Ewing Marion Kauffman Foundation, a nonprofit group that studies U.S. business start-ups, from 2007 to 2008 (the latest data available) new businesses launched by 55- to 64-year-olds grew 16 percent. All told, boomers in that age group started approximately 10,000 new businesses a month.[1] A certain number of these new business developers may be converting a hobby into a vocation, others are drawing on their experiences and skills to create a new service or product, and still others are following a passion to make a difference as entrepreneurs of social change. The trend is so strong that the Kauffman Foundation predicts that the country's aging workforce could be responsible for a boom in entrepreneurship: "Americans aged 55 to 64 form small businesses at the highest rate of any age group—28% higher than the adult average."[2]

FINANCIAL LITERACY

Many people, of all income levels and economic circumstances, find it hard to comprehend the complexities of Social Security and pensions, banking policies and practices, mortgage, insurance, and management of debt. The consequences of misunderstanding these basics are greater in times of economic uncertainty and life transitions. Without adequate financial literacy, more and more individuals, including those approaching retirement or recently retired, are at risk of economic insecurity or exploitation. The Presidential Advisory Council on Financial Literacy's 2008 Annual Report described financial literacy as among the causes of financial and credit crises.[3] The Employee Benefit Research Institute noted in 2010 that "individuals in the 50–70 year age group believe they are prepared for a comfortable retirement, but many have not saved enough to achieve that goal. Today, only 43% of Americans have calculated how much they need to save for retirement."[4]

The current recession has been a wake-up call for many baby boomers—especially those considering leaving full-time employment who have not saved enough for retirement or considered the number of postwork years they may need to finance. Planning for aging goes beyond having an IRA, a health proxy, and a will. It should include development of an individualized plan that aligns with personal and family assets and obligations. The need for planning is magnified as older adults create new pathways for retirement and envision productivity in new ways.

IMPLICATIONS FOR LIBRARIES

There are significant opportunities for libraries to position themselves as essential sources of information and assistance as older adults confront the financial issues outlined above. Libraries have core resources and services in place that can be enhanced and made more visible to meet the needs of an expanding 50+ population.

As one example, libraries already have strong credentials and sources to draw on as they work with older adults who own or are starting their own businesses. Nearly all libraries offer access to business development information in print and online, including proprietary databases, real-time reports and analysis of market trends, case studies, and other essential tools for business planning. Depending on their size, their community, and local economic conditions, many libraries augment collections with other services such as workshops, individualized financial counseling, and fee-based business development advice. Some libraries focus on basic business planning, others on entrepreneurship, and yet others on assistance in creating the networks that can enhance business activities and enlarge the local pool of business-related information. With increased demands for face-to-face assistance and counseling from businesses customers, many libraries have built partnerships with the U.S. Department of Labor, local chambers of commerce and other business associations, state economic development agencies, and groups such as SCORE that have a tradition of advising small businesses through the skills and experience of retired managers and executives.

As libraries perceive an increase in local business owners who are older adults or late-life entrepreneurs, they can, with relatively little investment, adapt their collections and services to ensure their relevance. They can also conduct targeted outreach to bring their resources to the attention of these patrons. In doing so they support local economic development while strengthening support from a key local constituency—older adult members of the business community.

With respect to financial literacy, libraries are also well positioned to respond to the needs of older patrons. In recent years many libraries have recognized the growing need for all people, not just low-literacy individuals and others outside the economic mainstream, to have a thorough understanding of financial basics and the tools they need for financial management. Libraries are responding, either by adapting or expanding existing offerings to ensure their relevance to midlife adults or by testing new programs targeted for 50+ patrons. Examples include New York Public Library's Campaign for Financial Literacy and Daly City (California) Library's Wi$eUp financial education program for baby boomers, both profiled below.

Midlife adults who are seeking ways to shift from a work-based income to one based on savings, to invest or protect investments, or to build new revenue streams can turn to libraries' existing print and digital resources and reference services. These constitute an important base from which libraries can expand work with older adults in the form of workshops, special software, and even one-to-one counseling. In addition, through partnerships with specialist organizations libraries can augment their collections and services. Two major national initiatives to strengthen investment education—Smart Investing @ your library and How Can I Afford Retirement?—demonstrate the value of collaboration. In both instances the library context enhances the educational offerings, providing additional information and assistance for participants during and beyond the programs.

Whatever the financial and business development needs of midlife adults—needs for information, education, reference assistance, or counseling—libraries have assets and services that can be highlighted or expanded. The following examples demonstrate some of the ways that libraries are starting to take advantage of this potential to serve as centers for financial education and business development for 50+ patrons.

Notes

1 Dane Stangler, *The Coming Entrepreneurship Boom*, Ewing Marion Kauffman Foundation, June 2009, p. 4, www.kauffman.org/uploadedfiles/the-coming-entrepreneurial-boom.pdf.

2. Ibid.

3. *President's Council on Financial Literacy*, Annual Report, 2008, www.jumpstart.org/assets/files/PACFL_ANNUAL_REPORT_1-16-09.pdf.

4. "43% of American Workers Have Less than 10k in Retirement Savings," GoBanking Rates.com, March 2010, www.gobankingrates.com/retirement/401k/43-of-american-workers-have-less-than-10k-in-retirement-savings.

Business Development Workshops for Older Business Owners

Orange County Public Libraries, California

http://egov.ocgov.com/ocgov/OC%20Public%20Libraries, www.score114.org

WHAT Business development assistance for older business owners is offered through the Orange County library system (OCPL) in partnership with SCORE, a national nonprofit dedicated to helping small businesses succeed.

GOAL To help 50+ adult business owners grow or improve their businesses.

Selected SCORE Business Workshops

Metropolitan Library Association, Minneapolis–St. Paul, Minnesota
The Metropolitan Library Association of the Twin Cities and WebJunction partnered with SCORE to offer a webinar on library community partnerships in support of business development. The program featured ways that Hennepin County Library works with a variety of partners to support entrepreneurs. The webinar, part of the larger series Small Business and Jobs, attracted adults of all ages. (www.melsa.org)

Oro Valley (Arizona) Public Library
Retired business experts counsel small business owners or those considering starting a business. The counseling is one-on-one, free, and confidential. The library provides space in its study room for the one-hour sessions. Participants can also take advantage of library business reference services and collections. (www.orovalleyaz.gov)

Pasco County (Florida) Library System
The Pasco County Library partners with its local SCORE affiliate to offer workshops on business development. The workshops are led by midlife volunteers with business experience; they attract both older and younger business owners. Topic titles have included "Starting a Business: Matching Your Ideas and Resources for Success"; "Introduction to QuickBooks" and "Advanced QuickBooks"; "How to Successfully Obtain a Business Loan;" and "How to Manage and Grow an Existing Business." (http://pascolibraries.org)

FEATURES OCPL has worked with the Orange County affiliate of the national organization SCORE for years to offer business development workshops and counseling to help entrepreneurs establish and expand successful businesses. In 2009, when OCPL was invited to submit a grant proposal to the California State Library's Transforming Life After 50 initiative, staff recognized that many 50+ adults in the county were small business owners who could benefit from free access to advice on strengthening their businesses. With grant funds the library increased the number and locations of SCORE workshops and marketed them to older adult business owners. As with all SCORE workshops, the OCPL programs were led by retired business experts, themselves 50+ adults.

The OCPL workshops have attracted an average of sixty-five participants. Demand is so great that staff have to turn people away occasionally. Workshops cover many of the typical topics offered by SCORE for general adult audiences, with titles such as "Retirement Planning for Small Business and Beyond;" "Starting a Small Business in California"; and "Fast Track to Internet Marketing." Other libraries across the country host SCORE workshops, but OCPL is one of the very few that has targeted older business owners.

PARTNERS AND FUNDING
OCPL partners with Orange County SCORE to offer the workshops for older business owners in multiple branch libraries. SCORE provides trained volunteers who bring unbiased business expertise and advice. The California State Library provided an LSTA grant to OCPL to cover expenses related to the workshops as part of the statewide Transforming Life After 50 program.

Campaign for Financial Literacy Now
New York Public Library, New York, New York
www.nypl.org

WHAT A partnership between New York Public Library, the McGraw-Hill companies, and several nonprofit organizations promotes the financial literacy of New Yorkers. Many libraries offer financial education programs for adults that touch on one or another aspect of planning and fiscal management, but New York Public offers an unusually comprehensive program, including many topics of particular value to midlife New Yorkers who are negotiating life transitions in an uncertain economy. The Campaign for Financial Literacy Now complements the library's Next Chapter initiative and is promoted on the *Next Chapter* blog (see chapter 2).

GOAL

To raise awareness about the critical importance of financial literacy and to provide greater access to financial literacy training, services, and information.

FEATURES

The Campaign for Financial Literacy aims to reach all New Yorkers, but there are numerous offerings that are particularly relevant to midlife and older adults, including presentations and workshops on such topics as investment choices and retirement and college savings. In addition to programs, the Campaign includes:

- Financial and economic literacy educational materials accessible online and through workshops and seminars
- Financial literacy resources at select library branch locations
- Financial literacy instruction through adult basic reading classes
- Teacher and student access to business and economic experts who bring real-world economic and personal finance issues to life

Debt education is a feature of the Campaign that has special interest for older adults. In conjunction with Fordham University, the library offered "10 Ways to Protect Your Money: Ideas to Keep Your Assets Safe, Avoid Scams and Safeguard Your Identity" at neighborhood libraries in the Bronx and Manhattan.

PARTNERS AND FUNDING

With McGraw-Hill as the primary partner and sponsor, the library has engaged other organizations and agencies to present specific Campaign features. The Debt Education series, for instance, was carried out in partnership with Fordham University Law School's Coalition on Debt Education.

Daly City Wi$eUP

Daly City Public Library, Daly City, California

www.dalycity.org/Page41.aspx

WHAT Wi$eUP at Daly City was a nine-part series on financial literacy based on the U.S. Department of Labor's Wi$eUp financial education program for generation X and Y women. The sustained nine-session series offered participants the chance for in-depth learning and discussion about issues they face in their midlife years. Although the Labor Department's core course concentrated on women, men were included in the Daly City program.

GOAL To improve participants' understanding and handling of their finances, from basic money management to insuring, investing, and retirement planning.

FEATURES Through collaboration with the local college and the national Wi$e-Up program, the library was able to engage academic and financial literacy experts to help lead individual programs. The nine sessions covered multiple financial topics facing midlife adults. The program was promoted through monthly utility bill mailings. As part of the project, library collections relevant to boomer interests were expanded at all four branch libraries.

PARTNERS AND FUNDING The Daly City Library partnered with Skyline College and the U.S. Department of Labor's Women's Bureau's (www.dol.gov/wb/). Wi$eUp Daly City was funded by an LSTA grant from the California State Library, as part of the statewide Transforming Life After 50 program.

Engaged Retirement
Princeton Public Library, Princeton, New Jersey
http://princetonlibrary.org

WHAT This speaker series offers a broad overview of the various aspects of retirement or major life change. The series has been jointly presented by the library and the Princeton Senior Center (www.princetonsenior.org) since 2009. The programs offer midlife adults the opportunity to learn about the latest thinking on such matters as investments and Medicare. The breadth of issues examined and variety of specialist perspectives make this series a useful model for other libraries.

GOAL To help older adults make informed choices regarding financial planning and other retirement preparation issues.

FEATURES Engaged Retirement is a monthly speaker series for people thinking about retiring or making other significant changes in their work or personal lives. Speakers address a variety of topics such as financial planning, legal matters such as wills and estates, moving and downsizing, volunteering, family relationships, and healthy aging. The presentations are focused on employees in the 55–70 age cohort.

PARTNERS AND FUNDING Princeton Public library and the Princeton Senior Center work closely together to attract high-caliber speakers and reach a wide potential audience. The two organizations cover expenses associated with the series.

Growing Dollars and $ense
Brooklyn Public Library, Brooklyn, New York
www.brooklynpubliclibrary.org

WHAT This series of programs developed by Brooklyn Public Library's Business Library promotes financial literacy as a means of financial protection. Offered for all adults, the series has attracted many who are recently retired or nearing retirement age.

GOAL To help adults "get smart" about their finances.

FEATURES Growing Dollars and $ense is based on the concept that financial planning today will directly influence financial freedom tomorrow. The program was developed after the recession of 2009, which negatively affected so many adults including those planning for or experiencing retirement. The library partnered with several specialist organizations in a joint effort to encourage financial literacy. The series features workshops, seminars, and one-on-one counseling sessions, covering topics from repairing credit to growing a nest egg.

Growing Dollars and $ense is one of dozens of programs offered by Brooklyn Business Library each year to assist with business startup and expansion, resource navigation, and financial and investment education. Many baby boomers and older adults take advantage of the Business Library's extensive research resources and participate in programs such as the Con Edison Power Breakfast series for business networking; the Entrepreneur series, which brings well-known entrepreneurs to the library to share their startup stories; or the PowerUp!Business Plan Competition. The Business Library also hosts an Entrepreneurs Expo that attracts older adult business owners as exhibitors and spectators.

PARTNERS AND FUNDING Partners for Growing Dollars and $ense are Mind Your Money, the Coalition for Debtor Education, and the New York City Office of Financial Empowerment. Support for the series is provided by the FIN-RA Investor Education Foundation through Smart Investing @ your library, in partnership with ALA.

How Can I Afford Retirement? Education in Your Community

National Program

www.investorprotection.org

WHAT Investor Protection Trust brings together state securities regulators' offices and public libraries in this national investor education program to provide educational seminars for community audiences. Although there are numerous agencies and businesses offering advice on retirement planning, the How Can I Afford Retirement? program demonstrates the special capacity of the library to mobilize experts from public agencies, introduce participants to print collections and online information, and link them to other local and national organizations with complementary resources. In addition, How Can I Afford Retirement? offers a template for program content that can be adapted by local libraries for their own communities.

How Can I Afford Retirement? Sample Sites

Boston (Massachusetts) Public Library
Boston Public offered How Can I Afford Retirement? over two years, partnering with the Massachusetts Securities Division and attracting over 1,700 participants. The library also offered "Spring into Action: A Day of Retirement Financial Planning" with expert speakers on asset allocation strategies and money management and created web pages with resources on retirement topics. Partners included Boston Public's Kirstein Business Library and the Financial Planning Association of Massachusetts. (www.bpl.org)

District of Columbia Public Library, Washington, D.C.
Library partners in D.C. were the Financial Planning Association of the National Capital Area and Howard University Law School. The library offered a fifth session with a hands-on tutorial on online investor education resources. (www.dclibrary.org)

Fayetteville Public Library and Central Arkansas Library System, Little Rock, Arkansas
Fayetteville and Central Arkansas library system presented the Investor Protection Trust series in partnership with the Garrison Financial Institute and the Sam M. Walton College of Business at the University of Arkansas. In Little Rock the programs were offered over two years at branch libraries. (www.faylib.org, www.cals.lib.ar.us)

Hennepin County Library, Minneapolis, Minnesota
The library offered a four-part series and created video clips of the series for expanded access. Partners included the Minnesota Department of Commerce, the Financial Planning Association of Minnesota, the Vital Aging Network, and Twin Cities Public Television. (www.hclib.org)

GOAL To provide access to objective, noncommercial information about investing for retirement so that people can make informed choices, avoid misleading investment advice and scams, and learn ways to better manage their retirement investments.

FEATURES How Can I Afford Retirement? is a four- or five-part series focused on the theme "You Can Do It." Sessions cover planning and investment issues, with titles including "Taking the Mystery Out of Retirement Planning and Closing the Gap: Investment"; and "Expense Strategies—Even for Late Starters."

Each event has several components, including a topical presentation by a financial expert, a briefing on library resources, small-group-facilitated discussions, and a question-and-answer session. Presenting libraries encourage use of the investor education resources developed for the series in their libraries and on their websites.

In some locations an additional online session is offered using the U.S. Department of Labor online workshop "Taking the Mystery Out of Retirement Planning" or other local resources. For instance, at the District of Columbia Public Library, the fifth session was held in the library's computer lab, providing a hands-on tutorial in using the online investor education resources available from the D.C. Public Library, the Social Security Administration, the U.S. Department of Labor, and other trusted sources.

The series is targeted toward individuals who are thinking about retirement or are recently retired. Local libraries adapt and market the program for maximum exposure in their communities.

PARTNERS AND FUNDING How Can I Afford Retirement? is a partnership between libraries and the Investor Protection Trust, which provides funding. Begun in 2006, the pilot phase of the program brought state securities regulators' offices together with libraries in twenty states to offer free seminars on investment education. The full program was launched at the Boston Public Library in 2008. Subsequently, it has been offered at other Massachusetts libraries and locations across the country. Each site has adapted the program to include local partners and other community-specific resources.

Retirement Planning Club for Women / Smart Investing @ your library

Newton Free Library, Newton, Massachusetts

www.newtonfreelibrary.net

WHAT As part of the national Smart Investing @ your library program (see below), Newton Free Library received funds to create the Retirement Planning Club for Women. The Club is open to all women, but the majority of participants are planning for their retirement or are recent retirees. The use of grant funds for organization of a financial planning group for women was unique within the Smart Investing @ your library program and may be a unique service in libraries nationwide.

Selected Smart Investing @ your library Sites

Ames (Iowa) Public Library
Ames is partnering with Iowa State University Extension to offer investment education appropriate to three life stages, including baby boomers. The project includes a general media campaign to increase awareness of investing and direct the public to the library for further education. There is a web presence with self-study materials and online classes. The library also offers in-person classes, investment clubs, and book clubs on investment issues. (www.amespubliclibrary.org)

Fargo (North Dakota) Public Library
Fargo is conducting an outreach campaign to seniors and others, especially new immigrant groups, in order to expand use of the library's financial literacy resources. Programs are offered on personal finance and investing, with attention to language and cultural barriers. Partners include Fargo Senior Services, the Immigrant Business Development Center, and the Tri-College University

Consortium. (www.cityoffargo .com/CityInfo/Departments/ Library)

Glendale (Arizona) Public Library
The library is offering multisession financial and investor education seminars at library and community locations, including courses on retirement planning. Partners include Neighborhood Housing Services of Phoenix, Glendale Community College, and the Carey School of Business at Arizona State University. (www.glendaleaz.com/ library)

Jacksonville (Florida) Public Library
Jacksonville focused its Smart Investing program on meeting the financial education needs of northeast Florida veterans and service members. Seminars and online resources were provided in partnership with Florida State College at Jacksonville's Military Education Institute and Veterans Center and the City of Jacksonville's Military and Veterans Office. More than three hundred people

attended one of the seminars on retirement planning. (http:// jpl.coj.net)

Libraries of Eastern Oregon, Fossil, Oregon
The fifty-one-member library system is presenting in-person and video conferences on a wide range of financial literacy topics through "broadcasts" to targeted populations of seniors including Latino and Native American residents. Partners include community colleges and other local agencies. The learning is reinforced through discussions in personal finance book clubs offered in English and Spanish. (www.librariesof easternoregon.org)

Loveland (Colorado) Public Library
Loveland is offering "Money Talks" at the library and on Loveland's cable TV station covering sixteen topics such as budgeting and retirement planning. One goal is to reach boomers and the Silent Generation. The key project partner is Colorado State University Extension. To help prevent financial

GOAL To improve the financial outlook for women by providing a club environment where they can learn about options for retirement and find the information they need to make effective choices.

FEATURES The core program consists of monthly meetings and presentations on key retirement issues from the perspective of women. In addition to the monthly events, Club participants use library resources, online and in person, to help them with their individual financial planning. Volunteer coaches recruited by the Newton Community Service Center's SOAR program are available for individual counseling. Community response to the program has been strong, and the library is continuing to support Club activities beyond the period of the grant.

fraud among older investors, the library is conducting outreach with the Loveland Police Department, Larimer County Office on Aging, Colorado AARP ElderWatch Project, and local volunteers. (www.ci.loveland.co.us/index.aspx?page=154)

Milwaukee (Wisconsin) Public Library
Milwaukee aims to expand access to investment resources and education to a broad population including older adults. It is improving finance collections at all branches, providing training to staff in the use of print and electronic investment sources, and partnering with organizations such as the Greater Milwaukee Literacy Center, which provides investment materials in Spanish. (www.mpl.org)

Multnomah County (Oregon) Library
Multnomah is working with the Oregon Society of CPAs and community organizations to help high-need audiences, including low-income older adults and others

susceptible to financial fraud. A "road show" team visits retirement centers and other nonprofits and provides hands-on learning on financial topics such as online banking and money management. (www.multcolib.org)

Naperville (Illinois) Public Library
The Naperville Library aims to build its identity as a valuable one-stop community resource on investment education for older adults and other community members. It is creating online video tutorials for beginning investors, offering interactive forums and collaborative programs with the local chamber of commerce and the Naperville Community Career Center. The library's website is being upgraded with investment research tools, and adult services librarians are being trained in investment research strategies. (www.naperville-lib.org)

Natrona County (Wyoming) Public Library
The library designed an intergenerational approach to financial

education focusing on teens, young adults, and boomers nearing retirement. A five-part series of forums held over ten weeks included investment fundamentals, savings tools, specific topics such as compounding, and options for retirement planning. (www.natronacountylibrary.org)

New Haven (Connecticut) Public Library
The library is integrating "Finances @ Fifty" as a permanent feature of its 50+ Transition Center, targeting adults who are planning their pre-and post-retirement options. The program includes financial literacy resources, discussion groups, and programs. The library was able to purchase a subscription for Morningstar Investment Research Center, which is available at all library branches and from patrons' home or office. Library staff and staff from the greater New Haven area libraries were trained to provide individual and group financial planning assistance to 50+ patrons. (www.newhaven library50plus.com)

In addition to the public service aspect of the project, the national grant program supported collection development and library staff development on issues of gender differences and financial literacy.

PARTNERS AND FUNDING The library partnered with the local organization Discovering What's Next (www.discoveringwhatsnext.org) and Newton Community Service Center's SOAR (www.ncscweb.org/programs/soar55) program to implement this project and also benefited from an association with the Center for Retirement Research at Boston College.

Organization of the Retirement Planning Club was made possible by a grant from the Financial Industry Regulatory Authority (www.finra.org) in partnership with ALA through Smart Investing @ your library (www.smartinvesting .ala.org).

Smart Investing @ your library
American Library Association / Financial Regulatory Authority
Investor Education Foundation
www.smartinvesting.ala.org, www.finra.org

WHAT This national grant program enables libraries to help people find the information they need to improve their financial decisions. Libraries use the funds to implement a variety of programs and create resources that increase patrons' access to and understanding of financial information. More than a quarter of the funded projects were geared to address the specific informational needs of 50+ adults. The program is a joint project of the Financial Industry Regulatory Authority (FINRA) Investor Education Foundation and ALA's Reference and User Services Association.

GOAL To build the capacity of public libraries to provide effective and unbiased investor education to the communities they serve.

FEATURES Smart Investing @ your library provides new models of library-based financial planning, some targeted for 50+ adults, that can be adapted for urban, suburban, and rural communities. Grantees receive one to two years of funding, along with assistance with program marketing, outreach, and evaluation provided by ALA. They offer diverse programs including lectures, workshops, and one-on-one education. Grantees partner with community organizations including universities, community centers, and local governments to expand their reach and impact. They also use the funds to augment library collections, train staff, and engage in promotional efforts so that diverse audiences have access to effective financial education resources.

FINRA and ALA started Smart Investing @ your library in 2007 with thirteen library grantees. Since then the program has funded forty-four libraries, strengthening their abilities during and beyond the grant period to help people make financial decisions. Of the sixty-two libraries funded through 2011, at least sixteen carried out programming specifically for 50+ groups.

According to former FINRA Foundation chairman Mary Schapiro, "libraries are an ideal conduit for individuals looking for unbiased information on investing."

PARTNERS AND FUNDING The program has been supported by the FINRA Investment Education Foundation for four years.

IN-BRIEF: FINANCIAL PLANNING AND BUSINESS DEVELOPMENT

Estate Planning, Elder Law, Trusts and Asset Protection
Queens (New York) Library Queens Library offered this series of presentations on strategies to help adults deal with aspects of elder law, such as power of attorney, estate and disability planning, and long-term care. The presenting specialists also reviewed how to reduce tax liabilities when dealing with an estate or trust, how to provide for heirs and charitable interests, and how to increase lifetime income. (www.queenslibrary.org)

Financial Education
J. Lewis Crozer Library, Chester, Pennsylvania The purpose of these workshops was to increase financial literacy among Chester's 50+ population while raising awareness of community resources. The library partnered with the Consumer Credit Counseling Service of Delaware County, and a representative from the local Social Security Administration office addressed benefits. The full series of workshops covered money management, loan information, and identity theft protection. (www.crozerlibrary.org)

Financial Planning Day
Science, Industry and Business Library, New York Public Library The Science, Industry and Business Library, New York's premier public resource for financial planning and business development, organized a full-day exposition featuring classes, database demonstrations, and one-to-one counseling. Some of the most popular classes, which were attended by midlife adults, were "Retirement Planning" and "Starting a Small Business." Cosponsors of the event, who sent representatives and provided advice and information, included the Better Business

Bureau of New York, Office of Financial Empowerment, and Financial Planning Association of New York. (www.nypl.org)

Learning How to Keep Financial Investments Safe

Pierce County (Washington) Library System Through a series of free presentations, "participants gain valuable techniques to safely and wisely select investments for their portfolio in today's challenging economic times." The series is of special interest to 50+ adults. It is one of many services offered by the library's Job and Business Center, including classes on small business development that also attract older adult entrepreneurs. (www.piercecountylibrary.org)

Money Matters: Retirement Rendezvous

Cuyahoga County (Ohio) Public Library Midlife adults are taught how to navigate their finances in this monthly series. Topics include retirement accounts, Social Security and pensions, compounding interest, and accessing benefits. The program announcement states "Knowing how to manage your money and make sound financial decisions creates a secure financial future. Join us and build your financial confidence." (www.cuyahogalibrary.org)

CHAPTER 12

THE 50+ PLACE

In the future, people may not need to come to the library for information.
But they will come in droves if they perceive it as a desirable place.

—Fred Kent, president, Project for Public Spaces

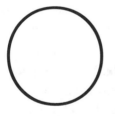ver the past thirty years the physical library has become more complex, with the addition of multiple systems for content storage and communications and multiple spaces for educational and civic functions. These changes are transformational, affecting the entire experience of the library as a physical destination. Simultaneously, scientific understanding of aging processes has increased, including knowledge of the factors that contribute to health and longevity. This too is transformational, raising societal awareness of the "bonus" years and approaches for optimizing those years.

50+ library services are at the intersection of these two developments. Trends in library design have implications for positive aging, and new knowledge of positive aging has implications for the design of libraries.

TRENDS

Aging Research

Beyond the numbers and the policy debates about aging, there are several trends in social planning and research on aging that have direct bearing on how librarians develop their libraries as places for midlife adults and positive aging.

Mental stimulation. Brain health and the fear of losing mental capacity are high on the list of concerns for baby boomers, a group that currently accounts for more than 25 percent of the U.S. population. Recent research on cognition and aging indicates that mental stimulation may aid in improving memory abilities, reasoning, attention focus, and other aspects of cognitive functioning:

> Mental stimulation that consists of cognitively challenging activities is a means to facilitate neural plasticity, which can increase cognitive reserve and result in maintained or improved cognitive functioning. . . . Effective mentally stimulating activities should be novel, cognitively challenging, and preferably enjoyable so that older adults remain engaged. *The mental stimulation must make participants' "brains sweat"—a corollary to physical exercise.*[1]

The concept of "brain health" is now well accepted, with many gerontologists, neurologists, and other experts recommending that aging adults consciously and regularly promote their brain health by participating in creative activities that foster cognitive stimulation and staying involved in physical or mental activities they enjoy.[2] These activities can be reinforced through the design of visually stimulating spaces that are flexible, colorful, and aesthetically pleasing.

Social interaction. Some researchers studying longevity are concentrating on the connections between social interaction and healthy aging. Studies repeatedly show that social isolation is a health risk and, conversely, that social interaction offers health benefits including, but not limited to, lower blood pressure, potentially reduced risk for cardiovascular problems, potentially reduced risk for Alzheimer's disease, and reduced risk for mental health issues such as depression.[3] Researchers identify social support and engagement as key behavioral and psychosocial factors that can enhance both mental and physical health.[4] Recognizing the importance of staying socially connected, aging experts note the value of "Third Places," places that are neither work nor home, places that offer a neutral, welcoming, alternative environment for all.[5] Some also note the value of new communications technologies and social media in helping older adults stay connected. Although direct, face-to-face contact seems to be optimal for midlife connections, today's new media can complement and extend direct contact for the benefit of 50+ generations.

Community engagement. For many 50+ adults, positive aging is related to the extent to which they feel purposeful and involved in a group or community. They want to "give back," do something meaningful, and stay civically connected.[6]

Recent studies document the health and emotional benefits of community service for older adults, including a 2010 study indicating that "older adults who volunteer and who engage in more hours of volunteering report higher levels of well-being."[7] For engagement to occur, individuals must find the appropriate connections. Institutions such as libraries can promote these connections both directly and indirectly.

Independence. Aging specialists often emphasize the importance of control in healthy aging. Loss of control, either physical or mental, leads to dependence.[8] Institutions working with adults at every stage in the life span need to be attentive to how they can reduce restrictions and enable self-direction. This principle has enormous implications for the design of public spaces, including libraries.

Livable communities. Some community planners are looking at how communities promote positive aging in terms of housing, transportation, educational and cultural opportunities, recreation, health supports, amenities, and public space. With the baby boom population expanding and more and more older adults aging in place—including those in naturally occurring retirement communities—there are greater pressures on all these elements of the community infrastructure. According to Partners for Livable Communities (http://livable .org), the goal is to develop "ageless" communities where age is no barrier to safety, mobility, or enjoyment. Librarians concerned with quality-of-life issues for 50+ adults must consider how the library adds features to other community elements that support residents' engagement in social and civic life. Access and siting are only two considerations; others include amenities, programs, and design of exterior and interior spaces.

LIBRARY DESIGN AND RENOVATION

Until relatively recently the "library" was a known quantity—a static enclosure housing information artifacts. The functions that took place within that enclosure were limited and predictable, consisting primarily of reading and research. Contemporary libraries are far more complex and offer seemingly infinite possibilities for individual exploration, expression, and community interaction. The following four trends in library design suggest ways in which library design today can support positive aging.

Multiple dimensions. Once autonomous, boundaried spaces, libraries are now multidimensional. They are both material environments and nodes within diverse networks that work together to give new meaning to the place itself. This transformation, which is ongoing, has implications for how librarians organize their services and programs for 50+ adults and for how these adults interact with their libraries. Increasingly, patrons can experience the library in more than one dimension: onsite reading and study; face-to-face group interactions; research using library equipment and networks; remote access to databases, texts, and community information; and online participation in forums, book clubs, or distance learning. To help 50 + adults take advantage of these multiple dimensions, librarians must pay close attention to the balance of physical and virtual experiences and the interplay between these dimensions.

Forum functions. Some library space freed up by the contraction of book collections is being allocated for computer labs, workstations, and laptop usage, but more and more space is being allocated for public events and group functions. Instead of a single community room, newer libraries feature varied spaces such as auditoriums, classrooms, meeting rooms, story gardens, galleries, and theaters for convening, performing, displaying, debating, and conversing. Through the use of videos and podcasts the activities within these spaces can be broadcast digitally, communicated to larger audiences beyond the library walls and, even, beyond the local community itself.

Transparency and connectivity. Whereas historically the library was a closed container, a stand-alone entity, the twenty-first-century library is open and transparent, enabling visual and physical contact with the local community and the natural environment through glass cladding, special views, courtyards or atriums, gardens, and even rooftop landscaping. These new libraries, deeply embedded within their environments, may be destination libraries, such as the central library in Salt Lake City, Utah; or key components of multiuse projects, such as the Montgomery County Library at the Rockville, Maryland, Town Center. They may be colocated with a school, museum, or senior center, such as the Mission Creek Branch of the San Francisco Public Library. Whatever the context, the new library is just as connected to its physical surroundings as it is connected electronically to local and global information networks.

Flexibility and self-directed services. As libraries have become more open, with fewer physical boundaries between service areas and generally more porous spatial layouts, they have also become less restrictive in the ways patrons function within these spaces. Self-directed services are now common, with self-checkout devices, browsing areas, and computer labs just a few of the ways libraries are becoming more self-directed environments.

Amenities. Another trend in library design is the increase in amenities, transforming libraries into more pleasurable physical environments with opportunities for informal meeting, relaxation, and aesthetic inspiration. The coffee shop is but one example of this transformation. Twenty years ago the notion of a coffee shop in a library was anathema to most libraries and, even, to most patrons. Today library coffee shops are ubiquitous. Artwork is displayed in special galleries and throughout public areas. Color, signage, lighting, and furnishings are all increasingly important as the physical experience of the library takes on greater importance. New and renovated libraries, and their special features, are often marketed digitally both to draw people to the building and to signify the attractiveness of the library as a destination within the larger community.

Learning spaces. Along with the allocation of additional space for "forum functions," libraries are allocating additional space for educational functions that foster learning across the lifespan. These include learning spaces for preschoolers, afterschoolers, tweens, and teens. They also include spaces for older students and adults of all ages: study rooms, smart classrooms, workshops, and technology labs or digital commons. These spaces enable new opportunities for both formal and informal learning which, combined with electronic connections, increase learning opportunities exponentially.

> They wanted a gathering place where people with the same interests could meet to swap ideas, meet new people, exchange information and socialize in a relaxed setting.
>
> **—Baby boomer survey summary, Kern County (California) Public Library**

The increase in learning spaces is part of a larger societal emphasis on learning in which libraries are understood as key elements of a "learning society."[9] Whether the activities that take place within the learning spaces are initiated by the library, organized through a partnership with another educational institution, or developed by a patron group, they underscore the growing importance of the library as a hub for lifelong learning.

IMPLICATIONS FOR LIBRARIES

Both sets of trends outlined above have implications for 50+ services. The principles of positive aging can inform library design and renovation, and new approaches to library design can inform 50+ programs and services. As libraries start to examine how they can provide more effective environments for midlife adults, they must consider how to align these trends.

Fortunately, alignment is not a stretch. In fact, today's library design trends seem ready-made for baby boomers and other active older adults.

- Many of the new features and functions of libraries, such as increased spaces for group functions and face-to-face communication, along with increased options for electronic connectivity, are all congruent with key principles of healthy aging such as the importance of opportunities and spaces for social interaction, creative expression, and community participation. Intentional planning and programming of these spaces will help to animate libraries as 50+ places.

- Libraries that offer new opportunities and spaces for midlife learning—peer-led learning, informal learning, academic learning, self-directed learning—are libraries that are attentive to mental stimulation, one of the most important factors in positive aging. Brain expert Paul Nussbaum calls the library a "a clinic for the mind."[10]

- With respect to connectivity and the potential to use the library in a variety of dimensions, midlife adults are a key patron cohort that stands to benefit. They are seeking information and connections as well as face-to-face interaction. The new library offers options for usage that match the widely varying communication habits and capacities of 50+ adults and their growing demand for connectivity.

- The recent emphasis on amenities in libraries aligns with the new emphasis on livability in community and urban planning for older adults. New or renovated libraries that are deliberately designed as attractive and stimulating destinations for midlife adults can help to strengthen the overall community infrastructure for an aging America.

- The shift in libraries from restricted, staff-controlled spaces and services to more self-directed environments aligns with the importance of independence, options, and self-directed activities for healthy aging. Betty Turock, one of the first library leaders to advocate increased attention to older adults, stated: "We know from studies that older adults' learning activities are largely independent, self directed and self-paced. In the library elders travel at their own pace; are joint planners in their learning programs with librarians; assess their own needs and interests and set their own goals."[11]

This brief summary underscores the potential to link new knowledge of aging with library planning and design. However, despite that potential, the current landscape is uneven at best. With several stellar exceptions, such as the Tempe Public Library's Tempe Connections Café, profiled below, there has been much less attention paid to the physical aspects of the 50+ library than to programmatic activities. This is unfortunate, inasmuch as the most exciting and well-designed programs can suffer in a nonconducive environment.

There are obviously several reasons for a relative lack of attention to the library as place. Certainly current fiscal challenges are a primary barrier. Funds to reorganize or reequip a room or a floor are almost nonexistent. Time is also a factor. With pressure to expand direct service programs, planning for space reallocation and accommodation of new functions may seem impossible for an institution or department operating with minimal staff. The lack of staff training in midlife adult services is another challenge. Although there are (albeit very few) continuing education opportunities enabling librarians to acquire some basics of learning behaviors and the importance of peer involvement for 50+ adults, the kind of intensive training that would include study of space and place in relation to positive aging just does not exist for librarians. Finally, leadership is an issue. Space is turf, and reallocation of space assignments can be problematic internally. Library directors and administrators need to take the lead in reworking functional and physical priorities so that they reflect programmatic goals for midlife adults.

Beyond the practical and organizational challenges, there are other issues and questions that need to be answered before there is a clear model for the library as a 50+ place. Is it preferable to situate midlife adults in their own dedicated spaces, apart from young people, or to create spaces that are ageless and encourage intergenerational contact? What does a virtual space for midlife adults look like, and how can it reinforce the factors that promote healthy aging? Can we design library spaces for self-directed learning as well as social interaction? How can one space or even several spaces accommodate the diverse needs and interests of the multiple generations that make up the 50+ population?

Even in the face of these challenges and questions, given the extraordinary potential for libraries to become essential hubs for midlife adults, it is surprising to see how little investment there is in space development. A new life stage demands new approaches to space and place. It is not enough simply to relocate a reading group or health seminar to an unused corner of the reference area, expand large-print collections, purchase comfortable furniture, create a web page titled "50+," or hang a banner welcoming seniors. All of these may be appropriate in one or another community, but they do not reflect the realities of today's midlife adults. All too often the spaces that are developed to attract older adults end up reinforcing the stereotypes of aged persons as passive, infirm, and inactive. Baby boomers today are looking for action, challenge, and engagement.

Just as libraries across the country are redesigning early childhood areas to take advantage of new research on brain development and emerging literacy, and teen spaces to engage and empower adolescents as they mature, so they must start to redesign older adult areas on the basis of new knowledge of cognitive development and the factors that promote healthy aging. To fulfill their potential as 50+ places, libraries need to carry out a thoughtful process for allocation of space and development of physical features that matches a vision for programs and services for midlife adults. That vision needs to be grounded in what is known about how to optimize aging, it needs to be reflected in staff attitudes and practices, and it needs to be reinforced through appropriate language and internal and external marketing.

Despite the obstacles to change, there are some efforts under way to rethink libraries as places and spaces that are conducive to positive aging. They are small in number, but they do reflect the beginning of awareness that programming alone does not create the 50+ place. Just as other aspects of 50+ library services are works in progress, so, too, is the 50+ place.

Notes

1. David E. Vance et al., "Mental Stimulation, Neural Plasticity, and Aging: Implications for Nursing Research and Practice," *Journal of Neuroscience Nursing* 40, no. 4 (2008): 241–49.

2. See, for example, Gene Cohen, *The Mature Mind: The Positive Power of the Aging Brain* (New York: Basic Books, 2005).

3. "Chicago Healthy Aging and Social Relations Study (CHASRS)," University of Chicago Department of Psychology, http://psychology.uchicago.edu/people/faculty/cacioppo/CHASRS.shtml.

4. Margie E. Lachman and Stefan Agrigoroaei, "Optimizing Health: A Life-Span Approach," in *Boomers and Beyond: Reconsidering the Role of the Library*, ed. Pauline Rothstein and Diantha D. Schull (Chicago, American Library Association, 2010).

5. R. Oldenburg, *The Great Good Place: Cafes, Coffee Shops, Community Centers, Beauty Parlors, General Stores, Bars, Hangouts, and How They Get You through the Day* (St. Paul, MN: Paragon House, 1989).

6. Richard Wolf, "When Retiring Means Giving Back," *USA Today*, March 29, 2011, www.usatoday.com/printedition/news/20110128/1arestoflife28_cv.art.htm.

7. Fengyan Tang, Choi EunHee, and Nancy Morrow-Howell, "Organizational Support and Volunteering Benefits for Older Adults," *Gerontologist* 50, no. 5 (2010): 603–12.

8. *Older People: Independence and Well-Being*, a report cosponsored by the Audit Commission and Better Government for Older People, Public Sector National Report, London, 2004, www.audit-commission.gov.uk/nationalstudies/health/socialcare/Pages/olderpeople.aspx.

9. Robert Martin, "Libraries and Learning," *Advances in Librarianship* 28:83–93.

10. Paul Nussbaum, quoted by Yamila El-Khayat of the Arizona Health Sciences Library in "Librarians Are True Doctors: Reflections on the Arizona Adult Services Summit,"

National Network of Libraries of Medicine, http://nnlm.gov/psr/newsletter/2011/08/24/librarians-are-true-doctors-reflections-on-the-arizona-adult-services-summit.

11. Betty Turock, "Libraries, Older Adults and Senior Spaces," remarks at the opening of the Old Bridge Public Library Senior Space, www.infolink.org/seniorspaces/presentations/BTurock.pdf.

50+ Transition Center

New Haven Free Public Library, New Haven, Connecticut

www.cityofnewhaven.com/library

WHAT New Haven Free Public Library's 50+ Transition Center is a dedicated space for midlife adults on the main floor that serves as a meeting place, information resource, and gateway to other services and programs throughout the library. The Center has become an integral part of the library and the community, and it offers a strong signal to active older adults that the library is a place for learning and interaction. It is one of the first 50+ centers of its type to be developed.[1]

GOAL To be a "Third Place" where informal networks and individual research activities can coexist aided by support of helpful staff and professional advisors, and where people want to come to be connected with what is going on in the community and the world.

FEATURES The 50+ Transition Center is well located, near the main entrance to the library, adjacent to the business reference area. In addition to the actual space, there is a menu of information services, collections, programs, and events. The space includes sections for one-to-one conversations, informal meetings, librarian consultation, and browsing and book racks with current literature and periodicals. Special programs offered by the Center usually take place in a larger meeting space that is also on the main floor of the library. Outdoor programming can be on a patio just outside the Center, looking out onto the New Haven Green. According to Kate Cosgrove, Center manager, "we're trying to re-

> 50+ Transition Center: A Library-based special collection of resources and materials for older adults in various life transition stages who are seeking guidance, advice, direction and information as they make critical choices in their career, family, social, civic, and recreational lifestyles.
>
> **—New Haven Library, Center of Excellence and Innovation report**

spond to this age group. Many of them aren't interested in senior centers. The boomers and beyond don't want to be labeled as seniors. . . . today's 50-plus age group is active, working and wants to be challenged. People in this age group ask themselves, 'What next,' and the Center gives them a place for exploring the possibilities."[2]

Collections. Collection development has been part of New Haven's 50+ initiative, including identification of items in the library's regular collections relevant to the Center as well as acquisition of publications and electronic media related to life transitions, financial planning, health, recareering, travel, entrepreneurship, and volunteering. Library and Center staff have created a "catalog" of 50+ Transition Center collections that is identified as such within the library catalog and on the website.

Programs. The Center offers diverse programs that respond to patron recommendations as well as library and city initiatives. Initially programs focused on transitions and aging. As an example, in 2006 author Suzanne Braun Levine spoke about her book *Inventing the Rest of Our Lives: Women in Second Adulthood*. Subsequent programs have continued the theme of life transitions but have also included other topics appealing to midlife adults. In 2011, for instance, the Center hosted Jay Tunney, son of prizefighter Gene Tunney, speaking about his recent book *The Prizefighter and the Playwright*.

Informational programs are an important strand of special programming. During 2011 the Center focused on health and financial planning (see "Head to Toe," chapter 5, and "Finances @ Fifty," chapter 11). Regular informational events are presented on a wide array of topics, from "Ask a Lawyer" to "Tai Chi and Yoga." Different categories of programming are scheduled at consistent times to help patrons keep track of the varied offerings.

From the outset, the Center has helped midlife adults find ways to contribute to the community. Staff have created a service that matches individuals with local or library volunteer opportunities appropriate for their skills and experience.

Efforts to make the 50+ Transition Center visible include a special link to the Center from the library home page, program announcements, and flyers distributed by partner organizations and throughout the library.

PARTNERS AND FUNDING The library works with many partners to carry out its 50+ programming, including the Connecticut Department of Banking, Connecticut Attorney General's Office, Connecticut Public Television, Community Foundation of Greater New Haven, Connecticut AARP, Dialogue Project and Mediation Center of Greater New Haven, Gateway Community College, Office of Elderly Services, SCORE, Senior Service America, Quinnipiac University, University of New Haven, Albertus Magnus College, and Yale University.

Funding to launch the Center was provided by the Connecticut State Library through an LSTA grant in 2004. In-kind support for the Center during its development was made possible through operational funding from the City of New Haven. Libraries for the Future awarded a grant to the Center in 2006 as a national "Center for Excellence and Innovation in Productive Aging," through funding from Atlantic Philanthropies.

Notes

1. See the discussion by Doug Lord, "BOOM! The 50+ Transition Center at the New Haven Free Public Library," WebJunction, (orig.) March 23, 2007, www.webjunction .org/content/webjunction/documents/connecticut/BOOM_The_50_043_Transition _Center_at_the_New_Haven_Free_Public_Library.html.

2. Kate Cosgrove quoted in Pamela Loughlin, "New Haven Library Program Targets 50+ Age Group. New Haven Register." February 18, 2011, www.nhregister.com/articles/ 2011/02/18/news/aa3_ne50plus1021711.txt.

Central Senior Services
Free Library of Philadelphia, Philadelphia, Pennsylvania
www.freelibrary.org

WHAT Central Senior Services (CSS) is a dedicated space in the Parkway Central Branch of the Free Library with special staff, collections, equipment, and a conference area (see chapter 2). Since 2009 it has been both a place and a service hub. It complements a wide range of information and resources relevant to older adults that are dispersed through the library system and makes the library a more comfortable place for older adults to "visit, browse and interact."

GOAL To create a place for seniors that blends a warm, welcoming environment with state-of-the art knowledge and information resources.

FEATURES CSS is a focal point for the library's 50+ services as well as a physical space for meeting, relaxing, and learning. The unit is managed by dedicated staff including a full-time reference librarian. The 480-square-foot area is equipped with comfortable seating and laptop computers, and a semiprivate conference area allows for semiprivate meetings and consultations. CSS is adjacent to the library's access technology workstations for the visually impaired and the government publications department. There is a closed-circuit TV nearby and a video display screen that continuously loops announcements and program information. "While the events aim to offer spice for every taste, the heart of CSS is the space itself with its collections, furniture, and equipment. Comfortable chairs for leisure reading are essential as well as laptops with databases and Internet connections."[1]

CSS has a collection of materials addressing a range of topics relevant to 50+ adults in multiple formats. Through grant funding the collection has its own budget and receives updated material continuously.

The library offers numerous programs and events for midlife and other active older adults, many of which are organized by CSS staff. They range from monthly programs on health to discussions on public affairs and topical programs that link to citywide events. Within the CSS space there are special programs and services, including one-to-one computer tutoring with an experienced professional who volunteers his time three days a week.

The library decided to create CSS after a 2007 survey to assess the number and variety of library programs over a three-month period in relation to different age groups in the city. Only 1 percent of more than 3,500 public programs had been targeted to 65+ adults, despite the fact that older adults made up 14 percent of the current population and their numbers were expected to grow by 11 percent over the next twenty years. In addition to the disparity in programming vis-à-vis other age groups, the library realized that there was also a disparity in the allocation of spaces: "As we venture onto new ground, we are pushing to learn from others' experience as well as our own. We noticed that although countless libraries house children's areas and a good many have teen nooks, apparently only a relative few have senior areas."[2]

When CSS opened in 2009, the library carried out intensive publicity, with mailings, radio spots on public service station WHYY, and website announcements. Community response has been strong, with large numbers of 50+ adults of all ages and backgrounds taking advantage of the Center as a space for reading, learning, and meeting.

PARTNERS AND FUNDING CSS partners with numerous community organizations in presenting special programs, ranging from the Creative Arts and Aging Network to the Mayor's Office of Community Services (www.phila.gov/mocs) and the Philadelphia Corporation for Aging (www.pcacares.org). Within the library there is strong coordination with other departments serving adults, especially the department responsible for adult programming.

Free Library of Philadelphia received an LSTA startup grant of $26,500 administered through the State Office of Commonwealth Libraries and a grant of $143,621 from the Christian R. and Mary F. Lindback Foundation.

Notes

1. For details, see Martha Cornog and Tracey Ray, "The Free Library of Philadelphia's Senior Center: Comfy and Stimulating Public Libraries," Public Libraries Online, www.publiclibrariesonline.org/magazines/featured-articles/free-library-philadelphias-senior-center-comfy-and-stimulating.

2. Ibid.

Senior Spaces
New Jersey State Library
http://njstatelib.org

WHAT Senior Spaces was a statewide grant program of the New Jersey State Library carried out under contract with INFOLINK, the Eastern Regional Library Cooperative. Four libraries were selected for grants in 2010. Senior Spaces was based on the concept that a designated space would help libraries attract and serve more older adults and would provide a new focus for 50+ programs.

New Jersey is one of two states (see Senior Spaces: Pennsylvania, below) to invest in the Senior Spaces concept and program model. The New Jersey State Library has been a leader in promoting the importance of preparing spaces and strengthening programs for 50+ adults.

GOAL To motivate local libraries to "reinvent" their older adult services.

FEATURES The four New Jersey libraries that received funding in 2010 all transformed a portion of their facility into an area for "seniors of all ages" and developed an array of programs to attract individuals and groups. Each library carried out the initiative somewhat differently:

- East Brunswick Public Library focused on health information and health education, creating the Just for the Health of It project (see chapter 5) along with space and collections for older adults.
- Montclair Public Library focused on reading and technology, creating the MPL STARS (Montclair Public Library Seniors' Technology and Reading Space).
- West Caldwell Public Library created the Savvy Senior Center adjacent to the Reference Reading Room. It features a computer with instruction

tutorials. The library also set up its *Savvy Senior Spaces* blog to help older patrons stay abreast of activities at the library as well as find reference and other relevant information.

- Old Bridge Public Library was the inspiration for the statewide program, having created a successful project in 2007 known as Senior Spaces: The Library Place for Baby Boomers, Older Adults and Their Families. Old Bridge featured redevelopment of a space for older adults that was broken down into zones such as technology, community information, and memory. The project was developed by Allan Kleiman, a specialist in older adults services, "to accommodate the interests, needs, and concerns of baby boomers, their parents, and elderly customers."

Senior Spaces emerged from growing awareness by New Jersey State Library staff during 2006 and 2007 that one of the most important demographic trends in the state during the coming decades would be the aging of the population, including an increase in the number of baby boomers. Staff realized that the current model for "senior" services would need to be transformed to meet the needs of two or three generations of 50+ adults. The request for proposals for Senior Spaces grants states:

> Many libraries still view "seniors" with an ageist mindset, thinking of older adults as those folks residing in nursing homes. The baby boomers beginning to retire are looking towards their libraries to provide recreation, lifelong learning, civic engagement, ideas for second careers, and meaningful volunteer opportunities. Very few libraries in the INFOLINK region have specific programs for older adults and the baby boomers.[1]

A pilot Senior Spaces project at the Old Bridge Public Library seemed promising as a model for prompting transformation in spaces and services. Working with the INFOLINK Eastern Regional Library Cooperative, which was responsible for the implementation of the New Jersey Library Network, the state library provided initial support to help expand the Old Bridge Library project and to start a project in Montclair. Allan Kleiman, then older adult services specialist at Old Bridge, was hired by INFOLINK to provide consulting services. Additional Senior Space grants were later awarded to the West Caldwell Public Library and the East Brunswick Public Library.

PARTNERS AND FUNDING The New Jersey State Library partnered with INFO-LINK (Eastern Regional Library Cooperative) to fund and carry out the Senior

Spaces initiative, supported by an LSTA grant derived from the IMLS. Each library awarded a Senior Spaces grant worked with local partners to carry out programs. Friends groups and other local sponsors added support at most of the funded sites.

Note

1. Request for Proposal, INFOLINK Senior Spaces 2009-2010, December 18, 2008, http://seniorspaces.pbworks.com/f/SeniorSpacesRFP_FY2010.pdf (page 4).

Senior Spaces: Pennsylvania Style

Office of Commonwealth Libraries,

Harrisburg, Pennsylvania

www.portal.state.pa.us/portal/server.pt/community/ commonwealth_libraries/7225

WHAT A statewide grant program of the Pennsylvania Office of Commonwealth Libraries has supported development of six Senior Spaces in libraries. Similar to the Senior Spaces program carried out by the New Jersey State Library (see above), the initiative was based on the concept that libraries could attract and serve more 50+ adults by creating special places for meeting, learning, and browsing. The space itself was meant as a platform for programming relevant to the growing population of baby boomers and other active older adults.

With a critical mass of eleven libraries now participating, each with a Senior Space of some sort and increased programming based on local input, the grant initiative is having an impact on how Pennsylvania libraries work with older adults. Although much of the programming is a continuation of prior activities, some of the libraries are reaching out more specifically to the youngest of the older adults—baby boomers—and are adding more diverse topics, learning opportunities, and intergenerational activities.

Design and Services Showcase: Imagining the Possibilities!

Not long after the New Jersey State Library initiated its Senior Spaces project, the state of Pennsylvania undertook a similar initiative. Given these states' interests in transforming spaces and programs for older adults, and librarians' growing awareness of the need to reexamine their services and spaces for 50+ adults, *Library Journal* decided to organize its 2010 annual design showcase program around the concept of Senior Spaces.

In May 2010, working with INFOLINK and the INFOLINK Diversity Committee, *Library Journal* helped present "Design and Services Showcase: Imagine the Possibilities!" Held at the Montclair Public Library, one of New Jersey's Senior Spaces libraries, the daylong workshop drew librarians not only from across New Jersey but also from Pennsylvania, New York, and other Mid-Atlantic states. The workshop included presentations by New Jersey Senior Spaces librarians.

GOAL To help meet the need to create a space in the library for the three generations of older adults: the baby boomers who will be retiring, older adults who have retired, and the elderly.

FEATURES Pennsylvania has the third or fourth highest percentage of older adults in the nation. Nearly 16 percent of residents are 65 or older, and many more, 55 and over, are in the boomer pipeline. Recognizing the significance of this demographic fact, the Office of Commonwealth Libraries initiated a grant program starting in 2009 that aims to stimulate development of spaces and programs relevant to "the three generations" of older adults. The spaces and programs in libraries, Senior Spaces, were intended to address the needs of baby boomers while complementing ongoing outreach to seniors in other community or residential settings.

The grant program involved $4,000 grants, awarded competitively, for space and program development. According to Claudia Koenig of the Office of Com-

Selected Senior Spaces: Pennsylvania Style

Classic Corner
Cambria County Library, Johnstown
The 450-square-foot area was created with input from an advisory board of 50+ adults. Equipped with comfortable furniture, puzzles, board games, and a Wii game system, the space was designed to attract more baby boomers. In announcing the 2010 grant, the library's public relations coordinator, Trudy Myers, stated: "The area can be what the library and community would like it to be, with materials, information and programming that is interesting, useful and targeted to the older adults." Programs include author talks, vision screenings, and peer-led crafts and hobby groups. (www.cclsys.org)

Classic Corner
Osterhout Free Library,
Wilkes-Barre
The Osterhout Library offers a diverse menu of activities in its senior space, which attracts people from many generations. In the afternoons young people and

older adults play chess together or work on jigsaw puzzles, there are mixed-age groups for board games on Monday nights, people of different generations knit or crochet on Saturdays, and adults of all ages debate philosophical questions in the Socrates Café on Thursdays. (www.osterhout.lib.pa.us)

KEENage Korner
Peters Township Public Library
Peters Township Library has used the Senior Spaces grant to outfit a special area of the library as a focal point for 50+ activities. Program options include Wii sports (assisted by teenagers); clubs (GO Green Club, Cooking Club, book clubs); Technology Thursdays, in which 50+ adults can get one-on-one assistance with new communications devices; online courses; and classes and special presentations on varied topics, including "Financial Planning," a Laughter Class, and a presentation by the World Affairs Council of Pittsburgh. (www.ptlibrary.org)

Seasons/Senior Spaces
Sayre Library
Twenty-two percent of the population in Sayre is over the age of 60. The library director believes there is "a great, huge population that we can reach out and provide programs for." Following the intent of the state's Senior Spaces grant program, the library offers programs for all 50+ generations, including the elderly. Programs include computer classes, "meet the artist" events, special seminars, lectures on nutrition and fitness, and Wii bowling. (www.sayrepl.org)

Second Chapter Café
Whitehall Public Library, Whitehall
Nearly half the population of Whitehall is over age 45. Staff used their Senior Spaces grant to renovate a former all-purpose room, in which 50+ patrons can now read, socialize, watch movies, and learn how to use new technologies. The room is equipped with tables, comfortable chairs, board games, a flat-screen TV, headphones, DVDs, music CDs,

monwealth Libraries, the grant program emphasized development of a program plan in advance, organization of local advisory committees, community partnerships, and "programming, programming, programming."[1]

Over the first two years of the program, eleven grants were awarded. The grant recipients also received an additional $300 a year for three years to sustain their space and program development, and they received a technical assistance site visit from consultant Allan Kleiman, a specialist on older adult services. Each yearly cohort of grantees attended a workshop on older adult services, and they all were asked to speak at an annual Pennsylvania Library Association conference.

Each library used the funds in slightly different ways, depending on the size of their spaces, existing collections and programs, and specific community interests. Different titles for the spaces have emerged (one library ran a contest to name its senior space), and different focal activities. Some libraries have emphasized health education, others technology training.

e-readers, iPads, books, and Wii games. A Senior Spaces advisory board helped develop a schedule for daily programming, with events such as blood pressure screenings, movie showings, creative writing classes, and book discussions. National Honor Society students from the local high school are offering technology classes on how to use Facebook, iPads, iPods, and e-readers. Said library director Paula Kelly, "I don't think people are interested in staying home in their rocking chairs. . . . There's very much an interest in keeping their minds active and lifelong learning." (www.whitehallpubliclibrary.org)

Senior Space
Mt. Lebanon Public Library, Pittsburgh
The library offers classes and conversation opportunities on a variety of topics, such as Shakespeare, tai chi, and Spanish literature and conversation. Creative Connections is a series on contemporary topics that offers opportunities

for learning and socialization. The library also provides a home base for the "Readers' Theatre," a group of retired people who rehearse and perform at local retirement homes, community centers, and senior centers. The members meet monthly at the library to prepare their productions; they perform approximately eight times a year. (www.mtlebanonlibrary.org)

The Jones Zone
B. F. Jones Memorial Library, Aliquippa
The library used its Senior Spaces grant to create the Jones Zone for 50+ adults and to increase programs relevant to their interests. Programs include special events and a regular biweekly open forum discussion group called "Birds of a Feather" that offers participants the opportunity to learn about a historical or cultural topic while meeting together over coffee. Health and informational programs have included a six-part series titled "Arts and Wellness in

Motion." A recent grant from the Remmel Foundation supports intergenerational programming through a partnership with the Sweetwater Center for the Arts in Sewickley. The project involves art classes for adults 55 and older who partner with a school-age child. They work together each week in a different medium, such as digital photography, on specific projects. (www.beaverlibraries.org/aliquippa.asp)

Your Place
Frackville Free Public Library
In creating its senior space, Frackville librarians and their community advisors tried to present a "modern look, as in a book store." They collected many new books, both fiction and nonfiction, expanded their large-print books, and included audiobooks. Programming was redesigned to go beyond the existing adult reading group and knitters club to add computer classes, health programs, and Wii gaming. (www.frackvillelibrary.com)

> We're going to do a lot more programs for baby boomers and beyond, anything from computer classes, "Meet the Artist," "Meet the Author," special seminars, programs on fitness, nutrition—just a variety of programs. . . . And as baby boomers age, there's a great, huge population that we can reach out and provide programs for, so we're really fortunate to receive this funding.
>
> —Susan DePumpo Robinson, director, Sayre Library

PARTNERS AND FUNDING The Pennsylvania Office of Commonwealth Libraries encouraged local grantees to partner with local organizations, and local partnerships are extensive, ranging from the area Agencies on Aging to local workforce development groups and arts organizations. The Office of Commonwealth Libraries provided funding for the Senior Spaces initiative using LSTA monies derived from the IMLS. Some of the funded sites raised additional funds from their Friends groups or other local sponsors.

Note

1. For details and program illustrations, see Claudia Koenig, "Senior Spaces: Pennsylvania Style!" PowerPoint presentation, May 2010, http://seniorspaces.pbworks.com/f/Claudia Koenig_Presentation.ppt.

Tempe Connections Café

Tempe Public Library / Tempe Connections, Tempe, Arizona

www.tempe.gov/index.aspx?page=397, http://tempeconnections.org

WHAT A 2,000-square-foot café and meeting area on the main floor of Tempe Public Library serves as a hub for learning and social exchange for midlife adults. Tempe Connections is one of the most fully developed library-based service programs for 50+ adults in the country, and the Café component is a key reason for its success (see chapter 2). The Café provides a critical focal element—space—to the overall program. It functions as a "Third Place," providing opportunities for social interaction, learning, and intergenerational connections.

GOAL To provide a dedicated space for social exchange and programming for baby boomers and other active older adults and to generate revenues to support Tempe Connections programming.

FEATURES In 2004, when planning started for Tempe Connections, Tempe Public Library and its community partners envisioned a physical space where boomers and other mature adults could relax, socialize, surf the net, read, and connect with opportunities for work, service, and learning. Today, the Café is an inviting area used by adults of all ages. It is the hub for programming carried out by Tempe Connections, a nonprofit community-led organization that offers a wide array of programs and services for 50+ adults, including options for volunteering, informal learning programs, and seminars in life planning. In fact, the symbol for Tempe Connections is a coffee cup, and marketing materials feature the Café as a destination for midlife adults. The Tempe Connections website features these phrases: "Purpose, Programs, Participation"; "Brewed in One Place"; and "The rest of your life begins in a coffee cup."

Tempe Connections Café features a service counter with a variety of beverages and snacks, café seating, computer stations, and wi-fi throughout. Frequented by individuals and groups, the space is used for social exchange, reading, study, research, meetings, and programming. It is where individuals gather before and after formal programs or courses and where small groups convene for regular gatherings, such as the Mystery Lovers Club book discussions and Veterans' Coffee Hours.

> **Tempe Connections Café**
>
> This is a place for library patrons and Tempe residents of all ages to connect, converse and contribute. Café purchases go to support the programming and volunteer activities of Tempe Connections.
>
> —Tempe Connections website

In addition to the Café space there is an 800-square-foot program room and two outdoor patios that are used by Tempe Connections for 50+ programs.

PARTNERS AND FUNDING Operated by the Friends of the Tempe Public Library (www.tempefriends.org), Tempe Connections is a coalition of more than fifteen community organizations. In addition, many programs that take place at the Café and its adjacent meeting room are the result of collaborations and partnerships with diverse community organizations, such as the Maricopa County Workforce Development Office, Experience Corps, and Arizona State University's Osher Lifelong Learning Institute.

Through its Friends group, the library received a grant of $547,644 from the Virginia G. Piper Charitable Trust for construction and initial programming associated with the Café. The grant was part of a Next Chapter funding initiative undertaken by the Piper Trust in conjunction with Civic Ventures, a national think tank with the mission of helping society achieve the greatest return on experience. Today, the Friends operate the Café and program space, with all profits used for the support of Tempe Connections programs and services.

The Living Room: A Place for Adults!
Santa Monica Public Library, Santa Monica, California
http://smpl.org

WHAT This programming initiative was designed to position the library as a place for lifelong learning and social connections for baby boomers. Started in 20008, the project continues today, offering varied programs for both 50+ adults and older seniors.

GOAL To promote the library as a "community living room, a place to connect, get active and to learn."

FEATURES Developed with a 2008 grant through the California State Library's Transforming Life After 50 initiative, the library initially organized the Living Room to help baby boomers "rediscover" the library. Despite its title, the initiative focused on programming, offering twenty-eight concerts, lectures, and films in the first year. The library filmed three of the initial programs as webcasts and posted these to the library's website to build audiences.[1] They also tested two social media tools, Facebook and Twitter, to further their community outreach. Library staff also organized an adult advisory board whose members continue to advise the library regarding future programming ideas for 50+ adults.

The library continues to offer programs that meet boomer interests. Some programs are informational, such as a three-part mini-course titled "Boomer Education 101" on Social Security, Medicare, and other retirement-related issues. Others focus on health, offering topics such as nutritional supplements and memory. Still others offer opportunities to learn about green living, writing, folk music, and opera, including "Saturdays with the Los Angeles Opera."

By sustaining the Living Room programming over several years, Santa Monica Library has strengthened the library's identity as a learning center for midlife adults.

PARTNERS AND FUNDING The local Aging Alliance was a partner in offering several of the Transforming Life After 50 programs. Today programs often are presented jointly with community cultural and educational organizations. The initial new programs and related communications were supported by the California State Library through a Transforming Life After 50 grant made possible with LSTA funds.

Note

1. See a sample video at http://tla50resource.ning.com/video/santa-monica-public-library.

Transforming Life After 50: A Place and a Space

Kern County Library, Bakersfield, California

www.kerncountylibrary.org

WHAT Programs in this two-year project were tailored to the interests of local baby boomers, with dedicated spaces, collections, and Boomer Information kiosks at each of the seven Bakersfield library locations. Marketing via multiple media was extensive. The 2008/9 project was part of the statewide Transforming Life After 50 initiative. It helped to draw in new boomer patrons and established an ongoing partnership with Kern County Aging and Adult Services.

GOAL To respond to baby boomers' needs for library services and to create a "Place and Space" program especially for that age group.

FEATURES When Kern County Library decided to try to attract more boomers, staff started out with a community survey. The survey, which was posted on the library's website and distributed in all library locations, elicited more than three hundred print and electronic responses. According to Kristie Coons, project director, results showed that boomers were looking for a gathering place and for programs on a range of topics such as health, finances, life planning, and technology.

The Kern County Library Federal LSTA "Transforming Life After 50 Grant" gives us an opportunity to ask local boomers how we can better create a place and a space with the programs, resources, services and materials to engage you in lifelong opportunities for learning, cultural enrichment, and personal growth. We would greatly appreciate your input!

—Introduction to the Kern County Library Baby Boomer Survey, 2008

With grant funds the library was able to create dedicated spaces in all seven library locations, the focal points of which were information and resource kiosks known as Boomer Information Zones.

Using the feedback gained from residents, staff organized a series of programs at each location on such topics as recareering, health, financial planning, and computers. Over the course of the project nearly forty programs were offered, led by community experts who donated their time and expertise. To promote the programs to boomer audiences, the library used a variety of avenues: TV, radio, billboards, and print and digital methods in both Spanish and English. The programs were well received and attracted new patrons in the boomer age group.

Although intensive, targeted programming has not continued, some project elements continue to be maintained, such as collection development and the information kiosks. According to Shelley K. Gomez, deputy director of libraries, "the Boomer Information Kiosks have proved to be an identifiable area for information that relates to Boomers." Gomez also reports two factors that helped make the project a success: "the enthusiasm of staff and publicity in a broader arena."

PARTNERS AND FUNDING Initial project partners were the Bakersfield Museum of Art and Kern County Aging and Adult Services. The latter has continued to work with the library on information fairs and other projects. The initial community needs assessment and the resulting project were funded by an LSTA grant administered through the California State Library.

INDEX

You may also be interested in

THE LIBRARY MARKETING TOOLKIT

Ned Potter

Essential reading for anyone involved in promoting their library or information service, whether at an academic, public, or special library or in archives or records management. A useful guide for LIS students who need to understand the practice of library marketing.

ISBN: 978-1-85604-806-4
192 pages / 6" x 9"

A BOOK SALE HOW-TO GUIDE: MORE MONEY, LESS STRESS
Pat Ditzler and JoAnn Dumas
ISBN: 978-0-8389-1074-0

MANAGING LIBRARY VOLUNTEERS, 2ND EDITION
Preston Driggers and Eileen Dumas
ISBN: 978-0-8389-1064-1

GRASSROOTS LIBRARY ADVOCACY
Lauren Comito, Aliqae Geraci, and Christian Zabriskie
ISBN: 978-0-8389-1134-1

LIBRARIANS AS COMMUNITY PARTNERS: AN OUTREACH HANDBOOK
Carol Smallwood
ISBN: 978-0-8389-1006-1

BITE-SIZED MARKETING: REALISTIC SOLUTIONS FOR THE OVERWORKED LIBRARIAN
Nancy Dowd, Mary Evangeliste, and Jonathan Silberman
ISBN: 978-0-8389-1000-9

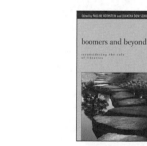

BOOMERS AND BEYOND: RECONSIDERING THE ROLE OF LIBRARIES
Pauline Rothstein and Diantha Dow Schull
ISBN: 978-0-8389-1014-6

Order today at alastore.ala.org or 866-746-7252!

ALA Store purchases fund advocacy, awareness, and accreditation programs for library professionals worldwide.